sharing the journey

LITERATURE

FOR YOUNG CHILDREN

David Yellin

OKLAHOMA STATE UNIVERSITY

Beverly A. DeVries

SOUTHERN NAZARENE UNIVERSITY

 Routledge
Taylor & Francis Group

LONDON AND NEW YORK

Library of Congress Cataloging-in-Publication Data

Yellin, David.
    Sharing the journey : literature for young children / David Yellin,
Beverly A. DeVries.
        p.   cm.
    Includes index.
    ISBN 978-1-934432-07-5
    1. Children's literature—Study and teaching.   2. Children's
literature—History and criticism.   3. Children—Books and reading.   I.
DeVries, Beverly A.   II. Title.
    PN1008.8.Y45 2011
    372.64—dc22

                                        2010038040

Please note: The authors and publisher have made every effort to provide current website addresses in this book. However, because web addresses change, it is inevitable that some of the URLs listed here will change following publication of this book.

We would like to thank the following publishers for granting us permission to reproduce these covers in our book:
pg. 14, *Lilly's Big Day:* Copyright © 2006 by Kevin Henkes. Used by permission of HarperCollins Publishers. ▪ **pg. 44,** *Crow Boy:* By Taro Yashima. Used by permission of Penguin Group (USA) Inc. All rights reserved. ▪ **pg. 71,** *If You Give a Pig a Pancake:* By Laura Numeroff. Illustrations copyright © 1998 by Felicia Bond. Used by permission of HarperCollins Publishers. ▪ **pg. 102,** *Sylvia Long's Mother Goose:* © 1999 by Sylvia Long. Used with permission of Chronicle Books LLC, San Francisco. Visit ChronicleBooks.com. ▪ **pg. 130,** *Fancy Nancy, Poison Ivy Expert:* By Jane O'Connor. Used by permission of HarperCollins Publishers. ▪ **pg. 152,** *The Grouchy Ladybug:* By Eric Carle. Copyright secured 1977 in countries signatory to International Copyright Union. Used by permission of HarperCollins Publishers. ▪ **pg. 176,** *The Egyptian Cinderella:* By Shirley Climo. Illustrations copyright © 1989 by Ruth Heller. Used by permission of Harper-Collins Publishers. ▪ **pg. 187,** *A Pride of African Tales:* By Donna L. Washington. Illustrations copyright © 2004 by James Ransome. Used by permission of HarperCollins Publishers. ▪ **pg. 229,** *Buffalo Bill and the Pony Express:* By Eleanor Coerr. Copyright © 1995 by Don Bolognese. Used by permission of HarperCollins Publishers. ▪ **pg. 256,** *Oceans:* By Seymour Simon. Used by permission of HarperCollins Publishers.

eResources are available at the following location: www.routledge.com/9781934432075

First published 2011 by Holcomb Hathaway, Publishers, Inc.

Published 2017 by Routledge
2 Park Square, Milton Park, Abingdon, Oxon OX14 4RN
711 Third Avenue, New York, NY 10017, USA

Routledge is an imprint of the Taylor & Francis Group, an informa business

Copyright © 2011 by Taylor & Francis

ISBN 978-1-934432-07-5 (pbk)

Brief Contents

Contents

2 Child Development and Literature   31

Literature for Infants and Toddlers   61

Poetry   93

Picture Books   117

6 Traditional and Modern Fantasy   167

Realistic and Historical Fiction   207

Informational Texts   243

appendices   282

See page 282 for a full list of appendix contents.

Preface

This book is intended for all those who work with and love young children: Head Start and Early Start instructors; preschool, kindergarten, and primary grade (1, 2, 3) teachers; daycare workers; preservice teachers; and also parents and other caregivers.

As elementary school curriculums continue to evolve, more and greater academic skill proficiency is asked of young children when they enter the primary grades. Two decades ago this was not the case. Today, however, the pressures on young children are great. For example, all states now require students to take standardized tests throughout the school year. This increased emphasis on testing has caused many teachers to feel they need to "teach to the test." It is important for parents and teachers alike to acknowledge that the students who do best on such tests are (1) children who are good readers, (2) children with a wide vocabulary, and (3) children who are critical thinkers. These are qualities developed early and best through wide reading and discussion of quality literature.

Today we know that the early years are the most important in a child's life in terms of later academic achievement and life fulfillment (Heckman, 2008). A healthy family environment and positive early school experiences tend to develop literate children who are emotionally stable, intellectually curious, and able to socialize easily with others. Unfortunately, the United States, once the leader in educational attainment, has actually seen a decline since the 1960s in the percentage of students who graduate from high school (Brooks, 2008).

The goal of *Sharing the Journey: Literature for Young Children* is to help those who educate young children to better appreciate literature, to recognize the value of sharing books on a regular basis with children, and to initiate creative and enjoyable activities that will motivate children to become lifelong readers who love books.

We hope that our book is readable and useful. We focus on the wonderful world of books for young children and ways for sharing those books and involving children in appealing book-related activities. The first two chapters introduce readers to literature for young children and how it relates to healthy child development. The remaining six chapters describe and discuss the various genres, or categories, of children's literature with an eye to involving young children in ways that will enhance their pleasure and understanding whenever literature is shared with them.

Each book chapter includes these resources:

- "Teaching Suggestions" offer ideas to help teachers use literature in a classroom or early childhood education setting.

- "Author Sketches" give a short biography of an influential author or illustrator and discuss their techniques and inspiration.
- "Journeying with Children's Literature" suggests ways for readers to apply the lessons of each chapter, encouraging them to interact with literature in the real world.
- "Activities to Use with Children" are for practicing and future teachers, parents, and caregivers to share with children to enhance their enjoyment and understanding of the books they read or hear.
- "Our Favorite Children's Books" lists the books we love best and includes descriptive annotations to help readers select books.
- "Children's Literature in This Chapter" provides an easy reference for those titles we discussed in the chapter, including authors and illustrators.

Acknowledgments

Our sincere thanks to our friend and colleague Mary E. Blake Jones, who contributed Chapter 4, Poetry, to this book. We would also like to thank the following reviewers, who offered input on the manuscript at various stages and helped us to improve this book: Anthony Applegate, Holy Family University; Terry Diana Benton, Youngstown State University; Patricia Dean, Salisbury University; Belinda Louie, University of Washington, Tacoma; Mary Napoli, Pennsylvania State University Harrisburg; Maria Offer, Bay Mills Community College; Martha Petry, Jackson Community College; Alison Preece, University of Victoria; Maureen Siera, St. Martin's College; Lawrence Sipe, University of Pennsylvania; Jeanne Swafford, Mississippi State University; Deborah Thompson, The College of New Jersey; and Maureen Walcavich, Edinboro University.

References

Brooks, D. (2008). "The Biggest Issue." *New York Times,* July 29, 2008.

Heckman, J. (2008, Aug. 25). "Schools, skills, and synapses." *VoxEU.org.* Retrieved Nov. 19, 2009, from http://www.voxeu.org/index.php?q=node/1564.

sharing the journey

LITERATURE

FOR YOUNG CHILDREN

Literature and the Young Child

Sharing Literature: AN EXAMPLE

When Ms. Lowry, the kindergarten teacher, starts to play the CD *One Two Buckle My Shoe*, the children begin to sing along and clean up the areas in which they have been playing. As they finish cleaning their areas, the children move to the big rug where Ms. Lowry is sitting on a chair by an easel with a copy of the big book *Shoes from Grandpa* (Fox, 1989). When all the children are gathered around her, Ms. Lowry explains that she is going to read a new book to them. She asks them to look closely at the cover to predict what will happen in the story. This discussion follows:

2 CHAPTER 1

Tyler: It could be about a neighbor and a little girl.

Morgan: It could be about a little girl begging her dad for a dog.

Jenna: It can't be a dad because the man looks too old. I think the man is like the one at the store where I go with my mom.

When there are no more suggestions, Ms. Lowry reads aloud: "Shoes from Grandpa by Mem Fox and illustrated by Patricia Mullins." She then asks what they thought would happen in the story. After another lively discussion where students offer up their best guesses, Ms. Lowry says, "Well, let's find out if any of us are correct."

The children listen intently. As the teacher reads the repeated line, "to go with the shoes from Grandpa" the third time, children begin to chime in with the line. When Ms. Lowry reads, "I'll get you a sweater when the weather gets wetter" the children begin to giggle and ask her to read it again. She rereads it and invites them to read it with her. They enjoy saying the tongue twister.

At the end of the book, Ms. Lowry asks what their favorite part of the story was. Some of the responses include these:

Emma: The funny hat she got.

Jordan: She got all those clothes and she wanted jeans.

Gabriel: I liked the long scarf she got.

Ben: I liked the part "gave her a sweater when the weather gets wetter" because it is funny and hard to say.

The teacher then asks what they can do to respond to the book. From their suggestions, it is obvious that the teacher has previously introduced the children to many different ways of responding to books. The children are not afraid to express their ideas because, like always, Ms. Lowry accepts all their ideas.

Jordan: I'm going to make a long scarf by making circles of paper and then pasting them together. You know, we did that at Valentine's Day. I'll make it all colors.

Morgan: I'm going to draw a funny hat like the one in the book.

Brandon: I could draw Jessie with all her funny clothes.

Gabriel: I'm copying the part "when the weather gets wetter" in my journal because I can read those words now.

Ben: I'm going to pretend I am Jessie and write a "thank you" to Grandpa.

Jenna: May I use the wallpaper books to make Jessie some funny socks?

Ms. Lowry: Of course!

Emma: (Somewhat angry) That's what I was going to do.

Ms. Lowry: Both of you can do that.

Paige: I'm going to fold paper to make Jessie a funny hat.

Emily: I want to do that too.

Ms. Lowry: That's great. Maybe you can help each other.

Tyler: I'm going to listen to the book at the listening table. (He knew that Ms. Lowry had recorded each book she read on a tape; many of these she had recorded herself to save money.)

Some students decide to do the same thing that a friend is doing. Ms. Lowry listens to every child's response and accepts everyone's idea. When all have shared their ideas, she tells them to get the materials they need and then go work quietly at their tables. As the children get up, she starts to play a CD of classical music softly. Once the children have their materials, she reminds them to work quietly so they can hear the music.

Introduction

"Read again! Please? Please?" This is a familiar plea of toddlers who have been listening to quality literature since birth. Young children quickly find the joy in listening to funny, suspenseful, or tender stories. Even decades after Margaret Wise Brown wrote *Goodnight Moon* (1947), children enjoy the lilting rhyme of "Goodnight room / Goodnight moon / Goodnight cow jumping over the moon." A century after Beatrix Potter wrote *The Tale of Peter Rabbit* (1902), children love to repeat the names Flopsy, Mopsy, Cottontail, and Peter and giggle when they hear of Peter's mischief, his running back to his mother's hole and finding that his mother loves him unconditionally, even though she does make him drink a dose of chamomile tea. Children also enjoy listening to Tomie dePaolo's *Strega Nona* (1979). Like Big Anthony, children often are tempted to do things they are specifically told *not* to do. Children agree that the punishment Strega Nona dished out to Big Anthony—eating all the extra pasta— is just, and they laugh when his stomach grows with each bite. As adults read *Is Your Mama a Llama?* (Guarino, 1997), children enjoy guessing what creature is being described. Children like to imagine with Lois Ehlert in *Leaf Man* (2005) that leaves can be real people or animals on an imaginary journey; and as they view the book's cover, they become aware of the many different types of leaves and often begin looking for them in their neighborhoods.

We hope this book takes you on an adventure, exploring quality books, both new and old, written for young children. We encourage you to find the books in your public library or campus curriculum library and examine them as they are discussed. By the end of the book, we hope you are able to distinguish quality literature and will have learned to share literature with young children in ways that help them develop a love of books. Enjoy this journey and continue to look for new books to share with children. And remember: quality children's literature offers readers something new to discover each time a book is read or reread.

This text is written for pre-service teachers and early-childhood caregivers, and we will focus on books for children from infancy through primary grades. In this chapter we offer a general overview of children's literature, discuss the importance of reading to infants and young children, briefly describe the genres of children's literature, describe basic traits of quality children's books, and explore how picture books can celebrate diversity and introduce children to new cultures. In Chapter 2, we highlight developmental theories to guide you as you select books for children. In Chapters 3 through 8, we discuss specific characteristics of quality fiction and nonfiction children's books and give lots of examples and ways to use them in your classroom.

What Is Children's Literature?

The answer to this question seems simple: children's literature is written for children and offers themes and information appropriate for the intended age range. Although the American Library Association (ALA, www.ala.org) defines "children" as persons from birth through 14 years of age, this book focuses on literature for children from infancy through third grade. ALA states that a book for children "is one for which children are a potential audience. The book displays respect for children's understandings, abilities, and appreciations" (American Library Association, 2005, p. 1 of 11). The ALA defines the story picture book for children as a book with "a collective unity of story-line, theme or concept, developed through the series of pictures of which the book is comprised" (ALA, 2005, p. 1 of 11). Authors who write effectively for infants through primary grades understand children's stages of linguistic, cognitive, moral, and social development. They also understand children's curiosity, and the length of children's attention span. Quality books intended for this age level offer text that is appropriate for this age and illustrations that help children understand the text. Caregivers and teachers need the skills to recognize quality children's literature because many books on the market do not meet the standard of *quality literature*. Characteristics of quality children's literature are discussed later in this chapter.

Literature for young children may be categorized in a number of ways. Books can be categorized into fiction (story) or nonfiction (informational), into picture books or chapter books, and into prose or poetry. Both picture books and chapter books can be fiction or nonfiction, and both can be prose or poetry. Fiction and nonfiction are two broad categories; each broad category can be broken down by genre. Genres are distinct types of literary works, related by form, technique, and sometimes by subject matter. All genres available for adults—for example, science fiction, historical fiction, biography and other informational books—are also available for children.

Nonfiction books for young children contain factual information about their world. They include biography, autobiography, and concept books about colors, numbers, shapes, the alphabet, animals, nature, history, explorers, national leaders, heroes, and places around the world.

Fiction for infants through primary grades includes many genres: tall tales, legends, fairy tales, realistic fiction, historical fiction, science fiction, fantasy, fables, and others. Fantasy is a common genre of authors who write for very young children because they can use animals to personify all the emotions, needs, antics, and adventures of young children. For example, Max and Ruby, the lovable bunnies, Arthur, the aardvark, and Spot, the puppy, appear humanlike in their actions and emotions. Many fiction books for young children include humor. Two longtime humorous favorites for young children are Winnie-the-Pooh, who finds himself in many hilarious situations because of his love of honey, and Curious George, who is often caught in funny situations because of his curiosity. More recently, Coleen Salley has created a humorous opossum character in her Epossumondas series.

Fiction picture books for young children are often written in rhyme, which helps young children become aware of the beautiful lilt and sounds of the English language. Nancy White Carlstrom's *Guess Who's Coming, Jesse Bear* (2002) begins with Mama Bear talking on the telephone and Jesse Bear wondering the following:

> Who is Mama talking to?
> Who will come to play?
> Will it be tomorrow,
> Or will it be today? (unpaged)

Eve Bunting describes a house created by a ring of sunflowers in *Sunflower House* (1996):

> Their petals open wide and spread
> a golden roof above my head.
> My friends come rushing down to see
> the sunflower house, hand grown by me. (unpaged)

In the next section we explore why reading to young children can have such a positive impact on their lives.

The Importance of Adults Reading to Infants and Children

Much of children's literature written for infants on up to children in the primary grades is intended to be read to children by adults. Ideally, adults first introduce children to the wonderful world of books by holding them on their laps and reading to them at a very young age. Jim Trelease (2006), an advocate for reading aloud to children, suggests that mothers begin to read to their babies on the day they are born and then continue to read to them every day thereafter. Researchers (Nagy & Scott, 2004; Stanovich, 2004; Ruddell, 2004) have documented many benefits of reading aloud to infants and young children. Besides discovering that books are a treasure house of entertainment and information, children learn oral language, concepts of print, story language, new vocabulary, world knowledge, the patterns and structure of written language, new ideas, and the conventions of a variety of genres (Fisher, Flood, Lapp, & Frey, 2004). "The single most important activity for building knowledge required for [children's] eventual success in reading is reading aloud to [them]" (Anderson, Hiebert, Scott, & Wilkinson, 1985, p. 23). Oliver Van DeMille, another advocate of reading to children, believes that

> In teaching a young child to read, there is no substitute for 'lap reading.' . . . It is here that through parent bonding and memorable moments a child gains a rapport with books as his friends and teachers, grows comfortable and familiar with the symbols of language on the page, gains a curiosity and drive to encounter the secrets of the pages not yet turned, and ultimately the confidence that reading must be within his reach, for it has always been a part of his life, and his parents have not only mastered it but communicate in word and deed that he will too, in due time. (Van DeMille, 2000, p. 91)

As toddlers move from laps to small-group reading settings, they continue to enjoy books read aloud to them by adults. When children enter preschool and the primary grades, expressive, fluent, enthusiastic reading by an adult continues to encourage children to become successful readers. Fisher, Flood, Lapp, and Frey (2004) found that teachers who were effective during read-alouds did the following:

1. chose books that interested the child and that matched the child's developmental, emotional, and social maturation
2. practiced reading the book so that due emphasis was given to important parts
3. established a purpose for listening
4. made predictions based on book cover and/or title
5. modeled fluent reading
6. read with expression and animation that held the child's interest
7. at the end of reading a book, revisited the children's predictions by comparing them to what actually happened
8. stopped occasionally and led thoughtful discussion so that the child focused on specific aspects of the book
9. encouraged the child to do independent reading and writing if appropriate

As teachers and caregivers of young children, we can and should use these guidelines as we read to children. However, to share literature most effectively with young children, we must learn to choose quality literature. And the first step toward this end is to understand the various genres available.

Books for Infancy Through Primary Grades

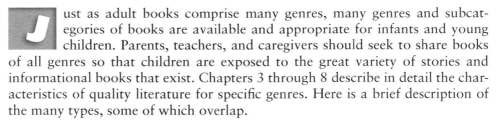ust as adult books comprise many genres, many genres and subcategories of books are available and appropriate for infants and young children. Parents, teachers, and caregivers should seek to share books of all genres so that children are exposed to the great variety of stories and informational books that exist. Chapters 3 through 8 describe in detail the characteristics of quality literature for specific genres. Here is a brief description of the many types, some of which overlap.

- *Mother Goose and nursery rhymes.* Mother Goose stories are succinct and told in rhyme, often with much nonsense. The humor and witty language appeals to young children as adults read the rhymes to them.
- *Poetry.* Poems are written in verse and are rich with alliteration and figurative language. A few of the many types of poetry for children are concrete, free verse, haiku, tanka, clerihew, diamante, couplets, and limericks.
- *Interactive books.* This subcategory of books has tabs and flaps and things to scratch and sniff that encourage infants and toddlers to interact with the book. Many are board books (made of hard, durable cardboard) or vinyl books.
- *Concept books.* These books help children discriminate among different letters, numbers, colors, shapes, and other concepts such as opposites and

sizes. There are four main formats: (1) word–picture format, (2) theme books, (3) simple narrative, and (4) riddles or simple puzzles.

- *Picture books.* These books include the elements of a good story and have themes, illustrations, vocabulary, and a style appropriate for the audience's age. The plot and description of characters are conveyed through text as well as pictures. The length of most picture books is around 32 pages.

- *Wordless books.* In wordless books the illustrations tell the entire story, although some have a few words at the beginning. Wordless books for young children have plots that are easy for children to follow, but the complex illustrations may be symbolic, giving readers an opportunity to make inferences.

- *Informational books.* Informational books share facts about the world in which children live. Topics range from science to famous people, from history to inventions. Photographs, illustrations, and diagrams support the text's information.

- *Biographies.* In biographies, authors write about other people, not about themselves. In fictionalized biographies, authors write about people who really lived, but much of the story line is invented.

- *Autobiographies.* Authors write about their own life experiences in autobiographies. Some authors write autobiographically about one incident of their lives but use a name other than their own, such as in *The Art Lesson* (1997) by Tomie dePaola and *The Friend* (2004) by Sarah Stewart.

- *Fantasy: Traditional and modern.* In fantasy, the characters, plot, and/or setting are not possible in the real world. Traditional fantasy includes fairies, talking animals, and magic. Stories may be myths (about gods and goddesses), legends (about the exaggerated feats of heroes), or tall tales (about characters of extraordinary abilities and their deeds). Modern fantasy includes science fiction, where time or place is set in the future or somewhere other than Earth.

- *Contemporary realistic fiction.* In contemporary realistic fiction the characters, setting, plots, and action portray real-world experiences or issues. Stories can be adventures, mysteries, or narratives of everyday events.

- *Historical realistic fiction.* In historical realistic fiction characters, plots, and action reflect life in the past. Stories can include real people and real incidents with some fictional elements or include only fictional characters and fictional incidents.

- *Multicultural literature.* Many books celebrate diversity, introducing children to other cultures and traditions in a positive way. Quality multicultural books are free of stereotyping and reflect the wonderful diversity across cultures.

As you can see, teachers and caregivers can choose from a great variety of books. One genre is not better than another, but some books are of higher quality than others. Quality books beg to be read again and again by both children and adults, while lesser books lack this quality. The next section describes the characteristics of quality books, both fiction and nonfiction.

Characteristics of Quality Children's Books

With thousands of books written for children each year, how do teachers and caregivers choose quality books? What is quality children's literature? Why do children want to read and reread some stories, while other stories fail to interest them? Even for adults, some stories are timeless, while others may seem flat and boring. As you select books, remember that the main purpose of quality fiction is to bring pleasure; if readers learn new information or better understand human nature from reading fiction, then they receive a bonus (Lukens, 2003). The main purpose of nonfiction, on the other hand, is to inform and expand the reader's knowledge.

In this section, we examine the general characteristics of quality children's books. Later chapters discuss in more detail the characteristics of quality literature for particular genres. The chapters that discuss fiction and nonfiction picture books will also discuss characteristics of quality artwork.

General characteristics found in all types of quality children's books include these:

1. Rich vocabulary that builds children's lexicon.
2. Topics that are important and interesting to children (for example: making friends, settling conflicts, and learning facts about the world around them and elsewhere).
3. Stories that are of interest to the intended age group (for example, infants and toddlers enjoy stories about parents' unconditional love and concept books about the alphabet, numbers, colors, and shapes, while older children love fictional books in which the main character overcomes conflict or informational books about how things work and what they are made of).
4. Cover and opening pages that give hints about plot, setting, or characters, which help readers make predictions about the rest of the story.
5. Binding that is sturdy enough to withstand rough handling.
6. Artwork throughout that is appealing, imaginative, dramatic, and intriguing.
7. Illustrations that support the story and supplement the text.

Quality Fiction

In realistic and historical fiction, the story is not factual, but it is plausible; the author imagines a story that could possibly happen now or in the past. The characters appear to be real people, and the setting appears to be a real place. However, in fantasy anything is possible. Whatever the differences of genre, all quality fiction has certain characteristics that teachers and caregivers should look for when selecting literature.

Like adult literature, children's literature includes seven literary elements: character, plot, setting, theme, point of view, tone, and style. You may have had courses in literature in which you studied the elements of fiction; these elements are considered in more detail in Chapter 5. In the next section, we give an overview of these elements so that you can keep them in mind when choosing books. Appendix B.3 includes a checklist to help you in selecting fiction books.

The characters are believable

What makes for quality characters in fiction is that readers find them believable. Just like real people, fictional characters must have a distinctive appearance, have variable moods, and react in characteristic ways to different situations. They must have strong emotions, feelings, likes, and dislikes. At the end of the story, readers should have empathy for most of the characters, especially the main character.

Quality characters are usually not stereotypes. For example, all librarians are not stern individuals who are constantly shushing people, all farmers do not wear overalls, all urban families are not dysfunctional, and all suburban families are not affluent. However, in traditional fantasy, characters are often stereotypical—wolves, foxes, witches, goblins, and stepmothers are all evil. Sheep, princesses, and little children are usually sweet and innocent.

The plot is interesting

Plot is the sequence of actions in a story. It is what holds readers' interest. Just as stories have different types of characters, so too do they have different types of plots. Quality literature avoids plots that feature sensationalism, coincidences, and sentimentality. Sensationalism occurs when the suspense of the plot creates an immediate but superficial emotional response. For example, a story in which a young boy is lost in a forest at night by himself and encounters a big brown bear can be sensationalist if the entire book is one episode after another, in which the boy tries to run away but encounters all sorts of obstacles, such as a pitfall, a river, or a cliff.

Coincidences do sometimes happen in real life, but a story with contrived coincidences often leaves readers skeptical about its plausibility. For example, if a young girl is attempting to save money to buy her mother a birthday gift and finds on the day of her mother's birthday that she is twenty-five cents short, it would seem contrived if she found a quarter lying on the sidewalk as a windfall resolution.

Sentimentality occurs in a plot when the author attempts to play too much on readers' emotions. For example, imagine a protagonist who is a young cancer victim in a children's hospital on her birthday. Her parents, siblings, grandparents, friends, and neighbors come with gifts. She accepts all the gifts; but after opening them all, she states that she has a gift for each one of them. She returns all the gifts to the givers because she will not be needing them and wants all of them to remember her by them. That is likely to be too sentimental for young readers. When choosing books for children, watch for and avoid books that rely on these techniques.

Teachers and caregivers should remember that in realistic fiction and historical fiction, the plot must fit the time period. For example, it is not plausible that stories set in the 1800s include young people traveling alone on an airplane to grandma's house or children desiring Big Wheels for their birthday. In quality literature, the plot, no matter what type, will keep the young child wanting the

Before reading further . . .

Before reading on, take a few minutes to reflect on a character you remember from a children's book or from a novel you recently read. What made the character memorable to you? A favorite character for one of this book's authors (one who normally despises spiders) is Charlotte from *Charlotte's Web* (White, 1952). Charlotte is capable of doing everything humans can do and has all the emotions of humans. While reading the book, a reader forgets that Charlotte is a spider because her actions, thoughts, and speech are so human. Readers feel as though they could converse with Charlotte, and she would sympathize and give wise advice. If after reading a book you have such strong feelings about a character, you know that the author developed a quality character.

Throughout this book, we discuss many different characters who face all kinds of situations. When considering the characters in a children's book, consider what characteristics, if any, makes them believable. Are the characters likely to elicit strong feelings from young children who interact with the book? Are children likely to relate to the protagonist?

parent or caregiver to continue reading. If a plot is not interesting, a child, like any adult, will want to close the book and find a different story.

The theme reflects children's interests

Theme is the meaning or "unifying truth" of the story (Lukens, 2003, p. 87). It is the message (often unspoken) about discovering oneself, about society, about human nature, about death and dying, about friendship, or about other aspects of living. "Theme provides a dimension to the story that goes beyond the action of the plot" (Kiefer, Hepler, & Hickman, 2007, p. 16).

Quality themes arise from plots that are plausible to young children and from characters that have all the emotions of humans. Quality themes engage children's interests and address their needs, such as friendship (Rohmann's *My Friend Rabbit,* 2002), sibling rivalry (Well's *McDuff and the Baby,* 1997), and the successful completion of tasks (McPhail's *Something Special,* 1989). Other themes may reflect events in their lives; for example, the humorous events of *Epossumondas* (Salley, 2006) or the disappointing events of *Alexander and the Terrible, Horrible, No Good, Very Bad Day* (Viorst, 1972). For children in primary grades, themes of adventure and heroism are appealing.

The setting fits the story

The third element of literature is setting, which is the time and place of the action. Quality settings support the plot and fit the time period. In some stories the setting may be the source of conflict such as a stormy day out at sea (e.g., *Sailor Bear,* Waddell, 1992) or a forest at night (*Let's Go Home, Little Bear,* Waddell, 1991). Settings may set the mood of the story such as a snowy day (*Magic Winter,* Monks, 2004), or an attic (*In the Attic,* Oram, 1984), or a crowded city street (*Make Way for Duckling,* McCloskey, 1941). Quality settings suit the action and characters. Later in this book, we explain that in historical fiction the setting is integral and must be accurate in order for the story to be believable.

Quality settings should also be integrated into the plot and should not require long descriptions. In picture books typically no long description of setting is warranted because young children want action, not detailed descriptions of setting.

The point of view is logical

Point of view is the perspective, "the eyes" through which the story is told. A story can be told from four different points of view—first person, omniscient, limited omniscient, and objective—which will be discussed further in Chapter 5.

Stories must be told from a logical point of view. For example, if the story is about a young child's visit to his grandparents' house, the logical point of view would be first person, as in *Pennies for Elephants* (Judge, 2009). However, if the story is about a female character meeting many different people in various settings and their reactions to her, the most logical point of view would be omniscient so that readers understand how all the people feel about the main character; an example is *The Mysterious Tadpole* (Kellogg, 2002). Generally, point of view should not suddenly switch during the story. Moreover, in most cases it would be illogical, for example, for a story about a young infant to be told in first person because infants cannot speak.

The tone is consistent and appropriate

Tone refers to the author's attitude toward the readers or the subject of a literary work. The author's choice of words and the illustrator's use of color and drawing style help create a tone. In quality literature all elements work in conjunction to create a consistent tone that convinces readers that the story could have, did, or will happen. The tone of a story can be serious, humorous, lighthearted, gentle, or suspenseful.

Examine *The Mysterious Tadpole* (Kellogg, 2002). On the first page, readers can predict a lighthearted, humorous story when they encounter Uncle McAllister dressed in his colorful Scottish kilt and Louis's parents' perplexed facial expressions when they see the gift, a tadpole that Uncle McAllister has given Louis. The light colors on each page suggest a cheery mood even though the swimmers, coach, and parents are exasperated with Alphonse the tadpole. The language, pictures, and color palette all set the tone in this delightful humorous tale.

In both *The Mysterious Tadpole* and *Come On, Rain* (Hesse, 1999) the tone is a product of both language and pictures. In *The Mysterious Tadpole,* the language is concise because the illustrations tell so much of the story. The tone of the story is evident in the facial expressions of the characters as they encounter Alphonse. Their faces express the parents' and other adults' exasperation with Alphonse, while Louis's facial expressions show his delight and concern for Alphonse. In the more verbally evocative *Come On, Rain* tone is created through words that describe a hot day, when "sweat trickles down" mother's neck. Later the exuberance of neighbors tromping through puddles is described as a romp and reel "in the moisty green air" (unpaged).

> ### Before reading further . . .
>
> As you read children's books, take time to reflect on the tone of the book. Determine what language the author used to create the tone. How were the character and setting described? Did the author use poetry in the story to give a quiet rhythm or a jaunty rhythm? What figures of speech did the author use? Did the art in the picture book enhance the tone? These are some questions to ask yourself as you determine the tone of a story.

The writing and illustrating styles are descriptive

Style refers to how the author arranges words into sentences and positions text on the page. Since many books written for children are read aloud by caregivers and teachers, adults should look for books in which the author uses descriptive, vivid, concrete words to create pictures in the minds of listeners. For example, look at the vivid vocabulary John Rocco uses in *Wolf! Wolf!* (2007):

> After a tiring climb and two stubbed toes, the old wolf came to a clearing.
> "What's this? A boy? With goats!" the old wolf drooled with excitement. "Surely he can spare *one* for a hungry wolf."
> Before he could step into the meadow, a group of villagers came clambering up the hillside. (unpaged)

"Tiring climb," "stubbed toes," "drooled," and "clambering" all give a vivid, concise picture of the hungry wolf and concerned villagers. This concise use of language builds excitement in readers.

Language with internal rhythm, rhyme, and onomatopoeia (words that sound like what they mean) appeals to many children. Listen to the rhythm and rhyme in *Tugga-Tugga Tugboat* (Lewis, 2006): "Early morning SCOOT! SCOOT! Whistle warning! TOOT! TOOT! Tanker turning. TOOT! TOOT!

Water churning. SCOOT! SCOOT!" (unpaged). Adults and children can hear and see the tugboat chugging along.

Style also refers to the way that an illustrator depicts events in a story. Whatever style an author uses, in quality children's literature the story and accompanying illustration must work together to convey action and mood vividly. For example, in *Mrs. McTats and Her Houseful of Cats* (2001), Alyssa Satin Capucilli uses rhyme to convey a peaceful yet whimsical story of Mrs. McTats, who lives with one cat: "In a small, cozy cottage / lived Mrs. McTats. / She lived all alone / except for one cat."

Joan Rankin, the illustrator, captures the scene with Mrs. McTats, a plump older lady, sleeping peacefully on a cushioned lawn chair in front of her thatched roof cottage with her cat snoozing by her feet. Rankin uses muted shades of aqua and green in a full-spread illustration of a small peaceful village of thatched roof cottages, a barn, and a little church in the background. The soft green trees around Mrs. McTat's cottage have their branches outstretched as if they are arms welcoming visitors. Indeed, we later learn that Mrs. McTats welcomes two or more cats into her home each day to share in her meal. She names each whimsical-looking cat, beginning with a "B" name and ending with a "Y" name. Finally, the last scratch at the door brings a dog, whom she names "Zoom." Capucilli's book also uses lively, descriptive language to describe the food Mrs. McTats buys each day: "plump fish" and "scrumptious dish." The illustrations, rhyme, and descriptive language all convey one message—this is a happy woman who shares her home with playful cats and a dog.

No matter how young the child, it is never too early to discuss an author's or illustrator's style. Pick any one of Tomie dePaola's books in which he is the main character—for example *Oliver Button is a Sissy* (1979), *The Baby Sister* (1996), *Tom* (1993), and *The Art Lesson* (1989)—or Patricia Polaco's books, such as *Some Birthday* (1991), and *Babushka's Doll* (1995), and ask children what they see in the books. Or discuss Jan Brett's use of borders and inserts in many of her books. Figure 1.1 provides a checklist to use when considering a book's style.

FIGURE 1.1   Determining the quality and nature of a book's style.

TEXT

- Does the author use figurative language?

- Are the sentences short and simple or long and complex, or are they a combination of both kinds?

- Does the author use questions and answers to tell the story?

- Does the author use rhyme?

- Does the author use rich language in a manner that readers will be able to surmise the meaning of a new word from the context of the story?

ILLUSTRATIONS

- Does the illustrator use bold colors or pastels?

- Are the illustrations realistic or are they whimsical?

- Are the pictures boxed with black lines, or do the pictures fill the entire page?

- Does the illustrator use lots of white space, or does color fill each page so that even the words are printed in color?

- Are all the words the same size and color, or does the author use different sizes and colors to emphasize words?

Tomie dePaola was born in Meriden, Connecticut, in 1934. He now lives in New London, New Hampshire. By age four, he knew he wanted to write and illustrate stories, sing, and tap dance. He has done all of these things. More than 40 years ago dePaola illustrated his first book, *Sound,* a science book that he did not write. The first book that he wrote and illustrated was *The Wonderful Dragon of Timlin* in 1966. He now has written and illustrated over 200 books that have sold over 6 million copies worldwide.

Some of dePaola's stories are about his relationship with his grandparents and family (e.g., *Tom, Nana Upstairs, Nana Downstairs, My Baby Sister*). His Irish and Italian background is the focus of many of his stories (e.g., *Song of the Blackbird, Tony's Bread, Fin M'Coul*). Some of his favorite characters are Strega Nona, with her magic powers, and Big Anthony, who always manages to get into trouble. He has also retold and illustrated many folktales (e.g., *The Blue Bonnet, The Paintbrush*). His stories about grandparents and family typically depict loving relationships among family members, and his stories are often funny. Tomie dePaola also writes easy chapter books for young readers, such as *26 Fairmount Avenue* (1999) and *Here We All Are* (2000).

The text and art work together

The words and the art in picture books that tell a story must be unified. The illustrations should extend the story or help explain the information. For example, in *I.Q. Goes to School* (Fraser, 2002), the class does not understand why I.Q.'s plants never grow even though the other children's plants are flourishing. The illustration explains the reason—I.Q. is seen sitting next to his flower pot that is labeled with his name, eating the plant. Later in the book when the teacher announces that I.Q. is going to camp with her during the summer to be the camp pet, the text indicates that "I.Q. already knew he didn't want to be the camp pet" (unpaged). The text and illustrations on the following page indicate that "He wanted to be a camper" (unpaged). The illustrations depict I.Q. dreaming of fishing, hiking, and rowing a boat.

To extend or augment the story, artists in children's books use media, techniques, and styles found in all of art. *Medium* refers to the materials used, such as watercolor, oil, acrylics, ink, pencils, clay, crayons, charcoal, pastels, tissue paper, cardboard, linoleum, tree bark, leaves, seeds, and many other materials. *Technique* refers to the methods used, including painting, etching, woodcuts, linoleum cuts, airbrush, collage, patchwork, embroidery, and photography. Examples of children's books that use these various techniques and others are listed in Figure 1.2.

The book's *style* is the end result of pairing medium and technique with the author's and illustrator's specific content, as we discussed earlier.

Effective illustrators strive to use the positive space (the area filled with design or color), the main picture, the negative space (empty areas surrounding an object), and the background in such a manner that the end result is aesthetically pleasing and corresponds with the text, style, and mood of the story. Artists often use fine lines to depict delicate, smooth moods and broad black lines to depict gloom and despair or boldness. Kevin Henkes in *Old Bear* (2008) uses the colors of each season to depict Old Bear dreaming during his long winter's nap. The double-page picture of spring is all in pastel colors with the text in

FIGURE 1.2   Examples of medium and techniques used in children's literature.

Pen and ink. Steven Kellogg's *The Day Jimmy's Boa Ate the Wash* (1980); Kevin Henkes's *Lilly's Big Day* (2005)

Acrylics. David Shannon's *No! David!* (1995)

Pencil. Brian Selznick's *The Invention of Hugo Cabret* (2007)

Watercolor. All of Marc Brown's Arthur books

Oil. Jan Brett's *Armadillo Rodeo* (1993)

Fabric. Jan Brett's *Hedges's Surprise* (2000)

Charcoal. Kevin Henkes's *Kitten's First Full Moon* (2004)

Cross-hatching. Ron Barrett's illustrations in *Cloudy with a Chance of Meatballs* (J. Barrett, 1982)

Woodcut. Eve Chwast's illustrations in *Grandma's Latkes* (M. Drucker, 1996); Mary Azarian's illustrations in *Snowflake Bentley* (J.B. Martin, 1998)

Collage. Simms Taback's *Joseph Had a Little Coat* (2003)

Natural objects. Lois Elhert's *Snowballs* (1999)

Linoleum cuts. Leslie Evan's illustrations in *Winter* (S. Schnur, 2002)

Photographs. Janet Kerr's photographs in *The Quiet Little Farm* (2000); J. Carl R. Sams II & Jean Stoick's photographs in *Stranger in the Woods* (1999); photographs from the Metropolitan Museum of Art Photograph Studio in *Can You Find It Inside?* (J. Schulte, 2005)

Scratchboard. Brian Pinkney's illustrations in *Duke Ellington* (A. Pinkney, 2006); Beth Krommes's illustrations in *The House in the Night* (Swanson, 2008)

Paper pulp. Denise Fleming's *Beetle Bop* (2007)

Computer. Don Wood's illustrations in *Jubal's Wish* (A. Wood, 2000)

lavender; the summer scene is predominately green with green letters; the fall scene is red-orange with red-orange letters; the winter scene is white and blue with blue letters. Each season is accompanied by peaceful text about Old Bear's pleasant dreams. Marjorie Priceman in *Zin! Zin! Zin! A Violin* (Moss, 1995) uses curvy lines to accentuate the poetry describing the musical instruments. Colors convey warmth, coolness, personality traits, moods, and feeling. David Diaz in *Smoky Night* (Bunting, 1994) uses broad black outlines around his illustrations and dark colors and collage to depict the gloom and chaos that hung over Los Angeles during the fires caused by the riots. Kevin Henkes used charcoal in *Kitten's First Full Moon* (2004) to depict the time of day—night—in which the story takes place. Caldecott winner Chris Raschka captures the happiness of children with grandparents in Norton Juster's *The Hello, Goodbye Window* (2005) by using bold bright colors throughout the illustrations.

Some author–illustrators like Graham Base use the borders on each page to extend the story or give clues to the developing mystery. The clues engage the reader by requiring them to become detectives. The border surrounds the text and illustrations. Other author–illustrators like Jan Brett use inserts, little illustrations that are separate from the page illustrations, to tell readers what is happening in a scene not being discussed on that page. The insert may show what another character is doing in another place while the main action is depicted on the page, or an insert may predict what action is about to happen. Readers get to "read" multiple levels of action when they "read" the inserts.

Figure 1.3 offers a checklist of unifying traits found in quality picture books.

Checklist of unifying traits found in quality picture books.	FIGURE 1.3

○ Lines augment and complement the action and mood of the text.

○ Shapes suggest feelings, mood, and ideas of the text.

○ Texture supports the movement, action, and feelings of the text.

○ Color expresses the characters, moods, and emotions of the text.

○ Unity exists among lines, colors, shapes, and texture.

Quality Nonfiction

Often teachers and caregivers read only fiction to young children, assuming children prefer a good story. However, children also love to learn about the world that surrounds them and about different places to explore; for this reason they also enjoy nonfiction or informational books. Nonfiction teaches children about their world and how to do things or care for things. It piques interest in technology and science. Nonfiction entices young children to do age-appropriate experiments; to classify animals, plants, and objects; and to explore and appreciate cultures and civilizations of the past and present.

Nonfiction for young children comes in many different forms: concept books, survey books, nonfiction picture books, how-to books and craft books, experiment and activity books, identification books, life cycle books, biographies, autobiographies, and photographic essays.

Quality nonfiction books share a number of requirements with fiction:

1. The information for each age level must be clearly and accurately explained.
2. The book must be age-appropriate.
3. The illustrations must enhance, augment, extend, and/or complement the text.
4. The text must build on what readers already know so they expand their schemata.
5. Authors and illustrations need to be aware of the depth of information that is appropriate for different age levels. (Anders & Lloyd, 1996)

In addition to these requirements, nonfiction must also be accurate, organized in a way that is logical, designed in an appealing way supportive of content, and written in an engaging style. Appendix B.4 includes a checklist to help you choose quality nonfiction books. While Chapter 8 looks at these characteristics in more detail, we look briefly at these qualities below.

The nonfiction elements are accurate

Unlike fiction, nonfiction must have accurate, up-to-date facts and illustrations. In order for nonfiction to be accurate, the information must be consistent with current knowledge. Researchers and scientists are constantly gaining new insights, so information is always changing. Technology and new discoveries change facts. Societies also change, so books about cultures also must be up-to-date and provide relevant content. For example, a book about Austria that depicts all women in long dresses with aprons and all men in lederhosen, green Austrian wool jackets, and felts hats would be erroneous. However, if the author focused on one small town in Austria observing holidays in which Austrians wear their native dress, the information would be correct.

Adults are responsible for making sure books are accurate. Young children may understand if information is incorrect about some books if they are familiar with the topic, but they will not be able to judge the accuracy of new topics. One way adults can check for accuracy is to look at the publication date. Any book written about space and other scientific topics may be inaccurate if the publication date is 10 or more years old. Other times, adults can tell the information is inaccurate because the information shared in a particular book contradicts their previous knowledge. If information is new because of research findings, authors will often explain how the old information conflicts with new research. This can help adults decide whether the new information is correct. Checking the credentials of the author and illustrator is another way adults can check for accuracy. Most informational books will describe the author's background, explaining why the author is an expert on the topic.

The organization aids comprehension

For young children, nonfiction must be presented in a way that is easy to comprehend and that connects to their prior knowledge. The text should not read like an encyclopedia, in which the passages are merely a "parade of fact" (Palmer & Stewart, 1997). Just giving a laundry list of facts makes it difficult for readers to fit them into a meaningful whole. If new facts are just listed without showing their interconnections, readers do not grasp or remember the information (Meyer & Poon, 2004). For readers to make connections between concepts, quality nonfiction is usually organized in one of the following ways: compare/contrast, sequence, cause/effect, problem/solution (Meyer & Poon, 2004).

Authors should present new information by building one fact logically upon the next; children need to be able to follow the presentation of information. The information must be presented in an engaging manner so that children will want to continue listening or keep reading. Quality nonfiction uses age-appropriate information so that as children listen to or read informational books, they can connect prior knowledge with the new information presented. Authors must consider what most children know at a certain age so that they neither "talk down" to the child nor give so much new information that the young child cannot follow along.

The style is age-appropriate

The language and sentence structure in nonfiction should be appropriate for the intended audience's age. Long sentences with embedded clauses and phrases may be too complicated for young children to grasp; however, complex sentences that show relationships are easier for readers to grasp than short simple sentences that do not express relationships (Meyer & Poon, 2004). Vivid nouns, verbs, and adjectives help young children create images in their minds.

Authors of quality nonfiction books use technical terms, but they provide explanations or definitions of the terms so that children understand them. If the term is difficult to pronounce, a phonetic spelling of the word is provided. For example, in *Owls* (2005) Gail Gibbons gives the pronunciation of two different types of owls in the narrative and clearly describes how differently the two owls look from each another. Notice how the accented syllable is given in all capital letters:

> Owls with round facial disks are STRIGIDAE (STRI-juh-dee) owls. Owls with heart-shaped facial disks are TYTONIDAE (tie-TON-ih-dee) owls. (p. 9)

The design is appealing

As with fiction, nonfiction must be appealing to the eyes as children open the pages, or they will quickly close the book and choose another one (Allington, 2001; Palmer & Stewart, 1997). The layout of the page should be appropriate for the intended age group. For young children larger print with white spaces on the page is more appealing than a page crowded with text. Large colorful illustrations or photographs are more appealing than small graphs or figures.

As with the text, the illustrations must be accurate as well. They should be clear and well-labeled. They can be artful but should have accurate colors. Captions under photographs and illustrations should augment or clarify information given in the text. If plants and animals are photographed or illustrated in their natural setting, readers learn not only information about the plant or animal, but also learn about the habitat. Maps that show where the featured animal, plant, or country is located help children see whether they live near the focal topic.

Creative techniques can greatly enhance readers' understanding. For instance, some books effectively use overlays—transparent pages containing drawings—so that when readers turn each transparent page the illustration changes. In *Color* (1995), Ruth Heller used overlays to demonstrate how color is added to books and other printed materials. Readers can see the step-by-step process of how one color is first printed, how other colors are added, and finally how the whole is finished with black outlines around the pictures.

The design can also integrate resources such as a table of contents, a glossary, an index, and chapters. For example, in *Sea Turtle* (Carlin, 2008), the table of contents is divided into four chapters—"Meet the Sea Turtle," "Sea Turtle Skills," "Mother Sea Turtle," and "Baby Sea Turtle." The table of contents helps readers quickly decide if the information sounds interesting or if the book provides the information they are seeking. Readers can choose to read only one chapter and know on what page it begins. Children are never too young to learn about these aids found in informational books.

Finding Books on Your Own

Now that you have an idea of what constitutes quality picture and informational books, you should feel more confident in approaching the children's section of a bookstore. One of the most important parts of selecting a quality book is being able to see it for yourself. Ideally, you should be able to see the book in person so that you can judge the quality of text, illustrations, and construction. If this is not possible, try to see a selection of the pages by looking online.

The following chapters, which discuss children's literature of various genres in more detail and offer hundreds of examples, will help you build a strong foundation for selecting and using children's literature. For now, Figure 1.4 offers a few guidelines for evaluating a children's book initially.

FIGURE 1.4   Scanning books for quality.

FICTION

1. Check the title to see if it is captivating and encourages readers to make predictions about the action.

2. Check the opening pages to see if children can make predictions about the characters and/or action.

3. Scan the pages to see if the illustrations are visually appealing.

4. Check to see if the print size is age-appropriate.

5. Read the first page to see if the vocabulary is engaging—Is there rhyme? Is there rhythm? Are there figures of speech or other engaging literacy devices?

6. Read the first page to see if illustrations complement or extend the text.

7. Read the last page to see if the end has an element of surprise.

8. Read the last page to see if it (text or illustration) encourages the reader to read a possible sequel.

NONFICTION

1. Check copyright date to see if it is current.

2. Check the jacket to see if there is any information about the author's qualifications.

3. Read the table of contents for main topics.

4. Check to see if there is a glossary to help young readers with definitions.

5. Scan the pages to see if there is visual appeal. Does it have white spaces? Colorful illustrations? Detailed figures or diagrams? Appropriate type size? Headings and subheadings?

6. Read the first page to see if the text is engaging.

7. Check several pages to make sure the information is accurate.

Celebrating Diversity with Books

In recent years authors have become more conscious of avoiding gender and racial biases in fiction and nonfiction. It is important that both genders and all races are represented in all professions. It is important for young children to see female doctors and male nurses of all races, to see both female and male dancers, engineers, politicians, scientists, teachers, mechanics, and so on.

Just as teachers and caregivers carefully select fiction and nonfiction, when searching for quality multicultural books, they should remember that such books celebrate both the uniqueness of people and the commonalities of humankind. For example, all humans have needs, emotions, and desires, even though everyone's needs, emotions, and desires are not the same. Young children's literature should celebrate diversity so that readers achieve a cross-cultural understanding and acquire accurate knowledge about other cultures. There are books written especially to make readers aware of other cultures, and we address those books and the issues that surround multicultural literature in the next sections.

Celebrate the Uniqueness of Individuals

Books that focus on a culture should not make general statements about people or customs because not all people in a culture experience the same life. Books that focus on one family's activities and attitudes within a culture instead of generalizing about those of an entire culture are usually more authentic, and books

Virginia Stroud's artwork depicts her Cherokee and Creek descent. She says she paints for her people because she wants her culture to survive. In her culture, individuality is not as important as a person's role in the group. Thus she does not paint facial features on her characters; viewers recognize characters through their clothing and roles. Her artwork is known as ledger art or pictorial images. She first relates stories of her culture through a series of pictures, and then adds the text or story. Her use of turquoise, other blues, green, and pink reflect her culture.

that show there are differences even within a culture are also more authentic. Patricia and Frederick McKissack in *Christmas in the Big House, Christmas in the Quarter* (1994) depict differences in Christmas celebrations between slaves and slave owners. Instead of making a general statement about how Americans celebrated Christmas during the 1800s, the authors show one plantation with two opposing ways of celebrating the holiday.

Authors Writing About Their Own Cultures

Some authors weave their own culture into fiction and nonfiction books. Because they have experienced the culture from the "inside," they can give their own perspective of the culture. Their stories may be written with more accuracy and passion than from an author looking from the "outside." For example, Allen Say, a Japanese American, has written some books based on his family's experiences. *Grandfather's Journey* (1992), a Caldecott Honor book, captures the emotional tug of his grandfather's love for his native Japan and his new home, America. Three of his other books that include Japanese characters are *Emma's Rug* (2003), *Allison* (2004), and *Tea with Milk* (1999). The books annotated in Appendix A.2 exemplify just a few of the many cultures represented in children's literature.

The fastest growing group in the United States is the Spanish-speaking community; many living in the Southwest region of the United States have come from Mexico. Many of these children find themselves submerged in English-speaking schools reading literature based on Anglo-American culture but still wanting books about their native culture or in their native language. Publishers have responded to this need by translating popular books written for young children into Spanish. One example is the Clifford series, but, as you may know, Clifford does not depict Mexican culture. As an alternative, there are children's books by Mexican American authors such as Carman Lomas Garza, Sandra Cisneros, Amada Irma Perez, Gary Soto, and Harriet Rohmer.

As with any culture, when selecting African American literature, it is important to check that the characters are not stereotyped, and caregivers and teachers must take care that the themes are appropriate for young children. Andrea Pinkney, Brian Pinkney, Jerry Pinkney, Jacqueline Woodson, Patricia and Fred McKissack, Joyce Carol Thomas, Nikka Grimes, and John Steptoe are a few of the award-winning African American authors and/or illustrators who capture African American life in an accurate manner.

author sketch

Brian Pinkney is proud to tell readers about his parents—Jerry Pinkney, illustrator of children's books, and Gloria Jean Pinkney, author of children's books. Like his father, he married an author of children's books: Andrea Davis Pinkney. Brian Pinkney's signature technique is scratchboard. He begins by covering a whiteboard with black. He then scratches off his picture. Lastly, he adds watercolors, pastels, or acrylics to color the picture. As he works, he uses photographs, slides, and live models to capture the emotions of his characters, which appear lifelike. Some of his books are about famous African American people, while others feature fictitious African American characters.

Authors Writing About Another Culture

Multicultural books are often written by authors who are of a different culture than the one they are writing about. The perspective of someone who is looking into the culture is different from that of someone who has lived within the culture. Many authors often have good intentions, but it can be difficult for them to capture the sights, sounds, smells, feelings, and emotions as authentically as authors who have heard stories told by their grandparents or have lived in the culture themselves. For example, a European American would not have the background experience to write with firsthand authority about the injustice of segregation for African American children once forbidden to attend white schools, to drink from white drinking fountains, or to sit in the front of a bus. Teachers and caregivers should be sure to include books written by authors who belong to the culture portrayed so that the perspective is one of inside knowledge. This is not to say that quality multicultural literature cannot be written by an author who does not share the culture of the characters. Instead, it is important for teachers and caregivers to be aware of the background and experience of the author of multicultural books.

Many quality books are written by authors who have spent significant time in the other culture that they write about. One such author is Demi Hitz. Her Chinese philosophy of art—to capture life on paper—comes from her studies at the China Institute and from her second husband Taesi Jesse Huang, who shares his childhood stories with Demi. Another example is Deborah Duvall, who grew up in the Cherokee Nation, and works closely with Cherokee tribes. Her books include the Grandmother Stories series, illustrated by Murv Jacob: *The Great Ball Game of the Birds and Animals* (2002), *How Medicine Came to the People* (2003), *How Rabbit Lost His Tail* (2003), *Rabbit and the Bears* (2004), *Rabbit Goes Duck Hunting* (2004), and *Rabbit and the Wolves* (2005). These are retellings of ancient tales that use Cherokee words for the animals. Murv Jacobs's intricate black ink illustrations depict the stories effectively. In evaluating multicultural books, you can start with the same quality standards that apply to all picture books (such as those shown in Appendices B.3 and B.4). Multicultural books must still be age-appropriate, and the illustrations must complement or augment the text. Look for books that provide a positive portrayal of the culture. In addition, the depictions of culture must be accurate, and the text and illustrations must be free of stereotypes.

Foundations of Children's Literature Activities

At the end of each of the chapters that follow, we will share activities that teachers and other caregivers can do with young children as they read and share books. Our suggested activities are based on Louise Rosenblatt's transactional theory and also draw on Howard Gardner's theory of multiple intelligences, both of which we discuss below.

Louise Rosenblatt's Transactional Theory

> Every reading act is an event, or a transaction involving a particular reader and a particular pattern of signs, a text, and occurring at a particular time in a particular context . . . The "meaning" does not reside ready-made "in" the text or "in" the reader but happens or comes into being during the transaction between reader and text.
>
> *Rosenblatt, 1994a, p. 1063*

A student of languages, literature and anthropology, Rosenblatt is noted for two major books, *Literature as Exploration* (1996) and *The Reader, the Text, the Poem: The Transactional Theory of the Literary Work* (1994b). Both of these works were originally written more than 30 years ago and have been reissued numerous times because of their continued importance to modern reading theory.

Here we only summarize briefly Rosenblatt's theory of literature and how one reads. Although her work's original goal was to explain how adults read, in recent time educators at the primary and elementary levels have used transactional theory to explain what happens in the classroom when very young children encounter books for the first time (Hancock, 2004).

Reader response

To best understand the importance of Rosenblatt's transactional theory it is necessary to contrast her work with more traditional approaches to reading theory. A traditional approach to reading is to check children's comprehension of the story by seeing if they can answer questions about the text and draw inferences from it. In this response to literature, teachers or caregivers are seeking the one "correct" answer. Children are not encouraged to ask questions or tell why they liked or disliked the story.

In contrast, Rosenblatt (2004) argued that every reader responds differently to a text because of his or her different background knowledge and experiences. Each reader brings a unique set of experiences, prior knowledge, reading ability, vocabulary, understanding, and personal values to the text being read. The "reader response" is the dynamic transaction that takes place between an individual reader and a text that results in understanding or a meaningful interpretation. We use the term *dynamic* to indicate that the reading event includes active involvement on the part of the reader, and the response of the reader to the text may change from one reading to another based on, again, the reader's prior experiences, personal contact with similar texts, and emotional state at the time of the reading.

Readers' prior experiences include their past language experiences as well as the "public" and "private" meaning they have of words. According to Rosenblatt (1994b), the public meaning is the meaning from dictionaries, while the private meaning is derived from all of one's past experiences. Public and private meanings are not strictly synonymous with "cognitive" and "affective" (emotional) meanings. Public meanings can have affective connotations because of the way a particular community or culture uses a word. For example, many children say "cool" to mean that something is outstanding even though dictionaries classify this meaning as slang. Likewise, the private meaning of a word for one child may not agree with the dictionary's meaning. For example, Jordan's father often uses the word "humdinger" when talking about his motorcycle. Three-year-old Jordan begins to assume the word "humdinger" refers to any motorcycle. Later, after a perfect day at the lake, his father says, "What a humdinger of a day!" Jordan now needs to change his private meaning of the word "humdinger" from motorcycle to something very special. An individual's private meanings are constantly changing based on life experiences and encounters with oral and written language. This is a personal approach to reading that can only be understood in terms of an individual reader interacting with a specific text at a given moment.

Efferent and aesthetic reading

Another major contribution of Rosenblatt's transactional theory is the idea that there are different ways of approaching the same text. This is the distinction between *efferent reading* and *aesthetic reading*.

When children engage in efferent reading, they are primarily trying to gain information from a text. Reading to learn facts is the hallmark of informational books. For example, Seymour Simon has written dozens of fascinating informational science books. His book *Jupiter* (1985) has facts and photographs that enthrall young and old alike. His book *Deserts* (1990) takes readers to all parts of the world and explains how deserts are formed and how they support incredibly diverse forms of life. Anne Ylvisaker's science book, *Your Stomach* (2002), shares interesting information about the alimentary canal and the importance of stomach acids in breaking down food for easy digestion. Kids of all ages love Megan Rocker's *How It Happens at the Fireworks Factory* (2004), an inside look at how firecrackers small and large are made. Finally, Gail Gibbons shows readers how a camera works and how to take great pictures in *Click: A Book About Cameras and Taking Pictures* (1997).

However, efferent reading is not restricted to informational texts alone; rather, it is one way of reading or approaching a book. For example, although the main purpose of fiction is entertainment, readers can gain much information from reading works of fiction. *Turtle Spring* (1998), a picture book with great illustrations by Deborah Zagwyn, tells the story of Clee and her pet turtle. Many young children empathize with Clee when she mistakenly believes her hibernating turtle has died. However, from this book children also learn much about the seasons, farm crops, and animal hibernation. Thus, efferent reading refers to the type of focus a reader brings to a text.

Rosenblatt identified another type of reading, aesthetic reading, in which the focus is on the feelings that occur as a reader reads. Literature evokes strong feelings, and when feelings, emotions, and personal thoughts become the focus of why and how one reads, aesthetic reading is taking place. When young children listen to *Shelia Rae, the Brave* (Henkes, 1988), they may identify with Shelia Rae, who is fearless, or they may compare Shelia Rae with classmates or neighborhood children who always appear to be confident. Shelia Rae bravely confronts any challenge and is proud to announce her bravery to others. As the story unfolds, children react emotionally to the plight of Shelia Rae as she becomes lost when she takes a new route home from school. Later, children are relieved to learn that Shelia Rae's timid little sister is there to show Shelia Rae the way home. In *More Bunny Trouble* by Hans Wilhelm (1989), young bunny Ralph is put in charge of his little sister Emily. Ralph gets so involved in painting Easter eggs that he forgets to keep a close watch on Emily, who wanders off into the tall grass of a big field and gets lost. Ralph is frantic, and children share Ralph's emotions as he searches for his sister.

The aesthetic stance can also be taken when reading informational books. Greg Mortenson and Susan Roth's true story *Listen to the Wind: The Story of Dr. Greg and Three Cups of Tea* (2009) evokes strong emotions from children as they realize that children in the village of Korphe, Pakistan, did not have a school to attend until Greg Mortenson stumbled upon the village after becoming lost while climbing a mountain. Readers are amazed to find out that even the children help to build the school by wedging slivers of stones into the cement of the walls. Many children are so moved as they read this story that they save and collect pennies to contribute to Pennies for Peace so they can help other Pakistani villages build schools.

The idea of efferent and aesthetic reading is more complex than merely acknowledging the distinction between the two types of reading because both types of reading can occur at the same time. There is never a complete separation but rather a shifting of focus. For example, when we learn about the facts of segregation in *The Other Side* (Woodson, 2001), the efferent stance may be our focus. But in reading the same book, our focus may become aesthetic once we get caught up in the dilemma of two neighborhood children who long to play together. It seems unfair that a law made by grown-ups can keep them from jumping rope and swinging together.

Efferent and aesthetic stances are also dynamic. At times an individual reader extracts information from the text, and, at other times, deep emotions are evoked by the same text. When we say a person is taking an efferent or aesthetic stance to a book, we are referring to the particular focus of that person at a given time. For example, consider a grandfather, Mr. Whitebear, reading to his granddaughter, Sarah. The poem he reads is Shel Silverstein's "Sarah Cynthia Sylvia Stout Would Not Take the Garbage Out"(1974). For a while, every time Mr. Whitebear reads the poem, Sarah laughs and asks for him to read it again. However, one particular day when Mr. Whitebear begins to recite it, Sarah angrily says, "Stop saying that stupid poem!" Mr. Whitebear cannot quite figure out why Sarah has such an outburst. Later, he discovers that Sarah's mother recently punished her for not taking out the garbage. Sarah's reaction was obviously a result of her life experience: she understood that standing garbage has an unpleasant smell (efferent reading), and she recalls the punishment she received for being disobedient (aesthetic reading).

Each individual child interprets or extracts meaning from a text based on what he or she brings to it. And much of that individual interpretation depends on prior contact (either through reading or listening) with other literature. Thus a child who is exposed to literature on a regular basis can more easily extract and personalize meaning from any given piece of literature. Without intending to do so, Rosenblatt became one of the early advocates of teaching young children to read through exposure to great children's literature.

As teachers and caregivers share books with children, they must remember that the reading event will be unique for each child. They should give ample time for young children to respond to the text. According to Rosenblatt, the response should be expressed in multiple ways—in speech, writing, art, drama, dance, and so on. At the end of each chapter we suggest a number of different activities to lead children in. As you conduct these activities, you may find that children want to modify them to fit their creative thinking. Let them do so; allow them to decide how to respond to the book.

Howard Gardner's Theory of Multiple Intelligences

The second theory that provides a foundation for the lessons in later chapters is the theory of multiple intelligences. Howard Gardner (1983) concluded that humans have multiple intelligences. When he first formed his theory, he posited seven different intelligences: *linguistic, logical-mathematical, spatial, kinesthetic, musical, intrapersonal,* and *interpersonal.* Later he added *naturalistic* and *existential* intelligences. Figure 1.5 offers a brief definition of each intelligence and the abilities associated with each.

According to Gardner's theory, all humans with normal intelligence possess all of these intelligences in varying degrees, with one or two of the intelligences being dominant. As a result, humans typically have abilities in one or two areas that come easy to them; thus they are inclined to engage in activities that use those intelligences. For example, someone with a dominant musical intelligence enjoys musical activities and may learn information, such as the order of the alphabet, more easily through song.

FIGURE 1.5   Howard Gardner's multiple intelligences briefly described.

Linguistic: Ability to use and manipulate languages.

Logical-Mathematical: Ability to understand causes and effects, to calculate easily and to think abstractly.

Spatial: Ability to represent spatial arrangements in one's mind.

Kinesthetic: Ability to use one's body.

Musical: Ability to hear rhythms and melodies.

Intrapersonal: Ability to understand oneself.

Interpersonal: Ability to interact with and understand others.

Naturalistic: Ability to discriminate among things of the natural world.

Existential: Ability to understand philosophies and theories.

Howard Gardner believes that humans can and should develop all intelligences; they should not merely engage in activities that support their dominant ones. This goal has great implication for teachers and caregivers, who should provide activities that encourage children to develop all intelligences but should also give ample opportunity for children to engage in activities that use their dominant intelligences.

Each chapter in this book will include activities to help children develop all the intelligences. We encourage you to use a number of different activities with each book read and always to listen to the child as they respond.

Conclusion

Children's literature encompasses the many genres of adult literature, and all quality fiction shares certain literary elements. Because so many new books are published each year for children, it is important to learn to identify and select *quality* books in a variety of genres. Books expand children's worlds by introducing them to other cultures; books expand children's vocabularies; books help children solve problems by showing them how others solve similar problems. Books give children the opportunity to laugh at the humor in daily life. Through quality books, children learn about many scientific and historical concepts. Books also introduce children to artists and styles of art. Quality fiction and nonfiction should be age-appropriate, have visual appeal, support current research, celebrate diversity, and depict all cultures fairly. Illustrations support, expand, and/or explain the text.

Louise Rosenblatt's transactional theory has it that all children respond uniquely to literature based on their past experiences and their emotional state at the time of reading. Therefore, teachers and caregivers must not insist that all students respond to literature in the same way.

Howard Gardner's theory of multiple intelligences posits that children must be given opportunities to respond to literature in a variety of ways so their dominant and lesser intelligences can grow.

journeying WITH CHILDREN'S LITERATURE

Engage in one or two of the following activities, individually or in small groups, to begin your journey into the study of literature for young children.

1. Go to your public library or curriculum library on campus and find some wordless books. Share the books with a small group of classmates and compare your responses to it. Then discuss the quality of each book.

2. As you read this chapter, you may have encountered authors or illustrators you do not know. Go to the library, find some of their books, and read them. Take notes on what you noticed about the style of writing or the illustration.

3. Select a children's storybook with two or three of your classmates. Each of you should read the story and then discuss whether you liked or disliked

the book, including your favorite part of the book. After you have shared your ideas about the book, take time to discuss the quality of the book: its characters, plot, point of view, setting, theme, style, and tone. Discuss whether the elements cohere with one another.

4. If you know little about Howard Gardner or Louise Rosenblatt, find one of their books in your campus library and read it so that you become more familiar with their theories.

5. Using a search engine, visit the websites of the following author–illustrators: Mo Willems, Eric Hill, Denise Fleming, and Don Wood. Read about their life, their work, and their sources of inspiration. Also observe what medium and technique they use in their illustrations. Keep a notebook on all that you learn about the authors–illustrators.

6. Begin two annotated bibliographies of children's books—one of fiction and the other of nonfiction. (See samples of annotated bibliographies in the sections "Our Favorite Children's Books.")

activities TO SHARE WITH CHILDREN

At the end of each chapter, we suggest activities that you can do with children. Many of these ideas can be used with a variety of books. We encourage you to try these ideas with children of varying ages and write notes to yourself about how you modified the activity to make it more age-appropriate.

1. Read Mem Fox's *The Magic Hat* (2002, illus. Trica Tusa) to kindergarteners. First, spend a few minutes discussing their favorite parts of the book, encouraging input. Next, invite them to stand up and, when you read the lines, "It moved like this, it moved like that! It spun through the air . . . ," have them move creatively like they think the hat would move. Next, invite them to share what they would do with a magic hat. Finally, have them draw and decorate their own magic hat.

2. After sharing with children the letters found in Alma Flor Ada's book *Dear Peter Rabbit* (1994), share a letter that you have written, pretending you are a character from a folktale writing to a character from another tale just as Ada did. Then invite students to choose a character, pair them up, and have them write and then exchange friendly letters as their book character personas. This activity is intended for second or third graders. With first graders, have them dictate a letter as you write it on a big flip chart so they can see it.

3. Read aloud the classic *Stone Soup* (retold by Stewig, 1991). Discuss the many different vegetables that can go into a soup. Give students modeling clay and have them create a vegetable that they can add to the soup. When they are finished, read the story again and have the students dramatize it, each adding his or her vegetable to the soup. Explain that while the villagers are waiting for the soup to cook, they decide to sing songs and dance around the pot so the time goes faster. Engage children in jump rope jingles such as "Teddy Bear, Teddy Bear, Touch the Ground" to include movement in the activity.

4. Let students hear the story *Caps for Sale* (Slobodkina, 1940) and see its illustrations of towering hats. Afterward, give each student a white paper plate. Demonstrate how they can cut out the center and wear it as a hat on their head. (If you are doing this with kindergarteners or younger children, consider cutting out the circle before giving the "cap" to the children.) Invite children to decorate their cap. After the children have completed their caps, read the story again and have one child play the peddler and the other children first be villagers and then, later in the story, become the monkeys. As you read the story, encourage the children to act like the villagers who are buying caps and later to act like a monkey in the tree as they throw down their caps.

5. After sharing *Rainbow Fish* (Pfister, 1992) with the students, invite them to help you create a class mural of the sea. After discussing with the children all the creatures and plants found in the ocean, provide them with yarn, paper, shell pasta, glitter, foil, and any other material they may want to create their mural.

our favorite CHILDREN'S BOOKS

Bunting, E. (1994). *Sunshine Home*. Illus. D. deGroat. New York: Clarion Books.

Timmy and his parents visit his grandmother, who just moved to Sunshine Home, a nursing home. Bunting's humor, honesty, and sensitivity gives the family hope that Grandma will be happy in her new home if she cannot return to her old home. deGroat's watercolor illustrations are realistic.

Creech, S. (2005). *Who's that Baby?* Illus. D. Diaz. New York: HarperCollins.

Babies see, hear, think, and feel many things. These poems express what a baby means to parents. The beautiful illustrations of David Diaz capture the emotions of the poems. This is a wonderful book for caregivers to read to infants and other young children.

DePaola, T. (2005). *Stagestruck*. New York: Putnam.

Tommy is very disappointed when he does not get the part of Peter Rabbit in the school play. He desires to be the star of the show but finds it hard to be a star while only playing the part of Mopsy. Tommy, however, does manage to steal the audience's attention during the play but is puzzled when his teacher and mother do not shout: "Bravo, Tommy!"

Ehlert, L. (2005). *Leaf Man*. San Diego: Harcourt Children's Books.

This story with its colorful illustrations is about the Leaf Man who has "got to go where the wind blows." The narrator follows the flight of Leaf Man as he blows toward the marsh and over meadows and other imagined places.

Fleming, D. (2007). *Beetle Bop*. Illus. D. Fleming. San Diego: Harcourt Children's Books.

This rhyming text reveals the great variety of beetles and their swirling, humming, crashing activities. Fleming's paper pulp illustrations are large and bright.

Henkes, K. (2004). *Kitten's First Full Moon*. New York: Greenwillow.

> One night Kitten steps outside and mistakes the full moon for a bowl of milk. The adventure begins as Kitten tries to reach for it.

Say, A. (2004). *Allison*. New York: Houghton Mifflin/Walter Books.

> In this story about adoption, Allison receives a kimono like the one her doll wears. She then realizes that she and her doll look different from her parents. Allison goes through a period of trauma until the day she adopts a cat and begins to appreciate the family that loves her. Say's realistic illustrations augment the story.

Seymour, S. (2004). *Cats*. New York: HarperCollins.

> Many young children have cats for pets. Through the book's sharp photographs and crisply written text, children learn some very interesting facts about different breeds of cats as well as how to feed and care for them.

Sierra, J. (2004). *Wild About Books*. Illus. M. Brown. New York: Knopf.

> Molly McGrew accidentally drives her bookmobile into the zoo. While she is there, she finds a unique book for each animal in the zoo. The fanciful paintings of Marc Brown accompany the rhymed story nicely.

Stewart, S. (2004). *The Friend*. New York: Farrar, Straus, and Giroux.

> When Annabelle's parents leave for a trip, she is left at home with her best friends, her teddy bear, and the housekeeper, Beatrice (Bea) Smith. Bea permits Annabelle to help her with the cleaning and cooking so that Bea can then take her to the beach. This story of friendship is told in rhyme.

children's literature IN THIS CHAPTER

Ada, A. F. (1994). *Dear Peter Rabbit*. Illus. Leslie Tryon. New York: Atheneum Books for Young Readers.

Barrett, J. (1982). *Cloudy with a chance of meatballs*. Illus. Ron Barrett. New York: Aladdin.

Brett, J. (1993). *Armadillo rodeo*. Illus. Jan Brett. New York: G. P. Putnam's Sons.

Brett, J. (2000). *Hedges's surprise*. Illus. Jan Brett. New York: G. P. Putnam's Sons.

Briggs, J. (1998). *Snowflake Bentley*. Illus. Martin & Mary Azarian. Boston: Houghton Mifflin.

Brown, M. (1947). *Goodnight moon*. Illus. Clement Hurd. New York: HarperTrophy.

Bunting, E. (1994). *Smoky night*. Illus. David Diaz. San Diego: Voyager Books/Harcourt Brace.

Bunting, E. (1996). *Sunflower house*. Illus. Kathryn Hewitt. San Diego: Voyager Books.

Capucilli, A. S. (2001). *Mrs. McTats and her houseful of cats*. Illus. Joan Randin. New York: Margaret K. McElderry Book.

Carlin, L. (2008). *Sea turtles*. Illus. Lydia Carlin. New York: Scholastic.

Carlstrom, N. W. (2002). *Guess who's coming, Jesse Bear*. Illus. Bruce Degen. New York: Aladdin Paperbacks.

dePaloa, T. (1966). *The wonderful dragon of Timlin*. Indianapolis, IN: Bobbs-Merrill.

dePaola, T. (1979). *Strega Nona*. Illus. Tomie dePaola. New York: G. P. Putnam's Sons.

dePaola, T. (1979). *Oliver Button is a sissy*. Illus. Tomie dePaola. Orlando: Harcourt Brace Jovanovich.

dePaola, T. (1989). *The art lesson*. Illus. Tomie dePaola. New York: G. P. Putnam's Sons.

dePaola, T. (1993). *Tom*. Illus. Tomie dePaola. New York: G. P. Putnam's Sons.

dePaola, T. (1996). *The baby sister*. Illus. Tomie dePaola. New York: Putnam & Grosset Group.

dePaloa, T. (1999). *26 Fairmount Avenue*. New York: G.P. Putnam's Sons.

dePaloa, T. (2000). *Here we all are*. New York: G.P. Putnam's Sons.

Drucher, M. (1996). *Grandma's latkes*. Illus. Eve Chwast. New York: Scholastic.

Duvall, D. (2002). *The great ball game of the birds and animals*. Albuquerque, NM: University of New Mexico Press.

Duvall, D. (2003). *How medicine came to the people*. Albuquerque, NM: University of New Mexico Press.

Duvall, D. (2003). *How rabbit lost his tail*. Albuquerque, NM: University of New Mexico Press.

Duvall, D. (2004). *Rabbit and the bears*. Albuquerque, NM: University of New Mexico Press.

Duvall, D. (2004). *Rabbit goes duck hunting*. Albuquerque, NM: University of New Mexico Press.

Duvall, D. (2005). *Rabbit and the wolves*. Albuquerque, NM: University of New Mexico Press.

Ehlert, L. (1999). *Snowball*. Illus. Lois Ehlert. San Diego: Voyager/Harcourt Brace.

Ehlert, L. (2005). *Leaf man*. Illus. Lois Ehlert. San Diego: Voyager/Harcourt Brace.

Fleming, D. (2007). *Beetle bop*. Illus. Denise Fleming. Orlando: Harcourt.

Fox, M. (1989). *Shoes from Grandpa*. Illus. Patricia Mullins. New York: Scholastic.

Fraser, M. A. (2002). *I.Q. goes to school*. Illus. Mary Ann Fraser. New York: Walker Publishing.

Gibbons, G. (1995). *The pumpkin book*. Illus. Gail Gibbons. New York: Scholastic.

Gibbons, G. (1997). *Click: A box about cameras*. Illus. Gail Gibbons. New York: Little, Brown.

Gibbons, G. (2005). *Owls*. Illus. Gail Gibbons. New York: Holiday House.

Guarino, D. (1997; 2004 reprint). *Is your mama a llama?* Illus. Steven Kellogg. New York: Scholastic.

Heller, R. (1995). *Color*. Illus. Ruth Keller. New York: Scholastic.

Henkes, K. (1996). *Shelia Rae, the brave*. Illus. Kevin Henkes. New York: Greenwillow Books.

Henkes, K. (2004). *Kitten's first full moon*. Illus. Kevin Henkes. New York: Greenwillow Books.

Henkes, K. (2005). *Lily's big day*. Illus. Kevin Henkes. New York: Greenwillow.

Henkes, K. (2008). *Old bear*. Illus. Kevin Henkes. New York: Greenwillow.

Hesse, K. (1999). *Come on, rain!* Illus. Jon Muth. New York: Scholastic.

Judge, L. (2009). *Pennies for elephants*. Illus. Lita Judge. New York: Hyperion Books.

Juster, N. (2005). *The hello, goodbye window*. Illus. Chris Raschka. New York: Hyperion Books for Children.

Kellogg, S. (1980). *The day Jimmy's boa ate the wash*. New York: Puffin.

Kellogg, S. (2002). *The mysterious tadpole*. Illus. Steven Kellogg. New York: Dial Books for Young Readers.

Kerr, J. (2000). *The quiet little farm*. Illus. Janet Kerr. New York: Henry Holt & Co.

Lewis, K. (2006). *Tugga-tugga tugboat*. Illus. Daniel Kirk. New York: Hyperion Books for Children.

Martin, J. B. (1998). *Snowflake Bentley*. Illus. M. Azarian. New York: Houghton Mifflin.

McKissack, P., & McKissack, F. (1994). *Christmas in the big house, Christmas in the quarter*. Illus. John Thompson. New York: Scholastic.

Monks, J. (2005). *Magic winter*. Illus. Julia Monks. New York: Scholastic Hippo.

Mortenson, G., & Roth, S. L. (2009). *Listen to the wind: The story of Dr. Greg & three cups of tea*. Illus. Susan L. Roth. New York: Dial Books for Young Readers.

Moss, L. (1995). *Zin! Zin! Zin! A violin*. Illus. Marjorie Priceman. New York: Aladdin.

Noble, T. H. (1980). *The day Jimmy's boa ate the wash*. Illus. Steven Kellogg. New York: A Puffin Pied Piper.

Oram, H. (1984). *In the attic*. Illus. Satoshi Kitamura. New York: Andersen Press.

Pallotta, J., & Cassie, B. (1995). *The butterfly alphabet book*. Illus. Mark Astella. New York: Charlesbridge Publishers.

Pinkney, A. (1998). *Duke Ellington*. Illus. Brian Pinkney. New York: Hyperion Books for Children.

Potter, B. (1902). *The tale of Peter Rabbit*. Illus. Beatrix Potter. London: F. Warne & Co.

Polacco, P. (1991). *Some birthday*. Illus. Patricia Polacco. New York: Simon & Schuster.

Polacco, P. (1990). *Babushka's doll*. Illus. Patricia Polacco. New York: Aladdin Paperbacks.

Polacco, P. (2007). *Ginger and Petunia*. Illus. Patricia Polacco. New York: Philomel Books.

Rocco, J. (2007). *Wolf! Wolf!* Illus. John Rocco. New York: Hyperion Books for Children.

Rocker, M. (2004). *How it happens at the fireworks factory*. Illus. Diane & Robert Wolfe. Minneapolis: The Oliver Press.

Salley, C. (2002). *Why Epossumondas has no hair on his tail*. Illus. Janet Stevens. San Diego, CA: Harcourt.

Salley, C. (2006). *Epossumondas*. Illus. Janet Stevens. Orlando: Harcourt.

Sams, C. R. II, & Stoick, J. (2000). *Stranger in the woods*. Illus. Carl R. Sams II & Jean Stoick. Milford, MI: Carl R. Sams II Photography.

Say, A. (1997). *Allison*. Illus. Allen Say. Boston: Houghton Mifflin.

Say, A. (2003). *Emma's rug.* Illus. Allen Say. Boston: Houghton Mifflin.

Say, A. (1993). *Grandfather's journey.* Illus. Allen Say. Boston: Houghton Mifflin.

Say, A. (1999). *Tea with milk.* Illus. Allen Say. Boston: Houghton Mifflin.

Schnur, S. (2003). *In winter: An alphabet acrostic.* Illus. Leslie Evans. New York: Clarion Books.

Schulte, J. (2005). *Can you find it inside?* Illus. photos by the Metropolitan Museum of Art Photography Studio. New York: Abrams.

Selznick, B. (2007). *The invention of Hugo Cabret.* Illus. Brain Selznick. New York: Scholastic.

Shannon, D. (1998). *No, David.* Illus. David Shannon. New York: Big Sky Press.

Simon, S. (1985). *Jupiter.* Illus. Seymour Simon. New York: HarperTrophy.

Simon, S. (1997). *Deserts.* Illus. Seymour Simon. New York: HarperTrophy.

Slobodkina, E. (1940). *Caps for sale.* Illus. Esphyr Slobodkina. New York: Scholastic.

Stewart, S. (2004). *The Friend.* Illus. David Small. New York: Farrar, Straus, and Giroux.

Stewig, J. W. (1991). (Retold by John Warren Stewig). *Stone Soup.* Illus. Margot Tomes. New York: Trumpet Club.

Swanson, S. M. (2008). *The house in the night.* Illus. Beth Krommes. Boston: Houghton Mifflin.

Taback. S. (2003). *Joseph had a little coat.* Illus. Simms Taback. New York: Viking Juvenile.

Waddell, M. (1995). *Let's go home, Little Bear.* Illus. Barbara Firth. New York: Candlewick.

Waddell, M. (1996). *Sailor bear.* Illus. Virginia Austin. New York: Walker Books.

White, E. B. (1952). *Charlotte's web.* Illus. Garth Williams. New York: Harper & Row.

Wilhelm, H. (1989). *More bunny trouble.* New York: Scholastic Paperbacks.

Wood, A. (2000). *Jubal's wish.* Illus. Don Wood. New York: Blue Sky Press.

Woodson, J. (2001). *The other side.* Illus. E. B. Lewis. New York: G. P. Putnam's Sons.

Ylvisaker, A. (2002). *Your stomach.* Illus. Robert Wolfe. New York: Capstone Press.

Zagwyn, D. T. (2001). *Turtle spring.* Illus. Deborah T. Zagwyn. New York: Tricycle Press.

Child Development and Literature

Chapter

2

Sharing Literature: AN EXAMPLE

Mrs. Chung runs a preschool for 3- and 4-year-olds. Lately she has noticed that the boys and girls are arguing over who plays with what toys. Though all the toys belong to the preschool, Richie grabs a truck and says, "This is mine. You can't have it." Belinda grabs blocks from Francie and says, "Mine, mine," while Francie begins to cry. So this day, Mrs. Chung gathers the children together for a read-aloud chat and book.

"Boys and girls, you know I am not happy when people don't share their toys. The toys are for everyone to play with and share. So what should we do when someone has

a toy? " She waits and waits. The children look at her without responding. Finally one hand goes up. "Yes, Jessica."

"We should share our toys," Jessica says in a tiny voice and looks around at the other children for approval. The rest of the group continues to stare at Mrs. Chung. Mrs. Chung is thinking, *This is not going well.*

"Yes, Jessica, that's right. We should share." Mrs. Chung looks at the group, hoping for a glimmer of understanding. Nothing. Finally, she says, "I've got a book here I want to read to you. It's called *The Pigeon Finds a Hot Dog* (Willems, 2004). The class giggles as a group. Mrs. Chung says, "Listen closely to see what the pigeon does with his hot dog when a little bird comes along."

In the book, a pigeon finds a delicious hot dog. But when another bird wants to know what the hot dog tastes like, the pigeon insists, "It's mine, mine, mine." In the end the pigeon gives in and shares with the bird.

The group listens to Mrs. Chung read the book and enjoys the funny pictures. At the end of the story Mrs. Chung asks, "Why do you think the pigeon shared the hot dog with the bird?"

"Because it's big enough for both of them?" says Francie. Mrs. Chung is not sure if that is a statement or a question.

"Yes, that's true, it is a big hot dog," says Mrs. Chung. "Richie, what would you do if you had the hot dog?"

Richie looks at the picture of the pigeon. "I'd take a big bite and give the birdie a little bite." He looks at Mrs. Chung with a smile on his face.

"That's a good idea, Richie. So you would share it, wouldn't you?" Richie nods.

Mrs. Chung wonders if he, or any of the other children, really got the idea of sharing. However, as a savvy teacher she knows this is a first step in the right direction. Learning to share with others may take youngsters like Richie a while, with progress mixed with setbacks. Mrs. Chung knows that at this age children are still learning how to balance autonomy and civility.

Introduction

I n Chapter 1 you were introduced to the wonderful world of children's literature. Beginning with infancy and continuing through the early years with parents and other caregivers, on into preschool and through the primary grades, literature plays a major role in the linguistic, cognitive, social, and moral development of children. Therefore parents, caregivers, preschool educators, and primary-school teachers must be aware of the significant role that literature can play in the healthy development of a young child. In this chapter we briefly review some of the major theories of child development and relate those theories to language and literacy development in young children.

James Comer, of the Yale Child Study Center, first contended in the 1960s that the purpose of schooling is to support the healthy development of children (Comer, 2005). To do that, all teachers must understand how children develop and how development relates to success in school. Teachers and parents of young children are constantly making decisions throughout the day based on their unconscious and conscious understanding of how children learn, grow, and develop. Comer (2005) also argued that sharing and talking about books with young children "leads to reflection, which promotes better thinking, better management of feelings, and more desirable social behavior" (p. 761).

Comer found that a positive school culture promotes physical, social, emotional, and ethical development in children, as well as linguistic and intellectual development. However, he and his colleagues also found that many colleges of education did not sufficiently prepare future teachers to understand the importance of child development in its relation to language and literacy development (Comer, 2004; Shonkoff and Phillips, 2000). Teachers, parents, and guardians alike need to be aware of the stages of child development as they read with children. Such knowledge helps them select age-appropriate literature and lead children in successful book discussions.

The late 20th century and early 21st century have seen extraordinary breakthroughs in brain research and our understanding of development in utero, scientific advances made possible by sophisticated imaging technology. Such knowledge helps us understand how children develop physically, cognitively, and emotionally; as well it suggests the best ways for parents and others to raise and teach children. Furthermore, much of this scientific research is available to parents, caregivers, and teachers via the Internet, whereas only two decades ago such knowledge was the preserve of experts. We briefly review some major points in this research in the sections to follow.

The Role of Literature in Healthy Child Development

Children's literature (whether read aloud to children or read by them) makes a positive difference in their overall development. This is especially true for general literacy development. Delores Durkin (1966) established the importance of reading aloud to young children as a reason why some children come to school already knowing how to read. Gordon Wells (1985) saw adults reading and sharing books with children as central to children's acquisition of literacy and adaptation to the world beyond their home, school, and community. The amount of time young children were read to, along with their general access to children's literature books, correlates positively with their success in learning to read and later academic achievement in school (Anderson, Wilson, & Fielding, 1988; Krashen, 1993; Anderson, 1996; Shin, 2004). Particularly for economically disadvantaged infants and young children, having access to books and being read to regularly (isolated skills instruction) has a statistically significant benefit for their literacy development and later scholastic achievement (Neuman, 1999).

Linguistic development, social development, psychological development, and emotional development are inseparable from cognitive and literacy development. Academic achievement is about developing the whole child, as Howard Gardner (1993) reminds us, not simply teaching them to read and write or imparting factual knowledge. How children control their impulses, manage anger, handle relationships with others, deal with success and failure, and develop their unique talents are all part of child development and are key to their scholastic success (Gardner, 1993; Goleman, 1995). Children's literature, for the broad view of human nature it presents and the discussions and activities it gives rise to, promotes children's growth and development (Glazer, 2000).

Talking about books helps children develop concepts about objects (such as their size, shape, and color), places (such as the home, school, park, and doctor's office), occupations (such as a firefighter, lawyer, dentist, mechanic) and nature (such as animals, plants, mountains, rivers, and beaches). In addition, reading aloud and discussing literature can have even greater benefits in the development of a child's intellect, personality, and emotional well-being.

According to the renowned child psychologist Bruno Bettelheim (1989), "our greatest need and most difficult achievement is to find meaning in our lives" (p. 3). Achieving a meaningful existence does not happen overnight, nor is it something automatic. Rather, human development occurs gradually, one event at a time, culminating in a mature adult who has experienced the world and understands his or her place in it. Children first come to understand themselves, then others, then, finally, they come to understand their place in the greater world. As Bettelheim explains, "Our positive feelings give us the strength to develop our rationality; only hope for the future can sustain us in the adversities we unavoidably encounter" (p. 4).

Early Physical Development

Let's begin with a child's basic physical development. The head and neck develop before the arms and legs; this is so because the regions in the brain that control activity "move from head to toe." While lying on her stomach, a baby will first raise her head, then her chest, and eventually sit up as her neck and back muscles grow stronger. Rolling over requires that multiple parts of the brain operate in unison.

Pediatricians stress that for normal physical growth babies need opportunities to do things on their own. Exploring the environment and solving problems they encounter are crucial to normal biological development of the brain. Synapses in the brain (connections between neurons necessary for learning and understanding) are formed by experience, experimentation, and human contact.

When children learn to walk (between ages 1 and 2), they are called *toddlers*. The toddler stage is marked by walking, talking, and exploring the environment; thus the child's home environment should be safe to explore. Gross motor development occurs through large body movements. In years 3, 4, and 5, children's gross motor development continues, so physical activities should be encouraged. The toddler who used to enjoy solitary play now becomes the young child who enjoys playing and interacting with other children. Visit http://pediatrics.about.com/od/agesandstages/u/agesandstages.htm or www.Wholefamily.com for more information on these developmental stages.

Pediatricians tell new parents not to worry over every developmental milestone; reaching a milestone early or late has little significance on a child's later cognitive and physical abilities. For example, the normal age range for walking without support is 12 to 18 months, but some toddlers walk earlier and some later. Furthermore, periodic regression in motor development is also normal. Once a child begins to walk, the brain's "postural reorganization" may cause a child to revert temporarily to reaching out and holding things with both hands (Raymond, 2000a).

Children's Literature About Physical Development

The books discussed in this section can be used by teachers and caregivers to talk about physical development with young children. James Comer (2005) found that teachers who were familiar with children's physical and emotional development were better able to use literature to get children to reflect on and talk about these important topics.

Step By Step by Bruce McMillan (1987) takes readers one photograph at a time through the development of "Evan," from 4 months to 14 months. In large print, with only one or two words per page, the book shows Evan sleeping, waking, kicking, and, later on, kneeling, sitting, standing up, and, eventually, running. This book makes for a great introduction to literacy in pairing pictures with words. Teachers or caregivers can point to the picture of Evan sleeping and ask a child, "What is the baby doing in this picture?" Then they can point to the word that corresponds with the picture.

In Amy Hest's *The Babies Are Coming* (1997) one dozen babies live in "tall apartment houses with fast elevators and squat buildings with winding stairs, in houses that are jumbled up and messed up, in houses neat and grand . . ." (p. 2). The illustrations show the babies crawling, dancing, peeking, singing, and yawning as they are bundled up in heavy snowsuits, mittens, and boots. On a snowy day they are all going to the library for story hour. Teachers or caregivers can then ask children questions: "Can you guess where the babies are headed?" "What do you like to wear on a blustery, cold winter day?" Asking children to talk about books is one way to help them enjoy and better understand the stories read to them.

Sometimes parent and child alike worry when a child's development does not keep pace with that of a kid down the block. In *Leo the Late Bloomer* by Robert Kraus (1971), Leo the lion cub can't do anything right: he's a sloppy eater, doesn't speak, and can't read either. His father is worried but his mother isn't. She says that there's nothing wrong with Leo; he's just a late bloomer. Someone reading the book to a child might ask these questions: "What do you think are some of Leo's problems?" "What do you predict will happen later in the story?" "How do you feel about Leo's problems and his later successes?" As you may recall from Chapter 1, Louise Rosenblatt (1994b) argues that books should be enjoyed and discussed on both the efferent (informational) and aesthetic (emotional) levels. Thus questions should try to engage children on both levels.

In *Don't Worry, Dear* by Joan Fassler (1971) Jenny is too small to do things for herself like ringing her own doorbell. At night she wets the bed.

The bigger kids down the block make fun of her because she stutters when she talks and always sucks her thumb. When her three aunts come to visit, they all have many suggestions for how to help Jenny with her problems. But Jenny's mother isn't worried about her. Instead she plays with Jenny and her stuffed animals, pretending that the animals really can talk back to Jenny. Little by little, Jenny feels better about herself. Bed-wetting, thumb sucking, and other early childhood issues are common for many children. Reading this book aloud and discussing it with children may help them cope better with their own frustrations.

Not all children are born without physical challenges. Jeanne Lee retells an ancient Cambodian tale in *Silent Lotus* (1991). This beautifully illustrated picture book follows the life of Lotus, who cannot hear or speak. Her parents pray to the gods for a sign of what will happen to their daughter. Years pass and Lotus grows into a beautiful young lady, kind in spirit and skilled in many tasks. One day at the famous temple of Angkor Wat she sees the temple dancers and feels the vibrations of the drums and cymbals. An old woman agrees to teach Lotus the intricate movements of the dances that tell the ancient stories of the Cambodian people. Lotus's life is transformed and her parents' prayers are answered. If you read this book to children, get out the tap sticks, drums, and dance with them. We encourage this because there are also distinct connections between musical knowledge and academic performance (Lamb & Gregory, 1993). Thus musical and movement intelligences should be nurtured as well (Gardner, 1993).

Cognitive Development

In this section we discuss some of the theories underlying children's cognitive or intellectual growth. Parents and teachers alike have their own theories as to how children learn and what the best conditions are for learning, but through the work of scientists in the field of human learning who collect large amounts of data, we can generalize stages across a general population (Miller, 2002).

Cognitive learning theories focus on the internal, mental processes of the brain to make sense of the world; this is in contrast to behaviorist theories, which focus on external, observable behaviors, conditioned by stimulus, response, and reinforcement. We shall briefly review the work of three leading cognitive learning theorists: Jean Piaget, Lev Vygotsky, and Jerome Bruner.

The Work of Jean Piaget

Jean Piaget, the great Swiss psychologist, gathered observational data on infants and young children over many years and formulated a theory for how children grow intellectually. His work has influenced so many others that scholars today consider him the most important figure in the field of developmental psychology (Miller, 2002). Piaget's theory is that children's intellectual growth parallels their physical growth. Based on an innate view of intellectual growth, Piaget's experiments led him to conclude that children learn as an adaptation to their physical and social environment (Piaget & Inhelder, 1969). For example, Piaget demonstrated that very young children believe that pouring liquid from a tall thin glass into a short squat glass reduces the amount of the liquid. Older children, however, recognize that the shape of the glass does not affect the amount of the liquid poured into it. Thus older children show cognitive development because they grasp the law of conservation of mass. Applying logic, they override the misperception that the taller container holds more liquid. They know that the amount of liquid does not change when poured from one container into the other.

According to Piaget, adaptation involves two important processes: *assimilation* and *accommodation*. Assimilation is the mental interpretation of a new experience in light of previous experiences. The child adds new information to existing categories or schemata in his memory. This is one reason why it is so important to read aloud to young children, for they add new information to their schemata in the process. For example, a child who lives in the city with a pet dog has some knowledge of four-legged animals. But an encounter with a calf in the country causes a mental adaptation whereby the child adds new knowledge about four-legged animals: i.e., not all quadrupeds are dogs.

But what happens when a child encounters an experience totally unrelated to an existing knowledge base? A new schema (along with a mental label) must then be created; Piaget called this *accommodation*. For example, a child's first ride in an airplane can be a scary event; many questions must be answered to reassure the youngster that, yes, this huge metal object flies above the clouds without falling. Cognitive development is the interplay between assimilation and accommodation as children adapt to a changing environment. A child seeks "to exist in harmony with its environment" (Goldhaber, 2000, p. 188). This harmony, the driving force behind adaptation, Piaget called *equilibrium*.

Piaget made the strong claim that a child's cognitive growth proceeds through a series of distinct intellectual stages (Piaget, 1974). See Figure 2.1 for Piaget's first three stages and their relationship to reading.

Stages of cognitive development.	FIGURE 2.1

Stage 1: Sensorimotor intelligence (roughly birth to 2 years). Infants learn about the real world through their senses by touching, grasping, smelling, and tasting. Letters made of plastic, felt, or stuffed bunting allow young children to feel the shape of the letters.

Stage 2: Preoperational intelligence (roughly 2 years to 7 years). Children at this stage can use symbols and words to represent objects, events, and ideas. Children learn words from seeing them in their daily environment: for example, street names, names of familiar businesses, names of products in the grocery store. Environmental print aids their emergent literacy. Children learn the names and sounds of the letters by listening to books read aloud.

Stage 3: Concrete operational intelligence (roughly 7 to 11 years). More systematic and logical thinking occurs based on children's manipulation of real objects and their engagement in physical activities. Formal instruction in learning to read is emphasized in the school curriculum, and independent, free reading time also increases.

The Work of Lev Vygotsky

Lev Vygotsky was born in Russia in 1896, the same year Jean Piaget was born in Switzerland. Vygotsky was influenced by Piaget's developmental theory that innate forces drive the intellectual growth of children. However, Vygotsky argued that starting around age 2, external or cultural forces play as great if not a greater role in children's cognitive development as internal ones. Vygotsky spent much time observing young children at play and also engaging them in various problem-solving situations. From his observations, he argued for the importance of intellectual symbols such as speech, writing, and math in developing higher levels of thought and abstract reasoning. These ideas influenced Howard Gardner many years later when he worked out his theory of multiple intelligences.

Speech, in particular, was of paramount significance for Vygotsky. He explained how the development of speech changes the ways a child acts upon and interprets the world (Vygotsky, 1962). Young children use speech to direct their parents to help them complete tasks. Later, children talk out loud to themselves as they play, a behavior Vygotsky termed *egocentric speech.* Still later, according to Vygotsky, comes *inner speech,* in which young children rehearse their thought processes by talking with themselves inside their own heads. This is a central part of problem solving and intellectual growth; even as adults, we use inner speech to help us solve difficult problems before we act.

As Vygotsky studied the cognitive growth of infants, preschool children, and primary-grade children, he became more convinced of the important role that adults play in children's mental growth. Unlike Piaget, who was concerned with the individual child, Vygotsky saw intellectual attainment as the outcome of interactions between children and adults in specific social settings (Crain, 2000; Miller, 2002). For this reason we refer to Vygotsky's work as the *sociocultural* or *social interaction theory* of cognitive development.

You may recall from Chapter 1 that Louise Rosenblatt (1994b, 1995) argued that learning to read involves not only a child and an adult but also the unique interaction that takes place between a specific child and a specific book at the time of reading. It is this literate and social interaction between child and adult, and among groups of young children, that lies at the heart of literacy acquisition.

Another of Vygotsky's major contributions toward understanding cognitive development is the notion of a *zone of proximal development* (1978). Working in the early years of intelligence testing, Vygotsky noted that intelligence tests measured what an individual child could achieve using her intelligence alone; however, with a little help from an adult, that same child could solve problems that she could not have solved by herself. The amount of assistance a child needed from an adult to solve a problem varied, but the potential for assisted improvement was what he called the zone of proximal development, a child's potential for enhanced performance made possible by adult assistance.

When adults interact with young children over picture books, they are helping to actuate the zone of proximal development by leading children to explore literature through what Louise Rosenblatt called efferent and aesthetic responses. And when children are encouraged to respond to books through a variety of activities (art, dance, song, etc.), they are also developing their multiple intelligences.

The Work of Jerome Bruner

Jerome Bruner, an American psychologist, was influenced by the work of Piaget and Vygotsky. Bruner believed that children's minds develop in three stages. The *enactive stage* comes first. At this stage, infants learn only through their own actions. The *iconic stage* occurs when children use imagery to assist their thought processes. The third stage, the *symbolic stage,* occurs when children connect their own thoughts to the real world through language. Like Vygotsky, Bruner placed great importance on language for the development of intelligence (Bruner, 1965, 1971). Bruner believed that language played an important part in the development of reason because language frees "the mind from total dependence on the appearance of reality" by allowing a child to talk about things he experienced in the past or things he might encounter in the future (Yellin et al., 2008, p. 125).

Another term associated with Bruner's theory of cognitive development as it relates to language development, is *schemata*. The brain utilizes both short-term memory and long-term memory to store information for later use in problem solving. Retrieving thousands of individual bits of information would prove overwhelming, so the brain creates categories or schemata in order to store and recall knowledge (Bruner, 1983). Language, by giving things a verbal label, aids in the storage and retrieval process; in fact without such labels, recall of information would be nearly impossible.

Like Vygotsky, Bruner saw children's interaction with adults as crucial to both their linguistic and cognitive growth. When children carry on dialogues with adults in real-world situations (e.g., making a model airplane or taking a nature walk), they can build on the adult's greater knowledge, experience, and language complexity. The assistance that the adult provides is verbal instructions and modeling. Bruner termed this *scaffolding* (1987), which is one way of describing what occurs in Vygotsky's zone of proximal development. Caregivers provide early scaffolding experiences to infants when they work together in the kitchen making dinner or in the garage fixing a broken toy. Teachers provide scaffolding in the classroom when they verbally explain and visually demonstrate complex concepts such as addition in arithmetic or punctuation in writing.

Following in the footsteps of Piaget, Vygotsky, and Bruner, modern learning theorists have developed the *information processing theory* to help explain how young children learn.

Information Processing Theory

Information processing theory is the most valuable theory for our purposes of examining child development and learning for two reasons. First, it incorporates the latest work on brain research from the fields of both medicine and education, and it applies the findings to how children learn. Second, it is a clear explanation of a very complex process, one that both teachers and caregivers can understand and bring to bear in their work with young children.

The theory focuses on how new knowledge is processed, stored, and later retrieved from memory. There are three parts to this process: sensory registers, short-term memory, and long-term memory. Understanding how these three parts interoperate is key to understanding how the brain works, how infants and young children acquire new knowledge, and how school-age children process print and learn new information.

Sensory registers

An infant is surrounded by stimuli. Immediately after birth, a child's major sensory registers (smell, touch, taste, hearing, and vision) are all operative. There is even evidence that the sensory registers are operating before birth: for example, sounds penetrating the womb are registered in the growing baby's auditory cortex; also babies in utero can perceive the smell of the mother's amniotic fluid (Raymond, 2000b). The senses of smell, touch, and taste introduce babies to the world. Each new stimulus in the environment sets off a multitude of brain wave activity. Touch, for example, is crucial for later cognitive and physical development; neonatal research has shown that premature infants who are regularly massaged gain weight faster than infants who are not. Auditory neurons allow the brain to process phonemes, the building blocks of language, and very rapidly these auditory neurons focus on retaining the phonemes repeatedly heard (English has around 44 phonemes) and rejecting phonemes not heard in their environment. As the last sense to develop, vision continues to sharpen until around age 9 (Raymond, 2000b).

The sensory registers receive information, but only for a brief time—seconds usually. But it is the ability to hold on to sensory information that allows you to read this sentence and retain the information from the previous one (Eggen & Kauchak, 1992). However, true cognitive growth requires the brain to hold on to information for a longer period of time. And that requires short-term memory.

Short-term memory

Short-term memory, also called "working memory," takes information (stimuli) from the senses and stores it temporarily in the brain. It also helps the brain make decisions regarding what to retain and what to ignore. Separate bits of information can be combined into chunks for easier storage. For example, we remember a friend's phone number in two or three chunks of information rather than as seven or ten separate digits.

The important point to remember about short-term memory is that it has inherent limitations in both capacity and duration. Much of what passes through short-term memory is soon forgotten. An example of this is a first grader who phonetically decodes a sentence slowly, one word at a time, and then, when asked what the sentence means, draws a blank. Another example is the confusion caused by asking a child multiple questions before she has had a chance to think and respond to the first question.

Long-term memory

Long-term memory allows us to store information on a permanent basis to retrieve as we live our daily lives. It is like a giant archive of information made of two types of memory:

- *Episodic memory* is our mental record of our personal life, imprinted with people, places, things, and even smells that we encountered in the past. As we constantly add new impressions to this memory collection, older ones may become fuzzy. However, certain significant events in our lives help us to retain important information. We can all probably remember where we were when we heard the tragic news of September 11, 2001.

- *Semantic memory* is what allows us to remember facts, concepts, generalizations, and rules. It is a great repository of information that we use to solve problems and make decisions (Eggen & Kauchak, 1992).

Memory and learning to read

We know that both short-term memory and long-term memory are involved when children learn how to read. The most cogent explanation of this relationship comes from the work of psycholinguist Frank Smith (1988). First, short-term memory receives symbols (input) and allows a child to produce sounds (output). But clearly this is only an initial, rudimentary stage of reading. Plus, as was noted earlier, short-term memory is intrinsically limited in its capacity and duration. Thus, true reading (understanding for meaning) requires long-term memory: it is here that the brain stores and organizes relevant information from our past experiences. Long-term memory comprises our collection of spelling rules, knowledge of sight vocabulary, and our understanding of grammar and syntax, as well as our familiarity with books and print. Most important of all, it is long-term memory that helps us decide if what we read makes sense. If it does not make sense, we reread the material to understand it.

Information processing theory is relatively new compared to the research of Jean Piaget, Lev Vygotsky, Jerome Bruner, and others who focused on how infants, toddlers, and children develop cognitively. Their work in cognitive development is the foundation upon which most early childhood programs are based today.

Children's Literature About Cognitive Development

It is no surprise that the best way for parents, caregivers, and teachers to help children acquire and organize new knowledge is by reading aloud to them. By reading to children, adults model (scaffold) many processes: fluency and intonation, the connection of print to sound, and the vicarious flights of fancy that good books occasion. For example, all children deal with fears and must learn how to handle their emotions. In *Jeremy's First Haircut* (Girard, 1986), a little boy is afraid to go to the barbershop for his first haircut. But in the end he enjoys the experience. Fear of the dark is discussed in the fiction picture book *Who's Afraid of the Dark?* (Hamilton, 1983). And author Kimura Yuichi writes about children facing their fear of storms and fear of animals in *One Stormy Night* (2003). Reading books such as these to children and discussing them is one of the best ways to help them handle their fears and, in turn, grow and develop.

Social and Moral Development

ust as children develop physically, they develop socially and morally, too. Successful social development is most evident in a child's ability to establish friendships with other children. Moral development is seen when children make choices that adults may deem either right or wrong. It is important for caregivers to remember that this development takes place gradually and cannot be rushed.

Social Development

Social development in young children was theorized in the well-known work of Erik Erikson. As a teacher of young children in Vienna, Austria, Erikson came under the influence of Sigmund Freud. However, in his own work he moved beyond Freud's psychoanalytic theories to incorporate social and cultural influences in personality development (Crain, 2000; Miller, 2002).

Erikson's major contribution was a psychosocial description of the stages of human life from birth to old age. For each stage Erikson saw the individual as adjusting (or not adjusting) to certain conflicts encountered in the social/cultural environment (Erikson, 1963). Figure 2.2 briefly describes only the first three stages of Erikson's work, which are the ones most relevant to teachers and caregivers of young children.

In the 1980s and 1990s, child psychologists, researchers, and educators began to integrate the work of Vygotsky, Piaget, Bruner, Erikson, and Kohlberg to prescribe ways that parents, caregivers, and teachers could promote healthy development in preschool and school-age children. During this time new research aimed at helping children become more responsible, outgoing, helpful, considerate, and generally sociable (Solomon et al., 1992). Preschool and primary school programs were developed to improve children's social skills, promote their tolerance in the face of frustration, and teach them self-control (Greenberg et al., 1995).

FIGURE 2.2 Erickson's first three stages of life.

Stage 1: Trust vs. mistrust (from birth to around age 1). Infants learn to trust or mistrust their environment through their relationships with caregivers. If the infant's basic needs for food, comfort, and attention are met, they perceive the world as trustworthy. What a baby wants most is consistency and predictability. If mistrust develops in the infant, this may cause later feelings of suspicion toward the world in general.

Stage 2: Autonomy vs. shame and doubt (roughly from ages 1 to 3). Around age 2 the child develops a sense of autonomy or independence. The child can hold tightly to objects or throw them away. He can help dress himself or throw a tantrum. This is where parents (or society's rules) step in. Though autonomy is encouraged, the child also learns there are right and wrong ways to behave. Breaking the rules leads to feelings of shame and doubt. The pull between the need for autonomy and feelings of shame and doubt leads to normal conflicts that the child must resolve during day-to-day activities.

Stage 3: Initiative vs. guilt (roughly from age 3 to age 6). As the child explores the world and initiates actions, he or she gains a sense of self-confidence. A girl wants to be more like her mother. A boy wants to be more like his father. Sometimes such ambitions run up against social taboos; a classic example in Freudian psychoanalysis is the Oedipus Complex. Parental and societal controls are becoming part of the child's self-controlling behavior to avoid feelings of guilt.

Quality picture books can encourage children to talk about their interests, their fears, their friends, and the world around them. Engaging in activities with other children around books—activities such as simple art projects, constructions, dance and musical performances—present further opportunities for children's social development.

Moral Development

The work of Lawrence Kohlberg (1984) has influenced educators' thinking about moral development in children and adolescents. He presented children with a moral dilemma; for example, a person who steals food in order to feed his starving family. Then Kohlberg asked, "Was the person right or wrong?" What Kohlberg sought from his subjects was the reasoning behind their response, why they thought the person in the story did what he did. His research led Kohlberg to describe six stages of moral development. Figure 2.3 describes only the first two stages, which apply to young children.

Adults read picture books aloud and ask questions that may require young children to respond based on their moral understanding. Similarly, adults respond differently to children of different ages based on their understanding of the stages of social and moral development. Observing young children at play helps adults assess how children understand the world in terms of right and wrong. Knowledge of Kohlberg's stages should help teachers and caregivers better guide children in self-reflection on their behavior (Crain, 2000; Kohlberg, 1984).

Children's Literature About Social and Moral Development

Teachers and caregivers of young children need to understand the totality of social, emotional, and cognitive growth for healthy development. Reading to young children and discussing important issues with them is just one way children learn how to deal with their feelings, emotions, and frustrations, as well as how to get along with others and find their own place in the world. Many different types of children's books can be used by teachers and caregivers to help children grow socially and emotionally. The following brief descriptions of books to be shared with young children will give you some ideas for how to use books to help children cope with their feelings.

Kohlberg's first two moral development stages. **FIGURE 2.3**

Stage 1: Punishment and obedience (approximately ages 1 to 5). In this first stage young children explain right and wrong based on the consequence of an action. They don't steal things because they don't want to get punished. Children obey the rules out of fear of adult authority.

Stage 2: The individual and exchange (approximately ages 6 to 12). At the second stage children still worry about the consequences of an action, but they also consider their self-interest. Will doing something for someone else invite reciprocation or cooperation? Right and wrong are therefore colored by how an individual thinks he or she may benefit from an action.

Anxieties bring about similar doubts in all children: "Will other children like me?" "How will I fit in with the group?" Two books that deal with these adjustments are *Archibald Frisby* and *Crow Boy. Archibald Frisby* (Chesworth, 1994) tells the story of a young boy who is different. He doesn't like to play the kinds of games that other kids play. Instead, his only interest is science. His mother is worried that he won't make friends, and her solution is to send Archibald to camp. But at camp Archibald not only continues to pursue his fascination with science, he also becomes a favorite among his fellow campers and a leader in their adventures. Children who have interests different from those of their classmates will be able to relate to Archibald and should be encouraged by adults to develop their unique talents.

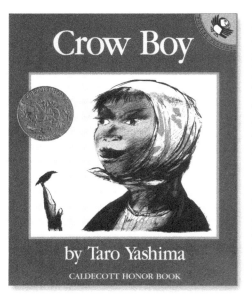

In *Crow Boy,* by Taro Yashima (1983), Chibi is a tiny Japanese boy attending school for the first time. He is very shy and afraid of everything. He acts strangely, and the other children make fun of him. But Chibi also has a special gift for imitating birds that live in his remote mountain village. With the help of a kind teacher, the other children are led to understand who Chibi is and why he acts as he does. We are all different in some ways, and we all have gifts to share with others. Teachers and caregivers can help bring out children's special gifts and develop their multiple intelligences.

Some books deal with gender roles and stereotyping. This is an emotional and often confusing issue for young children as they grow up. Teachers can use the following books to initiate discussions and get children thinking about how they are alike, how they are different, and how they view various roles we play in life.

In the *Paper Bag Princess,* Robert Munsch (1980) reverses the classic fairy tale involving a prince and princess. Princess Elizabeth's castle is destroyed, and she is carried off by a fire-breathing dragon, wearing only a dirty paper bag. Clever Elizabeth, however, manages to save herself through a number of tricks she pulls on the dragon, and she eventually returns to Prince Ronald. But prim and proper Ronald is shocked by her dirty appearance and lack of ladylike clothes. Elizabeth quickly realizes that she does not need Ronald to save her from dragons or anything else in the world. Discussing with young children how traditional gender roles are reversed in this story can lead children to try their hand at rewriting other stories and recognizing that not all of life's roles need follow traditional scripts or stereotypes. Our society has changed radically from a time when girls did not play competitive sports, and boys weren't supposed to know how to cook.

Another book in this same vein is *Max* by Rachel Isadora (1976). Max loves to play baseball, while his sister goes to ballet class. One day, before his baseball game, Max decides to peek in on his sister's ballet class and decides to join in. In the end, Max decides that he can do both ballet and baseball, as the one helps him do the other better.

The Caldecott Honor book *When Sophie Gets Angry—Really, Really Angry . . .* by Molly Bang (1999) is a picture book that shows how one little girl deals with her anger. Sophie loves to play with her toys, especially her toy gorilla. But one day her sister takes her toy and will not give it back. This makes Sophie so angry that she gets red and wants to explode like a volcano. Young children can

Rachel Isadora   www.harpercollinschildrens.com/HarperChildrens/Kids/AuthorsAndIllustrators/ContributorDetail.aspx?Cld=17066

Rachel Isadora was born in New York City in 1953. All her life she wanted to be a dancer. She attended the American School of Ballet and eventually danced with the Boston Ballet Company. However, a foot injury cut her dancing career short. It was then that she turned to writing and illustrating children's books. Her book *Max* (1976), tells the story of a young boy who loves to play baseball. In *Opening Night* (1984) readers go behind the scenes with a young girl at her first ballet performance. *Ben's Trumpet* (1979) was selected as a Caldecott Honor book. She also writes stories based on her many trips to Africa and the Caribbean.

relate to Sophie's anger and her relationship with her sister. They want to talk about a time they were really, really angry or perhaps draw pictures of something that got them so mad they didn't know what to say. Books like this give teachers and caregivers a chance to talk about feeling anger and coping with it.

Everyone has bad days, days when nothing seems to go right. In *Alexander and the Terrible, Horrible, No Good, Very Bad Day,* by Judith Viorst (1972), the title character Alexander has one such awful day. He wakes up with gum in his hair; he then gets the worst seat in the car pool; later he even embarrasses himself at school in front of the whole class. Kids laugh at all the things that go wrong in Alexander's day, but they may want to share their own misadventures too. Adults, too, can share with children stories about their own very bad days. Children also enjoy pantomiming or play acting out their very bad days. Coping with such days is a major part of how children mature and learn that, while there will be some days like Alexander's, better ones will follow.

The poet Ogden Nash has created a real hero in Isabel. *The Adventures of Isabel* (1991) tells of a young child who faces down one fright after another: bears, witches, even a visit to the doctor. But brave Isabel manages to get through them all unscathed. The illustrations by James Marshall should inspire young children to draw pictures of their own fears and their triumphs over them. For preschool and primary-grade children, drawing and finger painting are great ways to communicate their feelings. Caregivers and teachers can then ask them to talk about their drawings, which, in turn, can inspire them to write their own stories.

Every child has done something she later regretted. In *Lilly's Purple Plastic Purse* (Henkes, 1996), Lilly loves school but also loves her new purple plastic purse. She brings it to school one day to show it off to her friends, but the consequences are not good. This is a good book for prompting prediction by asking students, "What will she do now?" Also, teachers can ask questions that exercise problem-solving abilities: "How could she have handled the situation differently?" "What might she do the next time she has a favorite toy to share with her friends at school?"

One of the most difficult events that simultaneously evokes powerful and confusing emotions is the death of a loved one. The loss of a loved one is difficult for children at any age. *Some of the Pieces* by Melissa Madenski (1991) is a serious story about how a young boy must deal with the death of his father. Madenski's story allows children to talk about death and dying and the good memories they can cherish after someone (or some pet) they loved has passed away.

Language Development

y 18 months a child is learning 12 new words a day, and by age 2, a child may have command of nearly 2,000 words. How exactly this process takes place remains a debate among linguists and child specialists. There are many theories explaining how young children acquire and develop their language, the most widely accepted being the behaviorist, the innatist, and the sociocultural theories. However there is agreement among theorists that the early years of language development are critical. For example, if children with hearing impairments (the most common cause of childhood language problems) are identified and treated within the first 6 months, they will likely develop normal speech and language (Cowley, 2000).

Behaviorist Theory

The behaviorist theory of B. F. Skinner (1957) is among the oldest theories of language acquisition and remains one of the most popular. In the behaviorist view, the actions and interactions between parents and child are the environmental factors that imprint oral language in a baby's mind. The focus is on parents and caregivers interacting with children in a controlled environment, such as the home. A father communicates with his infant daughter, depending on the situation, in a positive or negative tone of voice. His communication is the stimulus that triggers behavior such as crying, smiling, or babbling from the baby. When a child says "mama," the stimulus can trigger an ecstatic response from his mother: "Oh, honey, yes, Mama will give you a hug!" These communicative interactions between parent and child are also referred to as the *stimulus-response theory* of language acquisition.

A baby imitates what she hears at home, memorizing words and grammar rules, and she adjusts her spoken language based on feedback from others. A controlled environment, imitation of language, and response to a stimulus are the hallmarks of behaviorism. However, not all scholars accept the premise that babies learn everything through imitation or that it is feasible for infants to memorize such huge amounts of linguistic information.

Innatist Theory

The innatist theory, also known as the nativistic or predetermined theory (Machado, 2006), is an alternative to behaviorism. Associated with the work of Noam Chomsky, innatism holds that every newborn child possesses the mental ability to acquire language; that is, the human brain, unlike any other animal's brain, is preprogrammed to learn language. Chomsky calls this the *language acquisition device*, or LAD. LAD allows very young children to speak phrases and sentences they have never heard before, overgeneralizing common forms (such as believing plausibly, though incorrectly, that all nouns take an "s" to form the plural: *sheeps, deers, peoples*) and otherwise using language in creative ways that go way beyond mere imitation of what they have heard (Cowley, 2000). The innatist position does acknowledge that a stimulating, supportive environment is still necessary to spark language acquisition. There have been extreme cases of child abuse where LAD languishes in disuse, such as the infamous case of Genie (pseudonym). Genie was a young girl confined in a barren room, terrorized by her father, and denied contact with human language or love until she was rescued at age 13 (Curtiss, 1977). It was only after Genie was rescued and placed in a hospital setting with caring specialists that she began to acquire limited language.

Pragmatic or Sociocultural Theory

This theory argues that some combination of innate abilities and a positive language environment most likely explains how infants acquire oral language. It acknowledges that children possess an inborn capacity for acquiring language. But it also contends that other language users (adults) interacting with infants in ordinary situations shape their language learning.

As previously discussed, Lev Vygotsky (1976) was an early believer of the importance of social interactions in children's development; he believed that when young children interact with adults, social exchanges trigger inner speech or verbal thoughts that later become spoken language. Inner speech is a child's way of rehearsing for overt language production. Even as adults we speak to ourselves either out loud or in our minds. But the key to understanding pragmatic theory is recognizing the powerful emotional and linguistic impact that positive social interactions at home and at school have upon a child's language development (Golinkoff & Hirsh-Patek, 1999; Lieberman, 1993).

Stages of Communication and Language Acquisition

Language acquisition (from birth through age 6, approximately) and language development (from age 6 through adolescence) are key periods of literacy development. Here we briefly review the stages that children pass through in acquiring and developing their speaking skills and relate them to the ability to read.

Courtney Cazden (1972), Ursula Bellugi (1971), and Roger Brown (1970), all three of Harvard University, described the stages through which infants and young children pass in their journey toward fluent speech. Later work by Ferreiro and Teberosky (1982) and Marie Clay (1982, 1991, 2001), plus countless pediatricians, such as T. Berry Brazelton (1983), advanced the scientific study of young children's development of oral language.

Paralinguistic stage

Communication in newborns begins with hearing. Babies hear the voice of their mothers and fathers, the sounds of the radio, television, and fire engines wailing outside. How do we know this? Because of the facial expressions and the crying response of infants. Facial expressions (such as smiling) are part of what we call *paralinguistic,* or nonverbal responses; hand and arm gestures and body movements, such as shrugging one's shoulders, are other examples of paralinguistic communicative signs.

Gazing, crying, and cooing are the early signs that a baby is communicating. Furthermore, the pitch of others' voices elicits specific responses from infants. For example, strident voices cause babies to cry, but soft, soothing sounds from a caregiver elicit cooing. Crying, in particular, triggers a parent's concern and attention (Machado, 2006).

Before reading further . . .

TELEVISION AND THE HEALTHY HOME LANGUAGE ENVIRONMENT

Perhaps one of the most researched areas of home influences on young children's early oral language development and later reading development is television. The controversy surrounding the impact of television viewing on children's language development and reading achievement is not new. Marie Winn's controversial book *The Plug-in Drug* (1985) argued that television is essentially a passive medium that inhibits interacting with others. In 1988 Susan Neuman reported on a series of research studies on young children and heavy television watching; the latter she defined as 4 or more hours per day and 30 hours or more per week. The studies showed a significant negative effect on young children's vocabulary development and reading ability. Neuman's explanation for this negative effect is known as the *displacement effect:* children who watch lots of television could be doing other things such as playing games, playing sports, looking at picture books, reading books, drawing, and talking with their parents. Also, Singer and his colleagues (1988) found that in children ages 5 through 8, heavy television watching resulted in what they termed "concentration deprivation," or an inability to attend to adult language and school tasks; children with concentration deprivation had a more limited vocabulary and greater problems in learning to read than other children.

Compared to the decades of the late twentieth century, there is much less research being done today on the effects of television on children's oral language development and later reading achievement. This is so because television has been accepted as an inevitable factor in children's lives, at both home and at school. However, the controversy surrounding television and young children does continue.

Two of the more recent and large sample studies regarding television and young children had mixed findings. Wright and colleagues (2001) concluded that the effect of television on children is related to the content viewed. When young children view educational and informational programs with their parents, who discuss the content with them, television has a positive impact. However, when young children (ages 2 and 3) watch cartoons and other noneducational programs without parents present, such viewing has a negative effect on their intellectual development. The researchers also acknowledged that even when parents and children watch television together, it limits opportunities for social interactions critical to psychosocial development. Finally, Anderson and Pempek (2005), in a review of research studies, reported mixed results, too. Some studies found that television watching was negatively associated with language development, attention span, and cognitive abilities. They also noted that the American Academy of Pediatrics has recommended that children younger than 24 months not be exposed to television. Figure 2.4 presents some humorous young children's books about television that can lead to interesting parent–child discussions about how the family spends its time at home.

Clearly, television can entertain and inform children in many positive ways. However, in addition to affecting language development and reading proficiency, studies have also linked heavy television watching (more than 20 hours per week) in preschool and primary-school children to increased violent behavior, decreased attention span, emotional trauma, and even obesity (Christakis, 2004; Elias, 2004; Huesmann, et al., 2003; Koolstra, et al., 1997). In the home, parents can offset some of the negative influences of television by talking to their children and reading to them.

Babbling stage

When babies babble, they are testing various speech sounds—vowels, consonants, syllables—even imitating the rhythm of speech they hear around them. Pitch and intonation, too, make up their language environment. Within 6 months babies are aware of and are reproducing the phonemes (smallest units of language) of

| Books that turn couch potatoes into bookworms. | FIGURE 2.4 |

- *When the TV Broke* by Harriet Ziefert (1993) tells of little Jeffrey, who watches television every single day of the week, until one Saturday it stops working. Jeffrey is at a loss over what to do with his time on Monday, Tuesday, and Wednesday, anxiously waiting for the television to be fixed. Finally, on Thursday he decides to help his mother bake cookies. On Friday, he begins building an imaginary city. By the time the television is fixed Jeffrey is too busy doing other things to watch it. After reading this book, parents and teachers can read a how-to book. For example, in *A Cow, a Bee, a Cookie and Me,* by Meredith Hooper (1997), little Ben and his grandmother bake honey cookies. This picture book takes you on a real adventure to find the ingredients you need to bake cookies (e.g., cinnamon, which comes from the bark of a tropical tree).

- *Library Lil* by Suzann Williams (1997) is a funny, fanciful romp about a librarian in a town where no one reads but everyone watches television. Going house to house in her bookmobile she eventually converts the whole town into readers, until a motorcycle gang demands that they all watch pro wrestling on television. The confrontation between the gang and the librarian makes children cheer for Lil. A field trip to the local library would make a great follow-up to this book.

- If kids like *Library Lil,* they will also like *Aunt Chip and the Great Triple Creek Dam Affair* (1996) by Patricia Polacco. Aunt Chip is the former librarian of a town whose residents built a television tower and used books as tables, chairs, and even as materials to build a dam, rather than as reading material. Aunt Chip warns the townspeople of serious consequences if the children don't learn how to read. Polacco's colorful, zany illustrations will stimulate children to talk about the book and reflect on what happens when books are misused.

what will become their native language (Begley, 1996). And from then on, in interactions with adults, babies gradually begin to repeat certain sounds and ignore others that are not part of the language or languages spoken around them.

Holophrase stage

Somewhere around the end of the first year, a baby emits the first recognizable word, a thrilling moment for every parent. Linguists call this a *holophrase.* Although heard as one word (i.e., "Daddy," "Mommy," "no"), a holophrase actually carries meaning beyond one word alone. Utilizing "volume, intonation, facial expression, bodily gesture" the one-word holophrase can signify an entire sentence or many sentences, depending on the situation (Yellin et al., 2008, p. 134). For example, when a little baby sees her mother at the kitchen stove she holds her hands up and wails, "Mommy." Mother knows that what she is trying to say is "Mommy, I'm hungry, feed me."

Pivot-open stage

The next stage, pivot-open, occurs around 18 to 24 months. Pivot–open is described as the two-word stage of language acquisition. The pivot word, of a limited grammatical class such as the personal pronouns *my, your,* and *me,* serves as a lever to which open or unlimited grammatical terms such as nouns can attach. Thus a baby begins constructing simple two-word utterances like "My milk," "My Daddy," "Your cookie," "Your toy." As with the holophrase stage, the two-word pivot–open stage actually represents a longer, more complex sentence such as "My milk spilled on the table and I want more" (Yellin et al., 2008).

During this period of language growth, children and their caregivers should be playing with language, reciting riddles and songs, and sharing favorite bedtime stories. Language play is fun and it lays the foundation for a positive emotional response to learning language. Think of the familiar rhyme, "This little piggie went to market," in which the toes are pressed as the rhyme is recited. Too often language education is only thought of in terms of formal lessons (e.g., grammar work sheets), but singsong play can be an informal lesson of considerable importance.

Telegraphic speech stage

Occurring around the second year, telegraphic speech is characterized by three or more words. For linguists this is the most fascinating of all the stages, fascinating because the 2-year-old is now stringing together meaningful multi-word units according to highly abstract and complex grammatical rules they have never been explicitly taught. Children 2½ years old have a vocabulary of 2,000-plus words, and they link noun phrases to verb phrases accurately long before they understand the concept of syntax. The sentences still sound like baby talk, "Me want a cookie now," but the message is clear. Behaving like little linguists, infants tackle grammar long before they learn to use a fork (Cowley, 2000).

Language Pattern Development

Clearly, then, the telegraphic stage of language acquisition demonstrates the creative powers of children to master language. However, it is also clear that this process cannot take place in isolation. For the child's language patterns to resemble those of an adult, three kinds of interaction must occur: *language reduction, language expansion,* and *language extension.*

A young child hears and understands language to a much greater degree than he can produce it. When hearing adult speech and attempting to communicate back, for example, the young child automatically shortens lengthy adult syntax to something more manageable. Thus, when mother says, "Don't bother me now, I'm fixing your dinner. It's chicken noodle soup, your favorite," the child replies "Hmm, chicken noodle is good." This is known as language reduction.

The flipside, language expansion, occurs when a caregiver takes a short, truncated child's sentence like "Where my doggie?" and stretches it into "I don't know where your doggie is." Rather than talking baby talk back to her child, the mother or father takes the child's question and elaborates it into a fully formed, grammatically correct response. Finally, language extension occurs naturally when a parent or teacher chats at length with a child, using fully formed adult sentences to complement and extend the child's shorter phrases. In the example above, perhaps the caregiver responded at greater length: "I don't know where your doggie is. Perhaps he's hiding in the other room. Let's go look for him." This would be an example of language extension.

For normal language development to take place, a supportive home language environment must exist. This means that adults talk regularly with a child. This unconscious "teaching" that parents and caregivers do is part of what sociologists call the "hidden curriculum" of the home. This refers to the everyday routines—play, chores, lunch and dinnertime conversations, even the physical

author sketch

Mo Willems   http://mowillemsstuff.blogspot.com

Mo Willems's artistic abilities are various. Not only is he an author of children's books, he also produces music theater and makes wire sculptures and carved ceramics. He was born in 1968 and was raised in New Orleans, where he attended the Isidore Newman School. He then attended and graduated from New York University's Tisch School for the Arts. He started his artistic career as a writer and animator for _Sesame Street, The Off-Beats, Sheep in the Big City,_ and _Codename: Kids Next Door._ He also performed stand-up comedy for some time. Besides three Caldecott Honor awards, he has won six Emmy Awards and the Carnegie Medal.

Some of Mo's books include _Don't Let the Pigeon Drive the Bus!,_ a Caldecott Honor book, _Knuffle Bunny: A Cautionary Tale, Knuffle Bunny Too: A Case of Mistaken Identity,_ and the Elephant and Piggie series for young readers. Each one of these books is humorous; the text, often presented in speech bubbles, matches his witty illustrations. In the Knuffle Bunny books, he uses photographs of his Brooklyn neighborhood as the background for his cartoonlike illustrations.

objects of the home (i.e., radio, television, computer, books, magazines)—that help shape a child's learning in the preschool years (McInerney & McInerney, 1998). In terms of later language development and successful academic achievement, the hidden curriculum of the home exercises a powerful influence.

Children's Literature About Language Development

Clearly books can make a difference in children's lives and their language development. However, it is up to adults to bring those books into the child's world. A humorous book that depicts early language development of language in children is Mo Willems's _Knuffle Bunny: A Cautionary Tale_ (2004). In this tale, Trixie is attempting to communicate with her dad about her beloved bunny gone missing. However, her dad cannot understand her nonsense words even though he understands that she is very upset and is trying to get him to understand. It is not until they return to the Laundromat that she speaks her first words: "Knuffle Bunny." Her dad then understands Trixie.

In Fred Hiatt's picture book _Baby Talk_ (1999), older brother Joey gets a new baby brother. Only he can't understand a thing he's saying. "WAAH, WAAH," the baby wails. "Ageek," says the baby. "Ada agoo," says the baby. Eventually, as Joey spends more time with his baby brother, he begins to understand what he is saying. Soon Joey is able to translate baby brother's babbling to his mother when they go shopping at the supermarket. Babbling is a natural stage of language acquisition. Parents and caregivers can understand the meaning behind the babblings of their children. This book can be used to explain to children how their infant siblings' strange sounds are really their way of communicating.

In a series of great animal photographs, the photographer Ylla Koffler helps tell the story of Oliver the Ostrich, who would not speak (_Look Who's Talking,_ Bonsall, 1962). When Oliver first arrived at the zoo, he was alone and scared. Young children going to school for the first time will be able to relate to Oliver's feelings. The other animals in the zoo wondered why Oliver didn't speak. The camels thought he had bad manners. The pelicans thought Oliver wasn't very smart.

51

FIGURE 2.5 Stuttering resources.

- **Stuttering Foundation of America,** 3100 Walnut Grove Road, Suite 603, Memphis, TN 38111, phone: 1-800-992-9392, website: www.stuttersfa.org
- **National Stuttering Association,** 5100 East LaPalma, Suite 208, Anaheim, CA 92807, website: www.nsastutter.org
- **The Stuttering Home Page,** Minnesota State University, Mankato, MN, 56001, website: www.stutteringhomepage.com

Parents and caregivers can ask young children to infer the reason why Oliver does not speak and to talk about their own anxieties about the first day of school.

Stuttering, a common occurrence for young children learning to speak, is the subject of *Ben Has Something to Say* (Lears, 2000). Ben won't read aloud in school or speak to neighbors on the street. People think he's just very shy, but the truth is that Ben is embarrassed to speak because of his severe stuttering. Only his dad and his speech therapist understand his problem and support Ben's efforts to talk. Ben wants to talk, but it takes the love of a dog to force him to make the effort. This easy to understand book gives teachers of young children an opportunity to discuss this important topic with children in a nonthreatening manner. Parents, caregivers, and teachers need to be patient with children who stutter and focus on what the child is trying to say, not how he is saying it.

Stuttering is a common but somewhat puzzling speech impediment that affects many in early childhood. Stuttering is definitely a communication disorder, but it is very complex in nature, making it hard to predict which children will stutter. It is not the result of a brain defect or of poor parenting. Some authorities believe it is related to emotional stress in a child's life, but other experts disagree. See Figure 2.5 for more resources on stuttering.

Literacy Development

Just as there are stages of language development, so too are there stages of literacy development that children go through. The discussion earlier in this chapter on cognitive, physical, and social development, along with language development, provides a foundation for understanding literacy acquisition in young children, but there are few absolutes in the teaching–learning transaction. Learning to read varies in relation to children's personality and abilities, their home environment, preschool experiences, familiarity with community resources such as libraries, and myriad other factors. Thus, all children do not learn to read on the same schedule. Some children acquire knowledge of the alphabet letters and sounds as early as 3 or 4 years of age, while other children enter kindergarten and first grade without knowing basic sound–symbol relationships. Parents, caregivers, and teachers should keep this in mind and not expect all youngsters to acquire literacy skills at the same age or rate.

For our discussions, we have categorized the stages of literacy development in three age groups: infants and toddlers (birth through year 3), preschool and kindergarten (years 4 and 5), and early primary grades (years 6, 7, and 8). Within the infant and toddler group, we make a finer subdivision according to age.

Infants and Toddlers

Lamaze International (2003) has identified three stages of babies' literacy development. For each stage, particular types of books are appropriate. Books for infants and toddlers are discussed at greater length in Chapter 4.

Stage one: Birth to 9 months

During stage one, as adults read to infants, the infants begin to understand the purpose of a book—an object that brings pleasure, that entertains, and that provides a vicarious experience to the reader or listener; this is the beginning of the aesthetic response described by Louise Rosenblatt (1994b). During these first 9 months infants learn through their senses, so they like to explore books with their hands and mouths. They are attracted to contrasting colors, shapes, and sizes. For this first stage, ideal books are small so they fit in small hands; they are also washable, made of soft cloth or plastic, in which case they can go into a bathtub. These books should be free of small detachable objects that babies could choke on. *Baby's Day: A Cloth Book* (Katz, 2007) is a good example of a colorful book that is safe for babies. Another good book for babies is *My First Taggies Book: Sweet Dreams* (2003), written and illustrated by Kaori Watanabe. It is made of soft fleece with eight different looped ribbons for babies to pull. A different animal is featured on each page along with simple text such as "Sweet dreams, little kitty."

Stage two: 9 to 18 months

During this stage, babies begin to recognize familiar objects in books, as well as people portrayed in books in family roles such as mommies and daddies. Since babies react to texture and sounds, ideal books for them at this stage give them opportunities to touch, push, and listen. There are many books featuring textures. One example is Rosemary Wells's (2004) *McDuff's Favorite Things,* which is a small book that lets babies feel McDuff's fluffy tail, his terrycloth towel, his leather collar, his soft blanket, and his knobby bone. During stage two, infants begin to turn pages, point, and repeat what adults read, so ideally books have text that names distinguishable objects featured in illustrations. One example is Disney's (Feldman, 2003) *Pooh and Friends: Animals,* which is a small board book with simple illustrations. On page 1 the word "sheep" appears in a question above a picture of a sheep, "What does a sheep say?" And Pooh provides the answer: "Bah, bah!" (unpaged).

Stage three: 18 months to 3 years

This stage is referred to as the toddler stage. During this stage children can identify objects when an adult points them out on the page. They can also now comprehend simple plots and enjoy rhyming words. This is also the stage in which toddlers begin to enjoy interactive peek-a-boo books that require them to lift flaps. Eric Hill's many "Spot" books delight toddlers. Each of the Spot books requires infants to lift a flap to find out the answers to questions. Toddlers may also enjoy imitating animal sounds, train whistles, truck motors, and car horns. Rosemary Wells has written many books for toddlers. Her books are short, written in rhyme, and have themes that encourage language development, cognitive development, and social skills. Two of her books that fit this description are *Only You* (2003) and *Shy Charles* (2001).

For all three of these stages, teachers and caregivers should choose books that encourage adult–child interaction. As caregivers read books, they can point to the various objects in the illustrations and point to the words so that children begin to follow along, understanding that one reads from left to right and top to bottom. As they listen to stories being read to them, children begin to hear the cadence of their language and its wonderful sounds. They also recognize the reality that the written world refers to.

Preschool and Kindergarten

Walker (2004) and O'Donnell and Wood (2004) describe the early stages of literacy prior to and during school. Beginning with the preschool years and kindergarten, a new phase of literacy development unfolds, often referred to as the *emergent literacy stage*. The child has been talking and using language for a number of years by this point. Oral communication has been the means by which the child gets her basic needs met (instrumental language), directs the actions of other people (regulatory language), and maintains social relationships (interactional language). The ends and means of understanding of language is what linguist Michael Halliday (1977) referred to as the "functions of language." Halliday described seven functions of language based on observing his infant son Nigel.

In the emergent literacy stage the child is beginning to recognize print as part of the communication system that older children and adults use. Printed words in a book represent spoken words, and more important, meaningful concepts. For example, when a mother reads a story about Winnie-the-Pooh aloud, her 5-year-old daughter talks about her own teddy bear. Her mother can point out the words "teddy bear" in another book, *Ira Sleeps Over,* and say, "Look, this is the word *teddy bear* just like your own bear." What were once meaningless black marks on a white page are becoming meaningful symbols we call *sight words*.

Emergent literacy through sight word knowledge is furthered in the child's environment as she comes to recognize street names in the neighborhood (Apple Lane), restaurant signs (Hardee's), and food package names in the grocery store (Cap'n Crunch). Language and reading are now part of the dynamic responses of each child and will form the later building blocks of what Rosenblatt (1994b) termed transactional response theory, the unique way in which a person interacts with a book.

Some of the first books children read with the help of an adult are *rebus* books. Rebus books have a picture for key characters and objects. The key at the beginning of the books indicate what word they must "read" when they see the particular picture. *The Bag I'm Taking to Grandma's* (1995) by Shirley Neitzel is a rebus book with a cumulative text. Each picture item is introduced as the story unfolds, and then the pictures become part of the overall story. Figure 2.6 offers an example of a rebus sentence.

An example rebus.   FIGURE 2.6

Today is my first day of school. I packed my with all the supplies I need for class,

including new  , my tasty [sandwich] , and my favorite [book] .

I wanted to take my [dog] but he would not like to sit still in class.

After children read rebus books with adults and chime in with known words or phrases, they begin to read picture books independently; in other words, they are becoming emergent readers. Many of these books have controlled vocabulary, predictable story patterns, repetitive words and phrases, and/or cumulative texts. The purpose of these books is for young children to experience success in reading while at the same time interact with the story line in their own unique way; encouraging young children to interpret books for themselves is a very important part of comprehension.

Controlling the vocabulary in beginning readers goes back many years. Sometimes the vocabulary was controlled to such an extent that the language sounded stilted and unnatural, as in the early Dick and Jane readers: "Look, look. See Spot. See Spot run." Today's early readers may control vocabulary, but the language is more natural and the story line is interesting.

Books with controlled vocabulary often use words found in the Dolch list, the 200 most commonly founds words in books, magazines, and newspapers. Often these words belong to word families, also called phonograms (e.g., *and, sand, land, band,* and so on) or words that can be phonetically sounded out. Many of Dr. Seuss's books—*One, Fish, Two Fish, Red Fish, Blue Fish* (1960), *A B C* (1963), and *Fox in Socks* (1963)—have controlled vocabulary. Books that use phonograms also make the text easier for emergent readers. Dr. Seuss's *Green Eggs and Ham* (1960) has many phonograms and only 50 different words. Denise Fleming used rhyming words in her book *In the Tall, Tall, Grass* (1991): *scurry/hurry, strum/drum, slide/glide,* and *crunch/munch* to make the text easy for emergent readers. Authors also use repetitive words for emergent readers. Rhyming sounds and repetitive words make it easier for young children to remember text. Karen Pandells's, *I Love you, Sun, I Love You, Moon* (1994), for example, has simple repetitive sentences with one word different in each sentence. Tomie dePaola's simple illustrations aid young readers:

> I love you, Sun.
> I love you, Sheep,
> I love you, Wind.
> I love you, Tree. (unpaged)

Anthony Browne's *I Like Books* (1988) and *Things I Like* (1989) also have simple repetitive phrases and clear illustrations that complement the text. Though simple, such books should not discourage parents and caregivers from stretching their child's imagination by asking, "What things do you love?"

Mem Fox's *Time for Bed* (1993) uses repetition and rhyme. Each page features a mother animal with its baby and a rhyming verse like this one:

It's time to sleep, little snake, little snake,
Good gracious me, you're still awake.
It's time to sleep, little pup, little pup,
If you don't sleep soon the sun will be up! (unpaged)

Today publishers recognize the importance of easy-to-read nonfiction books. These books are designed for beginning readers. They cover many topics, ranging from history, places, and cultures around the world, to even simple science experiments. Many are written to be read by an adult to a child. Others have simple enough vocabulary, excluding technical terms, that emergent and beginning readers can experience success. Nonfiction books for children have clear illustrations that support the text and large print with adequate space between words and between lines. HarperCollins, Crowell, Greenwillow, and Random House are only a few of the publishers with a wide selection of easy-to-read informational books.

Primary Grades

Walker (2004) identified two stages of literacy development that occur during the primary grades (one through three). Walker referred to the first stage as the *grounded stage*. In school, reading is the subject most emphasized in terms of importance and time allotted. Children not only hear stories read aloud by their teacher but receive lessons in how to decode words (sounding them out letter by letter) and how to recognize common patterns in words (for example, the "ing" pattern at the end of verbs). Children not only learn that words are composed of sounds and letters (the alphabetic principle) but that English words are based on syllabic patterns and consonant blends that speakers can enunciate: thus "thr" and "ath" are accepted, whereas "dcr" or "qlk" are now rejected. By focusing on reading for meaning, and decoding words to make sense within a story, students are mentally accepting reading as a form of communication. Teachers further emphasize this by adding writing activities, another communication tool, to parallel reading instruction. Writing about books they read furthers children's comprehension and enriches their individual responses to books, as Louise Rosenblatt (1994b) has theorized.

The next stage of literacy development, called the *expanding stage,* begins around grade three and involves the young child with longer passages of print. No longer restricted to decoding unknown words and applying sight word knowledge, the child now starts tackling sentences, paragraphs, and chapters. Familiarity with various punctuation marks is necessary for extended comprehension of longer texts. Word order or sentence structure, emphasized in grammar lessons, further aids reading comprehension. Recognizing that English sentences have common patterns, just like English words follow common patterns, is a major cognitive leap forward in literacy acquisition. This knowledge frees the child from dependency on adults and gives her the confidence to take risks by reading more challenging books. Using context clues within sentences to figure out the meaning of unknown words is now another major strategy she applies automatically while reading.

Once children experience success with simple picture books, they can enjoy reading short, simple chapter books. These chapter books have more text than pictures; however, there are some illustrations so that there are no two consecutive pages of just words. The print is larger than adult chapter books, and the double-spaced lines make it easier for beginning readers to keep their place as they read. Some early chapter book favorites of children are Arnold Lobel's Frog and Toad series, E. H. Minarik's Little Bear series, E. T. Hurd's Johnny Lion series, and Cynthia Rylant's Henry and Mudge series.

Books for beginning readers with experience include Peggy Parish's Amelia Bedelia series, Paula Danziger's Amber Brown series, and The American Girl collection, written by various authors. Tomie dePaola and Marc Brown both write chapter books based on beloved characters from their picture books.

Conclusion

In this chapter we have reviewed some of the major aspects of child development, including physical development and oral language development. We have also reviewed some of the well-known work in psychosocial development, moral development, and emotional intelligence. Healthy child development, when children learn to cope with real-life situations, is what we wish for all children. Understanding these theories of human development from birth through the early years of school helps parents, caregivers, and teachers nurture children to achieve their true potential. Listening to, reading, and sharing good children's literature books help children not only grow in language, social, emotional, and moral aspects but also bridge the gap from infancy into early literacy. As children hear and read more and more books, they respond more fully in different ways: through their discussions with teachers and other adults, in writing, in art activities, and through dramatic playacting. Who could imagine a life without books!

journeying WITH CHILDREN'S LITERATURE

1. Online, look up additional information about Jean Piaget, Eric Erickson, and Lawrence Kohlberg.
2. Sit down and read through Daniel Goleman's *Emotional Intelligence: Why It Can Matter More Than IQ* (2006).
3. Using the Internet, search for "ProTeacher! Emergent Literacy—Early Years." The results should provide some ideas for emergent literacy activities. After you have read about some of the activities, begin an investigation of your own community. List the most popular store names, street names, businesses, and historic points of interest. Then create posters for your classroom that could be displayed as a way of building children's emergent literacy through sight vocabulary.
4. Begin an annotated bibliography of children's books that focus on children overcoming a childhood problem, such as coping with a physical disability or dealing with issues such as shyness, moving to a new school, making friends, losing a pet or a loved one.

activities TO SHARE WITH CHILDREN

1. Read aloud from any of the books mentioned under social and emotional development. Then ask the children to draw their feelings as the listened to the book.
2. With the children, create simple paper bag, sock, or stick puppets and ask the children to act out their feelings after listening to a book read aloud to them.
3. Role-play a scene from a book read aloud, such as *When Sophie Gets Angry, Really Angry,* that deals with childhood emotions.
4. Discuss David Shannon's *No David!* with a preschool child. The text is simple, but the illustrations depict situations that many young children experience.

our favorite CHILDREN'S BOOKS

dePaola, T. (1978). *The Popcorn Book.* New York: Holiday House.

In a simple, clear, and easily understood fashion, this book explores the history of popcorn, from ancient time to the modern day. It even includes two great ways to make popcorn at home or in a classroom with children.

Fox, M. (1985). *Wilfred Gordon McDonald Partridge.* New York: Kane Miller.

A little boy with a long and unusual name lives next door to a retirement home. Everyday he likes to play with his friends who live there. This is a great book for introducing young children to the elderly and explaining how things change when you get really old.

Fox, M. (1994). *Sophie.* Illus. A. Robinson. New York: Harcourt Brace.

This is a beautifully illustrated multicultural picture book about little Sophie and her loving Grandpa. But as Sophie grew older and bigger, Grandpa became older and smaller. This book tells a tender story dealing with the death of a loved one.

Henkes, K. (1991). *Chrysanthemum.* New York: Scholastic.

Little Chrysanthemum was looking forward to the first day of school until the children made fun of her unusual and very long first name. A kind and wise teacher saves the day for Chrysanthemum.

Lasky, K. (1997). *She's Wearing a Dead Bird on Her Head!* Illus. D. Catrow. New York: Hyperion Paperbacks for Children.

This is a beautifully illustrated, informative, and, at the same time, humorous book. It tells the story of two Boston ladies who are horrified by the latest fashion: women wearing stuffed birds on their hats. Their campaign to correct this outrage actually led to the formation of the first Audubon Society chapter.

Lester, H. (1988). *Tacky the Penguin.* Illus. L. Munsinger. New York: Trumpet Club.

Tacky lives in an icy land, but he's not like other penguins. He can't march straight or dive gracefully. He is an odd bird. But in the end he saves the day and joins his friends.

Penn, A. (1993). *The Kissing Hand*. Illus. R. Harper & N. Leak. Terre Haute, IN: Tanglewood Press.

> Chester Raccoon doesn't want to go to school. It will mean leaving his friends and his toys and his mother. But a wise mother raccoon shows Chester how much fun school will be by giving him a very old and special secret to carry with him.

Tinkham, K. (2007). *Hair for Mama*. Illus. A. Bates. New York: Dial Books for Young Readers.

> Marcus is excited with October coming because that is when the whole Carter family take a family picture. Only this year Mama has cancer and is losing her hair.

Wells, R. (2000). *Timothy Goes to School*. New York: Viking.

> Timothy raccoon is off to school wearing his new sunsuit. But it's not what he hoped it would be. The other kids make fun of his clothes. And then he finds a friend.

children's literature IN THIS CHAPTER

Bang, M. (1999). *When Sophie gets angry—really, really angry . . .* New York: Blue Sky Press.

Bonsall, C. N. (1962). *Look who's talking*. Illus. Ylla. New York: Harper & Brothers.

Browne, A. (1988). *I like books*. New York: Scholastic.

Browne, A. (1989). *Things I like*. New York: Random House Children's Books.

Chesworth, M. (1994). *Archibald Frisby*. New York: Farrar, Straus & Giroux.

Dr. Seuss. (1960). *Green eggs and ham*. New York: Random House Books for Young Readers.

Dr. Seuss. (1960). *One, fish, two fish, red fish, blue fish*. New York: Random House Books for Young Readers.

Dr. Seuss. (1963). *A B C*. New York: Random House Books for Young Readers.

Dr. Seuss. (1963). *Fox in socks*. New York: Random House Books for Young Readers.

Fassler, J. (1973). *Don't worry, dear*. New York: Behavioral Publications.

Feldman, T. (2003). *My very first encyclopedia with Winnie-the-Pooh and friends: Animals*. New York: Disney Press.

Fleming, D. (1991). *In the tall, tall, grass*. New York: Henry Holt.

Fox, M. (1994). *Sophie*. New York: Trumpet Club.

Fox, M. (1993). *Time for bed*. Illus. Jane Dyer. Adelaide, Australia: Omnibus Books.

Fox, M. (1985). *Wilfred Gordon McDonald Partridge*. New York: Kane Miller.

Girard, L. (1986). *Jeremy's first haircut*. Illus. M. Begin. New York: Albert Whitman Publishers.

Hamilton, M. (1983). *Who's afraid of the dark?* Illus. Patience Brewster. New York: Avon Books.

Henkes, K. (1991). *Chrysanthemum*. New York: Scholastic.

Henkes, K. (1996). *Lilly's purple plastic purse*. New York: Greenwillow.

Hest, A. (1997). *The babies are coming*. New York: Knopf Books for Young Readers.

Hiatt, F. (1999). *Baby talk*. Illus. Mark Graham. New York: Margaret K. McElderry Books.

Hooper, M. (1997). *A cow, a bee, a cookie and me*. Illus. Alison Bartlett. New York: Kingfisher.

Isadora, R. (1976). *Max*. New York: MacMillan.

Isadora, R. (1979). *Ben's trumpet*. New York: Greenwillow Books.

Isadora, R. (1984). *Opening night*. New York: William & Morrow.

Katz, K. (2007). *Baby's day: A cloth book*. New York: HarperTrophy.

Kraus, R. (1971). *Leo the late bloomer*. Illus. Jose Aruego. New York: Windmill Books.

Lasky, K. (1997). *She's wearing a dead bird on her head!* New York: Hyperion Books.

Lears, L. (2000). *Ben has something to say*. Morton Grove, IL: Albert Whitman.

Lee, J. (1991). *Silent lotus*. New York: Farrar, Straus & Giroux.

Lester, H. (1988). *Tacky the penguin*. New York: Trumpet Club.

Madenski, M. (1991). *Some of the pieces*. Boston: Little, Brown.

McMillan, B. (1987). *Step by step*. New York: Lothrop Lee & Shepard.

Munsch, R. (1980). *Paper bag princess*. Illus. Michael Martchenko. Toronto: Annick.

Nash, O. (1991). *The adventures of Isabel*. Illus. James Marshall. Boston: Little, Brown.

Neitzel, S. (1995). *The bag I'm taking to Grandma's*. Illus. Nancy Winslow Parker. New York: Greenwillow.

Pandell, K. (1994). *I love you, sun, I love you, moon*. Illus. Tomie dePaola. New York: Putnam Juvenile.

Polacco, P. (1996). *Aunt Chip and the great Triple Creek Dam affair*. New York: Philomel.

Viorst, J. (1972). *Alexander and the terrible, horrible, no good, very bad day*. Kingsport, TN: Kingsport Press.

Waber, B. (1975). *Ira sleeps over*. New York: Houghton Mifflin Harcourt.

Watanabe, K. (2003). *My first taggies book: Sweet dreams*. New York: Cartwheel.

Wells, R. (2000). *Timothy goes to school*. New York: Puffin.

Wells, R. (2001). *Shy Charles*. New York: Puffin.

Wells, R. (2003). *Only you*. New York: Viking Juvenile.

Wells, R. (2004). *McDuff's favorite things*. Illus. Susan Jeffers. New York: Hyperion Books.

Willems, M. (2004). *Knuffle bunny: A cautionary tale*. New York: Hyperion Books.

Willems, M. (2004). *The pigeon finds a hot dog*. New York: Hyperion Books.

Williams, S. (1997). *Library Lil*. Illus. Steven Kellogg. New York: Dial Books for Young Readers.

Yashima, T. (1983). *Crow boy*. Darby, PA: Diane Publishing.

Yuichi, K. (2003). *One stormy night*. Japan: Kodansha International.

Ziefert, H. (1993). *When the TV broke*. Illus. Mavis Smith. New York: Puffin.

Literature for Infants and Toddlers

Sharing Literature: AN EXAMPLE

Recently Beverly has been volunteering as a childcare worker at a single mom's convention and has been watching a group of 3-year-old children. The toddlers do not know each other and have never been together as a group. When nap time comes, of course, no one is tired or wants to stop playing. So today Beverly asks if they want her to read them a book, and all of them readily gather around her on the floor. She picks up Eric Carle's *The Very Hungry Caterpillar*, shows them the picture, and asks them what they think the story will be about. Responses come readily:

"A green bug!"
"A wiggly worm."
"A funny-lookin' worm."

When Beverly reads aloud the title, author, and illustrator, one little girl asks, "What's a capkiller?"

"It's a caterpillar," one little boy corrected. "Cat—ter—pil—er. Say it." Beverly suggests that everyone say the word together as she counts each syllable on her fingers.

Beverly reads and discusses each page. The toddlers love the holes in the pages; all want to put their fingers through them. After completing the story, Beverly asks what their favorite part was. One says she loved the last page when the caterpillar became a butterfly; another loved the page where the caterpillar ate all the different foods.

Since the children were still wide awake, Beverly asks if they would like to act out the story. She tells each toddler to find a spot in the room so they all can move around. She says that she will act it out, too.

First, everyone rolls up into a little ball to become a quiet egg.

Next, everyone "cracks open" and becomes a caterpillar, eating their favorite foods. As the toddlers are moving around and pretending to eat, Beverly asks them what they are eating. She hears "watermelon," "hamburgers," "popcorn," "ice cream," "apples," and other foods not mentioned in the book.

After the "caterpillars" are good and full, they begin spinning cocoons. One toddler starts to roll over and over, and soon others are rolling over and over. Beverly reminds them that caterpillars are quiet inside their cocoons.

Without her prompting, they begin to break out of their cocoons and start flying around like butterflies. After flying around for some time, they want to hear another book.

Introduction

Scene: Maternity ward in a large city hospital. Mothers and fathers holding newborns in their arms.

Mother #1:   Hush, little baby, don't say a word. Momma's gonna buy you a mockingbird. Momma loves you, loves you, loves you!

Mother #2:   Rock-a-bye, baby, in the tree top. You are so cute!

Father #1:   Hi, little sweetheart! Say, "hi" to your big brother and your mommy!

Father #2:   Welcome to this world, little guy. Daddy is going to read you a book by one of my favorite authors. Listen! "It is the long vacation in the regions of Chancery Lane. The good ships Law and Equity, those teak-built, copper-bottomed, iron-fastened, brazen-face, and not by any means fast-sailing Clippers, are laid up in ordinary . . . (Dickens, 1853).

All of the parents in this scene are giving their newborns two priceless gifts—love and words! The last father understands the importance of newborns hearing our complex language with its rich vocabulary.

Some parents may think that the book the second father is reading is too advanced for infants since the baby cannot comprehend it. Of course, the baby cannot comprehend Charles Dickens's *Bleak House,* but neither can they comprehend the messages from the other parents we mentioned! Many educators such as Jim Trelease (2006), an advocate of lap reading, believe that parents and other caregivers should begin reading, just like they begin talking, to babies on the day they are born.

This chapter focuses on books that are appropriate for the first two stages of childhood: infancy and the toddler years. Because so many books are written for this age range, this entire chapter is devoted to them. As noted earlier in Chapter 2, infants experience many changes quickly in their first year, hitting developmental milestones month after month. Therefore, preschool teachers and caregivers must constantly find new books to read to children that are appropriate to their developmental stage in its many dimensions: physical, cognitive, emotional, social, moral, linguistic.

In this chapter we explain ways that parents and caregivers can share books. We look at the types of books to select and present some of the many quality books available for infants and toddlers. These earliest years are the ones spent with parents or some other caregiver in a non-structured (informal) learning environment. During these first three years, children learn to converse in their native language. To do so, they must master many tasks, such as learning to pronounce thousands of words, learning the meaning of the words, and learning how to sequence words into sentences. To facilitate children's literacy, caregivers not only talk to their infants, sing songs and recite rhymes to them, they also read books to them.

This is not the only chapter in which we discuss books for infants and toddlers. The chapters that discuss fiction, nonfiction, fantasy, and historical fiction mention titles appropriate for infants and toddlers.

The Importance of Reading to Infants and Toddlers

A study by Cox, Fang, and Otto (2004) found that preschoolers develop a *literate register* when they have had many experiences with books; such experiences include parents and caregivers reading to children and also children handling books by themselves. Children's literate register is their knowledge of the language of books. For example, in narrative text, children become aware of the typical structure of conversations: when characters talk, an author uses tag lines such as "she said" or "John said." They learn that some stories begin with "Once upon a time" and end with "They lived happily ever after." When children begin to use these phrases, as they retell stories or make up their own, caregivers and teachers know that children are developing a literate register. When nursery rhymes and other poems are shared with infants, toddlers, and preschoolers, they may invent nonsense phrases that end with a rhyme because they are aware that many nursery rhymes and poems rhyme. Developing a literate register during the toddler stage, at preschool, and in kindergarten, children later become successful readers in the primary grades (Stanovich, 2004).

In their research, Mason, Herman, and Au (1991) found that having prior experience with text greatly affects children's ability to read. They found that if children have been exposed to stories at home, by the time they enter kindergarten they

- understand syntax, story grammars, and other text structures.
- know how to use picture clues to figure out meaning.
- understand that stories have sequence.
- have a sophisticated vocabulary.

Researchers also found that children who were read to by parents were able to read before formal or structured instruction (Tobin, 1981). They also scored higher on reading tests in elementary grades (Sulzy & Teale, 1987) and had a world knowledge that other children did not have (Ruddell & Ruddell, 1994).

As indicated earlier, Trelease (2006) contends that parents should begin talking and reading to a child as soon as the child is born. Even though infants do not understand what is being said or read to them, they begin to recognize the cadence and rhythm of language.

It is also important that infants hear well-written stories with a rich vocabulary and complex sentences. Infants and toddlers learn new vocabulary as they hear it repeatedly in context. Our basic lexicon (words we use in daily conversation) consists of approximately 5,000 words. Approximately another 5,000 words are used less frequently in conversation. Thus children are exposed to approximately 10,000 words through conversation. In contrast, quality literature exposes children to a much richer vocabulary than conversation can provide (Ruddell & Ruddell, 1994). Books use another 10,000 words that are considered "rare." Examples of these rare words are *dozing, slumbering, snoring,* and *cozy* in *The Napping House* (Wood, 1984) and *growling, slithered, prickles,* and *awed* in Winnie-the-Pooh stories. It is estimated that parents use only nine rare words per 1,000 words when conversing with a 3-year-old, while quality children's literature uses approximately 27 rare words per 1,000 (Trelease, 2001).

Vygotsky (1962, 1976) and Heath (2004) found that infants learn language through conversation. Trelease (2006) agrees that conversation is critical in developing children's language skills; however, he posits that conversation is inferior to reading in its vocabulary. Also, most conversation with infants is characterized by short simple sentences joined by *and*—sentences such as "Let's have some toast and eat some cereal." In contrast, reading quality literature lets infants hear complex sentences. Note how Marcus Pfister includes both simple and complex sentences in *Hopper* (1991): "When he had finished cleaning himself, he ran over to Nick, who was still sleeping soundly under a bush. [complex sentence] Hopper tickled his nose and tapped his ears. [simple sentence] But when Nick refused to wake up, Hopper just pulled him out from under the bush [complex sentence]" (unpaged).

Trelease (2001) believes that every time a parent reads literature to a child, five things happen:

1. Both the child and parent enjoy the time together because reading is a pleasure.
2. Learning is taking place.
3. The child is hearing and learning new words in context.

4. The memory skills of the child are developing.

5. The child's mental processing abilities are developing.

The American Association of Pediatrics (AAP) agrees with Stanovich (2004) and Cox et al. (2004) that reading to infants not only aids the development of a literate register, it also "encourages a solidifying emotional bond between parent and child" (AAP, 2005, p. 1 of 3). The AAP (1997) even encourages pediatricians to prescribe specific types of reading activities to parents.

The International Reading Association (IRA) also understands the importance of sharing quality books with children and offers tips for both educators and caregivers (see Figure 3.1).

Tips for reading books with very young children.	**FIGURE** 3.1

From the IRA (2003, p. 166):

- First preview the story by pointing out the sequence of detailed illustrations. Acquaint young listeners with characters, plot, and setting.
- Make reading a regularly scheduled daily activity just like eating and naps.
- Always hold the book upright and begin at the beginning so that infants become familiar with how to handle books.
- As soon as an infant is capable of pointing, ask her to point to the characters, setting, and action as you read.
- Take time to enjoy language by repeating words with interesting sounds, rhyme, or repetition.
- Permit the child to "read" the story to you by turning the pages, looking, and pointing to pictures.
- Take time to discuss how the characters feel as things happen in the story.
- Always take the time to enjoy the book without rushing through it.
- As soon as possible, take the child to the library each week for story time. Toddlers can learn how to share story time and space with other children during these visits.
- When a toddler is old enough, permit him to respond to the book by drawing, finger painting, or sculpting modeling clay.

Additional tips:

- Do not read in a monotone voice. Use inflection to keep an infant's attention.
- Choose books with a rich vocabulary; do not shy away from books with an advanced vocabulary.
- Enunciate all words clearly. Infants and toddlers repeat what they hear.
- When discussing pictures, use correct names for the objects depicted. For example, distinguish between a cow and horse rather than referring to both as simply "animals."
- Be sure to discuss the books with infants and toddlers. Listen as they vocalize.
- Sing nursery rhymes and other songs to infants and toddlers. Songs also introduce words not used in normal daily activities.

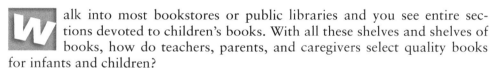

Before reading further . . .

NEUROSCIENCE RESEARCH SUPPORTS EARLY READING

Not only have educational researchers found that reading stimulates language development and cognitive growth—neuroscientists have also revealed that reading to an infant daily stimulates the growth of the infant's brain. Brain imaging technology helps researchers study the workings and growth of the human brain and has elucidated how crucial reading and other early language experiences are to brain development. AAP reported the following scientific findings at a White House summit in 1997:

- As a caregiver reads to an infant, thousands of growing cells in the infant's brain respond. New cells are formed and the connections among existing cells are strengthened.

- Early exposure to books and stories is positively correlated with a child's success in learning to read.

- Environmental influences, such as reading quality literature, stimulate a child's literacy development.

- Infants who are read to find learning to read easier than do infants who are not read to.

- The National Commission on Reading claims that reading to a child is the single-most important activity for developing the child's reading skills.

Selecting Literature for Infants and Toddlers

Walk into most bookstores or public libraries and you see entire sections devoted to children's books. With all these shelves and shelves of books, how do teachers, parents, and caregivers select quality books for infants and children?

First, consider the age and maturation of the child. As mentioned, the rapid growth in a child's first 36 months of life (Berk, 2006) means that infants' and toddlers' physical, social, cognitive, and language skills change each week, and this must be taken into consideration when looking at potential books.

Once the developmental level of the child is taken into consideration, review the features of the book and imagine how a child might interact with them. We look closely at some of the characteristics of quality books for infant and toddlers in the sections to follow. Appendix B.2 also offers a checklist that can be used while examining books for this age group.

Choose Books That Provide Sensory Stimulation

Piaget (1964) found that infants learn through sensory stimulation, which includes touching, seeing, hearing, tasting, smelling. Thus, at about 2 months, infants begin to explore books with their hands and mouths. There are many books with texture that appeals to an infant's desire to touch and taste objects. In Saltzberg's *Baby's Animal Kisses* (2001), infants can kiss or touch and feel a wrinkly elephant, a bumpy alligator, a hairy gorilla, a smooth seal pup, a velvety cow, a rubbery fish, and a fuzzy panda cub. In *Let's Play Ball* (Romanell,

2008), infants and toddlers feel bumpy rocks, a leather ball, soft grass, slick water, rough dirt, and scratchy wheat. In *Busy Baby* (Watt, 2005), readers can feel the baby's soft blanket on each page.

Choose Books That a Child Can Manipulate

Because infants begin to grasp objects at 3 months (Berk, 2006), ideal books for children between 3 and 18 months are ones that have parts to manipulate. These interactive, accessorized books foster children's social, physical, and intellectual development. These books promote social development because they encourage toddlers to interact with the reader. Preschool teachers and caregivers can read and point to the objects and invite the child to touch, pull, push, and point to the objects and repeat words or phrases. David Carter's book *Feely Bugs* (1995), in addition to its descriptive text, features bugs made from material that readers can feel. "Feathery bugs" are insects with pink and green feathers for the child to touch. "Lacy bugs" have lacy material on their wings, and "leather bugs" are centipedes whose bodies are pieces of red leather. These interactive books also help children develop their fine motor skills.

Another good book for toddlers is *My First Taggies Book: Sweet Dreams* (2003), written and illustrated by Kaori Watanabe. It is made from soft fleece and has eight different looped ribbons for infants to pull. A different animal— kitten, bunny, puppy, and so on—is featured on each page along with simple text like "Sweet dreams, little kitty." With *Tails* (Van Fleet, 2003), children touch tails of different textures, pull tabs to see the tails move, and scratch and sniff a skunk's tail.

Interactive books can encourage a child's intellectual development because many of them introduce children to concepts, such as opposites, and to simple arithmetic. In *Tails,* for example, the tails of the different critters demonstrate opposites and give children chances to count. The text rhymes, and Van Fleet introduces children to words not often used in conversation: "Tails furry, Tails spiny, Tails rainbow-hued and shiny. Tails stand up, Tails drag, Tails frisky— way, way, way!" (unpaged). *Toes, Ears, & Nose!* (Bauer, 2003), a lift-the-flap board book, introduces children to various body parts. A child lifts the flap to find that fingers are behind mittens, ears are under a hat, and toes are inside boots. The children are from different cultures, and Karen Katz, the illustrator, uses bright colors to make this a cheerful book. Eric Hill's Spot series also delights toddlers. In all the Spot books, toddlers must flip flaps to find answers to simple questions. Young children are attracted to the friendly little brown dog. Figure 3.2 lists some of Eric Hill's Spot books.

Toddlers soon begin to enjoy interacting with peek-a-boo books. In *Peek-a-Zoo!* (Cimarusti, 2003) children must guess what animal is under each flap. The text on each page is "Guess who?" Under each flap, the answer begins with "Peek-a-" and ends with the sound that animal makes. For example, the lion says, "Peek-a-roar!" Two similar books by Cimarusti are *Peek-a-Moo!* (1998) and *Peek-a-Pet!* (2004). With these books, toddlers get to touch and feel various animals. The text states the animal's name and gives the sound each animal makes. Toddlers enjoy imitating animal sounds.

FIGURE 3.2   Eric Hill's Spot books.

Spot Visits His Grandparents. (1996). Readers flip flaps to find out all the fun activities that Spot does with his grandparents.

Spot Helps Out. (1999). This books features all the things that Spot does to help his parents.

Spot Looks at Colors: Board Book. (2003). Each page reveals a new color with items of that color.

Spot Looks at Shapes: Board Book. (2003). Everything Spot looks at has a familiar shape, such as a circle, a square, a rectangle, a star, and others.

Spot's First Words: Board Book. (2003). One of Spot's favorite words is featured on each page. Some of the words featured are *apple, sock, hat,* and *train.*

Spot Goes Splash! (2003). Every page shows where Spot likes to splash—in the garden, at the beach, in puddles, and even in the bathtub.

Spot Goes to the Park. (2005). Readers flip flaps to find out what Spot sees and experiences at the park.

Spot: Night-Night, Spot. (2005). Like most infants and toddlers, Spot does not like to go to bed. He would much rather stay up and play with his toys.

Choose Books Made of Appropriate Materials

As mentioned in Chapter 2, ideal books for children this age are washable cloth books and wipeable vinyl books. Again, make sure there are no loose or detachable objects that could cause a child to choke. *Three Little Ducks* (Jugran, 2006) is a small, eight-page vinyl book in which one duck goes "flip flop" and another goes "quack quack." *Toys* (Field, 2002) and *Clothes* (Field, 2002) are each 10-page, small washable cloth books. Each page has one object and its name. For example, individual pages in *Toys* show a toy car, tractor, boat, and so forth. On each page in *Clothes*, one item of clothing appears with its name printed below it. If you visit your local public library or the children's section of a bookstore, you will find many concept books and storybooks made of sturdy cardboard. Toddlers can easily turn the pages without tearing them up. But keep cardboard books away from the bathtub!

Choose Books That Enrich Children's Vocabulary

It is also important for parents and caregivers to remember that research has shown that infants prefer hearing novel words over familiar words (Saffran, Aslin, & Newport, 1996). Therefore, adults should look for books that build toddlers' listening vocabulary: for example, books that use verbs such as "grumbled," "muttered," "screamed," or "demanded" over ordinary alternatives like "said" or "asked." Denise Fleming carefully chooses vivid words in her books. For example, *In the Small, Small Pond* (1998) includes phrases like "waddle, wade, geese parade." *Waddle* and *wade* are more descriptive verbs than *walk* and *swim*. In *Fuzzy Fuzzy Fuzzy! A Touch, Scratch, & Tickle* (2003), Sandra Boynton uses descriptive less common verbs like "tousle," "scratch," "stroke," and "tickle" to encourage children to find and touch the various animal parts.

In the previously mentioned *Feely Bugs* (Carter, 1995), each page has an adjective paired with the word "bugs." The adjectives are not words typical of everyday conversation: "velvety," "wrinkly," "bristly," "crinkly," and "glittery." Marcus Pfister, in *Hopper* (1991), also uses words not often heard in daily conversation: "Hopper <u>bounded</u> away and his mother ran back and forth across the field to <u>distract</u> the falcon" (unpaged). Ruth Brown, in *Baba* (1997), also employs a rich vocabulary: "'Baba, Baba,' she <u>sobbed,</u> holding up the very last <u>strand</u> of her blanket. It was totally <u>unraveled</u>" (unpaged). Again, we see uncommon words, both nouns and verbs.

When adults select books for children, they should never shy away from books that have words children do not know. As we discussed earlier in this chapter, our conversational vocabulary is limited, but quality literature introduces children to a far richer vocabulary. If the meaning of the word is not easily discerned from the context of the story, adults can take the time to repeat and define the word. Adults can also ask a child to repeat new words; this increases the child's expressive (oral) vocabulary. The child can then begin to use the new words himself.

Choose Books That Introduce Concepts of Print

Infants and toddlers can be introduced to the basic functions of print as soon as caregivers begin reading to them (Harste, Burke, & Woodward, 1994). In order for them to understand how to interact with print, caregivers and preschool teachers should point to words and sweep their fingers across each line so that children begin to comprehend the orientation and logic of print:

- that the sticks and circles (letters) are words that adults read.
- that words and pictures are different.
- that one reads from left to right and top to bottom.
- that one holds a book right side up and reads from page one to book's end.

The reader should always share the title, author, and illustrator of books. As soon as the child is capable of making predictions, show the cover of the book to the child and ask her to predict what the book is about. The adult may need to model such forecasting until the child can join in with predictions of her own.

As soon as the child is able, caregivers can invite him to turn pages, point, and repeat words read. Ideal books for children at this stage have words or phrases paired with clearly distinguishable objects. One example is *Bright Baby Colors* (Priddy, 2004), a small board book with one color word on each page: "gold" is paired with a picture of gold stars; "orange" accompanies a picture of an orange fish. In Priddy's *Bright Baby Animals* (2005), each page has a photograph of an animal with only the animal's name below it. Priddy has a small collection of similar books: *Bright Baby First Words, First Concepts: Shapes,* and *First Concepts: Numbers.*

During the toddler years, children can locate objects in a book when an adult prompts them. Some books are made with this in mind. *I Spy Little Bunnies* (Marzollo, 2001) is a small board book with simple text on left-hand pages and a photograph filled with objects on right-hand pages. For example, on the first left-hand page, the text reads "I spy a camel, and a bunny's red nose." On the facing page is a photo of an open book with many pictures, including the camel, some marbles, jacks, writing paper, and the bunny with the red nose. This book can introduce toddlers to the fact that books are read from left to right and that pictures communicate in conjunction with text. First, read the text on the left-hand page, pointing out the words. Then, ask the child to locate the object named in the picture on the right-hand page. The objects are easy for adults to find, but toddlers will need to study the picture carefully to locate them. This book is a wonderful book for caregivers and a child to interact with.

Can You Find It Inside? (Schulte, 2005) is a similar search-and-find book in which readers are invited to find objects in works of art. Each open page has a rhyming verse of questions asking children to scrutinize a masterpiece art work on the opposite page for the objects named. Some objects are obvious, while others take more time to find.

Choose Books That Reflect a Child's Everyday Experiences

Toddlers learn about the world around them through both firsthand experience and also through books that represent a world familiar to them. In *SHHHHH! Everyone's Sleeping* (Markes, 2005), toddlers learn about people's jobs through rhythmic verses: "The doctor is sleeping. Everyone feels well" (unpaged). Each person is asleep in a setting that suggests his or her occupation. For example, the grocer's headboard is a head of lettuce.

Some books reflect children's everyday dilemmas. It is important to select books in which the protagonist makes choices about issues that toddlers face. For example, many children have a difficult time sitting still, and they often make a mess without even trying. *Wiggle* (Cronin, 2005) and *Oops! (Oops!)* (Shannon, 2005) are two good books for a child who is restless or prone to accidents. In *Wiggle* (Cronin, 2005), a puppy wiggles from the time he gets up to the time he lies down under the moon. Like the puppy, many children have a hard time sitting still. When this book is shared with them, children realize that others experience the same things they do. In the small board book *Oops! (Oops!)* (2005), David Shannon portrays the many little accidents that toddlers often make, such as spilling milk or throwing a ball off target. The delightful pictures tell the story of many a child.

Choose Books That Reflect Appropriate Themes

Quality books for toddlers, both serious and humorous, frequently have pro-social themes, such as obedience, honesty, kindness, helpfulness, politeness, and generosity. The best books are those that are not didactic; that is, they don't *explicitly* state what is right or wrong. Instead, they have plots in which the protagonist learns to make a wise choice or learns how to get along with others. The protagonist must learn the importance of social skills such as being honest, kind, or friendly.

Young children are often confronted with having to share parents with a new sibling. Maribeth Boelts's *You're a Brother, Little Bunny!* (2001) addresses this problem by having the main character Little Bunny constantly saying, "If we didn't have a baby . . ." and then listing everything he thinks he could do— go out and play or make noise. His parents are aware of his jealousy, so they have a reasonable solution for Little Bunny that makes him feel important and loved. Because many toddlers become jealous upon the arrival of a new sibling, this story and others like it help toddlers learn how other children deal with the same issue.

Another appropriate theme for toddlers is unconditional love. Many books are favorites of adults and children alike because they demonstrate love despite trouble or mistakes. In *I Love You Through and Through* (Shustak, 2005), a little child is loved when he is silent or talking, when he giggles or cries, is silly or mad; he is loved consistently from day to day. Other favorites with the same theme are *Hula Lullaby* (Kono, 2005), *The Runaway Bunny* (Brown, 1942), *Guess How Much I Love You* (McBratney, 1994), *Love You Forever* (Munsch, 1986), and *The Tale of Peter Rabbit* (Potter, 1902).

Choose Books with Simple Plots

Infants and toddlers live in the present moment, and straightforward plots appeal to them. In *Pooh Goes Visiting* (a mini-board book) (Milne, 1996) the plot is chronologically linear and thus easy for toddlers to follow: Pooh visits Rabbit and eats too much honey. He gets stuck in the door when he is going to leave. All of the friends of the forest come to pull Pooh out. In another children's favorite, *Corduroy* (Freeman, 1968) the title character, Corduroy, a toy bear on a shelf in a department store, has not been bought because a button is missing from his suspenders. So on the night the story takes place, Corduroy searches for his button throughout the store. In *If You Give a Pig a Pancake* (Numeroff, 2003), the sequence of wants is also easy for toddlers to follow because the action is logical in terms of cause and effect. First, the pigs need syrup and then a bath because they get sticky. The story continues with logical consequences: bubbles for their bath, a rubber duck, and so on.

Choose Books with Rhymes

Rhyming books facilitate toddlers' awareness of sounds in the English language (Sadlier, 2000), especially when the adult reader emphasizes the rhyming words by rereading them. For example, after reading a page from *Jesse Bear, What Will You Wear?* (Carlstrom, 1986)—"My shirt of red / Pulled over my head / Over my head in the morning" (unpaged)—the adult can reread the words "red" and "head" and then encourage the toddler to repeat the words. Another of Nancy White Carlstrom's Jesse Bear rhyming books is *How Do You Say It Today, Jesse Bear?* (1992). Each month, Jesse Bear says "I love you" with a different rhyme. March's rhyme is "With colors that fly / Long tails in the sky, / I say it with kites today" (unpaged). Again the adult reader can repeat the rhyming words—"fly" and "sky"—and add other words such as "pie," "my," "by," and "cry." With this book, the adult can ask the toddler how she could say "I love you" and talk about why Jesse Bear flies kites in March and makes Valentines in February. Some other Jesse Bear books describing everyday experiences that feature rhyme are *Guess Who's Coming, Jesse Bear* (1998), *Better Not Get Wet, Jesse Bear* (1997), *It's About Time, Jesse Bear* (1998), *Let's Count It Out, Jesse Bear* (1997), *Happy Birthday, Jesse Bear* (1994), and *What a Scare, Jesse Bear* (2002).

Nancy White Carlstrom has written over 55 books for young children, including the popular Jesse Bear series. She writes about humorous everyday events in children's lives; most of which are written in lilting rhyme, so children want to repeat them.

Nancy grew up without a television, which, she has said, caused her to use her imagination to create her own fantasies. While working in the children's section of her local public library, she decided to become an author of children's books. She attended Wheaton College and taught school in Pittsburgh, Penn., and Gloucester, Mass. She has worked with children in the West Indies, in West Africa, and in the Yucatan, where she worked with children with Down's syndrome. She now lives in Seattle and manages The Secret Garden, a children's bookstore.

Nancy White Carlstrom has won many awards for her books, including the International Reading Association/ Children's Book Council award in 1987 for *Jesse Bear, What Will You Wear?* and the National Council for Teachers of English notable book designation in 1991 for *Goodbye Geese*.

Authors of concept books, which we discuss later in the chapter, often use rhyme. *One Green Frog* is filled with rhyme that teaches counting concepts (Hooker, 1978). One page from the book reads:

Eight quick, brown mice look for things to eat,
scuttling through the house on soft and dainty feet. (unpaged)

After reading the page, the adult can repeat the rhyming words *eat* and *feet* and encourage the toddler to repeat those words. In order to emphasize rhyme, the adult reader can add other words to the list like *meat* or *greet*. This book encourages the toddler to count the different creatures on each page.

Rosemary Wells has written many books in rhyme for infants and toddlers. *Carry me!* (2006) is a story that emphasizes the love between a young child and her parents. While sharing this book, parents can emphasize the rhyming pairs: *bees* and *peas, air* and *chair,* and others.

Choose Books with Humor

Toddlers also begin to enjoy humorous books that feature *onomatopoeia,* words that sound like their meaning: for example, "zoom," "crash," "bang," and "crackle." *The Snowball* (Sternberg, 2007) features animals and is filled with onomatopoeia, as the polar bears go thump-thump-galumping and skit-skat-skadoole through the snow. This book also increase children's vocabulary by using words such as *stomp, clomping, flump, rumps, feathery, sculpt,* and *swooping.* Parents and teachers can have children say the words and invent playful onomatopoeia words of their own.

Duck on a Bike (Shannon, 2002) begins with a duck seeing a parked bike, which is a temptation to ride. The barn animals say the duck is zany for riding a bike, but when they themselves are given the opportunity to ride, they change their minds. In this story the animals say one thing to the duck as he rides by, but their facial expressions suggest something different. Parents can talk with their child about why the characters say one thing but really think something different.

Choose Books with Repetitive Text

Books with repetitive text have phrases or words that recur throughout the book. When young children begin to talk, preschool teachers and caregivers can begin selecting books with repetitive text and encourage toddlers to chime in with the repeated phrases. As they read to children, adults should point to the words so that a child can make the connection between spoken words and their graphic equivalents. They should also encourage the child's responses by pausing and reading the repeated phrases a little slower so the child can chime in. Later, when familiar with the story, the child can read the repeated words and phrases by himself. *I Went Walking* (Williams, 1989) is an old favorite of children, as they love to chime in with the text "I went walking. What did you see?" that appears on every other page.

Bill Martin, Jr., has written a number of books that follow a similar pattern. *Brown Bear, Brown Bear, What Do You See?* (1996) asks the same question on every other page: "Brown, Bear, Brown Bear, what do you see?" And each answer follows a formula: "I see a [name of animal] looking at me." Each page features an animal of a different color. *Polar Bear, Polar Bear, What Do You Hear?* (1997) and *Panda Bear, Panda Bear, What Do You See?* (2003) follow the same question and answer pattern. With such a book, children can predict the answer to each question. Eric Carle, the illustrator of these books, provides large colorful animals on a simple white background, drawn in such a way as to appeal to young children.

From Head to Toe Board Book (Carle, 1999) also has two repetitive lines. The animal asks "Can you do it?" The child responds, "I can do it!" The animal performs simple movements such as touching his head or touching his toes, which encourages the adult and child to get up and replicate the movements. In Eric Carle's *The Very Busy Spider* (1984), each page has a different animal asking a question of the spider, but the answer is always the same: "The spider didn't answer. She was very busy spinning her web." However, at the end of the story, readers see that she completed her web and "caught a fly . . . just like that!" The short, simple sentences are easy for young children to read along with the adult. With older toddlers, caregivers can help them follow the steps of how spiders make a web by tracing their fingers on the raised web in the book. Or caregivers can draw the web with white glue and have children lay yarn over the lines to create a yarn web.

Mem Fox in *The Magic Hat* (2002) uses the refrain "Oh, the magic hat, the magic hat! It moved like this, it moved like that! It spun through the air!" Each time the hat lands on a person, that person turns into an animal. The pictures and text give clues as to what animal the person becomes. The adult and toddler can also take time to get out of the chair and move around by imitating how the characters "move like this and move like that." The zany story pleases both adults and young children.

In *Can You Make a Piggy Giggle?* (Ashman, 2002), a little boy is attempting to make a grumpy pig laugh. He tries many antics such as reading riddles and playing in the mud. With each antic, the little boy asks a different animal: "Can you make a piggy giggle?" Instead of the piggy giggling, the other animals begin to laugh. However, the pig never does. The text repeats itself each time another animal is introduced to the audience.

Eric Carle   www.eric-carle.com

Eric Carle was born in Syracuse, New York. His parents moved to Germany when he was 6, and he graduated from a prestigious art school in Stuttgart. He moved back to New York when he was 23 years old and worked for the *New York Times* as a graphic designer. Today he lives in Northampton, Massachusetts.

The first book he illustrated was *Brown Bear, Brown Bear, What Do You See?* His first children's book was *1, 2, 3, to the Zoo.* He is best known for his many books about insects—*The Very Hungry Caterpillar, The Very Quiet Cricket,* *The Very Lonely Firefly, The Very Grouchy Ladybug,* and *The Very Busy Spider.* He wants children to learn about the world around them; therefore, most of his books not only tell delightful stories, they contain information that interests young children. He has illustrated more than 70 books. Many of his books have been translated into 18 languages, and *The Very Hungry Caterpillar* has been translated into 30. Readers easily recognize his artwork. He paints paper, cuts it, and layers it to form collages. His brightly colored papers create bright, cheerful books for children.

The repetitive phrase "Oh, lovely mud" in *Mrs. Wishy-Washy* (Crowley, 1980) is another phrase that children quickly pick up as caregivers read the hilarious story of Mrs. Wishy-Washy washing animals that walk through a mud puddle. Of course, after she has washed them, they walk right back into the mud puddle. More books with repetitive text are listed in Appendix A.8.

We have discussed 11 considerations that can guide you as you select books for children. In the next section, we discuss two major categories of books for infants and toddlers and offer advice on how to select quality books.

Categories of Books for Infants and Toddlers

Caregivers and parents should select books from many different categories so that infants and toddlers become aware of all the information and entertainment that books can provide. One category of books written mainly for infants and toddlers is concept books. These books are written for the purpose of exposing infants and toddlers to different concepts, such as the alphabet or counting. Another category of books appropriate for very young children is storybooks, which are discussed briefly later in this chapter and in more detail in Chapter 5. In addition to these two categories adults should also share poetry (see Chapter 4), fairy tales (Chapter 6), or informational books (Chapter 8).

Concept Books

Concept books are books that expose children to basic ideas and mental operations such as the alphabet, counting, colors, shapes, and making comparisons. Quality concept books also introduce children to objects both familiar and unfamiliar to them. They thus extend their world knowledge by building on what they already know. Quality concept books also have a rich vocabulary, as you will see in the following discussion. Some of these books are intended for infants, depicting one item per page: a letter, numeral, color, or shape. Similar books for toddlers may be more complex, asking readers to count the objects on the page or to find a particular color. Caregivers and parents should select books from many different concept categories so that infants and toddlers become aware of all that can be learned by reading.

Many of these concept books not only introduce toddlers to a concept, they also introduce them to animals and objects not found in their immediate surroundings. When reading, caregivers can engage toddlers by having them repeat the alphabet, count the objects, or find objects around them of the same color as is named in the book. As soon as the child can talk, caregivers should invite children to participate and make these times of learning fun so children will want to read more books.

As adults share concept books with children, they are teaching more than the book's specific topic. Concept books engage children in many ways:

- children learn the order of numbers and the alphabet (Labbo, Love, Prior, Hubbard, & Ryan, 2006).
- they visualize each concept, which makes it easier for them to comprehend.
- they become motivated to learn about their world (Murphy, 1999; Shatzer, 2008).
- they develop oral language as they discuss the books with adults; details in the illustrations are often subjects of discussion (Labbo et al., 2006).
- they ask about unfamiliar objects in the illustrations, and the answer often expands their vocabulary (Beck, McKeown, & Kucan, 2002), elaborates their schemata (Labbo et al., 2006) and improves their listening skills (Morrow & Gambrell, 2002).

The key to such development is dialogic reading. This means the adult cues the child as follows: (1) asking "what" questions, (2) following the child's answer with more questions, (3) repeating the child's response, and (4) giving appropriate feedback (Lane & Wright, 2007).

Alphabet books

Alphabet books are wonderful books to share with infants and toddlers because they not only introduce young children to the 26 letters, they also introduce them to unfamiliar objects and new concepts. Children learn sequencing and visual discrimination as adults discuss the content and trace letters with their fingers. As you peruse alphabet books, you will find that many use rhyme and alliteration, which, as we have explained, increases language development and encourages a love of language. As with all lap reading, sharing books with children should be a time of pleasure.

Four types of alphabet books for infants and toddlers are (1) word–picture format, (2) theme books, (3) rhyming, and (4) riddle or puzzle books.

Word–picture alphabet books. The word–picture format is intended for infants who are being introduced to the alphabet. In most books, each page displays the uppercase and lowercase version of the letter with one or two objects represent-

Before reading further . . .

USING ALPHABET CONCEPT BOOKS EFFECTIVELY

When caregivers and teachers share alphabet books with children, children "acquire a foundational understanding of sound–symbol relationships as they explore why certain letters are accompanied by specific illustrations and words" (Labbo et al., 2006, p. 14). This foundational understanding is vital for students' literacy development (Adams, 1990; Snow, Burns, & Griffin, 1998; Duncan & Seymour, 2000; Labbo, et al., 2006). Their understanding must extend beyond reciting the alphabet; children must learn to recognize and distinguish the shape of each letter, and they should know letter–sound relationships. Just sharing alphabet books with children does not guarantee that they will learn to identify the letters or learn the sounds of each letter (DeTemple & Snow, 2003). Adults should point out the shape of the letters by tracing the child's finger over each one. This focuses their attention on the physical shape of each letter (Bradley & Jones, 2007; Justice & Ezell, 2004; Lane & Wright, 2007). Adults should say each letter and have the child repeat it so that the child also attends to the letter name (Bradley & Jones, 2007). As adults say the name of objects that begin with each letter, the child learns the letter–sound relationship (Mason, 1984).

Bradley and Jones (2007) found that preschool kindergarten teachers who share alphabet books effectively with their students emphasize the content of the book (e.g., letter shapes and sounds); they also pose thoughtful questions when reading. By encouraging children to comment during the reading, teachers can have a greater impact on student learning than they would by simply reading them aloud. The researchers also found that the best alphabet books to use with children are ones with alliteration in the phrases; that way children hear letter sounds repeatedly. They also found that when the letter is printed in simple type, it is easier for children to learn its shape than when the type is fancy. They also found that alphabet books featuring multiple sounds of a letter (e.g., "A" is for *apron* and *alligator*) tend to develop children's understanding of letters more so than books with single-sound examples.

The least effective books for learning the alphabet are alphabet books that feature stories (e.g., *The Alphabet Tree,* Lionni, 1968) because the discussion usually centers around the story instead of around the letters (Bradley & Jones, 2007).

ed that begin with that letter. Pinto's *The Alphabet Room* (2003) is a very simple book for infants. Each uppercase letter is shown on the left-hand side of the spread. On the opposite page are objects with names beginning with the letter. Readers open flaps to find the same objects in another setting. For example, "A" is accompanied by three green apples that are displayed on a white background. Under the flap are three green apples on the floor. *Touch and Feel: ABC* by DK Publishing (2000) is a small board book intended for little hands. Each double-page spread reveals five letters, each with one photo that depicts each letter. All photos are clearly displayed on a white background.

To use these word–picture alphabet books as teaching tools, it is advantageous for teachers and caregivers to point to the letter as they say the letter and then point to the object as they name the object. Adults should give infants plenty of time to study the object and the letter. When parents and caregivers see that toddlers are ready, they can show them, step by step, the way to draw the letters. Parents can invite children to draw the letters with crayons or thick pencils.

Theme alphabet books. Theme alphabet books focus on one category, such as trains, daily routines, food, animals, and so one. For example, *Alfie's ABC*

Jerry Pallotta, known as the alphabet man, has written more than 20 alphabet books that feature science and nature. His boyhood years spent at Peggoty Beach in Scituate, Massachusetts, were a perfect setting to stimulate his curiosity. Everything about the ocean interested him. He researched, wrote, designed, edited, and self-published his first four alphabet books through his own publishing company, Peggoty Beach Books. Now that he no longer publishes his own books, he spends his time in doing research. It is this extensive research that makes his books quality concept books. They are great sources for accurate information about a wide range of topics. According to Pallotta, the page for letter "X" in each book is the most difficult because for many topics, an "X" word is hard to come by.

(Hughes, 1997) is a book about Alfie and his sister looking for items that begin with each letter. On the "I" page, Alfie and his sister are looking for insects under a rock. The text states: "I is for the insects Alfie loves to find under rocks." All of the pages focus on a daily activity of Alfie and his friends. *Eating the Alphabet* (Ehlert, 1989) concentrates on fruits and vegetables. Each letter is written in upper and lowercase. Each letter has a two-page spread of illustrations and single words of fruits and vegetables that begin with the letter. The books encourage discussion between the child and the adult because there are only single words. In this book, children are introduced to many different kinds and fruits and vegetables.

Jerry Pallotta has created many theme alphabet books and some are well-suited for toddlers. *The Icky Bug* (1986) has one short paragraph about different bugs. The *Ocean Alphabet Book* (1986) has a short paragraph about different fish and plants found in oceans, each corresponding with a particular letter. *The Furry Alphabet Book* (1991) has a short paragraph about different furry animals, with each animal corresponding with a letter. The pictures are detailed so preschool teachers and toddlers can discuss the setting of each bug, animal, or sea creature. Each of his books has a wide variety of information to discuss with inquiring young minds.

Rhyming alphabet books. Some ABC books have rhymes or simple stories for each letter. *Alphabears* (1984), by Kathleen Hague, is a poetic text showing different types of teddy bears for each letter. For example, the "Q" page has the following text:

> Q is for Quimbly, a soft quilted bear
> Who was sewn by hand with much love and care.

K Is for Kissing a Cool Kangaroo (Andreae, 2002) uses rhyme and alliteration for each letter. For example, on the open page for *G* and *H*, the upper and lowercase *G* is displayed on the left-hand page with the text: "g is for giant, whose garden is grown wild." On the same page is pictured a large giant sleeping under a tree in his garden. Elsewhere on the same page are pictured a goose, a goat, a giraffe, and a gorilla. This book gives "readers" an opportunity to find all the objects that begin with the featured letter.

Riddle or puzzle alphabet books. Riddle or puzzle ABC books are also interactive. *The Alphabet Tale* (1994) by Jan Garten introduces each letter by showing just the animal's tail. Before turning the page, children need to predict what animal will appear on the following page. The shape of the tail and children's knowledge of the alphabet's sequence help them predict each animal to come. As they turn the page, they see the entire animal that represents the letter.

Math concept books

It is our belief that the best way for children to learn about numbers and learn to count is by manipulating objects. However, books that illustrate numbers vividly can reinforce number concepts to infants and toddlers. Counting books, like alphabet books, help children with sequencing and visual discrimination. Many of these books also expand children's worlds by introducing them to interesting but unfamiliar objects. Often the narration is written in rhyme and features a rich vocabulary; thus the text facilitates children's language development. To use these books as teaching tools, preschool teachers and caregivers can point to the numeral, trace it with a finger, and then say it aloud. Then they can point to the objects as they name them. The three main categories of math concept books are (1) one-to-one correspondence, (2) simple counting, and (3) story books.

One-to-one correspondence counting books. Most infants are first introduced to one-to-one correspondence books. These books acquaint young children with the numbers 1 through 10 using vivid, clear illustrations that help children grasp

Before reading further . . .

SHARING MATH CONCEPT BOOKS WITH YOUNG CHILDREN

Math concept books are wonderful ways for toddlers to learn to recognize the shape of numbers and how to count. When adults engage toddlers in tracing the numbers on the page, toddlers become aware of the unique features of each letter (Shatzer, 2008). Toddlers develop number sense as adults engage them in pointing and counting the objects on the page (Shatzer, 2008). Math concept books help toddlers connect a number and its concept when the illustrations display the shape of the number and a quantity of objects corresponding to the number (Labbo et al., 2006). Shatzer (2008) found that kindergarteners enjoy counting books with rhyme, rhythm, and excellent illustrations. And they like math concept books with stories that feature a favorite character such as Oliva in *Oliva Counts* (Falconer, 2002) or the chimps in *Cha-Cha Chimps* (Durango, 2006). As with any concept book, adults should engage the child in dialogic reading.

Math concept books with stories "can be the vehicle for providing meaningful context of learning mathematics as it helps learners value mathematics, [and] encourages learners to be mathematical problem solvers . . ." (Shatzer, 2008, p. 650). Math concept storybooks provide children a meaningful context for using math in daily living. With these books, math is humanized: readers see the characters following recipes, measuring length or weight, and graphing. Through the visualization of math concepts, children better understand concepts and thus retain the knowledge about them (Raymond, 1995). Math concept books help students explain the reasoning and strategies needed to solve puzzles that are common in these books (Clarke, 2002). Research also shows that not only does children's interest in math increase when teachers engage them in math storybooks, the children's math scores increase as well (Jennings, 1992).

the concept of counting. For example, Slaughter's *1 2 3* (2003) is a one-to-one correspondence book. To illustrate the number eight, Slaughter has the numeral "8" on the left-hand page and eight beach balls on the right-hand page. When sharing this book with an infant, the caregiver could say, "eight" while tracing the numeral eight. Then the caregiver could point to the beach balls and slowly count them aloud. When teachers or caregivers repeat the sequence, the child has an opportunity to commit it to memory.

Simple counting concept books. Many simple counting concepts books for toddlers spell out the numbers in addition to presenting numerals; thus children are introduced to the numeral as well as its verbal counterpart. Many of these books also facilitate children's cognitive growth by introducing them to new objects. For example, in *Kipper's Book of Numbers* (Inkpen, 1994), toddlers are introduced to some uncommon animals. For example, two playful hedgehogs appear under the text "2 Two hedgehogs." Throughout the book, Inkpen uses very simple illustrations and simple text, thus giving the caregiver the opportunity to talk about the hedgehog's physical appearance and antics.

In *Count Me a Rhyme* (2006), Jane Yolen uses a poem for each of the first 10 numbers. Each page has the Arabic numeral and the Roman numeral. Yolen introduces other terms associated with the numeral. For example, for the number four, she has the "4" and "IV" with words "quartet" and "foursome." The poem that accompanies the numerals begins as follows.

Four Slow Snails
A slow of snails,
One, two, three, four,
As up the leaning grass
They snore. (p. 16)

The numeral is depicted along with a beautiful photograph of four snails on a blade of grass. Jason Stemple's photographs of nature add to the serenity of the poems. Not only can caregivers count the snails with a toddler, they can also repeat the rhyming words: "four" and "snore," "creep" and "asleep," "door" and "four." Teachers and caregivers can discuss snails to enlarge a toddler's world knowledge.

Tomie dePaola's *Marcos Counts: One, Two, Three* (2003) introduces infants and toddlers to counting in Spanish. The numbers from 1 to 10 are in both English and Spanish. This is a great way for caregivers to introduce English-speaking children to another language and a great way for Spanish-speaking children to hear both their native language and the English language.

Other simple concept counting books help children learn information about the world around them. For example, children learn about whooping cranes in Mary Beth Owen's *Counting Cranes* (1993). For all counting books, caregivers should count out the objects for each number and give the child time to point to each one while studying the page. Sharing the books and pointing out details trains children to be observant.

Some counting books introduce toddlers to subtraction. In these books the toddler learns to count backwards or to subtract. An example of a book that counts backwards from 10 is *Countdown to Spring* by Schulman (2002). This book has questions that ask readers to find objects on the page. For

Lois Ehlert, a master of collage art, was born and raised in Beaver Dam, Wisconsin, and now lives in Milwaukee. Her mother, a good seamstress, taught Lois how to use the sewing machine when she was only 8 years old. Her father had a workshop, which provided her scrap lumber and other materials to create her art. From an early age she created art with scraps of material and natural objects instead of construction paper. She preferred to create pictures by cutting instead of drawing.

She is a graduate of the University of Wisconsin and the Layton School of Art. She has been an art teacher, designer, and of course a talented illustrator of children's books. She has written and illustrated many books and has also illustrated books by other authors.

In her illustrations, she takes white paper and paints it to get the exact color she wants for her illustrations. She then cuts out individual pieces of the colored paper and glues them to create her collages. She also uses natural objects such as dried corn, yarn, pine needles, and other materials. In *Eating the Alphabet,* each kernel of Indian corn is affixed to a separate piece of paper. To create *Leaf Man,* she collected autumn leaves, copied them on a color copier, and then used those pieces to create the many creatures found in the book.

Some other well-known books written and illustrated by Ehlert are *Feathers for Lunch, Nuts to You!, Fish Eyes, Painting a Rainbow, Mole Hill, Snowballs, Color Zoo, Color Farm, Red Leaf, Green Leaf,* and *Growing Vegetable Soup.* Some titles illustrated by Ehlert are *Chicka Chicka Boom Boom, Thump, Thump, Rat-A-Tat Tat, Moon Rope,* and *A Pair of Socks.*

example, on the first page for the number 10, the text states: "10 ladybugs crawling all around the crocuses. Can you count them?" Again, readers are encouraged to interact and respond to the text by answering the question and counting aloud.

Toddlers learn the concept of adding by listening to Lois Ehlert's *Fish Eyes: A Book You Can Count On* (1990), which features a little black fish who takes the reader on a journey through the ocean. They discover different numbers of various types of fish, and each time the little black fish adds himself to the number to make one more.

Other books encourage toddlers to manipulate objects as they read the story. Because children tend to put things into their mouths, food is safer to manipulate than other objects. *Cheerios* (Wade, 1981) is a board book that permits infants to put Cheerios into indented circles on the pages. Caregivers should engage the child by reading the question on each page and then counting the number of Cheerios that the child puts into the holes.

Math concept storybooks. In these books, there is a story in which the characters are engaged in some type of number activity. In *Pigs Will Be Pigs* (Axelrod & McGinley-Nally, 1994), toddlers are introduced to the value of currency as the pigs collect money and then go to a restaurant to "pig out." In *Pigs on a Blanket* (Axelrod, 1996), children learn to tell time as the pigs go to the beach. Amy Axelrod also tells a delightful story of pigs using math while cooking in her book *Pigs in the Pantry* (1997). In *How High Is Pepperoni?* (1995) children measure objects in their environment. All of these books have fun, humorous stories to introduce toddlers to the various concepts of math. Appendix A.10 provides a list of counting books written for infants and toddlers.

Color concept books

Concept books featuring colors are aimed at different age levels. Books written for infants have photographs or illustrations that clearly depict the color. For example, *Maisy's Colors* (Cousins, 1997) is a small board book that has a simple phrase on the left-hand page and a colored object on the opposing side. Page one has the phrase "brown horse" with a brown horse illustrated on the other side. After reading this page, teachers or caregivers could point to other brown objects in the room so that infants generalize the color *brown* as an inherent quality of things that comes in many shades. Infants have to learn the difference between the color words and the object words.

Eric Carle's *My Very First Book of Colors* (2005) is another small board book about colors intended for infants. The top half of each page is brightly colored with a picture below of an object of the same color. For example, *blue* is bright blue on the top with a bluebird on the bottom, and the *purple* page has bright purple on the top with a cluster of grapes beneath.

When reading *Zoe's Hats: A Book of Colors and Patterns* (Holm, 2003), caregivers can expand a toddler's knowledge not only by discussing the colors, but also by discussing the different hats worn by different people. This book with big, bright, bold illustrations has a simple phrase accompanying each illustrated hat. For example, "red hat" is under a picture of a red Santa Claus hat. "Brown hat" is under a picture of a brown cowboy hat. All the hats are worn by a smiling child. This book is a great teaching tool to use with toddlers because, at the end of the book, the hats reappear and children are asked to name the color of each one. Caregivers can also permit toddlers to pick their favorite hat and say why it is their favorite. Caregivers might also invite toddlers to use their imagination and draw a hat they would like to wear.

Some color concept books include a story that is age-appropriate for toddlers. *Babar's Book of Color* (De Brunhoff, 2004) is the story of Babar the elephant inviting his children to choose a color and to paint something of that color. Babar's daughter Flora paints 11 gray elephants for her picture. This is a great book to use before inviting toddlers to also draw their own pictures. Caregivers can extend the discussion by asking the child about their favorite color and the feeling it evokes.

Another color concept book shows children how mixing the primary colors creates new colors. *Mouse Paint* (Walsh, 1989) is a story of white mice, climbing into buckets of primary paints and then creating new colors by stepping into the different colored puddles made by the other mice. After reading this book, teachers and caregivers can invite toddlers to experiment with finger paint, creating their own color combinations.

Some color concept books introduce children to other cultures. *A Rainbow All Around Me* (Pinkney, 2002) features photographs of people from many cultures. For example, *green* has four pictures of a Native American child; in the first photograph she is dressed in green and holding a green apple; in the second photograph she is spreading a green and white checkered tablecloth on the green grass; in the third picture she is sitting on the tablecloth; the last photograph shows her toes in the green grass. The text reads: "Green. Fresh. Soft blades. Ticklin' your Toes Barefoot in the park."

There are many quality color concept books that introduce infants and toddlers to the wonderful world of color. Appendix A.11 provides a list of color concept books intended for infants and toddlers.

Shape concept books

Concept books are also written to teach infants and toddlers about shapes. For example, *Touch and Feel: Shapes* by DK Publishing (2000) includes shapes such as circles, squares, and triangles. A shape and the word for it are accompanied by objects that represent the shape. The *circle* page, for example, is accompanied by a plate, a tennis ball, and a "bumpy orange" that readers can touch. All photographs are displayed on a white background so it is easy for readers to understand the concept.

Some shape concept books written for toddlers encourage readers to examine shapes found in their environment. *So Many Circles, So Many Squares* (Hoban, 1998) and *Shapes, Shapes, Shapes* (Hoban, 1986) have beautiful photographs of round, square, and triangular objects, such as bicycle tires, radishes, cubes, square signs, musical triangles, and boat sails. Since there are no words, children and adults are encouraged to discuss the pictures.

Another quality book about shapes is Eric Carle's *My Very First Book of Shapes* (1974). It is a board book that asks children to match a shape with a picture that resembles the shape. Each page is cut in half. For example, on the first open page, the word *circle* is on the left-hand page and a big black circle is on the upper right-hand page. The readers must flip the bottom half of the pages until they find a shape that matches it, in this case a picture of the sun. The featured shapes are circle, semicircle, square, squiggle, triangle, dome, almond, diamond, rectangle, and crescent.

After sharing any book about shapes, caregivers can take a toddler on a walk around the house, the neighborhood, or a park to find similar shapes in different objects. Parents can also demonstrate how to combine and embellish shapes. See Figure 3.3 for a sample.

FIGURE 3.3 A sample demonstration of how shapes can be combined.

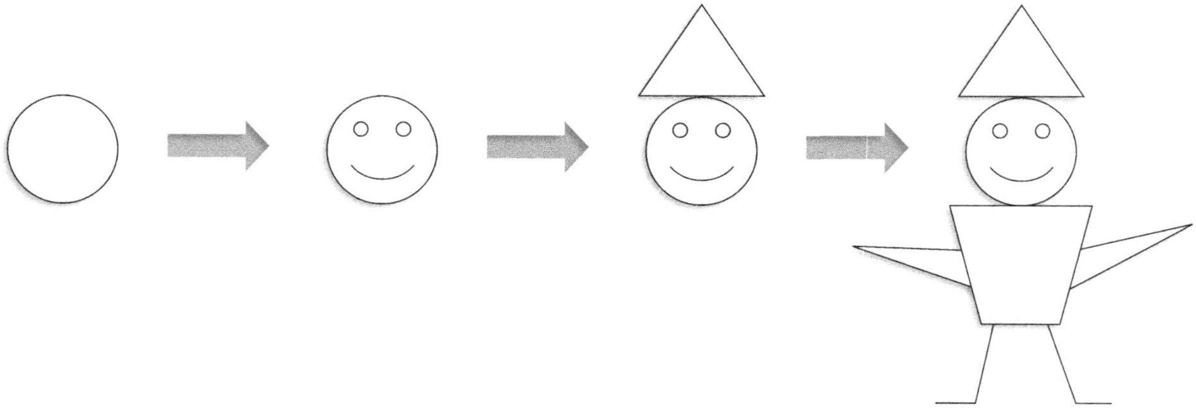

Comparison concept books

Other concepts featured in books for toddlers are opposites (for instance, up/down, cold/hot), sizes (tall, taller, tallest; small, smaller, smallest), and the five senses. In *First Concepts: Opposites* (Priddy, 2002), young children lift flaps to learn about opposites. For example, a "little" kitten is opposite of a "big" cat, and a train engine is "first" while a caboose is "last." In *Harry Bear and Friends: Opposites* (Kreloff, 2007), a sentence depicts big/little, near/far, up/down, front/back and alone/together. These board books are very sturdy to withstand rough handling. Because there is limited text, a teacher or caregiver has the opportunity to start a discussion about the featured objects and their functions.

In *Lift the Flap Sizes Board Book* (Millard, 2002), children lift a flap to find the opposite size beneath it. For example, one flap depicts a large doll in a nesting set, and beneath the flap is a small doll of the same set. Some of the objects are familiar and some may be unfamiliar to a young child. It is a perfect occasion for the teacher or caregiver to discuss unfamiliar objects with toddlers. The end of this chapter has a short list of shape and comparison concept books.

Storybooks

We have discussed the various types of concept books for infants and toddlers, but caregivers must never neglect to read stories to children. Chapter 5 discusses in great detail the many picture storybooks that are available for children in the primary grades. However, in this section, we discuss some books that are appropriate for infants and toddlers.

People of all ages love a great story. Sometimes stories have an engrossing plot, others have interesting characters, and still others thrill us with the imaginary world described therein. Through stories, infants and toddlers learn about themselves and about human relationships. They learn about grammar and hear a rich vocabulary.

Quality stories for this age group have all the elements of adult quality literature (see Chapters 1 and 5). The only difference is that these books are written with infants and toddlers specifically in mind and have themes appropriate for them. Of course, adults are often entertained and amused by quality children's literature. These stories have well-developed plots, which are usually chronological so that toddlers can easily follow the sequence of events. The characters are well-developed; often the characters are animals such as bears, rabbits, mice, sheep, monkeys, and elephants. The literary term for this is *anthropomorphism*, meaning that animals are given human characteristics. Two examples are Lily the mouse in Kevin Henkes's books and Marc Brown's character Arthur the aardvark.

Many stories appropriate for infants and toddlers deal with solving a problem so that adults can discuss with children what the characters did to solve it. For example, every child has failures when learning any new skill. *Little Buggy* (O'Malley, 2002) is about a little ladybug who is learning to fly. Two snails instill fear into the ladybug by telling him that he is way too little to fly. But through the encouragement of his father, the little ladybug learns to soar.

Nap time for toddlers often brings a struggle between caregivers and young children, who don't want to lie down. One book that covers this topic is *Little Brown Bear Won't Take a Nap!* (Dyer, 2002). When winter comes and it is time to hibernate, Little Brown Bear does not want to take a long nap. When he sees

Rosemary Wells was born in New York City and grew up on the shores of New Jersey. Her mother was a ballet dancer and her father was an actor and playwright. Rosemary began to draw at the age of 2, and her parents recognized her talent. She has been writing for more than 30 years and has written more than 60 books. In her books, she uses animals as characters. Some of her characters popular with children are Max and Ruby, Yoko, Noisy Nora, McDuffy, and Timothy. She also has nursery rhyme books and two large collections of Mother Goose titles. Her inspirations come from everyday incidents, from things she hears, and things she reads.

the geese flying overhead, he asks his parents if geese have to take a nap. They explain that geese fly south for the winter. Little Brown Bear decides to pack his suitcase and follow the geese. When he arrives down south, he enjoys the beach with the geese, but he soon becomes tired, builds a sand cave that is warm, and falls asleep. When spring arrives, his geese friends help him get back home. Even though Little Brown Bear leaves his parents, the plot is never scary for young children because the geese become his friends.

Many toddlers have great imaginations and they create imaginary friends. *Emma Kate* (Polacco, 2005) is a delightful story of Emma Kate and her imaginary friend, an elephant. The text is simple, and the illustrations are humorous. Polacco uses a soft pencil to draw the elephant, and most of the scenery she paints with bright watercolors. Emma Kate's dress, for instance, is bright red with blue flowers. Her parents understand her need to have an imaginary friend and keep telling her that she has such a wonderful imagination. After sharing this story, caregivers can discuss with toddlers whether they have an imaginary friend.

Some authors create a character and then write a series of individual stories about that character. Rosemary Wells creates many humorous stories with Max and Ruby. Max and Ruby often find themselves in situations that reflect toddlers' lives. In *Max Cleans Up* (2000), big sister Ruby is trying to help Max clean up his deplorably dirty room, but Max, when Ruby is not looking, attempts to put everything—Popsicles, sand, bubbles, ants, and more—in his pocket. When the room is finally clean, Ruby asks Max what he has in his bulging pocket. Max stands up, empties out his pocket, and says, "Everything!" Toddlers and adults can identify with this humorous event because toddlers seldom want to part with any of their "treasures." If a toddler has the same tendency as Max, parents can discuss why Max should not put all those sticky objects in his pocket. There is an annotated list of Rosemary Wells's other books found at the end of this chapter.

Young children enjoy such series because they enjoy hearing stories about their favorite characters in a number of scenarios. Some other favorite characters of infants and toddlers are Winnie-the-Pooh by A. A. Milne, Spot by Eric Hill, Little Critters by Mercer Mayer, Franklin by Paulette Bourgeois, Clifford by Norman Bridwell, Arthur by Marc Brown, Curious George by H. A. Rey, Madeline by Ludwig Bemelmans, and Carl by Alexander Day.

There are many other wonderful series written for young children. Appendix A.13 offers a short annotated list of them. We suggest that you begin your own annotated list, categorizing the books in a way that is most useful to you. Chapter 5 discusses other storybooks for children from infancy through third grade.

teaching suggestions
SHARING BOOKS

Parents and caregivers usually share books with infants and toddlers in an informal manner. The following teaching suggestions are for teachers who share books with preschoolers and other young students.

Tracing Letters and Numbers

With white glue, the teacher can draw each letter of the alphabet on a separate 4" x 6" index card. While the glue is still wet, the preschool or kindergarten children can place lima beans on the glue so they have a set of raised letters they can later trace. If a child has a difficult time writing one letter, the teacher can use the card to guide the child's finger over the raised letter. By guiding the child's finger, the teacher helps the child draw the letter using the correct motions (i.e., top to bottom or left to right) Another set of cards can be used to create the numerals 1 through 10.

Making a Class Alphabet Book

After sharing a number of alphabet books with preschool or kindergarten children and drawing attention to the initial letter of each of their names, the teacher can engage the children in making a class alphabet book. Using a digital camera, the teacher takes a picture of each student and prints it out on a color printer. The teacher then cuts out each picture and glues it on a piece of paper with the text: "__(Child's Name)__ loves to eat _____ and play _____." Each child writes his or her name in the first blank and dictates to the teacher a favorite food (written in the second blank) and a favorite activity (written in the third blank). The teacher then arranges the pages alphabetically by name.

It is quite likely that multiple children will have names that begin with the same letter (e.g., John, Jimmy, Jan) and other letters will have no names. This results in having multiple pages for some letters, while other letters are unrepresented. For the letters with no names, the teacher can have the children decide on an "imaginary" classmate with a name that begins with that letter. For example, the letter "V" may be blank. The children can find a picture of a person in a magazine, cut out the picture, and decide on a name for that person such as Victor or Violet. Then as a class they decide on the imaginary classmate's favorite food and play activity.

After all pages are complete, they are laminated and bound together using rings so that the booklet is durable. First, the book is shared in class by having each child read his or her own page. Later, have each child flip through all the pages. That way children learn to read the names of their classmates and learn about their favorite foods and activities. If a new classmate joins the class, the teacher can take a picture of the newcomer and have the student create a page that gets added to the class book.

Bundling Box Tops for Education

This strategy is good to use after sharing *How Much Is a Million?* (Schwartz, 2004). Joyce Shatzer (2008) believes that students need to see how math is used in their everyday lives. She and her students support the school's Parent–Teacher Association project Boxtops for Education. At the start of the day, she collects the box tops that the students brought to school. The children put the box tops into the "Ones" pocket on their number chart. When there are 10 box tops, they bundle them up and put the bundle into the "Tens" pocket. When they get 10 bundles in the "Tens" pocket, they put one big rubber band around the 10 bundles and put that bundle into the "Hundreds" pocket. Each year they strive to get 1 million box tops.

Creating a Class Book Using Montage

Montage (from the French for "putting together") can be used when children adhere small pieces of the same color paper to a surface, overlapping to create an object. This type of art project is great to develop children's fine motor skills as they learn about colors. Class books can be created for different seasons. For January, the class can create a book of favorite colored mittens; in March, a book of favorite colored kites; and in April, a book of favorite colored umbrellas. To create the book, each child is given a blank piece of paper. The teacher demonstrates how to draw the outline of a mitten by putting her hand flat on a piece of paper, with the four fingers close together and the thumb sticking out like a mitten. For the other months, the teacher draws the outline of a kite and umbrella. Then the teacher tells the children that they are to pick their favorite color and find pictures in a magazine with that color in it. They are to tear off pieces of the picture and then fill their outline with these overlapping swatches. The teacher should have a complete one on display so the children can see the finished product. Then the children write the sentence: "___*(Name)*'s___ favorite mitten is ___*(color)*___." The teacher can make the pages into a class book for the children to read.

Shapes Around the School

After sharing *When a Line Bends . . . A Shape Begins* (Greene, 2001), encourage children to look around the room to identify what shapes they see in the classroom. Also consider taking the class on a walk around the school and the schoolyard to find shapes, taking notes on what they find. When they get back to the classroom, ask them what they noticed and list their findings on the board. Assign one object to each child and have each child take a picture of the object with the digital camera. You may then create a slide show on the computer so everyone can view the class's collection of shapes.

Conclusion

Creating a special time to read to children, beginning on the day of their birth, is as important to their development as providing regular feedings. Reading stimulates infants' physical, cognitive, social, moral, and linguistic development. It does not matter during the first month that they do not understand what you read to them, just as they do not understand what you say to them either. However, reading to them instills the idea that reading is a pleasurable activity. It also helps them learn their native language—its cadence, its sounds, and, later, its vocabulary and grammar.

The choice of books for young children is enormous. You should try to include various types: concept books, poetry and nursery rhymes (Chapter 4), traditional fairy tales (Chapter 6), informational books (Chapter 8), as well as storybooks. Remember to select books with a rich vocabulary. A good resource for new books is your public library. Most public libraries provide a large selection of books for children. One thing to remember is to read and reread favorites to infants and toddlers while regularly introducing them to new books.

journeying WITH CHILDREN'S LITERATURE

1. Visit your local library and make a list or a spreadsheet of concept books: the alphabet, numbers, colors, shapes, and other concepts such as opposites. Be sure to include the author and/or illustrator, the copyright date, the publisher, and information about the books' contents. Categorize them according to age.

2. Go to a local bookstore and look through the infant books made of cloth, vinyl, or sturdy cardboard. With the bookstore manager's permission, make an annotated list of the ones you think are safe and appropriate for infants up to 9 months.

3. Go to a local daycare and ask the director if you may read to 1-, 2-, and 3-year olds. (Remember: all states require you to wear a nametag and check in at the front desk in order to work with children. Many places also require you to sign a statement giving the organization permission to do a background check on you. This is all done to protect the children.) Read the same book to children of each age group and record how each child responds to the book. Does every child respond differently to the book? Do you find validation for Louise Rosenblatt's transactional theory?

4. Visit a local daycare that looks after infants. Ask the director for permission to read/discuss books with their youngest infants on up to 2-year-olds. Be sure to choose appropriate books for the age. After spending time with each infant and toddler, record how the child responds to your reading. (Be sure to get the necessary permission.)

5. Read a color concept book to a small group of 2-year-olds. After each page, ask the children to find something in the room that is the same color as that on the page. Can every child do it? Make mental notes of the different ability levels of 2-year-olds.

activities TO SHARE WITH CHILDREN

1. Young children enjoy manipulating pieces on flannel boards. Caregivers can create felt farm animals that children can play with as they sing songs. Using white glue, adhere pictures of animals like those shown on the next page to pieces of felt. Create a small felt board by attaching a piece of flannel onto a sheet of cardboard. Children can put each animal on the board as they sing the verses to "Old MacDonald" or "The Farmer in

the Dell." Or, using the tune of "The Wheels on the Bus Go Round and Round," sing the following song: "The cows in the barn go moo, moo, moo. Moo, moo, moo, Moo, moo, moo. The cows in the barn go moo, moo, moo, all around the farm" (Smith, 1998). Similar verses can be invented for pigs, ducks, hens, horses, and sheep.

2. Most toddlers enjoy listening to Eric Carle's books about insects; two of his more popular ones are *The Very Hungry Caterpillar* and *The Grouchy Ladybug*. After reading the books, take the children outside to explore nature and examine the appearance of real caterpillars and ladybugs. Giving children a magnifying glass to examine the dots on a ladybug may help foster an interest in science.

3. After enjoying *The Grouchy Ladybug* and *Eye Spy a Ladybug! A Lift the Flap Book* with toddlers, give the children paper and have them draw the body of a ladybug with non-toxic, washable markers or crayons. For the legs, give each child six black pipe cleaners. Examine the picture of the ladybug in the book and help the children determine where the legs go. Then help them attach two short pipe cleaners on the head for antennas.

4. After reading one of the Clifford books with a child, have him or her draw two long tear-drop shaped ears. Cut out the ears for the child and cut a one-inch strip that is long enough to fit around the child's head. Using a glue stick, glue the band to fit the child's head size. Then glue the ears on the band. The next time you read a Clifford book, let the child wear the ears or act out one of Clifford's stories.

our favorite CHILDREN'S BOOKS

Bond, M. (1958). *Paddington Bear.* Illus. Peggy Fortnun. New York: Dell.

A little bear from Peru goes out on an adventure. He carries a tattered suitcase containing jars of marmalade and wears a tag around his neck with this message: "Please look after this bear." He arrives at Paddington Station where the Brown family finds him and takes him home to live with them.

Creech, S. (2003). *Who's That Baby?* Illus. David Diaz. New York: HarperCollins.

Babies see, hear, think, and feel so many things, but nothing quite as much as love. Creech's poems reflect the love and humor a baby brings to mothers, grandparents, and other family members.

Kono, E. E. (2005). *Hula Lullaby.* Illus. Erin Eitter Kono. New York: Little Brown.

Drummers' beats, ocean breezes, gentle swaying of tealeaf skirts, and Mother's warm arms lull the baby to sleep under Hawaiian starry skies.

McFarlane, S. (2004). *What's That Sound? On the Farm.* Illus. Kim Lafave. Allston, MA: Fitzhenry & Whiteside.

> Even toddlers who do not live on farms will experience the rumble of tractors, the quacking and splish splash of ducks, the snort and squeal of pigs, and other farm noises.

Melmed, L. K. (2005). *I Love You As Much . . .* Illus. Henri Sorensen. New York: HarperCollins.

> The realistic illustrations of Henri Sorensen and the gentle, lilting text of this lullaby celebrate the love between a mother and child.

Numeroff, L. (2003). *If You Give a Pig a Party.* Illus. Felicia Bond. New York: HarperCollins.

> This is one in a book series. In this one, the pig asks for balloons if you give her a party; then she asks for the house to be decorated and so on until she asks for a party dress. Then, of course, she asks for a party.

Roth, C. (2004). *Who Will Tuck Me in Tonight?* Illus. Valeri Gorbachev. LaVergne, TN: North–South Books.

> The entire story is a poem about farm animal mothers who attempt to tuck the lamb Wooly into bed. But no mother can do it properly but Mother Sheep.

Rowe, J. (2000). *Whose Ears?* Illus. Janette Rowe. New York: Greenwillow.

> This interactive book challenges the toddler to guess what animal has ears sticking out from the pages. The child must lift the flap to find the answers.

Willems, M. (2004). *Knuffle Bunny.* Illus. Mo Willems. New York: Scholastic.

> Trixie leaves Knuffle Bunny, her stuffed animal, at the laundromat and begins to babble to her father: "Aggle flaggle klabble." When her mother understands her babbles and Trixie sees Knuffle Bunny in the dryer, she says her first words: "Knuffle Bunny!" The speech bubbles with baby's babbles, and the black and white photographs of the street scenes gives adult and child lots to discuss.

Yolen, J. (2000). *Off We Go!* Illus. Lara Molk. New York: Little, Brown.

> This story is about baby critters and their mamas going to Grandmother's house. The sound-evoking text has readers listening to slithering snakes, hopping bunnies, and the dig-dig-digging of the moles.

children's literature IN THIS CHAPTER

Ashman, L. (2002). *Can you make a piggy giggle?* Illus. Henry Cole. New York: Dutton Juvenile.

Axelrod, A. (1994). *Pigs will be pigs.* Illus. Sharon McGinley-Nally. New York: Scholastic.

Axelrod, A. (1995). *How high is pepperoni?* New York: Scholastic.

Axelrod, A. (1996). *Pigs on a blanket.* Illus. Sharon McGinley-Nally New York: Scholastic.

Axelrod, A. (1997). *Pigs in a pantry.* Illus. Sharon McGinley-Nally New York: Scholastic.

Bauer, M. D. (2003). *Toes, ears, & nose!* Illus. Karen Katz. New York: Little Simon.

Benjamin, A. (1994). *Zoo's who board book.* Illus. A. Benjamin. New York: Simon & Schuster.

Boelt, M. (2001). *You're a brother, Little Bunny.* Illus. Kathy Parkinson. Morton Grove, IL: Albert Whitman & Co.

Bond, M. (1958). *Paddington Bear*. Illus. Peggy Fortnum. New York: Dell.

Boynton, S. (2003). *Fuzzy fuzzy fuzzy! A touch, scratch & tickle book*. Illus. Sandra Boynton. New York: Little Simon.

Brown, M. (1972). *Runaway bunny*. Illus. Clement Hurd. New York: HarperCollins.

Brown, R. (1997). *Baba*. Illus. Ruth Brown. London: Andersen Press.

Carle, E. (1969). *The very hungry caterpillar*. New York: Philomel.

Carle, E. (1977). *The grouchy ladybug*. Illus. Eric Carle. New York: Harper Trophy.

Carle, E. (1984). *The very busy spider*. Illus. Eric Carle. New York: Philomel.

Carle, E. (1999). *From head to toe board book*. Illus. Eric Carle. New York: Harper Festival.

Carle, E. (2005). *My very first book of colors*. Illus. Eric Carle. New York: Philomel.

Carle, E. (2005). *My very first book of shapes*. Illus. Eric Carle. New York: Philomel.

Carlstrom, N. W. (1986). *Jesse Bear, what will you wear?* Illus. Bruce Degen. New York: Simon & Schuster.

Carlstrom, N. W. (1992). *How do you say it today, Jesse Bear?* Illus. Bruce Degen. New York: Aladdin Paperbacks/Simon & Schuster.

Carlstrom, N. W. (1994). *Happy birthday, Jesse Bear*. Illus. Bruce Degen. New York: Aladdin Paperbacks/Simon & Schuster.

Carlstrom, N. W. (1997). *Better not get wet, Jesse Bear*. Illus. Bruce Degen. New York: Aladdin Paperbacks/Simon & Schuster.

Carlstrom, N. W. (1997). *Let's count it out, Jesse Bear*. Illus. Bruce Degen. New York: Aladdin Paperbacks/Simon & Schuster.

Carlstrom, N. W. (1998). *Guess who's coming, Jesse Bear*. Illus. Bruce Degen. New York: Aladdin Paperbacks/Simon & Schuster.

Carlstrom, N. W. (1998). *It's about time, Jesse Bear*. Illus. Bruce Degen. New York: Aladdin Paperbacks/Simon & Schuster.

Carlstrom, N. W. (2002). *What a scare, Jesse Bear*. Illus. Bruce Degen. New York: Aladdin Paperbacks/Simon & Schuster.

Carlstrom, N. W. (2003). *Goodbye geese*. Illus. Ed Young. New York: Aladdin Paperbacks/Simon & Schuster.

Carter, D. (1995). *Feely bugs: To touch and feel*. Illus. David Carter. New York: Little Simon.

Cimarusti, M. T. (1998). *Peek-a-moo!* Illus. Stephanie Petersen. New York: Dutton Juvenile.

Cimarusti, M. T. (2003). *Peek-a-zoo!* Illus. Stephanie Petersen. New York: Dutton Juvenile.

Cimarusti, M. T. (2004). *Peek-a-pet!* Illus. Stephanie Petersen. New York: Dutton Juvenile.

Cousins, L. (1997). *Maisy's colors*. Illus. Lucy Cousins. London: Walker Books.

Cowley, J. (1980). *Mrs. Wishy-Washy*. Illus. Elizabeth Fuller. New York: Philomel.

Cronin, D. (2005). *Wiggle*. Illus. Scott Menchin. New York: Atheneum Books for Young Readers.

De Brunhoff, L. (2004). *Babar's book of color*. Illus. Jean De Brunhoff. New York: Putnam.

dePaola, T. (2003). *Marcos colors: Red, yellow, blue*. Illus. Tomie dePaola. New York: G. P. Putnam's Sons.

DK Publishing. (2000). *Touch and feel: ABC*. New York: DK Publishing.

DK Publishing. (2000). *Touch and feel: Shapes*. New York: DK Publishing.

Durango, J. (2006). *Cha-cha-chimps*. Illus. Eleanor Taylor. New York: Simon & Schuster Children's Books.

Dyer, J. (2002). *Little brown bear won't take a nap*. Illus. Jane Dyer. New York: Little, Brown.

Ehlert, L. (1989). *Eating the alphabet: Fruits and vegetables from A to Z*. Illus. Lois Ehlert. New York: Trumpet Club.

Ehlert, L. (1992). *Painting a rainbow*. Illus. Lois Ehlert. New York: Voyager.

Ehlert, L. (1992). *Fish eyes: A book you can count on*. Illus. Lois Ehlert. San Diego: Voyager Books/Harcourt Brace.

Ehlert, L. (1997). *Color farm*. New York: Harper Festival.

Ehlert, L. (1997). *Color zoo*. New York: Harper Festival.

Falconer, I. (2002). *Olivia counts*. Illus. Ian Falconer. New York: Atheneum.

Field, E. (2002). *Clothes*. Wilton, CT: Tiger Tales Books.

Field, E. (2002). *Toys*. Wilton, CT: Tiger Tales Books.

Fleming, D. (1996). *In this small, small pond*. Illus. Denis Fleming. New York: Henry Holt.

Fox, M. (2002). *The magic hat*. Illus. Tricia Tusa. San Diego: Harcourt Brace.

Freeman, D. (1968). *Corduroy*. Illus. Don Freeman. New York: Scholastic.

Garten, J. (1994). *The alphabet tale*. Illus. Muriel Batherman. New York: Greenwillow.

Greene, R. (2001). *When a line bends . . . A shape begins*. Illus. James Kaczman. New York: Sandpiper.

Hague, K. (1984). *Alphabears: An ABC book*. Illus. Michael Hague. New York: Henry Holt.

Hill, E. (1996). *Spot visits his grandparents*. Illus. Eric Hill. New York: Putnam.

Hill, E. (1999). *Spot helps out.* Illus. Eric Hill. New York: Putnam.

Hill, E. (2003). *Spot's first words: Board book.* Illus. Eric Hill. New York: Putnam.

Hill, E. (2003). *Spot goes splash!* Illus. Eric Hill. New York: Putnam.

Hill, E. (2003). *Spot looks at colors: Board book.* Illus. Eric Hill. New York: Putnam.

Hill, E. (2003). *Spot looks at shapes: Board book.* Illus. Eric Hill. New York: Putnam.

Hill, E. (2005). *Spot goes to the park.* Illus. Eric Hill. New York: Putnam.

Hill, E. (2005). *Spot: night-night, Spot.* Illus. Eric Hill. New York: Putnam.

Hoban, T. (1986). *Shapes, shapes, shapes.* New York: Greenwillow.

Hoban, T. (1998). *So many circles, so many squares.* New York: Greenwillow.

Holm, S. (2003). *Zoe's hats: A book of colors and patterns.* Illus. Sharon Lane Holm. Honesdale, PA: Boyds Mill Press.

Hooker, Y. (1978). *One green frog.* Illus. Yvonne Hooker. New York: Grosset & Dunlap.

Hughes, S. (1999). *Alfie's ABC.* New York: Houghton Mifflin.

Inkpen, M. (1994). *Kipper's book of numbers.* Illus. Mick Inkpen. San Diego: Red Wagon Books: Harcourt Brace.

Jugran, J. (2006). *Three little ducks.* Illus. Barbara Vagnozzi. Norwalk, CT: Innovative Kids.

Kono, E. E. (2005). *Hula lullaby.* Illus. Erin Eitter Kono. New York: Little, Brown.

Kreloff, H. (2007). *Harry Bear and friends: Opposites.* Maplewood, NJ: Blue Apple Books.

Markes, J. (2005). *Shhhhh! Everybody's sleeping.* Illus. David Parkins. New York: HarperCollins.

Martin, B. Jr. (1996). *Brown Bear, Brown Bear, what do you see?* Illus. Eric Carle. New York: Scholastic.

Martin, B. Jr. (1997). *Polar Bear, Polar Bear, what do you hear?* Illus. Eric Carle. New York: Henry Holt.

Martin, B. Jr. (2003). *Panda Bear, Panda Bear, what do you see?* Illus. Eric Carle. New York: Harper Festival.

Marzollo, J. (2001). *I spy little bunnies.* Illus. Walter Wick. New York: Scholastic.

McBratney, S. (1994). *Guess how much I love you.* Cambridge, MA: Candlewick Press.

McCloskey, R. (1941). *Make way for ducklings.* Illus. Robert McCloskey. New York: Puffin.

Melmed, L. K. (2005). *I love you as much . . .* Illus. Henri Sorensen. New York: HarperCollins.

Millard, A. (2002). *Lift the flap sizes board book.* New York: DK Publishing.

Milne, A. A. (1996). *Pooh goes visiting.* New York: Dutton Juvenile/Penguin.

Milne, A. A. (2001). *Winnie-the-Pooh and friends.* Illus. Ernest H. Shepard. New York: Trustees of the Pooh Properties.

Munsch, R. (1986). *Love you forever.* New York: Firefly Books.

Numeroff, L. (2003). *If you give a pig a pancake.* Illus. Felicia Bond. New York: HarperCollins.

O'Malley, K. (2002). *Little buggy.* New York: Gulliver Books.

Oppenheim, J. (1989). *"Not now," said the cow.* New York: Bantam Little Rooster Books.

Owens, M. B. (1993). *Counting cranes.* Illus. Mary Beth Oloehs. New York: Little, Brown.

Pallotta, J. (1986). *The ocean alphabet book.* Illus. Frank Mazzola, Jr. Watertown, MA: Charlesbridge Publishing.

Pallotta, J. (1986). *The icky bug alphabet book.* Illus. Ralph Masiello. Watertown, MA: Charlesbridge Publishing.

Pallotta, J. (1990). *The furry alphabet book.* Illus. Edgar Stewart. Watertown, MA: Charlesbridge Publishing.

Pfister, M. (1991). *Hopper.* Illus. Marcus Pfister. New York: A Special Scholastic Edition.

Pinkney, S. (2002). *A rainbow all around me.* Illus. Miles Pinkney. New York: Cartwheel Books.

Pinto, S. (2003). *The alphabet room.* Illus. Sara Pint. New York: Bloomsbury USA Children's Books.

Polacco, P. (2005). *Emma Kate.* Illus. Patricia Polacco. New York: Philomel.

Potter, B. (1902). *The tale of Peter Rabbit.* Illus. Beatrix Potter. London: Penguin Books.

Priddy, R. (2002). *First concepts: Opposites.* London: Priddy Books.

Priddy, R. (2004). *Bright baby colors.* London: Priddy Books.

Priddy, R. (2004). *Bright baby first words.* London: Priddy Books.

Priddy, R. (2005). *Bright baby animals.* London: Priddy Books.

Romanell, S. (2008). *Let's play ball.* Illus. Hans deBeer. LaVergne, TN: North–South/Ingram Publishers.

Saltzberg, B. (2001). *Baby animal kisses.* Illus. Barney Saltzberg. San Diego: Red Wagon Books.

Schulman, J. (2002). *Countdown to spring.* Illus. Meilo So. New York: Random House.

Schulte, J. (2005). *Can you find it inside?* Illus. Jessica Schulte. New York: Harry H. Abrams.

Schwartz, D. M. (2004). *How much is a million?* Illus. Steven Kellogg. New York: HarperCollins.

Shannon, D. (2002). *Duck on a bike.* Illus. David Shannon. New York: Blue Sky Press.

Shannon, D. (2005). *Oops! (Oops!).* Illus. David Shannon. New York: Blue Sky Press.

Shustak, B. R. (2005). *I love you through and through.* Illus. Caroline Jay Church. San Diego: Cartwheel.

Slaughter, T. (2003). *1 2 3.* Illus. Tom Slaughter. Toronto, ON: Tundra Books.

Sternberg, D. (2007). *The snow ball.* Illus. Liz Conrad. New York: Penguin Young Readers Group.

Van Fleet, M. (2003). *Tails.* Illus. Matthew Van Fleet. Orlando: Harcourt.

Wade, L. (1999). *The Cheerios animal play book.* New York: Little Simon.

Walsh, E. S. (1989). *Mouse paint.* Illus. Ellen Stoll Walsh. New York: Trumpet Club.

Watanabe, K. (2003). *My first taggies book: Sweet dreams.* New York: Cartwheel/Scholastic.

Watt, F. (2005). *Busy baby.* Illus. Catharine MacKinnon. St. Louis: Usborne Books.

Wells, R. (2006). *Carry me.* New York: Puffin.

Wells, R. (2002). *Max cleans up.* New York: Puffin.

Willems, M. (2004). *Knuffle Bunny.* Illus. Mo Willems. New York: Scholastic.

Williams, S. (1989). *I went walking.* Illus. Julie Vivas. New York: Trumpet Club.

Wood, A. (1984). *The napping house.* Illus. Don Wood. San Diego: Harcourt Brace Jovanovich.

Yolen, J. (2006). *Count me a rhyme: Animal poems by the numbers.* Illus. Jason Stemple. Honesdale, PA: Boyds Mills Press.

Poetry

CHAPTER BY MARY E. BLAKE JONES

Sharing Literature: AN EXAMPLE

Sarah Stevens is trying to ignite a love of poetry in her second graders. She has decided that the surest way to do that is to utilize the humorous, silly, and often offbeat poems of Shel Silverstein. One of her personal favorites is "Sarah Cynthia Sylvia Stout Would Not Take the Garbage Out" from *Where the Sidewalk Ends* (1974). She thinks that it will appeal to her class because it features a child who refuses to do an unpleasant task and thus faces the consequences. She feels certain that many of her children may have had similar experiences and may well relate to Sarah Cynthia Sylvia Stout.

To begin Ms. Stevens gathers her group on the comfortable rug in front of a digital whiteboard connected to a class computer. Ms. Stevens had created her lesson materials on the computer prior to class and sent them directly to the board. Ms. Stevens proceeds to pull up a chart labeled, "THINGS I DON'T LIKE TO DO." Her first question to the children is, "What is something you really don't like to do around your house?" Immediately, hands go up and answers pour forth.

Caly: I hate to wash the dishes.

Jackson: I don't like to feed our animals.

Enrique: It's boring to set the table.

Bella: I think it's icky to put garbage in the trash.

Then Ms. Stevens asks, "What don't you like to do in the yard?" Again there is a flurry of replies.

Chad: Weeding the garden is awful.

Taneesha: So is watering the flowers.

Ryan: Picking up trash and branches isn't very good either.

The third question Ms. Stevens asks is "What's your least favorite chore in your room?" Many students say making their beds or picking up clothes and toys.

Before long the class has a chart that looks like the one in Figure 4.1.

After everyone finishes reading the chart to himself or herself, Ms. Stevens asks, "What do you think would happen if you didn't do these chores?"

After several children reply, "I don't know," one brave little girl ventures, "It might be a mess." Ms. Stevens takes that as her cue to introduce "Sarah Cynthia Sylvia Stout Would Not Take the Garbage Out." After reading the title, she asks the class, "What do you think happens to Sarah?"

Caly: The house begins to smell.

Ichiro: She gets buried in it.

Michael: It all will turn into compost.

Ms. Stevens records the answers on the digital whiteboard and begins to read with expression. The children are riveted through the whole reading:

And there in the garbage she did hate
Poor Sarah met an awful fate,
That I cannot right now relate
Because the hour is much too late. . . .
(Silverstein, 1974, p. 71)

Then they ask Ms. Stevens to read it again, twice. Once satisfied they have heard it correctly, some of the children begin to offer their versions of what had happened:

Sarah got buried in Cream of Wheat.
Sarah slipped on banana peels and broke her neck.
Sarah drowned in curdled milk.
Sarah was smothered by bubble gum and cellophane.

The class's "least favorite chore" chart.

FIGURE 4.1

THINGS I DON'T LIKE TO DO

HOME	YARD	ROOM
Wash the dishes	Mow the lawn	Pick up my clothes
Put dishes away	Rake the leaves	Make the bed
Walk the dog	Weed the garden	Put my toys away
Set the table	Water the flowers	Keep my desk clean
Feed the dog and cat		
Fold clothes		
Take out trash		

Ms. Stevens—who had earlier set up art stations with construction paper, markers, glue, and tissue paper squares that could be crumpled into pieces—took this opportunity to have the students work in pairs to create their vision of Sarah's last day. Each collage is given a title, such as the following:

Sarah Stout Gets Rubbed Out
Garbage Here, Garbage There, All That Garbage Everywhere
Sarah's Fate Rests Under a Plate
Ice Cream Cones Cover Sarah's Bones

After all the collages are complete, Ms. Stevens hangs them up all around the room.

Introduction

Poetry, elusive and lyrical, is the most powerful of all literature written for children. Its compact format requires that the language be structured and intense to evoke strong feelings and responses from young listeners. The beauty of poetry is that each listener's response is individual. As with adults, each child has his or her own interpretation of the poem at hand.

In addition to the emotional impact of poetry, another of its benefits for children comes from its artful use of language. The sounds, alliteration, rhyme, and rhythm of poetry all help young children become phonologically aware: that is, they become able to recognize differences in speech sounds and then begin to match them to print. As children progress from emergent to competent readers and writers, poetry encourages them to play with language and to use their imaginations to heighten reality or create a new reality that never existed before.

In this chapter we analyze the characteristics of children's poetry and explain the benefits of having them regularly interact with it. We include simple guidelines for evaluating and choosing good poetry for children. We limit our discussion of poetry to that which appeals to the very young: from Mother

Goose rhymes to narrative verse. Select poets and their works are described. In the last part of the chapter we suggest activities for sharing poetry with young children.

Poetry Defined

Experts claim that poetry defies "precise definition" (Kiefer, 2009, p. 341). And, in reality, it is difficult to pin down. A loose description of poetry would be this: language intended to evoke a feeling or create an experience. Poetry, with its lyrical cadences and rhythms, connects with children's reality and then intensifies and deepens it. Children, like adults, gain new insights from their encounters with poetry because of its powerful and moving use of language (Kiefer, 2009). Poems may be narrative or lyrical; both styles impact children's linguistic, emotional, and intellectual development. Poetry deserves a prominent place in the lives of young children.

Narrative Poems

Narrative poetry tells the story of an event or series of events. David Pelham's narratives appeal to children's sense of the ridiculous. In the Sam series, Pelham puts Sam's meals to rhyme. Pelham follows up *Sam's Sandwich* (1990) with the equally messy chocolate-flavored *Sam's Surprise* (1992). Next on the menu is *Sam's Snack* (1994), with tar-filled cookies. Then comes *Sam's Pizza* (1996), complete with slugs, baby eels, and sheeps' eyes. All the books are chock-full of silly verses and unsavory gastronomical images. In a different light, Pelham's *Skeleton in the Closet* (1998) provides a scary, humorous twist to Halloween.

Jack Prelutsky's dragons of *The Dragons Are Singing Tonight* (1993) might initially appear scary and menacing like thunderous Boom of "I am Boom!" However, most of the poems are stories about benign, sometimes sad, creatures that long for the old days when everyone believed in them and their powers. A more recent piece by Prelutsky that relates verse tales of various animals and people is *The Frogs Wore Red Suspenders* (2002). Several of the rhymes are about journeys: "Winnie Appleton who bounces a ball from Minneapolis to St. Paul and Barnaby Boone who drifts with his yellow balloon from El Paso to Fort Worth." Longer rhyming narratives come from Dr. Seuss. *The Cat in the Hat* (1985, 2005) tells the tale of a most unusual rainy afternoon, while *Green Eggs and Ham* (1960, 2005) portrays Sam-I-am's successful attempt to get the green eggs and ham eaten.

Lyrical Poems

Lyrical poetry presents a melody in words. More than other types of children's literature, poetry is about language—language as symbol, rhythm, image, and metaphor. The structured, intense, patterned language of poems evokes strong responses that are different for each reader (McKay, 1986). For example, how do you respond to Mary O'Neill's "What Is Red?" from *Hailstones and Halibut Bones* (1990):

Jack Prelutsky was born in Brooklyn, New York, and grew up in an apartment house in the Bronx. Even though he enjoyed playing with language as a child, he did not become a poet until he was 24 years old. He relates that he did not like poetry in grade school because he thought it was good for you but not enjoyable.

When Prelutsky was 24 years old, he decided to write a poem for each of the imaginary animals he had drawn. Editor and author Susan Hirschman thought these poems were very good and encouraged him to continue to write them; she then published his first book.

He has written many books of poems—*The New Kid on the Block* (1984), *Behold the Bold Umbrellaphant and Other Poems* (2006), *My Dog May Be a Genius* (2008), and numerous others. He has also collected two anthologies: *Random House Book of Poetry* (1983) and *Twentieth Century Children's Poetry Treasury* (1999). When asked where he gets his zany ideas, he has said that they come from anywhere, including his studio, which houses a collection of frogs and windup toys.

He is the first U. S. Children's Poet Laureate. The humor in his poems and his vivid vocabulary draw children and adults to read and love his poems. Besides being a poet, Prelutsky enjoys photography, carpentry, inventing games, creating collages, and making sculptures from found objects.

Red is a sunset
Blazy and bright
Red is feeling brave
With all your might
[...]
Fire-cracker, fire-engine
Fire-flicker red—
And when you're angry
Red runs through your head.
[...]
Red is a show-off
No doubt about it—
But can you imagine
Living without it? (unpaged)

   In response to this poem, children can create their own poetry books of the various colors; they also can illustrate the poems in a variety of media. The child who composes the lines, "Red is my hair / The balloons at the fair / And the sneakers I wear," has the option of illustrating them using vivid finger paints, a collage of tissue paper cut-outs, or even abstract figures made of red yarn. Poems allow children to come up with their own creative interpretations.

Elements of Poetry

The key elements in poetry—rhythm, rhyme, alliteration, assonance, image, and metaphor—are all conducive to children's language development. Early reading ability is related to awareness of rhyme and rhythm (Goswami, 2002). Interacting with nursery rhymes and rhythmical poetry has the potential to improve children's phonological awareness, word identification, and overall word decoding skills (Machado, 2007). Also, repetitive initial sounds, called *alliteration,* in poems help children identify and distinguish initial consonants in words they are decoding (Machado, 2007).

Poetry's figurative language—similes, metaphors, and personifications—lets children exercise their imaginations and visualize what they hear and read. The sound effects of poetry (rhythm, rhyme, alliteration, assonance) make many poems songlike (Kiefer, Hepler, & Hickman, 2007). Lines children recall can help them decode and identify new words. In coming sections we discuss these elements of poetry in more detail.

Rhythm

In poetry, rhythm can best be described as a recurring beat brought about by stresses and pauses in language. Children respond to the rhythm of Mother Goose rhymes from an early age (Kiefer, 2009). For example, take the cadence of this familiar traditional verse:

> Pease porridge hot,
> Pease porridge cold,
> Pease porridge in the pot,
> Nine days old.
> Some like it hot,
> Some like it cold,
> Some like it in the pot,
> Nine days old.

The rhythm of the poem may make children respond physically. They may start to clap their hands or play "patty cake" with each other. Such play helps develop eye–hand coordination. Clapping is a major part of *Clap Your Hands* by Lorinda Bryan Cauley (1992), poems written for very young children. Its rhythms are powerful, offering children many opportunities for clapping games and role-playing. Another example is Jack Prelutsky's (1986) rhythmic poetry:

> Rumpitty Tumpitty Rumpitty Tum,
> Buntington Bunny is beating the drum
> He twitches his nose as he tramps through the street,
> Stamping his Rumpitty Tumpitty feet.

Prelutsky's poetry provides ample opportunity for drumming and marching and engaging with the rhythm of its language. This engagement with the rhythm of words contributes to children's fluency in their own reading and, later, to the flow and cohesion of their writing. More books of poetry that include engaging rhythm are named in Appendix A.3.

Rhyme

Rhyme occurs when the accented syllable of the final words in successive lines of verse end in the same or similar sound. For example, *row* and *grow* in the poem about Miss Mary, below, both end in "o." While not all poetry rhymes (one exception is free verse), most traditional poems for very young children do rhyme. Notice the familiarity of the following Mother Goose rhyme:

> Mary, Mary, quite contrary
> How does your garden grow?
> With silver bells and cockle shells,
> And pretty maids all in a row.

Other more modern poems also incorporate sing-song rhyme. For example Shel Silverstein's (1964) *A Giraffe and a Half* is popular with young children. Another example is David Pelham's previously mentioned *Sam's Sandwich* (1990), which uses rhyme to make children laugh:

> Samantha gave Sam's hand a squeeze:
> "Just come and try this cheese"
> But in the pocket of his pants
> Sam had saved some big black ants (p. 5)

Jack Prelutsky (2002) continues in the same mode in *The Frogs Wore Red Suspenders:*

> The frogs wore red suspenders
> and the pigs wore purple vests,
> as they sang to all the chickens
> and the ducks upon their nests. (p. 8)

There are many collections of rhyming poetry available for children. Appendix A.4 includes some recommended poems and collections of poetry.

Alliteration

Alliteration helps children understand and internalize the sounds of particular letters. They can then use that knowledge to decode words they read. Alliteration is the use of identical initial vowel or consonant sounds in sequential words or syllables: "Seven snails and seven snakes swam," (Prelutsky, 2002, p. 59). Alliterative lines like this teach children about the sound of "s," something they can transfer to their own reading and writing. It is not unusual for young children to delight in creating tongue twisters like "Tall Tom talked to two tiny tigers ten times today."

Assonance

Assonance is the repetition of vowel sounds in stressed syllables. Good examples of assonance can be found in Mother Goose rhymes; "Handy Pandy, Jack-a-dandy" from "Handy Pandy" or "Doodle, doodle doo" from "The Lost Shoe" are recognizable examples. William Jay Smith (1987) writes this line: "I have a white cat whose name is Moon / He eats catfish from a wooden spoon" (p. 29), which provides a more modern example. Again, these verses help children recognize vowel sounds, which they apply when decoding words that enlarge their vocabulary.

Images

The language of poetry creates sensory and visual images that stimulate children's imaginations (Huck, Kiefer, Hepler, & Hickman, 2003). At times, poetry paints vivid verbal pictures. The best imagery takes into account the knowledge and experiences of children and then offers images they can relate to. Children easily relate to the culinary, gustatory visions of Jack Prelutsky's (1991) "Spaghetti! Spaghetti! Piled high in a mound. You wiggle, you wriggle, you squiggle around" (p. 4). Similes and metaphors may also evoke images. Similes use "like" or "as" to make explicit comparisons; metaphors describe one thing in terms of something else. Examples abound. While many think of Carl Sandburg (1982) as a poet for adults, his verses also delight children with their imagery: "Arithmetic is where numbers fly like pigeons in and out of your head" (p. 40) is a simile, while "The moon is a bucket of suds, yellow and smooth suds" (p. 74) is a metaphor. His description of fog coming in on cat feet may be his most famous analogy.

Colors abound in the imagery of poetry. After sharing *Hailstones and Halibut Bones* (O'Neill, 1990) with a second or third grade class, a teacher, using a flip chart, can put the color names at the top of different pages. She can then ask the children to name things of that particular color. For *blue*, she might get "ocean" or "sky"; for *red*, "heart" or "apple." After she has written down the responses, she can solicit a short phrase about each item or a phrase about how each color makes them feel. The teacher acts as scribe, writing down the children's ideas, one phrase per line. She could then give each child three pieces of paper and invite them to pick three of their favorite ideas and copy the phrases from the flip chart pages or write phrases of their own. Using watercolor, they could even illustrate each page.

Choosing Poems for Children

To introduce children to poetry, try to select poems they are likely to enjoy. Young children favor rhymed, metered, narrative verse, both traditional and contemporary (Fisher & Natarella, 1982). They can appreciate carefully chosen words and couplets or short verses that are easily remembered (Machado, 2007). This is why Mother Goose nursery rhymes are so popular with very young children. Content is also an important consideration; humorous verse involving children and animals is likely to please (Fisher & Natarella, 1982). Some examples are the popular "Mary Had a Little Lamb," "The Three Little Kittens," and "Little Boy Blue." Above all, poetry for children should be vivid in its images (Glazer, 2000).

Once children are familiar with poetry, teachers and caregivers can help youngsters appreciate other types of verse. They can learn to like poems that don't rhyme, that aren't about children or animals, and that are more lyrical than narrative.

Whenever making decisions about children's poetry, keep the following questions in mind:

- Is the poem appropriate for the age level of the children?
- Does the use of language (rhyme, rhythm, alliteration, assonance) suit the meaning of the poem?

- Are the poem's figures of speech ones the children can understand and enjoy?
- Are the sensory images vivid?
- Does the poet get his or her point across in a way likely to engage young children through rhythm, rhyme, or content? (adapted from Huck, Kiefer, Hepler, & Hickman, 2003, p. 68)

Appendix B.1 includes a checklist that can be used while previewing books online, in a store, or at a library. Once you have chosen poems to share, find ways to help young children engage with them. There are numerous online resources that can help you explore poetry. Figure 4.2 lists a few good ones.

Children's poetry websites.   FIGURE 4.2

www.storyit.com/Classics/JustPoems/index.htm

  The "Story It" website offers stories to listen to online and print out for families and teachers.

www2.scholastic.com/browse/article.jsp?id=1558

  Scholastic's website has ideas for young children to create their own poetry, with detailed explanations for each idea.

www.magneticpoetry.com/kidspoetry/index.htm

  This site is a place for children (grades K–8) to publish their own poetry and read poems written by other children.

http://poetry4kids.com/

  This website has a collection of funny poems, poems by Kenn Nesbitt, lesson plans, activities, games, podcasts, and links to other sites.

www.gigglepoetry.com/

  This site has a collection of poems from authors such as Bruce Lansky, Kenn Nesbitt, Ted Scheu, Bill Dodds, Robert Pottle, Charles Ghigna, Eric Ode, and others. It has word games, poetry theater, a feature called "ask the poet," and more.

www.readingrockets.org/calendar/poetry#learning

  This site includes links for teachers on how to teach language skills with poetry, and ideas for National Poetry Month.

www.poetryarchive.org/childrensarchive/home.do

  The children's poetry archive website is a search engine for poems, either by theme or poet. Includes three links to "ask the poet": Valerie Bloom, Spike Milligan, and Roald Dahl.

www.seussville.com/

  This interactive site has games based on themes in Dr. Seuss's books, a biography of Theodore Seuss Geisel (aka "Dr. Seuss"), a list of Dr. Seuss books, and a list of events celebrating reading, with information on where and when the events take place.

www.ncte.org/awards/poetry

  The portion of the National Council of Teachers of English website lists winners of their Award for Excellence in Poetry for Children, established in 1977.

Poetry Genres

Poetry choices for young children include Mother Goose rhymes, humorous poems, narrative poems, lyrical poems, limericks, free verse, shape poems, and poems from specific cultures.

Mother Goose Nursery Rhymes

Mother Goose nursery verses rhyme and have much repetition and alliteration. The patterns help children play with language and develop the phonemic awareness they need to become emergent readers and writers. A sample of these familiar rhymes is the following:

> Hot-cross buns!
> Hot-cross buns!
> One a penny, two a penny,
> Hot-cross buns!
> Hot-cross buns!
> Hot-cross buns!
> If ye have no daughters,
> Give them to your sons.

The patterned language of the poem, with five repetitions of "Hot-cross buns," helps young readers gain fluency because they know what to expect in the coming lines. The rhyming of "sons" in the last line with "buns" allows children to recognize that different combinations of letters can represent the same sound. Both teachers and children enjoy clapping out the rhythm as they repeat the lines.

Alliteration is everywhere in nursery rhymes: "Sing a song of sixpence," "Ring a ring o' roses," "Daffy-down dilly." Also, many rhymes (such as "Little Bo Peep," "Miss Muffet," and "The Three Little Kittens") tell a very concise story, thus helping young children develop their own sense of narrative. Notice how an entire tale is contained in just four lines:

> Little Boy Blue, come blow your horn!
> The sheep's in the meadow, the cow's in the corn.
> Where's the little boy that looks after the sheep?
> Under the haystack, fast asleep!

If you think Mother Goose rhymes are inappropriate for children because they seem outdated, you may be surprised to discover, in some of the books in Appendix A.5, modernized versions of the traditional nursery rhymes. Mother Goose rhymes are also available in electronic forms; some online resources related to nursery rhymes are provided in Figure 4.3.

The enduring popularity of Mother Goose rhymes is due partly to their slapstick humor (Kiefer, Hepler, & Hickman, 2007). Children can't resist the sonorous silliness of "Hey diddle, diddle, the cat and the fiddle" and the "cow

| Mother Goose websites. | FIGURE 4.3 |

www.mothergoose.com

> This site offers crafts, online games, clip art, tips for finding free stories and videos online, a link to all 362 Mother Goose nursery rhymes, and a list of other recommended Mother Goose websites.

www.enchantedlearning.com/Rhymes.html

> This website has coloring and print activities, and Mother Goose nursery rhymes to print out and use. There are also rebus rhymes, online painting games, and rhyming games.

www.mothergoosetime.com

> This website is for teachers or parents wishing to purchase learning modules or classroom activity kits that are informed by educational research. The merchandise covers all areas of learning, including writers' workshops, art, cooking, and other areas.

www.apples4theteacher.com/mother-goose-nursery-rhymes

> On this site Mother Goose nursery rhymes are broken down by theme: color words, telling time, days of the week, months of the year, holidays, and others. It also offers an alphabetical listing of all Mother Goose rhymes, along with riddles and character sketches.

www.fidella.com/trmg/contents.html

> This website is a complete transcription of *The Real Mother Goose* (1916), with wonderful pen and watercolor illustrations by Blanche Fisher Wright.

www.carlscorner.us.com/MotherGoose.htm

> This website has nursery rhymes with many teaching resources: a lesson planning matrix, sequenced activities, word searches, and worksheets. There is also a Mother Goose anthology to print out, Mother Goose "money" to print out, and Mother Goose recipes.

www.tlsbooks.com/nurseryrhymes.htm

> This website provides free coloring pages for many of the Mother Goose nursery rhymes and also includes a cut-and-paste activity that can be printed out.

jumping over the moon." Nursery rhymes let children enjoy the sound, sense, and nonsense of poetic language.

Humorous Poetry

Humorous poetry tends to be a favorite of young children (Fisher & Natarella, 1979). Some of the more humorous narrative poetry comes from writers like Shel Silverstein, Jack Prelutsky, Lewis Carroll, Edward Lear, David Pelham, Douglas Florian, and Dr. Seuss. Some recommended collections of humorous poems are provided in Appendix A.6. Classics like Lear's "The Owl and the Pussycat," which pairs an owl and a pussycat as unlikely sweethearts on a moonlight cruise, persist in their popularity because they posit unlikely, incongruous ideas and silly situations (Fisher & Natarella, 1979).

Another poet who produces both narrative and lyrical humorous poetry is Douglas Florian. He wrote the hilarious *Beast Feast* (1994), in which he de-

Born in Chicago on September 25, 1932, Shel Silverstein has entertained many children and adults around the world with his zany poems and black and white illustrations. His works have been translated into 20 different languages. Silverstein is not only a poet; he is also a cartoonist, songwriter, and playwright. During the 1950s, Silverstein was a cartoonist for the U.S. Army's *Stars and Stripes* while he was stationed in Japan and later Korea as a serviceman. In 1963, he wrote his first children's book *Lafcadio: The Lion Who Shot Back* (1963), followed the next year by *The Giving Tree* (1964). He also wrote and illustrated *Where the Sidewalk Ends* (1974), *A Light in the Attic* (1981), and *Falling Up* (1996). Shel Silverstein died in his home on May 9, 1999, but his books and poetry collections continue to be top sellers.

scribes a wide variety of fanciful animals in rhyming couplets. For example, the tubby toad is so plump that it doesn't even jump. Other silly animal portraits can be found in Florian's *Mammalabilia* (2000), *Bow Wow, Meow Meow* (2003), *Insectlopedia: Insect Poems and Paintings* (1998), and *Lizards, Frogs, and Polliwogs* (2001). More mature young readers might like *Zoo's Who* (2005), which catalogs a plethora of possible zoo animals.

Although most children enjoy humorous poems, Fisher and Natarella (1979) found that young children (in primary grades and younger) are not fond of limericks, such as those by Edward Lear. Fisher and Natarella (1979) surmised that sophisticated word play in limericks may be lost on young listeners (p. 382).

Classic Verse

Classic verse written in traditional metrical forms comes in both narrative and lyrical varieties. One of the most famous children's narrative poems is *'Twas The Night Before Christmas* by Clement Moore (1912), originally illustrated by Jesse Willcox Smith. Other classic narratives can be found in *The Complete Tales and Poems of Winnie-the-Pooh* (Milne, 2001), which collects all of the Pooh stories with the original Ernest H. Shepherd drawings in one volume. In *Winnie-the-Pooh* (Milne, reprint 1977) the lyrical poetry is often narrated by Pooh singing to himself:

> Floating in the Blue!
> It makes him very proud
> To be a little cloud. (p. 17)

Lyrical poems abound in Robert Louis Stevenson's *A Child's Garden of Verses* (2007). Although generally not suited for very young children, William Blake's lyrical poetry, such as the "Songs of Innocence" and the "Songs of Experience," has inspired another book of poetry: *A Visit to William Blake's Inn: Poems for Innocent and Experienced Travelers* (Willard, 1981). The pictures by Alice and Martin Provensen will delight more mature young children, and the rhymes, such as the following, will appeal to many:

> He wore a mackintosh and boots
> The tender green of onion shoots (p. 17)

Karla Kushkin and Myra Cohn Livingston both write traditional verse. Many of Kushkin's poems follow a narrative form. In *City Dog* (1998) she relates the tale of a city-living pooch's first encounter with country freedom; *The Animals and the Ark* (2002) focuses on animals and their survival through the storm. *Under My Hood I Have a Hat* (2004) describes the tribulations of a youngster who must struggle with layers and layers of winter clothing, so many in fact that she is afraid of falling and not being able to get up. Animals are common in Kushkin's verses, which is apparent from the titles of her works: *Dogs & Dragons, Trees & Dreams: A Collection of Poems* (1999), *Toots the Cat* (2005), and the interview-formatted *So What's It Like to Be a Cat* (2005).

Myra Cohn Livingston writes in a lyrical style. *B is for Baby: An Alphabet of Verses* (1996) provides verse for the youngest readers and captures the many actions, subtle and otherwise, of babies. Much of Livingston's work deals with moods and feelings. *There Was a Place and Other Poems* (1988) describes loss of all kinds and runs the emotional gamut from despair to joy. In *Light and Shadow* (1992) each poem begins with the word *light* and describes what light is able to do in various situations. In *Sky Songs* (1984) Livingston explores every aspect of the sky.

Poet Jane Yolen also writes narrative and lyrical verse. In the narrative volume, *Harvest Home* (2002), she writes harvest songs to relate the story of a Midwest family bringing in the wheat and celebrating the fruits of their labors. At the end of the book are notes explaining harvest in other parts of the world. Volumes by her suited for children in the primary grades are *Bird Watch: A Book of Poetry* (1999), which provides joyful verbal and visual images of various birds, and *Sky Scrape/City Scape: Poems of City Life* (1996), in which Yolen has compiled verses celebrating urban life from a multitude of well-known poets. For even younger readers there is *The Three Bears Holiday Rhyme Book* (1995), narrated primarily by the baby bear cub who ends the book with an account of his own birthday.

Free Verse

While young children seem to prefer rhymed verse (Fisher & Natarella, 1979), free verse deserves mention. Sometimes children need to be exposed to different forms of poetry to help them develop a taste for them (Vardell, 2006). Free verse breaks with poetic tradition and does not rhyme. However, it does have pattern and rhythm. Teachers can make young children aware of these patterns and rhythms, which are not as obvious as rhyme.

One good example is Carl Sandburg's "Fog," discussed earlier in this chapter. Much of Sandburg's poetry is written in free verse, yet its cadence draws readers in, as in "The stars tell nothing—and everything" (*Rainbows Are Made,* 1982, p. 74). Many of the poets who write narrative and lyrical verse also write free verse. One modern poet who has penned noteworthy free verse is Kristine O'Connell George. From her first book *The Great Frog Race* (1997) through the later *Hummingbird Nest: A Journal of Poems* (2004), George has consistently written in free verse. In *Old Elm Speaks: Tree Poems* (1998) she honors trees and sometimes narrates poems from the perspective of trees, as in "Oaks Introduction." In *Little Dog Poems* (1999) and *Little Dog and Duncan* (2001) George celebrates dogs, her own dog included, through small, tightly woven poems. *Toasting Marshmallows* (2001) contains poems about the magic of camping and feeling small and alone in a large universe. George proves that free verse can be appropriate for young readers. Most of her work is intended for 6- to 10-year-olds, although the Little Dog books are more appropriate for 4- to 8-year-olds.

Concrete/Shape Poems

Concrete or shape poems are ones where the poet uses the physical shape of the poem to convey meaning. Children not only enjoy these poems but also like to create them themselves (Vardell, 2006). A contemporary poet whose work includes concrete verses is J. Patrick Lewis, whose *Doodle Dandies: Poems That Take Shape* (2002) contains a variety of poems that wrap themselves into pictures. Another concrete poet is Paul Janeczko, who teamed with illustrator Chris Raschka to produce *A Poke in the I: A Collection of Concrete Poems* (2005). One poet whose body of work consists exclusively of concrete poetry is Joan Bransfield Graham. In *Splish Splash* (1994) the 21 water poems take the form of rippled lines that represent waves of the ocean, in one case, and white letters rising as steam from a black saucepan, in another. *Flicker Flash* (1999) gives similar treatment to the many forms of light in 23 concrete poems.

Ingenious texts like these often inspire imitation in children. However, sometimes the meaning of the poem gets lost in children's artwork. One way of focusing on meaning while still including shape is to introduce children to diamante poetry. A diamante is a seven-line poem that is written in the shape of a diamond (Tiedt, 1970). The diamond shape is simpler to create than the shape of a fish, say, so children are more likely to select words for their meaning rather than to fit the shape. The form of diamante is exemplified in Figure 4.4.

Once children have some experience with shaped poems, they can create their own shapes, such as a poem about a ball written in the shape of a ball.

FIGURE 4.4 The diamante format followed by an example.

DIAMANTE FORMAT	DIAMANTE EXAMPLE
Noun	Caterpillar
Adjective, Adjective	Soft, fuzzy
Participle, Participle, Participle	Slinking, creeping, crawling
Noun, Noun, Noun, Noun	Leaf, cocoon, branch, air
Participle, Participle, Participle	Flying, fluttering, flitting
Adjective, Adjective	Light, bright
Noun	Butterfly

Multicultural Poetry

oetry is also a way of reflecting the diversity of our society. There are many books featuring African American, Hispanic, Asian American, and Native American cultures that are written for young children. Moreover, there are books about cultures from around the world. For example, in *Festivals* (1996) Myra Cohn Livingston describes festivals for each month of the year from different cultures; the book starts with Chinese New Year and ends with the African American holiday Kwanzaa. In between these two holidays are others: Jewish Purim, Muslim Ramadan, and the Mexican holiday Day of the Dead. Some of the verses are rhymed; others are not. Another anthology that features many cultures is *Why Is the Sky?* (1997), edited by John Agard. The children's poems in this volume are about a variety of topics, including basic questions about nature, life, and death—things that are common to all people.

African American Cultures

There are many poets who write from an African American perspective. They range from Langston Hughes, whose works include *The Dream Keeper and Other Poems* (1996), to Arnold Adoff who compiled *My Black Me: A Beginning Book of Black Poetry* (1995). While the reading level of both texts is more appropriate for intermediate readers, younger children can benefit from hearing them read aloud. Three outstanding African American writers who have written poetry suitable for very young listeners and readers are Eloise Greenfield, Nikki Giovanni, and Walter Dean Myers.

One of the early works of Eloise Greenfield is *Honey I Love and Other Poems* (1986), which tells of the everyday experiences of an African American child. Greenfield's *Honey I Love* (2002) is the picture book version of the title poem in her 1986 collection. The poem recounts all the things that the main character, a girl, really loves—especially her cousin's Southern way of talking. Her *Night on Neighborhood Street* (1991) brings to life a place and all the people who live there. For very young children Greenfield has written *I Can Draw a Weeposaur and Other Dinosaurs* (2001), which captures the imagination of the young narrator–artist as she imagines fanciful dinosaurs, such as the "Messysaurus." Her *When the Horses Ride By: Children in the Times of War* (2006) takes on the complex issue of war and its impact on children. *Booklist* and *School Library Journal* specifically recommend this book for first and second graders as important and relevant in these times. With this work Greenfield moves beyond an African American perspective to a world perspective, as she showcases the experiences, both terrifying and triumphant, of children trapped in turmoil.

Nikki Giovanni has built a reputation as a major poet for adult readers. However, she has also created works for the very young. *The Genie in the Jar* (1998) is written for children ages 4 and older; it is a lyrical lullaby about the world of a young child and her mother. The world provides sanctuary, yet there are hints of the world beyond. She has also teamed up with illustrator Ashley Bryan to produce the exuberant *The Sun Is So Quiet* (1996), a read-aloud book that is celebratory in its verses and visions of children and nature. And, in the earlier *Spin a Soft Black Song* (1987), Giovanni manages to portray the unique perspective of a child expressing childlike views on life.

Eloise Greenfield was born in 1929 in Parmele, North Carolina, and grew up in a public housing development in Washington, D. C. Her home was only two minutes from the public library, where she spent much of her time as a child. She attended Miner Teachers College in Washington, D. C., a college for training African American teachers. Her first job as a typist for the U. S. Patent Office bored her, so she began to write. She desired to write books that expressed the truth about African American people; throughout her works, she tries to fight racism with words, and she depicts African American families that are strong and loving.

Her first book, *Bubbles* (1972), was followed by many other poetry books, picture books, and biographies. She has won many awards. Two of her award-winning books are *Rosa Parks* (1972) and *She Comes Bringing Me That Little Baby Girl* (1974). Her poetry collections include *In the Land of Word* (2003) and *The Friendly Forever* (2006), *Honey, I Love* (1978), *Water, Water* (1999), *Grandma's Joy* (1999), and many others. Greenfield has won the NCTE Award for Excellence in Poetry for Children. She has published over 38 children's books in all, in many genres: poetry, novels, picture books, and biographies.

Walter Dean Myers, a writer for older readers, has written *Here in Harlem: Poems in Many Voices* (2004). He has also written poetry celebrating childhood. *Brown Angels: An Album of Pictures and Verse* (1996) combines Victorian and early twentieth-century photos of African American children with verses that pay tribute to them. "Love That Boy," one of the poems in the collection, was the inspiration for the novel *Love That Dog* (2001) by Newbery Award winner Sharon Creech. In *Love That Dog*, Jack from Miss Stretchberry's room is a reluctant fifth grade poet, who is inspired by the words of Mr. Walter Dean Myers to compose a poem about his love for the dog he once had. A sequel to *Brown Angels* is *Glorious Angels: A Celebration of Children* (1997). Again using photos from the early 1900s, Myers features the experiences of children from a variety of families. His verses convey the universality of childhood, while the later *Angel to Angel: A Mother's Gift of Love* (2000) uses the same combination of pictures and verses to represent the bond between mother and child.

Hispanic and Latino Cultures

Hispanic and Latino cultures are represented in a wide variety of poetry books for young readers. Pat Mora brings Mexican American culture of the Southwest alive. In *Confetti* (1996) Mora portrays Southwestern culture and the desert environment from the viewpoint of a little girl, who intersperses Spanish words in English verses. Another book that explores the expanses of the Southwest in hybrid English and Spanish verse is *This Big Sky* (1998), in which Mora conveys the magical aura of place. Mora has also teamed up with woodcut artist David Frampton to produce a poetic tribute to St. Francis and the animals he loved. Mora's *The Song of Francis and the Animals* (2005) invites reading aloud, even singing its lyrical verse. Mora's most recent work for young children is *¡Marimba! Animales A to Z* (2006), in which animals have a Mexican fiesta at the zoo. One interesting feature of the book is that it uses cognates, words of common origin in different languages, to introduce Spanish and English together to young readers.

Francisco Alarcon has a quartet of books that celebrate the seasons in bilingual verse. In *Laughing Tomatoes: And Other Spring Poems* (2005) he has tortillas that applaud and tomatoes that laugh. *From the Bellybutton of the Moon: And Other Summer Poems* (2005) takes readers on a child's trip to visit his grandmother in Mexico, where he samples summer treats. The celebration of fall is the subject of *Angels Ride Bikes: And Other Fall Poems* (1999), which is also a tribute to the city of Los Angeles and urban life from a Mexican American perspective. The last book in the quartet is *Iguanas in the Snow* (2001), which is a celebration of another California city—San Francisco. Alarcon provides short, rhythmic vignettes of people and places, which are suited to reading aloud and which provide models for children's own attempts at writing poetry. Another bilingual book of poetry, not part of Alarcon's seasonal quartet, is *Poems to Dream Together: Poemas Para Sonar Juntos* (2005). The childhood dreams that Alarcon writes about are both mundane and universal. Told as daydreams and sleeping dreams, these children's verses offer a comprehensive vision of hope for the future.

Asian American Cultures

Asian American culture is featured in the work of Minfong Ho, whose works represent a Thai perspective. Ho's first, *Hush! A Thai Lullaby* (2000), is suitable for babies and preschoolers. In it, a mother keeps hushing all the animals (monkeys, a water buffalo, an elephant) around them to keep them from waking her sleeping child. Its call-and-response style, which appeals to young children, ends with the mother falling asleep and the child waking up. Ho's *Peek: A Thai Hide-and-Seek* (2004) involves a father and daughter playing *jut-ay* or peek-a-boo in the house, on the porch, and in the yard, which is a jungle. The rhymed verses and animal sounds invite child participation. In an earlier work, *Maples in the Mist: Poems for Children from the Tang Dynasty* (1996), Ho compiles and translates simple, unrhymed poems from China. Some themes of the poems, such as homesickness and death, may be difficult for the very young, but they will appreciate the watercolor pictures by Jean and Mou-Sien Tseng.

Janet Wong, of both Korean and Chinese ancestry, has written poetry featuring children of many ethnicities. Her works for young readers include *Night Garden: Poems from the World of Dreams* (2000) and *Knock on Wood: Poems About Superstitions* (2003). *Night Garden* explores dreams, good and bad ones, from a thoughtful perspective. These poems suggest that dreams are the imagination's way of helping us express our stories. Black cats, ghosts, and broken mirrors populate *Knock on Wood,* as do images of children from different time periods and ethnic groups. This book is a good selection around the time of Halloween. Even younger readers will appreciate Wong's *Grump* (2001) about an energetic baby and an exhausted mommy and *Hide & Seek* (2005), a counting book about a father and son playing hide-and-seek.

Native American Cultures

Poets who have collected Native American verse for children include Hettie Jones and Virginia Driving Hawk Sneve. In *The Tree Stands Shining: Poetry of the North American Indians* (1993) Jones compiles songs to the sun and songs about animals; these poems run the emotional gamut from joy to agony. The collection ends on a note of resilience. This collection is appropriate for children from age 4 through 8. Virginia Driving Hawk Sneve both writes and collects Native American poetry. In *Dancing Teepees: Poems of American Indian Youth* (1989) Sneve compiles poems from several groups: Sioux, Navajo, Apache, Hopi, Paiute, and Zuni. Many poems are about birth ceremonies and lullabies celebrating a new life; others are about preparing the young to embrace life, such as a poem about a young man facing his first hunt. Her poetry is appropriate for children in primary grades. Her later edited volume *Enduring Wisdom* (2003) is not a work of poetry per se; it is a collection of sayings from individuals of many tribes. What is interesting is that old sayings and new sayings, often appearing side by side, frequently express the same sentiment. Second and third graders will enjoy reading these sayings.

teaching suggestions
SHARING POETRY

We recommend three strategies for sharing poetry with children: reading it aloud, involving them in the reading, and then encouraging their responses to the reading.

Reading Poetry Aloud

Sylvia Vardell (2006) offers a number of tips for sharing poetry out loud:

1. Choose a poem that you yourself enjoy.
2. Practice reading it aloud before you share it.
3. Read the poem in a manner that accounts for line breaks and spaces.
4. Incorporate facial expressions and gestures into your recitation.
5. Feel free to repeat the poem as often as the children want to hear it.

Involving Children with Poetry

Decide how you would like to have the children involved:

- *Modeling*—you read the poem aloud
- *Unison*—everyone reads the poem
- *Refrain*—children repeat a certain section
- *Movement*—children add actions
- *Call-and-Response*—two groups alternate lines
- *Groups*—multiple groups read different lines
- *Solos*—individual children read separate lines
- *Two Voices*—two people read two different parts
- *Canon*—two groups start the same poem at differing times
- *Singing*—children sing the poem to songs they know (Vardell, 2006, p. 120)

Responding to Poetry

Finally, decide what to do next. Fortunately, there are many appropriate ways of responding to poems. Recommendations from Vardell (2006) include the following:

- Ask questions that probe feelings and opinions rather than facts.
- Encourage poetry circle discussions.
- Try partner dialogues or small-group discussions.
- Dramatize, role-play, or pantomime the poem.
- Set poems to music.
- Link poetry to the creation of different art forms.
- Use magnetic poetry kits to create 3-D poetry.
- Encourage children to write their own poetry by making them aware of different formats, such as a diamante poem (see Figure 3.4).
- Consider using poetry journals for both responses to and composition of original poetry.

Conclusion

While poetry remains the most powerful form of literature written for children, it has, in the past, been somewhat neglected in classrooms. The rhyme and rhythm of poetry help young children in their striving to become readers and writers. Teachers can use poetry to help children develop phonemic awareness (the ability to recognize the individual sounds that make up words), thereby increasing their syntactic knowledge and the size of their vocabulary. Most of all, teachers can help children learn to enjoy poetry (Vardell, 2006). Teachers can give children a chance to choose poems that they like and to respond to them in their own way.

journeying WITH CHILDREN'S LITERATURE

1. Explore ways of using poetry in conjunction with other subject areas. For example, Mother Goose rhymes can be used to teach children about math. They can determine how many bags of wool there are in "Baa, Baa, Black Sheep" or how many eggs are laid in "Hickety, Pickety My Fine Hen." See "Mathematics and Mother Goose" (Young & Maulding, 1994).
2. Find out about spoken word poetry as a way of engaging children with verse. Check out *Outspoken! How to Improve Writing and Speaking Skills Through Poetry Performance* by Sara Holbrook and Michael Salinger (2006). Another performance artist to look up is Brod Bagert, who has also authored multiple poetry books for children.
3. Identify any poets or illustrators in this chapter about whom you would like to know more. Add to your knowledge by checking out *Poetry Aloud Here!* by Sylvia Vardell (2006). Appendix A in Vardell's book has lists of poets for young people along with the poets' website addresses whenever available.
4. Explore the work of Lee Bennett Hopkins. A poet and an educator, he has written several resource books for teachers, including *Pass the Poetry Please* (1998) and *Days to Celebrate: A Full Year of Poetry, People, Holidays, History, Fascinating Facts, and More* (2004). Hopkins provides lots of tips for incorporating poetry in the curriculum.

5. Several books from the International Reading Association offer suggestions for incorporating storybooks and poetry into the classroom. Particularly good are *Scaffolding with Storybooks* by Justice and Pence (2005) and *Literature Links: Thematic Units Linking Read-Alouds and Computer Activities* by Labbo, Love, Prior, Hubbard, and Ryan (2006). Both texts describe activities specifically for poetry.

6. There are several prizes awarded to writers of children's poetry. The National Council of Teachers of English gives a poetry award every three years. The 2006 winner was Nikki Giovanni. The Lee Bennett Hopkins Award is given every three years to a promising new poet in recognition for a book-length poem. Finally, the Claudia Lewis Award is given every year for the best book of children's poetry. Check out *Poetry Aloud Here!* (2006) by Sylvia Vardell for more information about poets, poems, and poetry awards.

activities TO SHARE WITH CHILDREN

1. Read any of the color poems from *Hailstones and Halibut Bones* (1990) by Mary O'Neill. Then create a color display area in your preschool or kindergarten classroom where the children can display artwork in their favorite color (a bright yellow sun perhaps), their own poems, or rhymes about a favorite color.

2. Read several of the poems from *Beast Feast* (1994) by Douglas Florian. While you are reading the poems, be sure to emphasize the rhyming words, such as *feet* and *street,* and explain any new or unusual words (for example, *blubber* is the layer of fat that a whale has). After multiple readings, encourage youngsters to role-play the actions of their favorite animal, such as the tubby toad so fat and round that he can't even jump.

3. Gather poetry about food. Some examples would be "Spaghetti" by Shel Silverstein, *Spaghetti! Spaghetti!,* by Jack Prelutsky, *Sam's Sandwich, Sam's Snack,* and *Sam's Pizza* by David Pelham, and any number of Mother Goose rhymes. Then have a class feast featuring the foods in the poems.

4. Young children like exotic creatures such as dragons. Read them excerpts from Jack Prelutsky's *The Dragons Are Singing Tonight* (1993), paying special attention to the action poems "I Am Boom" and "The Dragons Are Singing Tonight." Help them create a dragon mural that will serve as a setting for them as they role-play the actions of "Boom," in which a dragon roars, dances, and booms like thunder. As a group, the children can then create their own "cacophonous chorus" of singing dragons on the one enchanted night of the year when they come out.

5. Music and poetry are a natural combination. The consistent rhythm of Mother Goose rhymes encourages children to clap their hands or tap their feet as they listen to the verses. Other poems, such as John Langstaff's "Oh, A Hunting We Will Go" and "Frog Went A-Courtin'" have already been set to music that children can sing along with. Encourage older children to make up their own verses to the songs.

our favorite CHILDREN'S BOOKS

Agard, J., & Nichols, G. (Eds.). (2002). *Under the Moon and Over the Sea.* New York: Oxfam.

> This collection for ages 4 to 8 is about Caribbean folklore, and it brings the cultures of the islands to life.

Bolden, T. (2003). *Rock of Ages.* New York: Dragonfly Books.

> This book, for ages 4 to 8, will make children want to get up and dance. This homage to African American churches fills readers with the spirit.

Bryan, A. (Illus.). (2001). *Ashley Bryan's ABC of African American Poetry.* New York: Aladdin.

> This book for ages 4 to 8 features a range of serious to silly verses on the alphabet.

Florian, D. (2001). *Lizards, Frogs and Polliwogs.* New York: Harcourt Children's Books.

> This book for ages 4 to 8 features humorous wordplay to describe mischievous creatures of all kinds.

Greenberg, D. (2002). *Bugs!* New York: Megan Tingley Books.

> For ages 4 to 8, these silly nonsense rhymes are disgusting to the point of being funny.

Greenfield, E. (1993). *Nathaniel Talking.* New York: Writers & Readers Publishing.

> This book describes life from a 9-year-old's perspective.

Gunning, M. (1999). *Not a Copper Penny in Me House: Poems from the Caribbean.* New York: Boyds Mills Press.

> For ages 9 to 12, this collection of poems captures the rhythmic speech of the islands.

Hennessy, B. G. (1992). *Sleep Tight.* New York: Viking.

> For infants to preschoolers, these soft and quiet verses have a lulling effect, creating an atmosphere of safety for children as they go to sleep.

James, S. (2005). *Days Like This: A Collection of Small Poems.* Cambridge, MA: Candlewick.

> For ages 4 to 8, these tender poems entertain readers with their accounts of both ordinary and special days in life.

Keats, E. J. (1999). *Over in the Meadow.* New York: Puffin.

> Children will learn to count from 1 to 10 in this wonderfully illustrated book. Infants and preschoolers will listen attentively as they hear of creatures, ranging from robins to frogs, that live in the meadow.

Moore, L. (2002). *I'm Small and Other Verses.* New York: Walker Books.

> For ages 2 to 6, these tender verses depict typical childhood concerns and pleasures.

Philip, N. (2002). *The Fish is Me!: Bathtime Rhymes.* New York: Clarion.

> In these 18 short poems, for ages 4 to 8, children will discover that bathtime can be fun.

Prelutsky, J. (2000). *It's Raining Pigs and Noodles*. Illus. J. Stevenson. New York: Greenwillow Books.

This book for ages 4 to 8 has crazy line drawings and clever wordplay.

Sierra, J. (1998). *Antarctic Antics: A Book of Penguin Poems*. Illus. J. Aruego and A. Dewey. New York: Gulliver Books.

For ages 4 to 8, this book has cartoonish drawings depicting the lives and habitats of emperor penguins in Antarctica.

Sklansky, A. (2002). *From the Doghouse: Poems to Chew On*. New York: Henry Holt.

These delightful poems for ages 4 to 8 are playful and colorful as well as irreverent.

Steptoe, J. (2001). *In Daddy's Arms I Am Tall: African Americans celebrating fathers*. New York: Lee & Low Books.

This book for infants and preschoolers features striking pictures of boys and their dads in a tribute to fatherhood.

Strickland, D. (1996). *Families: Poems Celebrating the African American Experience*. New York: Boyds Mills Press.

This upbeat book for ages 4 to 8 features attractive illustrations drawn in acrylic.

Swann, B. (1998). *The House with No Door: African riddle-poems*. New York: Browndeer Press.

These clever riddles for ages 4 to 8 may make readers laugh out loud.

Whipple, L. (1991). *Eric Carle's Dragons and Other Creatures that Never Were*. New York: Philomel.

This book featuring wonderful magical creatures, for ages 4 to 8, will intrigue young readers from cover to cover.

Young J. (2006). *R is for Rhyme: A Poetry Alphabet*. Chelsea, MI: Sleeping Bear Press.

These poems for ages 6 to 10 present factual information in a comical manner.

children's literature IN THIS CHAPTER

Adoff, A. (1995). *My black me: A beginning book of black poetry*. New York: Puffin.

Agard, J. (Ed.). (1997). *Why is the sky?* Illus. A. Klimowski. UK: Faber and Faber.

Alarcon, F. (1999). *Angels ride bikes: And other fall poems*. Illus. M. C. Gonzalez. San Francisco: Children's Book Press.

Alarcon, F. (2001). *Iguanas in the snow: And other winter poems*. Illus. M. C. Gonzalez. San Francisco: Children's Book Press.

Alarcon, F. (2005). *From the bellybutton of the moon: And other summer poems*. Illus. M. C. Gonzalez. San Francisco: Children's Book Press.

Alarcon, F. (2005). *Laughing tomatoes: And other spring poems*. Illus. M. C. Gonzalez. San Francisco: Children's Book Press.

Alarcon, F. (2005). *Poems to dream together*. Illus. P. Barragan. New York: Lee & Low Books.

Cauley, L. B. (1992). *Clap your hands*. New York: G. P. Putnam's Sons.

Creech, S. (2001). *Love that dog*. New York: HarperCollins.

Engelbreit, M. (2005). *Mary Engelbreit's Mother Goose*. New York: HarperCollins.

Florian, D. (1994). *Beast feast*. New York: Harcourt Children's Books.

Florian, D. (1998). *Insectlopedia: Insect poems and paintings*. New York: Harcourt Children's Books.

Florian, D. (2000). *Mammalabilia*. New York: Harcourt Children's Books.

Florian, D. (2001). *Lizards, frogs, and polliwogs*. New York: Harcourt Children's Books.

Florian, D. (2003). *Bow wow, meow meow*. New York: Harcourt Children's Books.

Florian, D. (2005). *Zoo's who*. New York: Harcourt Children's Books.

George, K. O. (1997). *The great frog race and other poems*. Illus. K. Kiesler. New York: Clarion.

George, K. O. (1998). *Old Elm speaks: Tree poems*. Illus. K. Kiesler. New York: Clarion.

George, K. O. (1999). *Little dog poems*. Illus. J. Otani. New York: Clarion.

George, K. O. (2001). *Toasting marshmallows: Camping poems*. Illus. K. Kiesler. New York: Clarion.

George, K. O. (2002). *Little dog and Duncan*. Illus. J. Otani. New York: Clarion.

George, K. O. (2004). *Hummingbird nest: A journal of poems*. Illus. B. Moser. New York: Harcourt.

Giovanni, N. (1998). *The genie in the jar*. Illus. C. Raschka. New York: Henry Holt.

Giovanni, N. (1987). *Spin a soft black song*. Illus. G. Martins. New York: Farrar, Straus & Giroux.

Giovanni, N. (1996). *The sun is so quiet: Poems*. Illus. A. Bryan. New York: Henry Holt.

Graham, J. B. (1999). *Flicker flash*. Illus. N. Davis. New York: Houghton Mifflin.

Graham, J. B. (1994). *Splish splash*. Illus. S. Scott. New York: Tichnor Fields.

Greenfield, E. (2002). *Honey I love*. Illus. J. S. Gilchrist. New York: Amistad.

Greenfield, E. (1986). *Honey I love and other poems*. Illus. L. Dillon & D. Dillon. New York: Harper Trophy.

Greenfield, E. (2001). *I can draw a Weeposaur and other dinosaurs*. Illus. J. S. Gilchrist. New York: Greenwillow.

Greenfield, E. (1991). *Night on neighborhood street*. Illus. J. S. Gilchrist. New York: Dial Books for Young Readers.

Greenfield, E. (2006). *When the horses ride by: Children in the times of war*. Illus. J. S. Gilchrist. New York: Lee & Low Books.

Ho, M. (2000). *Hush! A Thai lullaby*. Illus. H. Meade. New York: Scholastic.

Ho, M. (1996). *Maples in the mist: Poems for children from the Tang Dynasty*. Illus. M. S. Tseng. New York: Lothrop, Lee & Shepard Books.

Ho, M. (2004). *Peek!: A Thai hide-and-seek*. Illus. H. Meade. Cambridge, MA: Candlewick.

Hughes, L. (1996). *The dreamkeeper and other poems*. New York: Knopf Books for Young Readers.

Janeczko, P., (Ed.). (2005). *A poke in the I: A collection of concrete poems*. Illus. C. Raschka. Cambridge, MA: Candlewick.

Jones, H. (Ed.). (1993). *The trees stand shining: Poetry of North America*. Illus. R. A. Parker. New York: Dial.

Kuskin, K. (1998). *City dog*. New York: Clarion.

Kuskin, K. (1999). *Dogs & dragons, trees & dreams: A collection of poems*. New York: HarperCollins Children's Books.

Kuskin, K. (2002). *The animals and the ark*. New York: Atheneum.

Kuskin, K. (2004). *Under my hood I have a hat*. New York: Laura Geringer.

Kuskin, K. (2005). *Toots the cat*. New York: Henry Holt.

Kuskin, K. (2005). *So, what's it like to be a cat?* New York: Atheneum.

Lewis, J. P. (2002). *Doodle dandies*. Illus. L. Desimini. New York: Atheneum.

Livingston, M. C. (1996). *Festivals*. Illus. L. E. Fisher. New York: Holiday House.

Livingston, M. C. (1984). *Sky songs*. New York: Holiday House.

Livingston, M. C. (1988). *There was a place and other poems*. New York: Margaret K. McElderry.

Livingston, M. C. (1992). *Light and shadow*. New York: Holiday House.

Livingston, M. C. (1996). *B is for baby: An alphabet of verses*. New York: Margaret K. McElderry.

Milne, A. A. (1977). *Winnie-the-Pooh*. Illus. E. H. Shepard. New York: Dell Publishing.

Milne, A. A. (2001). *The complete tales and poems of Winnie-the-Pooh*. Illus. E. H. Shepard. New York: Dutton Juvenile.

Moore, C. (1912). *'Twas the night before Christmas*. New York: Houghton Mifflin.

Mora, P. (1996). *Confetti: Poems for children*. Illus. E. O. Sanchez. New York: Lee & Low Books.

Mora, P. (2006). *¡Marimba! Animals from A to Z*. Illus. D. Cushman. New York: Clarion.

Mora, P. (2005). *The song of Francis and the animals*. Illus. D. Frampton. New York: Eerdmans Books.

Mora, P. (1998). *This big sky*. Illus. S. Jenkins. New York: Lee & Low Books.

Myers, W. D. (2000). *Angel to angel: A mother's gift of love*. New York: Harper Trophy.

Myers, W. D. (1996). *Brown angels: An album of pictures and verse*. New York: HarperCollins.

Myers, W. D. (1997). *Glorious angels: A celebration of children*. New York: Harper Trophy.

Myers, W. D. (2004). *Here in Harlem: Poems in many voices*. New York: Holiday House.

O'Neill, M. (1990). *Hailstones and halibut bones*. New York: Doubleday.

Pelham, D. (1990). *Sam's sandwich*. New York: Dutton Children's Books.

Pelham, D. (1992). *Sam's surprise*. New York: Dutton Children's Books.

Pelham, D. (1994). *Sam's snack*. New York: Dutton Children's Books.

Pelham, D. (1996). *Sam's pizza*. New York: Dutton Children's Books.

Pelham, D. (1998). *Skeleton in the cupboard*. New York: Dutton Children's Books.

Prelutsky, J. (1986). *Ride a purple pelican*. Illus. G. Williams. New York: Greenwillow Books.

Prelutsky, J. (1991). *Spaghetti! Spaghetti!* Illus. L. McClelland. Bothell, WA: The Wright Group.

Prelutsky, J. (1993). *The dragons are singing tonight*. Illus. P. Sis. New York: Greenwillow Books.

Prelutsky, J. (2002). *The frogs wore red suspenders*. Illus. P. Mathers. New York: Greenwillow Books.

Sandburg, C. (1982). "Two moon fantasies." In L. B. Hopkins (Ed.), *Rainbows are made*. New York: Harcourt Brace & Company.

Sandburg, C. (1982). "Fog." In L. B. Hopkins (Ed.), *Rainbows are made*. New York: Harcourt Brace & Company.

Sandburg, C. (1982). "Stars." In L. B. Hopkins (Ed.), *Rainbows are made*. New York: Harcourt Brace & Company.

Seuss, Dr. (2005). *Green eggs and ham*. New York: Random House Books for Young Readers.

Seuss, Dr. (2005). *The cat in the hat*. New York: Random House Books for Young Readers.

Silverstein, S. (1964). *A giraffe and a half*. New York: HarperCollins.

Silverstein, S. (1964). *The giving tree*. New York: HarperCollins.

Silverstein, S. (1974). *Where the sidewalk ends*. New York: HarperCollins.

Silverstein, S. (1981). *A Light in the Attic*. New York: HarperCollins.

Silverstein, S. (1996). *Falling up*. New York: HarperCollins.

Smith, W. J. (1987). Moon. In M. C. Livingston & T. S. Hyman (Eds.), *Cat poems*. New York: Holiday Books.

Sneve, V. D. H. (Ed.). (1989). *Dancing teepees: Poems of American Indian youth*. Illus. S. Gammell. New York: Holiday House.

Sneve, V. D. H. (Ed.). (2003). *Enduring wisdom: Sayings from Native Americans*. Illus. S. Saint James. New York: Holiday House.

Stevenson, R. L. (2007). *A child's garden of verses*. Illus. B. McClintock. New York: HarperCollins.

Willard, N. (1981). *A trip to William Blake's inn*. Illus. A. Provensen & M. Provensen. New York: Harcourt Brace Jovanovich.

Wong, J. (2001). *Grump*. Illus. J. Wallace. New York: Margaret K. McElderry.

Wong, J. (2005). *Hide & Seek*. Illus. M. Chodos-Irvine. New York: Harcourt Children's Books.

Wong, J. (2003). *Knock on wood: Poems about superstitions*. Illus. J. Paschkis. New York: Margaret K. McElderry.

Wong, J. (2000). *Night garden: Poems from the world of dreams*. Illus. J. Paschkis. New York: Margaret K. McElderry.

Wright, B. F., illus. (1994). *The real Mother Goose*. New York: Scholastic.

Yolen, J. (1995). *The three bears holiday rhyme book*. Illus. J. Dyer. New York: Harcourt Children's Books.

Yolen, J. (1996). *Sky scrape/city scape: Poems of city life*. Illus. K. Condon. Honesdale, PA: Boyds Mills Press.

Yolen, J. (1999). *Bird watch*. Illus. T. Lewin. New York: Putnam Juvenile.

Yolen, J. (2002). *Harvest home*. Illus. G. Shed. New York: Silver Whistle.

Picture Books

Sharing Literature: AN EXAMPLE

Ms. Cho is a creative third grade teacher who loves books and loves to share books with her class in creative ways. Sometimes she dons a paper plate mask that resembles the character from the book and tells the story from behind the mask. Sometimes she prepares her own book jacket for a picture book and reads the flaps aloud so her students have an idea of what the story is about. Because she is creative, her students (with her help and encouragement) give creative book reports in teams.

It is mid-April and time for another set of book reports from Team Henkes. (Each time new teams are formed, each team is allowed to choose an author as their team name.) Each student from the team gives his or her own book report, based on a book of his or her choice. Only one team per week gives reports, usually on Friday afternoon. With only four reports being read each week, no one becomes tired of listening to the reports. Ms. Cho pops popcorn to make it an afternoon of entertainment. She always encourages the students to give "award-winning reports."

Ella is the first to give her report this week. She walks into the room with red galoshes, a cape over her shoulders, a handmade crown on her head, and a purple purse swinging on her arm. The children all respond, "Lilly's Purple Plastic Purse." Ella smiles, announces the title, author, and illustrator and proceeds to give her book report, using all the expressions Lilly used in the book. When she finishes, there is a big "BRAVO!" from the class.

Marie is next. She slips behind the puppet box (a large cardboard box with holes cut out to act as the stage for the puppets) available for students to use and pulls out two cloth puppets, one dressed like the country mouse and the other as the town mouse. She announces her book title and illustrator, hidden behind the puppet box with only the puppets "on stage," and then with great expression she acts out a dialogue between Jan Brett's town mouse and country mouse. Again there is a shout of "BRAVO!" after her performance.

Jacob, the next performer, has to slip out of the room for a minute. He comes back wearing a cloth diaper with blue safety pins fastened around his middle with a long tail of pink yarn trailing behind him. The class roars: "Epossumondas!" Jacob puts a cupcake, an empty container of butter, a stuffed dog, and an empty bag of bread on a table. He reenacts the entire story, telling it as Epossumondas' mother, but acting out the part of Epossumondas. After his performance, the students cry, "More! More!"

Juan is the last performer of the day. He walks quietly over to the corner, rolls out the overhead projector, and announces his project: "Today, you will see a movie of *The Old Woman Who Lived in a Vinegar Bottle* by Margaret Reid MacDonald. This version is illustrated by Juan Garcia." On the roller transparency he has meticulously drawn all the dream homes of the old woman. As he tells the story, he turns on the overhead and displays his drawings on the large screen. His classmates are amazed by his beautiful artwork; they knew he was a great artist but had no idea he could draw in such detail. At the end of his performance, their reaction is "WOW! You need to show that to the other third grade classes."

After the performances, as they eat popcorn, students give specific comments to the performers about what made their book report excellent. Ms. Cho has modeled for the children how to give helpful, honest critiques by first offering one or two comments on what was really good and why it was good. Then she offered one suggestion (not a put-down) for how the report could be made even better. By modeling this method of critique, she has prepared her students to give constructive comments.

Introduction

n quality picture storybooks the text and pictures are like a ballet. In ballet, the music provided by the orchestra must be in perfect harmony, while the dancers extend and interpret the story. Both the music and the dancers provide a mood and style that result in an aesthetically pleasing experience for the audience. In a quality picture book, both the text and illustrations must be in harmony as well. The resulting book "provides the child with a visual experience [and] has a collective unity of story-line, theme, or concept, developed through the series of pictures of which the book is comprised" (American Library Association, 2005, p. 1 of 11). A ballet or storybook is sometimes dramatic, sometimes funny, sometimes thought provoking, and always intriguing to the audience or reader. Both ballets and books evoke all sorts of human emotions.

For example, in Tchaikovsky's *The Nutcracker,* each dance provides a different story and a very different mood. In the scene in which mice go to battle with toys, the music is dramatic and pounding to evoke tension. The mice's dark costumes and their swift and forceful movements reflect the music. Later in the dance of the snowflakes, when the music is rich and romantic, the costumes are white and flowing, and the movements are smooth and fluttering. The music for the dance of the sugar-plum fairy is light and playful, and the dancers, dressed in bright costumes, dance lightly on their toes in short little steps to represent fairies fluttering in a playful manner.

In storybooks, the mood is created through text and illustrations. Stories with tension or conflict may have illustrations with dark colors and heavy black outlines. Authors choose words that help readers feel the tension. In *Smokey Night* (1994), Eve Bunting tells the story of families who must leave their apartment house during the Los Angeles riots and fires. Bunting creates the scene with vivid language:

> Outside, the sky is hazy orange. Flames pounce up the side of our building. Three fire engines scream to a stop. (unpaged)

David Diaz's illustrations have dark, heavy colors with black outlines; his collages of apartment objects depict the chaos of the scene. In *Zin! Zin! Zin! A Violin* (Moss, 1995), text and illustrations are fluid like the sounds of a musical instrument. Lloyd Moss chooses words in his rhymes to describe each instrument: "strings all soar," "reed implore," "brasses roar," and the violin goes Zin! Zin! Zin! In the accompanying illustrations, Marjorie Priceman uses lines and colors that fit each instrument. On the page with the violin, the performer's tuxedo tails sweep like the violin's bow; on the French horn page the performer's stance curves like the French horn itself.

In the gentle bedtime story *Can't You Sleep, Little Bear?* (Waddell, 1988), the soft pastel colors of the woodland complement the text:

> Big Bear lifted Little Bear and cuddled him and said ... "I've brought you the moon, Little Bear. The bright yellow moon and all the twinkly stars." (unpaged)

Every genre—fiction, nonfiction, poetry, and so on—can be found in picture books. In quality children's literature of any type, authors choose words carefully to fit the mood of the story, and the illustrators complement the story with appropriate style. This chapter looks at fiction picture books generally, while Chapters 6 through 8 examine specific genres of picture storybooks, including traditional and modern fantasy, historical and realistic fiction, and informational books. In this chapter, we look at the benefits of reading picture books to young children. We discuss the literary elements of quality books, the artistic quality of illustrations, and the unity between story and illustrations. We examine how pictures support, explain and extend the text, and how both work together to create quality literature. Following this discussion we provide information about selecting quality fiction for young children, considering both the story elements and the illustrations, as well as the unity between them. The chapter concludes with information about how to teach with picture storybooks.

The Benefits of Fiction Picture Books

The International Reading Association (IRA) and the National Association for Education of Young Children (NAEYC) understand the importance of exposing young children to a wide variety of genres, including fiction (Jacobson, 1998). We agree with IRA and NAEYC and believe there are many benefits to sharing and discussing fiction picture books with children. The primary purpose, of course, is to enjoy a story together and to share quality time. But during this time learning also occurs, and children at a very young age are developing a positive attitude toward learning (Gambrell, Morrow, & Pennington, 2002).

Educational researchers (Brown, Sullivan-Palincsar, & Armbruster, 2004; Forman & Cazden, 2004; Cox, Fang, & Otto, 2004; Neugebauer & Currie-Rubin, 2009) have studied the benefits of reading fiction to young children and found that fiction picture books integrate "cognition, social interaction, society, and culture" (Gee, 2004, p. 116). Reading and discussing picture books with children stimulates their cognitive growth and adds to their knowledge of the world.

Sharing picture fiction books with children also helps their language development; they learn that language is social (Gee, 2004). For example, different situations give different meaning to words. Take for example the word *lock*. If a story's setting is in Sault Ste. Marie, Michigan, *lock* could refer to the canal locks that connect Lake Huron to Lake Superior; and if the main character of the books is "locking through," it would mean that he was on a boat cruise, going through the locks. In another story about a bicycle, *lock* could mean the act of locking up the bicycle or putting on a lock on the bike to keep it from being stolen. Gee's (2004) research also showed that children learn about formal and informal language when fiction is shared with them. They experience the play on words found in humorous books, and in serious fiction they encounter a more somber or dramatic tone.

When fiction is shared with preschool children, they develop a literate register, the syntax and semantics common to literature (Cox et al., 2004). They learn that stories have settings, characters, and plots, which may involve a problem that needs to be resolved. Through listening, they learn that book language (in which complete sentences are used) is different from oral conversations (in which sentences are often not completed). Cox and colleagues (2004) did find in their study that children who heard many stories read to them used a literate register when retelling a story. This research also revealed that reading to and discussing stories with children help them become better readers.

Cognitively, young children's phonological awareness increases as caregivers and teachers read to and discuss rhyming books with children (Juel & Minden-Cupp, 2004; Stanovich, 2004). Sharing rhyming books such as Dr. Seuss's *There's a Wocket in My Pocket* (1974) and playing with the language during the reading help children become aware of sounds in words, which correlates positively with their early reading ability (Stanovich, 2004). Reading fiction also aids in the development of their vocabulary (Juel & Minden-Cupp, 2004; Stanovich, 2004). According to Beck (2004), there are three tiers of words. Tier 1 are words used daily in conversation that most children know. Tier 2 words are words used by adults that children understand because of the context of the conversation or text. Tier 3 words are uncommon words that may be unfamiliar to children but may be found in quality children's literature. Many of these tier 3 words must be discussed with children in order for them to understand them fully and make them part of their expressive vocabulary (Lane & Wright, 2007). English learners' vocabulary also develops during read-alouds (Neugebauer & Currien-Rubin, 2009; Adams, 1990). Their vocabulary was shown to increase at a faster rate when teachers took the time to provide explanations for words the English learners did not understand.

Children's listening comprehension also develops as they listen to and discuss books with adults (Stanovich, 2004). This is especially true when adult readers ask children to predict what will happen next and then stop to confirm the prediction or discuss why the prediction was incorrect (Fisher, Flood, Lapp, & Frey, 2004). Children's comprehension is enhanced when adults discuss the book before, during, and after reading (Fisher et al., 2004). It is important that during these discussions the adult values the child's interpretation of a story; if not, the child may be discouraged or may think that there is a right or wrong response to literature (Many, 2004). During the discussion, adults should aim to balance efferent questions (questions about information) with aesthetic questions (questions about children's emotions, mental images, and thoughts). That way children learn to make a connection between their own life and the story in the book (Many, 2004).

Sharing fiction picture books with children also develops their awareness of different cultures. When children listen to and discuss multicultural books, more occurs than a transaction between reader and text; as children construct the meaning of the text, they begin to take their "stances and identities within larger socio culture context" (Galda & Beach, 2004). They learn about people and communities in other parts of the world and learn the reasons why some people live differently than they do. When they hear stories of other cultures, children learn to accept differences instead of judging them (Gee, 2004).

It is important that parents, caregivers, and teachers read and engage infants, preschoolers, and primary-school children with quality fiction. During this mediated learning time, "cognition, social interaction, society, and culture" (Gee, 2004, p. 116) are integrated, which helps develop children's schemata. This in turn will aid them when they learn to read independently.

Elements of a Story

In Chapter 1, we introduced the seven main elements of a story: *characters, plot, theme, setting, point of view, tone,* and *style.* The best fiction integrates these elements seamlessly, as shown in Figure 5.1. Each element must be in unity with the others. Let's look more closely at these elements and how they take shape in picture books.

Characters

How many times have you started a novel and didn't want to put the book down because the characters had become a part of your life? You most likely empathized with the characters through their struggles or happy events. The characters became like real people in your mind. When this happens, the author has succeeded in creating quality literature. This happens, too, in quality picture books, even though they are just 16 to 32 pages long. Picture storybooks reveal the characters through their illustrations and through the text (by what they say and how they act and react, by what other characters say about them, and how the author describes them).

Often, it is the characters of a story that young children will remember, imitate, or name their stuffed animals after. Toy companies realize the popularity of some picture book characters and manufacture stuffed animals or dolls that resemble them. Peter Rabbit, Madeline, Curious George, Arthur, the Cat in the Hat, and Corduroy are only a few of the many storybook characters made into toys. They can be found in both bookstores and toy stores.

Young children usually empathize with the protagonist, the main character, but stories also have supporting characters or antagonists. Because authors reveal the entire personality of protagonists, they are known as *round characters,* who are either *dynamic* (changed in attitude or perspective over the course of the story) or *static* (unchanged over the course of the story). Antagonists usually are *flat;* that is, they are not fully developed, and readers do not get to know their entire personality.

FIGURE 5.1   Integration of the seven components of a story.

characters
plot
theme
setting
point of view
tone
style

When the seven components of a story are uniquely knitted together, the result is quality literature.

Kevin Henkes was born and grew up in Racine, Wisconsin. He loved to draw when he was very young, and he always knew he wanted to be an author and illustrator when he grew up. His parents and teachers encouraged him to draw because they recognized his talent. He wrote and illustrated his first book, *All Alone,* at a card table in his parents' home when he was 19 years old. When he went to New York City to find a publisher, Greenwillow Books bought it right away. Since then, he has written and illustrated many books.

He has created 14 lovable mice books with different characters. Some of them are Chester, Chrysanthemum, Lilly, Owen, Sheila Rae, Wendell, Sophie, and Wemberly. Changing the eyes, ears, and tails, he creates many different expressions on his characters. He also has written picture books with characters other than mice (e.g., *Shhhh, All Alone,* and *Kitten's First Full Moon,* which won the 2005 Caldecott Medal).

Protagonists as dynamic round characters

Round characters have multiple dimensions to their personality, just like real people do. Their actions, feelings, speech, and moods are believable. Dynamic characters change their personalities or beliefs because of what happens in the story. In quality literature, they change for reasons that readers can accept. Kevin Henkes has two books with dynamic round protagonists: Lilly (a mouse) in *Julius: The Baby of the World* (1990) and Wemberly in *Wemberly Worried* (2000). Readers see Lilly boiling with jealousy after Julius, her baby brother, is born. Lilly thinks his pink nose is slimy, his black eyes beady, and his white fur smelly when he needs his diaper changed. She makes loud crying noises like Julius, and when she is asked to tell him a story, she tells him the story of Julius, the Germ of the World. But when Cousin Garland comes for a visit and says that Julius is disgusting, Lilly changes her tune about Julius. She forces Cousin Garland to kiss, admire, and stroke Julius and to repeat after her: "JULIUS IS THE BABY OF THE WORLD!" (unpaged). Wemberly, on the other hand, is constantly worrying about everything. She is especially worried when she needs to go to school. However, on that first day she meets another shy girl who becomes her best friend, and she stops worrying. Wemberly becomes a happy child, who is able to pass on the lesson learned and tell her own teacher not to worry.

Other stories with round dynamic characters include *The Ticky-Tacky Doll* (Rylant, 2002), *Rosie and Tortoise* (Wild, 1999), *The Best Wind* (Williams, 2006), *Chester's Way* (Henkes, 1997), and *Mirette on the High Wire* (McCully, 1991).

Protagonists as static round characters

Static round characters do not change their personalities or beliefs throughout the story, yet they are round and fully developed. Mr. Mutt in *Help Me, Mr. Mutt!* (Stevens & Stevens Crummel, 2008) is a dog who is an expert in people problems. He is a static round character. Through the letters he writes to advise dogs who have problems with their masters, readers learn Mr. Mutt's opinions about dog food, masters who watch too much TV, masters who dress their dogs in holiday costumes, and many other situations. However, in these letters his opinions never change. Mr. Mutt never gives up his cynical attitude.

Patricia McKissack also creates a round static protagonist in *Goin' Someplace Special* (2001); readers see all the emotions of Tricia Ann, who stays positive and confident throughout the events of the story. The setting is Nashville in the 1950s when African Americans were confronted with the humiliations of segregation. Readers see Tricia Ann's feelings through text and illustrations as she is ejected from a hotel lobby, snubbed by a theater she cannot attend, and jeered at by another girl. Jerry Pinkney's facial expressions of Tricia Ann also portray her as a static round character. Readers see her eagerness as she goes out by herself, witness her confidence as she is humiliated by ejection and the jeers of others, and see the pure joy she radiates when she enters the public library, which her grandma calls "a doorway to freedom." The illustrations reflect the dress fashions of the 1950s and make the story realistic.

In *Plaidypus Lost* (Stevens-Crummel, 2004), the granddaughter of the story is also a static round character. Like many typical young children, she loves her stuffed animal Plaidypus, which her Grandma made for her. The granddaughter is believable because she acts like a real child, thinking her stuffed animal is real and has feelings. She takes it everywhere, talking to it as if the stuffed animal hears and understands her.

Some other stories with static round characters are *Night Noises* (Fox, 1989), *Wilfrid Gordon McDonald Partridge* (Fox, 1984), *Hopper's Treetop Adventure* (Pfister, 1997), *My Chincoteague Pony* (Jeffers, 2008), *When Lightning Comes in a Jar* (Polacco, 2002), *Dry Days Wet Night* (Boelts, M. 1994), and *The Little Bit Scary People* (Jenkins, 2008).

Teaching about protagonists

A good teaching principle is to introduce students to one character concept at a time (for example, the concept of a protagonist). Once the concept has been taught, teachers should always ask, "Who is the protagonist?" "What do we know about the protagonist that makes him or her a round character?" That way students become familiar with the literary terms and fully understand them. During discussion, teachers can review books that she has already read to them, asking them, "Who was the protagonist in *The Other Goose?*" (Kerr, 2002). When teachers know that most students have mastered the concept of protagonist, they can explain *dynamic* and read many stories in which the protagonist is dynamic. After each story, teachers need to give students ample opportunity to discuss why the protagonist is dynamic. Later, teachers can introduce *static* and read stories in which the protagonist is static. Again, teachers must give students opportunity to discuss why the protagonist is static and not dynamic.

When students have learned these literary concepts, teachers can have students fill out the graphic organizers (character profiles) found in Figure 5.2. When a student names a trait of a character, the teacher should encourage the student to find evidence of that trait in the story by asking, "Did other characters reveal that trait about the protagonist? Did the protagonist reveal that trait through action or through speech? Did the author state that the protagonist had that trait?" Readers learn about protagonists through what they say, how they act, how they feel toward others, and what others say about them. Charts such as the ones in Figure 5.2 can help readers recognize the traits that make a protagonist round and dynamic or static. Blank forms are available in Appendices C.1 and C.2 for you to copy and pass out to students.

Character profiles of a round dynamic protagonist and a round static protagonist. **FIGURE** 5.2

A round dynamic protagonist

BOOK
Julius: The Baby of the World

Beginning

TRAITS
Jealous of baby brother Julius

EVIDENCE
■ Yelled at Julius ■ Pinched his tail ■ Thought his nose was slimy, black eyes were beady ■ Thought he was disgusting

CHARACTER NAME
Lilly

CHANGING EVENT
Cousin Garland came to visit

End

TRAITS
Loved, admired, protective of Julius

EVIDENCE
■ Kissed his pink nose ■ Admired eyes ■ Stroked his fur ■ Made Cousin Garland repeat "Julius is the Baby of the World!"

Kevin Henkes' *Julius: The Baby of the World* (1990). New York: Greenwillow Books.

A round static protagonist

BOOK
Bently & Egg

CHARACTER NAME
Bently

TRAIT #1
Happy

EVIDENCE
He was extremely happy

TRAIT #2
Musical

EVIDENCE
He would sing his heart out

TRAIT #3
Loyal to friends

EVIDENCE
Through all types of danger, he went to rescue the egg of his best friend Kack Kack

William Joyce's *Bently & Egg* (1992). New York: Scholastic.

Antagonists as flat characters

Antagonists are often flat or not fully developed as characters, but they are still important to the story. This is because they create tension in the story by opposing the protagonist; they may also help readers better understand the protagonist. In quality literature, antagonists must be believable, and they are not always the "bad guys." For example, in *Epossumondas* (Salley, 2002), Epossumondas is the protagonist, but the readers get to know him through his mother's actions and her remarks about him. Epossumondas' mother, the antagonist, loves him unconditionally. Her actions and speech display unconditional love and are consistent throughout the book—no matter how much trouble Epossumondas gets into. Epossumondas' mother is believable because her unconditional love reflects a real mother's love for her young child. However, the mother is a flat character because readers do not learn anything else about her personality.

In *Possum Magic* (Fox, 1983), Hush is the main character, but there would be no story if Grandma Poss was not there to use her magic to make Hush disappear and to reappear. Belle is the protagonist in *The Friend* (Stewart, 2004), but the antagonist Bea, the housekeeper, is needed to show readers how love and family can be found in people that aren't relatives.

Teaching about antagonists

Just like when teachers facilitate children's understanding of round protagonists as either dynamic or static characters, teachers can discuss antagonists and their importance to the plot. After discussing characters such as Leonard P. Cage in *Clorinda* (Kinerk, 2003), *Soldier in Little Whistle's Medicine* (Rylant, 2002), the doctors in *A Bad Case of Stripes* (Shannon, 1998), and the Blue Whale in *Rainbow Fish and the Big Blue Whale* (Pfister, 1999), teachers can help primary grade students understand the importance of the flat antagonist by helping students complete the graphic organizer found in Figure 5.3. The graphic organizer should generate much discussion among the students. Teachers can begin the discussion by asking students some of the following questions: "Did the antagonist like or dislike the protagonist?" "What did the antagonist say about the protagonist that made you believe that?" "Can you find where in the story the antagonist says that?" Teachers can ask a student to find the exact page and sentence that supports her interpretation. As the student finds the evidence, the teacher can begin to complete the graphic organizer shown in Figure 5.3 on a digital white board or overhead so that it is large enough for all students to see it. A blank version is available in Appendix C.3.

Plot

Although children often remember and imitate characters, it is usually the plot of the story that initially stimulates and holds children's interest during reading. At its most basic, "The plot is the sequence of events or showing the characters in action" (Lukens, 2003, p. 59). If the plot has no suspense, young children will not sit to hear the entire story. In quality picture books, plots are basic; however, even in these short stories, plots must have tension or a surprise that is age-appropriate.

Character profile of a flat antagonist.	**FIGURE** 5.3

Flat Antagonist

BOOK
Clorinda

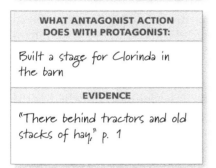

WHAT ANTAGONIST SAYS ABOUT PROTAGONIST:
He encourages Clorinda to dance
EVIDENCE
"Be bold and imaginative! Shoot for the sky! If it's dance that you love, then it's dance you should try!"

CHARACTER NAME
Leonard P. Cage, young farmhand

WHAT ANTAGONIST DOES TO PROTAGONIST:
Gives her cash to go to New York
EVIDENCE
"I'll help! Here's some cash for the flight!" p. 2

WHAT ANTAGONIST ACTION DOES WITH PROTAGONIST:
Built a stage for Clorinda in the barn
EVIDENCE
"There behind tractors and old stacks of hay," p. 1

RELATIONSHIP BETWEEN ANTAGONIST AND PROTAGONIST:
True friends
EVIDENCE
"You're a prince, Len" "I'll dance you my thanks." Clorinda said this after Len built her a bigger stage.

Robert Kinerk's *Clorinda* (2003). New York: Aladdin Paperbacks.

Conflict in plots

Plots typically revolve around some kind of conflict. In stories, readers encounter four main forms of conflict: (1) character versus character, (2) protagonist versus self, (3) protagonist versus society, and (4) protagonist versus nature. All of these types of conflict are common in fiction picture books.

Character versus character. Tension builds when a conflict develops between the protagonist and one or more other characters. This type of tension is found in children's literature and adult literature because humans of all ages have conflicts in their interactions with others. This type of plot is especially common in picture books, because as young children, who tend to be egotistic, socialize with others around them, they must learn to deal with others and their opinions.

Denise Fleming uses a cat and a dog to show the tension that often occurs in children's lives when a new sibling or friend changes their daily routine. In *Buster* (Fleming, 2003), problems arise between Buster, the happy dog, and Betty, the new kitten bought by Buster's masters, when Betty changes Buster's favorite radio station to her favorite station.

Young children are learning to follow their parents' rules; they are also learning that not all people have good intentions. Patricia McKissack uses a child and a person in disguise to create a story on the theme of listening to parents. In *Precious and the Boo Hag* (McKissack, 2005), Precious is told by her mother never to let anyone into the house when she is home alone. Tension arises in the story when the mysterious Boo Hag attempts to trick Precious into letting her into the house by disguising herself as different characters.

Janet Stevens uses wit to create conflict between Hare and lazy Bear in *Tops and Bottoms* (Stevens, 1995). Hare tricks lazy Bear out of his crops by asking Bear to choose which part of the crop he wants. When Bear wants the tops of the crop, Hare plants carrots, radishes, and beets. At the next planting, when Bear says he wants the bottoms, Hare plants lettuce, broccoli and celery. At the third planting, Lazy Bear says he wants both the tops and the bottoms at harvest. One more time, Hare tricks Bear by planting corn. Hare gives Bear the bottom roots and the top tassels and keeps the ears, the middle part of the plant. As young children listen to these stories, they hope that the protagonist will outwit the antagonist. Children hope that Hare will continue to outwit lazy Bear.

Some other titles with this type of conflict are *Hedgie's Surprise* (Brett, 2000), *Naked Mole Rat Gets Dressed* (Willems, 2008), *Too Many Toys* (Shannon, 2008), *Flossie and the Fox* (McKissack, 1986), and *Timothy Goes to School* (Wells, 2000).

Because these plots often reflect children's lives, caregivers and teachers can discuss with children how the protagonists resolved the conflict and whether the resolution was a wise choice. They can also discuss alternative ways the protagonist could have resolved the conflict or ask about a time when the children solved a problem they were having with someone else.

Protagonist versus self. Young readers, from the toddler years through primary grades, will find this kind of conflict as familiar as conflicts with others. Inner struggles are a part of life, and young children are learning how to resolve them. The main character may have done something wrong and is trying to decide if and how she should confess the wrongdoing. Inner conflict can also come about when the protagonist needs to overcome some inner fear. In children's books, authors attempt to teach positive moral development; thus, the protagonist usually does the correct action at the end of the story.

For example, in *Stagestruck* (dePaola, 2005) Tommy becomes upset when Miss Bird, the teacher, does not choose him to be Peter Rabbit in the class play but instead gives him the small part of Mopsy. Even though he cannot be the star, Tommy is determined to steal the audience's attention, and he does so very successfully by overacting. But he is shocked when his teacher and mother do not yell "Bravo!" with the rest of the audience. His mother explains that it was not nice of him to steal the show from Johnny, who played Peter Rabbit. Readers can see Tommy's struggle within himself: he really wanted to be the star; but after his mother and teacher talk with him, he realizes that his actions were harmful to Johnny. He decides that the right thing for him to do is to apologize to Johnny and Miss Bird.

In *Little Bunny's Pacifier Plan* (Boelts, 1999), Little Bunny is struggling inwardly with giving up his pacifier. His parents are encouraging him in all his attempts, but his love for his pacifier overtakes him at times, even though he know he needs to give it up so his teeth do not come in crooked. Finally, he overcomes his need to use a pacifier and gives it to his newborn cousin as a gift.

Other stories to share with children with this type of plot are *Thunder Cake* (Polacco, 1990), about overcoming a fear of thunderstorms; *Dry Days, Wet Nights* (Boelts, 1994), about overcoming the embarrassment of wetting the bed at night; *Rosie and Tortoise* (Wild, 1999), about overcoming the fear of hurting a newborn sibling because he is so tiny, and *There's a Nightmare in My Closet* (Mayer, 1968), about overcoming the fear of sleeping alone in a room. In each of these books, teachers should point out the conflict within the character and discuss the wisdom of the protagonist's actions.

Protagonist versus society. This type of plot is harder for very young children to grasp because they do not know or understand all the customs and rules of society. However, after they enter kindergarten and the primary grades, children do begin to learn that there are acts of injustice happening in the world around them and that the desires, values, or expectations of others often differ from their own. It is especially important in stories with this type of conflict that the conflict is realistic—that is, the plot depicts a struggle between the protagonist's values or desires and those of today's society; or, if it is historical fiction, the protagonist clashes with values of the era when the story is set.

One book that accomplishes this type of plot is *She's Wearing a Dead Bird on Her Head!* (Lasky, 1995). In this story, birds are being killed so high society women can wear feathers on their hats. At the end of the story, Harriet, Minna, and Augustus, the three friends who see the cruelty being done to birds, are able to get laws passed that make it illegal to hunt birds during their breeding season and illegal to import bird feathers from England and the tropics. The humorous illustrations make children cheer as Harriet, Minna, and Augustus win the battle over the societal custom of wearing hats decorated with bird feathers.

In *Oliver Button Is a Sissy* (dePaola, 1979), Oliver, the protagonist, is going against the common belief that dancing is not for boys. He proves society wrong when he enters a talent show. Oliver practices his tap dances routine and enters the contest even though boys in his class wrote "Oliver is a sissy" on the school wall. At the contest, Oliver's classmates are impressed with Oliver's ability to dance; even though he does not win first place, his friends consider him a star. In this story, Tomie dePaola demonstrates that protagonists do not have to win first place in a contest to be a winner.

In *Nana Hannah's Piano* (Bottner, 1996) the protagonist, a little boy who loves both piano lessons with Nana and playing baseball with his friends, struggles with his friends who thinks he should spend all his time playing baseball. The conflict between what society thinks—boys play ball and girls play piano—is resolved when his friends hear him play "Take Me Out to the Ballgame."

Other stories with similar tension include *Willie and the All-Stars* (Cooper, 2008), *Amazing Grace* (Hoffman, 1991), *The Moon Over Star* (Hutts Aston, 2008), *Grace for President* (DiPucchio, 2008), *Art from Her Heart* (Whitehead, 2008), *White Socks Only* (Coleman, 1999), *The Story of Ruby Bridges* (Cole, 2004), *The School Is Not White* (Rappaport, 2005), *Rosa* (Giovanni, 2007), *Freedom Summer* (Wiles, 2005), and *The Other Side* (Woodson, 2001).

When reading stories with this type of plot, teachers should talk about the struggle of the protagonists and their bravery to overcome the norm. This can open up discussion about things that the children may want to do but that others think they cannot do because they are inappropriate.

Protagonist versus nature. Children's stories in which the protagonist faces a problem with the natural world are often about a character getting lost in a storm or in a strange place. The protagonist must find a way to survive the elements of nature. For young children, the tension is resolved in such a way that they do not become afraid of nature's elements but rather learn to cope with them.

In *Twister* (Beard, 1999), two siblings left alone at home while their mother helps a neighbor are confronted with a tornado barreling down on their house. They run to the cellar for shelter as the twister strikes and "claws and chomps and pulls at [the] cellar door" (unpaged). Then suddenly all is quiet outside. The children open the cellar door to find all the damage the twister left behind. They find comfort as they fix the old porch swing and squeeze into it with their mother and the elderly neighbor, realizing that the twister destroyed buildings, trees, and other property, but it did not destroy them.

In *The Snow Lambs* (Gliori, 1995), Sam, his dad, and Bess the sheepdog are gathering their sheep when a snowstorm rolls in. Sam and his dad are able to make their way back to the farmhouse; however, Bess does not make it before dark. Sam

by Jane O'Connor
pictures based on the art of Robin Preiss Glasser

worries all during the night about Bess. In the one picture frame, readers see the action in the house while in another frame, readers see how Bess and one lost sheep are coping with the snowstorm. Young readers want to keep reading to see if Bess will survive the storm. In the morning, the conflict is resolved when Bess arrives at the front door with the little lamb.

In *Jubal's Wish* (Wood, 2001), Jubal the frog must make it through a terrible storm at sea. Readers empathize with Jubal as he contends with the strong wind and high waves while attempting to make his way to the ship where his friends are. The conflict is resolved when Jubal is pulled safely onto the wind-tossed ship. At the end of the story the storm subsides and all are safe.

Other stories in which the protagonist wrestles with nature are *Fancy Nancy: Poison Ivy Expert* (O'Connor, 2008), *Louise, the Adventure of a Chicken* (diCammillo, 2008), *Abe Lincoln Crosses a Creek* (Hopkinson, 2008), *Come on, Rain* (Hesse, 1999), *The Rain Came Down* (Shannon, 2000), *Tsunami!* (Kajikawa, 2009), *Earthquake* (Lee, 2001), and *Sailor Boy* (Waddell, 2005).

In primary grades, teachers can brainstorm with students possible plots in which the protagonist confronts nature and then invite them to write their own story.

Plot structures

Children's literature also offers a variety of plot structures. The three most common types are *progressive* plots, plots with *unresolved conflict,* and *episodic* plots.

Progressive plot. This type of plot structure is usually straightforward: the events of the story build to a climax and then the conflict is resolved. Many books for young children have a progressive plot because children love action. In picture books, the setting of the story is usually described briefly and the characters introduced in short order. The problem is often announced on the first page, and for the rest of the story the protagonist runs into obstacles while attempting to solve the problem. Once the problem is solved, the story quickly comes to an end. In a picture book the pictures show much of the action.

One example that follows this pattern is Marc Brown's *Arthur's Pet Business* (1990). Arthur wants a pet but must prove to his parents that he can be responsible with one. He agrees to take care of Perky, Mrs. Wood's nasty dog. Little episodes show Arthur struggling to take care of this dog. The climax comes when Mrs. Wood returns for Perky, but Perky is nowhere to be found. Everyone is in a panic as they attempt to find him. Finally a bark comes from under Arthur's bed where Perky is found with three puppies. In the resolution, Mrs. Wood pays Arthur for this work and gives him a puppy to keep. Of course, his parents now know he is responsible enough to care for a pet.

My Name Is Yoon (Recorvits, 2003), an Ezra Jack Keats New Illustrator Award book, is another story with a progressive plot. When Yoon, which means *shining wisdom* in Korean, goes to school and learns to write, she does not like how her name looks when written in English. She does not like the lines and circles standing all alone on the paper. She thinks her name looks happier on paper when written in Korean. She begins to substitute other English names that better fit her inner emotions. She first chooses "Cat" because she longs to cuddle with her mother. She then chooses "Bird," dreaming of flying back to Korea. Finally, she chooses "Cupcake," a name she thinks all her classmates will like. In the end, however, Yoon is unhappy with the name Cupcake and decides to go back to her given name.

Some stories with a progressive plot show how different characters in similar situations act or resolve the conflict. Many picture books have this type of plot. David McPhail's *Something Special* (1988) has a progressive plot that is appropriate for very young children. The story begins, "Everyone in Sam's family could do something special. Everyone but Sam" (unpaged). On the very first page, the problem is introduced. The text and the illustrations depict a very dejected Sam, a raccoon dressed in blue overalls and a red shirt. Each page shows someone from his family doing something special with Sam, on the facing page, attempting the same task and failing. There are 10 tasks that Sam attempts but fails to do. Finally, the climax comes when Sam, watching his mother paint a duck, hears her complain, "I just can't get it right" (unpaged). Sam suggests that she should make the paint greener like the ducks in the pond. He then begins to paint the duck for his mother, and she recognizes that he is very good at painting. He then paints a picture of an apple, a picture of his sister at the piano, and one of his sister and her trophy. At the end of the story, Sam has finally found his talent.

Another progressive plot story is Sharon Creech's *A Fine, Fine School* (2001) in which the principal loves his fine school so much that he decides to have school on Saturdays, then on Sundays, then on all holidays, and, finally, even during the summer. Through his illustrations, Harry Bliss shows the children and teachers becoming more depressed as each free day is taken from them. The climax of the story is when Tillie, a brave student, goes to Principal Keene and explains that, because she is in school all the time, her dog is not learning new tricks and her younger sibling is not learning how to swing and do other important activities.

Readers know from Principal Keene's facial expressions that he will go back to the original school calendar.

Other books with progressive plots are *Luba's Wren* (Polacco, 2002), *Epossumondas* (Salley, 2006), *Epossumondas Saves the Day* (Salley, 2006), *Buffalo Dreams* (Doner, 2000), *Henry and the Valentine Surprise* (Carlson, 2008), *Madeline and the Cats of Rome* (Bemelmans, 2008), *Doggone Dogs!* (Beaumont, 2008), *Skippyjon Jones in Mummy Trouble* (Schachner, 2008), and *Lester Fizz, Bubble-Gum Artist* (Spiro, 2008).

To help primary students with the sequencing of progressive plots, teachers can map out the action on a graphic organizer like those found in Figure 5.4 and Appendix C.4. Progressive plots are also easy for students to act out. Remember that Howard Gardner (1993) encourages teachers to give students opportunities to develop all of their multiple intelligences. When teachers give students opportunity to act out the stories, they develop their spatial intelligence through body movements; they develop their linguistic intelligence as they develop their stage voices; and they develop their interpersonal intelligence as they interact with others and learn to cooperate during the reenactment of the story. When teachers encourage students to develop story grammar maps, such as a "mountain" plot, students are given an opportunity to develop linguistic skills as they learn

FIGURE 5.4   A mountain plot based on *Epossumondas* (Salley, 2002).

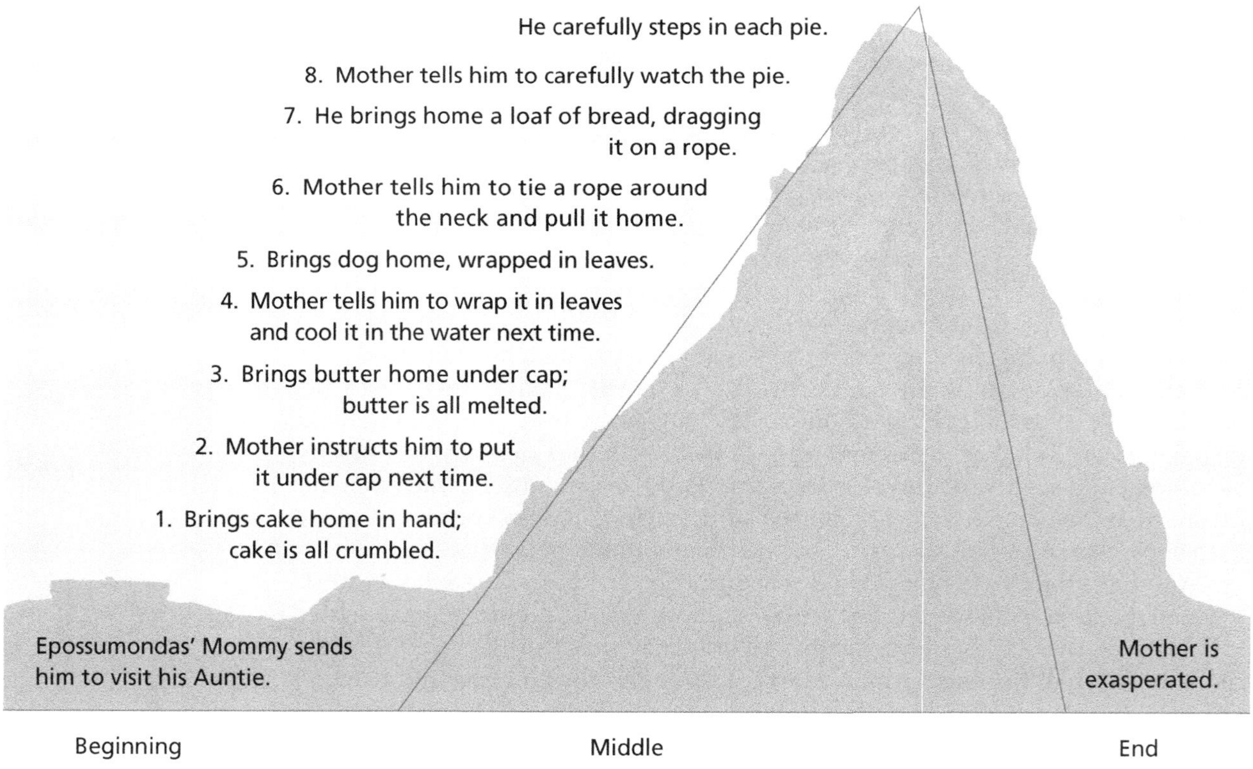

He carefully steps in each pie.

8. Mother tells him to carefully watch the pie.

7. He brings home a loaf of bread, dragging it on a rope.

6. Mother tells him to tie a rope around the neck and pull it home.

5. Brings dog home, wrapped in leaves.

4. Mother tells him to wrap it in leaves and cool it in the water next time.

3. Brings butter home under cap; butter is all melted.

2. Mother instructs him to put it under cap next time.

1. Brings cake home in hand; cake is all crumbled.

Epossumondas' Mommy sends him to visit his Auntie.

Mother is exasperated.

Beginning   Middle   End

Allen Say was born in Yokohama, Japan, to a Korean father and Japanese American mother. He had a difficult childhood after his parents divorced when he was 8 years old. His life as an artist began when he was 12 years old and became an apprentice to Noro Shimpel, a cartoonist. When he was 16, he moved with his father and his new family to California, where he enrolled in different art schools. After graduation from art school, he decided to return to Japan and was amazed to find how life had changed there. He moved back to California and began to paint signs, but he was unhappy painting other people's ideas. He started to study architecture at the University of California but was drafted into the army. While he was serving in the army in Germany, his commanding officer noticed Say's talent for photography. When he returned home after his tour in Germany, he began to write and illustrate. Many of Say's books are based on his life experiences. His stories often include the innocence of children and their fears of not being what they want to be. His lifelike illustrations often resemble photographs.

to paraphrase the ideas of the story and intrapersonal skills as they learn to work by themselves.

Unresolved conflict. In this plot structure, the story's conflict remains unfinished, which results in an open-ended story. This gives adults and children the opportunity to discuss what could possibly happen next. In *The Popcorn Shop* (Low, 1993), Nell's popcorn machine will not stop popping corn and soon popcorn fills the town. So, Nell gets a pizza dough machine with which "nothing can go wrong" (unpaged). However, on the last page, readers see Nell standing before a machine that has dough streaming out of it. Parents and children can surmise what will happen next. It is a wonderful book to nudge young children toward higher-level thinking. There is no right or wrong conclusion but plenty of room for speculation.

Another story for young children in which the conflict is not resolved is Allen Say's *Emma's Rug* (1996). Emma is an incredible artist; her parents recognize her talent from the time she is old enough to hold a pencil. However, when she arrives home one day and finds that her little rug, a source of inspiration, is shriveled and ragged after her mother washed it, she stops drawing and destroys her previous drawings. Some days later, Emma thinks she sees something move and rushes outside:

> She saw the eyes watching her and then the faces of creatures all round. She knew the faces and creatures from before, and thought she would never see again. "I can see you!" Emma cried with joy. The trees rustled, as if laughing. And then it was quiet. (p. 30)

The text ends abruptly, and readers are left to view all types of creatures hidden within the leaves of the trees. When they turn over the page, readers see Emma drawing again, but there is no text. Children can discuss with adults what they think Emma is drawing and why she started to draw again, even drawing their guess themselves.

Other stories with unresolved conflict include *Tuesday* (Wiesner, 1991), and *Flotsam* (Wiesner, 2000), *My Friend Rabbit* (Rohmann, 2002), and Mo Willems' *The Pigeon Wants a Puppy!* (2008).

133

Stories without resolutions allow children to improvise an ending. With *The Popcorn Shop* (Low, 1993), teachers can invite children to pretend that they are Nell with the malfunctioning pizza dough machine and act out the rest of the story. Since there is no correct ending, each child can imagine his own ending. Another story that has an open ending is *The Day the Goose Got Loose* (Linbergh, 1990).Children can pretend they are the geese flying away to another place. When they finally come to their destination, they can imagine what trouble the geese may cause upon their arrival.

Episodic plot. The third pattern, episodic plot, is a plot in which several discrete episodes are strung together with no explicit logic of cause and effect, though sometimes they are chronological. One action is linked to the next with no build up to a climax followed by a resolution. Children listen to these stories because they want to see what the characters will do next. This structure also reflects children's daily lives, showing how relationships are built among family members and friends. Episodic structures create quiet suspense by relating everyday events, including sibling rivalry, the fear of being alone, or the sorrow of losing a favorite toy.

Olivia (Falconer, 2000) has an episodic structure. In the story, the episodes show Olivia, a pig, acting like any normal active toddler. She scares her little brother, builds sand castles on the beach, refuses to take naps, paints on walls, needs a time out, and negotiates with her parents on reading many books before going to bed.

Some other popular books with this type of plot for infants are books in which young children and their mothers ask how deep their love is for each other. Barbara Joosse writes about Inuit culture in *Mama, Do You Love Me?* (1991). Even though her daughter might drop ptarmigan eggs, put salmon in her mother's parka, or turn into a polar bear, she has the unconditional love of her mother. In *The Runaway Bunny* (1942) Margaret Wise Brown uses a bunny to demonstrate that a mother will never let her child leave her even when the child attempts to run away. In *Guess How Much I Love You* (McBratney, 1994), Sam McBratney demonstrates how much Little Nutbrown Hare loves his mother and in turn how much Mother Hare loves her child. In the three stories, young children may think it impossible that a mother and child's love extends as far as the text implies; however, they discover that such love is unconditional.

Other episodic plots may be stories written as diaries or as first-person accounts. They can be personal reflections, a record of a character's personal life struggles, or a chronicle of adventures. *My Diary from Here to There* (Perez, 2002) relates a little girl's feelings about leaving her beloved Mexico. The story is based on the author's life experiences. Yang's *Hannah Is My Name* (2004) is told in first person. It records the author's experience of when she and her family moved from Taiwan. *First Day in Grapes* (2002) is King Perez's account of his first day as a fourth grader in yet another school.

Other stories with episodic plots are *Monsoon Afternoon* (Sheth, 2008), *My Dadima Wears a Sari* (Sheth, 2008), *The Hello, Goodbye Window* (Juster, 2005), and *Sam's Winter Hat* (Lamb, 2006).

Flashbacks in plots

Plots may also include techniques such as flashbacks in telling a story. Younger children need plots that are in chronological order and are believable or logical. They tend not to understand flashbacks (when the plot suddenly goes back in time), as older primary-school children do, unless the flashback is easy to follow. Most flashbacks in literature for young children take the form of a character retelling a story from the past to explain an event. For example, Colleen Salley's *Why Epossumondas Has No Hair on His Tail* (2004) has a flashback that is easy to follow. Epossumondas, a possum, is lamenting that he has no hair on his tail like skunks, foxes, and hares. Mama, a human, then begins to tell him the story of his great-great-grandpa Papapossum who did have a fluffy powder-puff tail until one day Bear and Hare became angry when he was eating all the persimmons in the tree. As Papapossum was attempting to escape from Bear, Bear chomped on Papapossum's tail and stretched the powder-puff tail until it was long with no hair. The story ends back in the porch swing with Mama hugging Epossumondas.

Cloudy with a Chance of Meatballs (Barrett, 1978) also begins with Grandpa telling his grandchildren a story about Chewandswallow, a town in which food rained from the sky each day so no one had to prepare any. The story ends with the children back in the bed, listening to Grandpa. Rosemary Wells uses flashback in *Max and Ruby's Midas* (1995). The story begins with Max wanting another cupcake, and Ruby telling him her version of the Midas touch.

A longtime favorite with a somewhat different flashback is *Where the Wild Things Are* (Sendak, 1963). In this story Max has a dream about a forest where wild things are after being sent to his room for saying to his mother, "I'll eat you up!"

Some other books with flashbacks are *Bad Day at Riverbend* (Van Allsburg, 1995), *The Keeping Quilt* (Polacco, 2001), *Tell Me a Story, Mama* (Johnson, 1989), and *Ben's Dream* (Van Allsburg, 1982). With all these books, caregivers and teachers may have to explain what is happening because sometimes children cannot follow the plot. Adults should give children time to ask questions and think about the action.

Theme

A story's central message can be a commentary about society, human nature, different cultures, social injustices, and everyday expectations. It answers the question "What does this story say about life?" Stories can have a primary theme and a secondary theme or themes. For example, in *Koala Lou* (Fox, 1988), the main theme is a mother's unconditional love for her child: Koala Lou's mother loves her even though Koala Lou does not win the race. A secondary theme also emerges: even though a person trains hard for a race, it does not mean she will automatically win.

After reading a story with a group of children, teachers can open discussion about the story's theme by asking *why* questions. For example, "Why do people still love us even if we don't always win or listen to their advice?" or "When shouldn't we tell the truth?" or "Why weren't different races permitted to play together?" Of course, teachers must always choose books with themes that are age-appropriate. For example, themes appropriate for toddlers are receiving the unconditional love of a parent, conquering fear of the dark and nighttime, and dealing with jealousy at the birth of a sibling. These themes are often part of toddlers' everyday lives. Books about racial prejudice are beyond their comprehension because they do not yet have the moral development to understand an injustice like racial discrimination. As children begin preschool, appropriate themes include conquering separation anxiety and learning to share with others; again, these themes are a part of their everyday lives. In the primary grades, some appropriate themes are accepting one's abilities and accepting others' differences, including racial differences.

Appendix A.16 lists books with common themes that appeal to young children. You may note that some of the publication dates go back a couple of decades. Quality literature is timeless. Themes that concerned children 50 years ago still concern children in the twenty-first century. Of course, each decade brings new themes to children's literature. As you browse this list, you can make your own list by adding other themes or adding books to the themes on this list.

In terms of their literary treatment, themes can be *explicit, implicit,* or *didactic.*

Explicit themes

Explicit themes are clearly stated by an author, such as in *Strega Nona* (dePaola, 1975), when Strega Nona announces to Big Anthony and the other villagers, "The punishment must fit the crime." Grandma in *Goin' Someplace Special* (McKissack, 2001) explicitly states the theme to her granddaughter Tricia Ann: "You are somebody, a human being—no better, no worse than anybody else in this world" (unpaged). Lou in *Clorinda* (Kinerk, 2003) states the theme of the story explicitly when he tells Clorinda that the audience is cheering even though Clorinda fell flat on her tummy during the ballet:

> They're doing all this because each understands
> the thing most important is making a try—
> you can't always triumph. You can't always fly.
> We gave it our best, but there's bound to be misses— (unpaged)

Implicit themes

Themes not directly stated, which the reader must infer from the text and illustrations, are implicit. For example, in *The Honest-to-Goodness Truth* (McKissack, 2000), Libby Louise Sullivan learns the importance of always telling the truth but must discern when the truth helps and when it hurts. Pointing to a hole in her friend's sock in public and telling her neighbor that her yard looks like a jungle are not truths that must be told. This theme is not explicitly stated, but through McKissack's storytelling and Giselle Potter's illustrations, young children understand that there is a difference between the right time and the wrong time to tell the truth.

Another story with an implicit theme is Deborah Wiles' *Freedom Summer* (2001), which has the implicit theme that the physical barriers created by racial prejudice can be overcome by a friendship that crosses racial divides. In this story, Joe, who is Caucasian, and his friend John Henry, who is African American, are excited about the Civil Rights Act because John Henry can now come along to the city swimming pool; however, when they get there, the city crews are filling it with asphalt because most whites do not want their children swimming with African Americans. Finally, the two friends courageously go into a once-segregated

Jan Brett grew up in Massachusetts and today lives in a Massachusetts coastal town. As a young child, Jan knew she wanted to be an illustrator. She spent much of her time drawing pictures with elaborate details. Jan Brett travels all over the world to research different countries so that the details in her pictures are accurate. Her books are easy to identify on account of her intricate borders and side panels. Since she loves to draw animals, many of her books are about animals.

Her pet is a hedgehog, and readers can find a hedgehog in many of her books.

Her first published book was *Fritz and the Beautiful Horses* (1981). One of her favorite books is *The Mitten* (1989), set in the Ukraine. *The Umbrella* (2004), a story based on the same folktale as *The Mitten,* is set in the Monteverde Cloud Forest of Costa Rica, with creatures from the cloud forest attempting to get into an umbrella instead of into a mitten. She also illustrates books written by other authors.

shop to buy ice pops because they understand that John Henry has the same rights as Joe. Together, they overcome the barriers of racial prejudice. The text and Jerome Lagarrigue's impressionistic illustrations capture a lazy summer's day, and the close-up portraits reveal the boys' emotions. The friendship of the two boys is stronger than the community's fears of desegregation.

Didactic themes

Themes can also be stated didactically. Didacticism in literature is when the sole purpose of a story is to instruct. The characters, setting, and plot are usually flat, and readers do not need to ponder what the theme is because the theme is, so to speak, "in the reader's face." Sometimes a story's main purpose is for children from one culture to appreciate people who are different from them, or for children to learn to be kind or gentle or forgiving. If a theme is didactic, it overpowers the plot and characters. Quality literature does not have didactic themes.

Setting

There are two types of settings—*integral* and *backdrop*. In an integral setting, the setting affects the characters, plot, and/or theme, while a backdrop setting does not affect the characters, plot, or theme. For example, the swamp in *Possum Stew* (Cushman, 1990) could be anywhere in the world; however, the setting in *Possum Magic* (Fox, 1983) is integral because all the animals are Australian.

Either type of setting can create a mood for the story. For example, a story that begins during the middle of the night in a cold, dark, damp cellar sets a different mood than a story that begins during a bright summer day on the beach. Sometimes a setting is used as a symbol. As in many fairy tales, stories set in a dark forest symbolize evil and danger, while those set in a garden symbolize beauty and peace.

Integral settings

Illustrators often help children visualize integral settings. Jan Brett, in *The Umbrella* (2004), vividly illustrates the physical features of all the animals and the many shades of green of the rainforest, using watercolor and gouache. The setting

Laura Numeroff grew up in Brooklyn, New York, surrounded by art, music, and books. She has said that her favorite possessions included a box of 64 crayons and her library card. As a child, some of her favorite books included *Eloise* by Kay Thompson, *Stuart Little* by E. B. White, *The Cat in the Hat* by Dr. Seuss, and books by Beverly Cleary.

Her *If You Give a Mouse a Cookie, If You Give a Moose a Muffin, If You Give a Pig a Pancake,* and other books with the same premise are read by many children. Her books have worldwide appeal and have been translated into many languages. She now lives with her two cats and dog and writes from her home office. She loves many animals but does not number a mouse, pig, or moose among them.

begins on the end pages with creatures peeking through ferns and other foliage found in a rainforest. In Brett's *Daisy Comes Home* (2002) the adventure begins with an event characteristic of its setting, an open-air market in China. Daisy the chicken is stolen. Brett's insets and borders are set apart with bamboo. The illustrations of houses, baskets, clothing, chopsticks, boats, villages, and landscape all reflect Chinese culture. The story could not be set in the Rocky Mountains at an American supermarket.

Integral settings are important to the plot and theme, so their description must be accurate. These settings must be true to the time period and region. It is important, for instance, that Jerry Pinkney's realistic illustrations evoke the 1950s in McKissack's *Goin' Someplace Special* (2001). Since it is set in Nashville in the 1950s during the era of racial segregation, everything must match the decade, from Tricia Ann's clothes to the finned cars. His watercolors successfully capture the era.

Some integral settings in picture books can be symbolic; the pictures are not meant to portray a specific place but instead create a mood. Deep, dark forests are usually places where evil lurks. Flower gardens are usually places of happiness and peace. Blue skies with white fluffy clouds suggest carefree days.

With integral settings, teachers should take time to draw children's attention to the pictures so they learn about different places. Teachers should encourage children to ask questions about the objects (e.g., "Whites Only" signs in books set during segregation) and the clothing characters are wearing in the illustrations. If teachers do not know much about the period in question, they can show students how to find information by reading other books or searching the Internet.

Backdrop settings

A backdrop setting is unimportant to the plot. The text usually does not describe the setting; rather the illustrator often creates it. For example, Jan Brett's *Gingerbread Baby* (1999) could be set in any country. However, Brett's illustrations show readers that the setting is not in the United States, but in Switzerland. The fact that the illustrations place the tale in Switzerland is not important to the story itself, but it adds uniqueness to the book. However, consistency and accuracy are as important to a backdrop setting as to an integral setting. Brett makes sure that each scene from each page represents the Swiss culture so that the story's setting is consistent throughout the book.

Felicia Bond in Laura Numeroff's *If You Give a Mouse a Cookie* (1985), *If You Give a Moose a Muffin* (1991), *If You Give a Pig a Pancake* (1998), *If You Take a Pig to School* (2003), *If You Give a Bear a Brownie* (2006), and *If You Give a Pig a Party* (2006) creates a happy setting in each story by placing the animal in a home or school, where, at the beginning of the story, all is neat and orderly. The setting in each of these stories does not need to be in a certain time or place in order to be plausible. In *If You Give a Mouse a Cookie*, the story begins in front of a neatly painted house.

Point of View

In Chapter 1 we defined point of view as the perspective from which the story is told. For children in the early grades, point of view is not an easy concept to grasp because they tend to focus on the plot and the characters, with little concern for who is telling the story. To teach what is meant by point of view, teachers should choose a story that uses first person because the pronoun "I" is used, and teachers can discuss with children who the "I" refers to in the story. First person is the easiest point of view for children to grasp when teachers are attempting to explain what the concept means.

First-person point of view

First-person point of view is told from one character's viewpoint, and the pronoun "I" is used. Readers may see the actions and dialogue of other characters, but they only know the thoughts, feelings, and motives of the character telling the story. First-person point of view is often difficult for very young children because they think the "I" in the story refers to themselves. However, some stories using first person are more easily understood by children because the situation in the story reflects their feelings and experiences. For example, many children have experiences similar to those of the little girl in *Some Birthday* (Polacco, 1991), whose parents are separated, who lives with her dad during the summer, and who fears her dad has forgotten her birthday, the most important day of the year for many children. Before reading the story, teachers can ask the children, "Have you ever feared that your family will forget your birthday?" "What did you do when you thought they forgot?" After the discussion, the teacher can invite children to listen to the story about a little girl who thinks her dad has forgotten her birthday and decides to do something about it.

One first-person point of view story that has become a favorite of many children is Mercer Mayer's *There's a Nightmare in My Closet* (1968). Most young children can relate to the boy's experience of thinking there is a scary being in the closet. The story is told from the boy's perspective. Another book for young children that uses first-person narration is *My First Day at Nursery School* (Edwards, 2002). Many young children can relate to the little girl's experience as she tells about her first day of school; she wants her mother back as soon as her mother leaves. She then relates how the toys draw her into the classroom, and by the end of the day she does not want to go home.

Judy Blume's *The Pain and the Great One* (1974) is a great book to teach first-person point of view because the story begins with the big sister telling the story: "My brother's a pain"; the second half of the book is told from the little brother's point of view: "My sister thinks she's so great just because she's older . . ." (unpaged). Teachers can point out how the story is much more believable because the sister and brother are telling it. They can explain how different and less interesting it would be to hear the story told from the third person: "The big sister thought her brother was a pain because her parents thought the little brother could do no wrong."

One book for primary students that effectively uses first person is *Freedom Summer* (Wiles, 2001). Joe begins this story with "John Henry Waddell is my best friend." He then goes on to tell of John Henry and his excitement when the Civil Rights Act was enacted because now the two boys can go anywhere together. Joe attempts to tell how John Henry felt when they noticed that the shops that were once segregated were now boarded up. Wiles tells this story through the eyes of a child so that readers understand how the boys felt and how they dealt effectively with the situation instead of becoming angry at the injustice of the time.

Third-person point of view

Many authors use third person, indicated by the use of the pronouns he, she, and they, to create *omniscient, limited omniscient,* and *objective* points of view.

Omniscient point of view. In this point of view, the author is all-knowing and therefore has access to all the actions, thoughts, desires, needs, and motives of all the characters. In Audrey Wood's *Rude Giants* (1993), readers know the thoughts and actions of the rude giants, of Gerdy the cow, of Beatrix the butter maid, and those of the villagers:

> The rude giants were clumsy, loud, and selfish. They trampled the flowers, quarreled until the birds stopped singing, and stole whatever they wanted from whomever they please. What will those rude giants do next? The villagers wondered. (unpaged)

In Gary Soto's *Chato's Kitchen* (1995), readers know all the thoughts and actions of the two cats Chato and Novio Boy, the dog Chorizo, and the members of the mouse family. Readers know that conniving Chato and Novio Boy are trying to get the mouse family to their house for a tasty meal. Readers see the mice innocently accept the dinner invitation from their neighbors and then prepare food to take along. Chorizo happily agrees to accompany the mouse family to dinner. When the mice arrive on the dog's back—his belly "bumping over the thresh-hold"—readers see the terror in Chato's and Novio Boy's faces as they "scampered from under the table, and leaped up the curtains where they meowed for their lives" (unpaged).

Limited omniscient point of view. Sometimes the author reveals only the thoughts and motives of one or two characters and presents the secondary characters as flat. Kevin Henkes uses limited omniscient in *Chrysanthemum* (1991). When Victoria says to Chrysanthemum, "I just cannot believe your name," readers get to know Chrysanthemum's inner thoughts when Henkes writes: "'Neither can I,' thought Chrysanthemum miserably."

Mem Fox in *Hunwick's Egg* (2005) reveals only the thoughts and feelings of Hunwick, a bandicoot, who finds an egg and cares for it and loves it. Readers see the other desert creatures, but they do not know what the creatures really think of Hunwick, who unconditionally loves the egg, which is really only a stone.

Objective point of view. Perhaps the most popular point of view in picture book stories is the objective point of view, when the author reveals only the actions and dialogue of the characters, not their thoughts and feelings. The story is told as if a camera is running, focusing in on all the sets, characters, and actions—those things that are outwardly observable. Readers see characters acting and reacting in situations, but they do not know anything about the characters' thoughts. They only find out what a character thinks by what the characters say or do. They must make inferences about a character's motives, feelings, and personality through the character's actions and dialogue.

In picture books, it is often the illustrations, not the text, that reveal characters' moods through facial expressions and body language. For example, in *Shouting!* (Thomas, 2007), a story of an African American worship service in the 1950s, the text does not reveal the inner thoughts and feelings of the elated Mama and other worshipers. However, the illustrations reveal an exuberant congregation, choir, and pastor wearing brightly colored clothes, hats, and robes, with hands lifted high as they shout, "Yes," "Hallelujah," and "Amen." The way the hands are raised and bodies bent suggests the emotions of the congregation, but the text describes the scene in a straightforward way:

> Mama was there for Sunday
> She danced stretching out the circle

In the primary grades, teachers can talk about how the story is told and ask open-ended questions such as, "Did you like the story as Joe told it in *Freedom Summer?*" "Did you like it when the author let you know what everyone was thinking?" "Did you like it that you knew what the protagonist was thinking but the other characters did not know the protagonist's thoughts?"

Open-ended questions will help children realize that authors use a particular point of view for a reason. After discussing point of view, teachers can invite students to write a story using first person. Teachers may need to help them understand that they become the character when they use the first person pronoun "I."

Tone

Tone can be defined as the author's attitude toward the subject and the reader. As discussed earlier, a book's tone can be formal, informal, playful, somber, whimsical, ironic, humorous, mournful, or reflective. Tone is created implicitly through word choice, imagery, sentence structure, and illustrations. Both text and illustrations create tone.

The text and illustrations in *Mei-Mei Loves the Morning* (Holloway & Tsubakiyama, 1999) create a reflective, happy tone. The simple sentences reveal a grandchild's love of morning because of her routines with her grandfather. After he prepares her rice porridge, they feed a songbird, ride to the park on his bicycle with a birdcage swinging from the handlebars, and visit with their friends. The impressionistic illustrations are accurate scenes of an area in urban China. The colors in the illustrations are light and cheerful like the text. The text and illustrations reveal a happy time for Mei-Mei and her grandfather.

The tone in *Cook-a-Doodle-Doo!* (Stevens & Crummel, 1999) is playful and whimsical. From the jacket to the title page to the last page of the story, the illustrations are brilliantly colored, depicting expressive animal characters wearing potholders and pans for hats. The text is also playful. On the title page the measuring cup is not a Pyrex cup, but a T-REX measuring cup. The text begins on a light note with incomplete sentences and a rooster complaining about what most roosters would enjoy.

> Peck. Peck. Peck.
> "Always chicken feed! Day after day—year after year—I'm sick of it!" squawked Big Brown Rooster. "Can we get something new to eat around here? Please? Nobody's listening. What's a hungry rooster to do?"

Silly Sally (Wood, 1992) is a zany story about Silly Sally going to town, walking backwards and upside down in frilly petticoats and wild curly hair. Each of the animals she meets joins her in the upside down and backwards walk. Wood uses short rhyming lines to add to the light tone: "On the way she met a loon / a silly loon / they sang a tune" (unpaged). The bright yellow, orange, green, and purple of the illustrations add to the nonsensical mood of the story.

Tone can change in a story, and illustrations and color can signal the change. Patricia Polacco's tone shifts throughout *Luba and the Wren* (1999). The story begins with Luba living with her parents in a humble home. Luba was "full of joy and free from care as all children should be" (unpaged). When Luba frees a wren from a net, the wren grants her a wish, which her parents have her use to get them a bigger house. However, trouble brews when her parents become greedy and ask for more with each wish. The illustrations at the beginning of the story are brilliant red, blue, and green, they are pleasing because the story is happy. However, when Luba returns to the forest each time her parents demand a larger house, the forest becomes darker, almost all black. When Luba returns from the forest the last time, she sees that the wren granted her wish by returning her parents to the run-down dacha (a country cottage). The illustrations contribute to the changing tone, creating a story that begins happy, turns gloomy, and ends happy again. Other books by Polacco that also use color to create mood are *Thunder Cake* (1990), *When Lightning Comes in a Jar* (2002), and *Picnic at Mudsock Meadow* (1992). Since many primary-school children love to illustrate their own stories, teachers can point out how illustrators use color to complement the mood of the story. They can encourage them to do the same as they write and illustrate stories.

Style

Style is the way the author writes and how the author says things. It includes word choice, grammatical structure, and the use of such literary devices as rhyme, puns, assonance and alliteration, onomatopoeia, similes and metaphors, personification, and imagery. We discuss these aspects of style in the sections to follow.

Word choice

Because picture storybooks are short (approximately 32 pages) authors need to choose words wisely so that they create the desired mood. Authors choose verbs that convey the intended action, descriptive adjectives, and specific nouns that trigger accurate visual images in readers' minds. Laura E. Williams in *The Best Winds* (2006) uses vivid verbs, ellipsis, and different sentence lengths to capture the sight when the winds are finally perfect for flying the kite. "The winds caught the kite and lifted it high . . . higher . . . almost to the clouds. Suddenly the kite plummeted. It swerved and mumped. It dived and swirled" (unpaged). Notice how the ellipses gives the reader time to imagine the kite rising higher into the sky. The reader can then imagine the kite plummeting and swerving.

Another example of stylistic word choice is in Lloyd Alexander's *How the Cat Swallowed Thunder* (2000). Read the following two short excerpts from the book and visualize the scene. The underlining is added to show what words could be discussed with young readers to increase their vocabulary. Adults can also explain how authors choose vivid words to create a mental picture in the readers' minds. The questions in brackets are added to give some ideas of the types of questions to use to begin the discussion.

> "The *besodden* Cat [What do you think a besodden cat looks like?] *seized* [How is *seized* different from *take?*] a mop hanging behind the door and *plied* it *desperately.* [What do you think *plied* means? How could someone ply a mop *desperately?*] By the time he had finished *swabbing* and *wringing,* wringing and swabbing, [Can you show me how you would swab and wring and wring and swab?] he was puffing from his efforts. The floor, at last, was clean and spotless." (unpaged, emphasis added)

Authors choose particular words in order to create and develop the mood for the reader. The words Gary Soto chooses in *Chato's Kitchen* (1995) create a humorous mood. The words are so well chosen that readers could read it without the pictures and visualize images in their mind that might resemble Susan Guevara's illustrations. Soto describes Chato as low riding with a tail that swings to the rhythm of the scampering mice's feet. When Chato eyes the mice, his eyes become "shifty" and he "raked his tongue over his lips and meowed a deep growling meow" (unpaged). When reading this, teachers can stop and invite students to make shifty eyes and rake their tongues and to make deep growling meow noises. Taking time for students to impersonate the characters and mime the action helps them understand the meaning of these words and gets them more involved in the story.

Soto then describes Chato's friend Novio Boy as a friend with "soft green eyes, sleek fur, and the loveliest growl . . . who also wore the flashiest cut collar—a leather one with real gems that sparkled at night when cars passed in the street" (unpaged). Novio Boy's speech fits his description: "Yo! Cool Cat of East Lost Homes. Whatcha doin'?" (unpaged). Chorizo the dog is described as "a low-road scraping dog" whose belly bumped over Chato's threshold. Again teachers can invite children to impersonate a low-road scraping dog. By going back to these sections to have students dramatize them, teachers can discuss how vivid language makes the story more entertaining. After sharing this story, teachers can return to certain pages and talk about the words that Soto uses—*shivered, scampered, rattled*—and write them on a piece of posterboard entitled "Interesting Words to Use When Writing" and post it so all children can refer to it.

Patricia McKissack in *Precious and the Boo Hag* (2005) also chooses words that fit the humorous mood of the story. Precious' brother described Boo Hag this way: "She's tricky and she's scary, and she tries to make you disobey yo' mama . . . She aine too smart, got no manners, hates clean water, can change her shape, and tells whoppers" (unpaged). When Boo Hag appears the first time at

Precious's window, she has "eyes of burning cinder and hair that shot out like lightning" (unpaged). Notice how the dialect helps develop the character and how dialect makes the story more entertaining. Teachers may need to explain what dialect is by explaining that all of us have a certain way of pronouncing words that sound right to us, but our pronunciation may sound strange to English speakers from other cultures or other regions of the country. Teachers should take care not to make derogatory comments about any dialect.

A. J. Wood uses very different word choice in *The Little Penguin* (2001); his words paint a dreamy picture in readers' mind. The story begins, "Far away in a land where there is only ice and snow . . ." Later when Little Penguin hatches, Wood describes Little Penguin as one "covered in tiny soft feathers as gray as the mist that rolled in from the faraway sea" (unpaged).

After sharing a story with students, teachers should take the time to discuss the words the author used to describe settings, characters, and actions. They can discuss how the language paints pictures in readers' minds and creates a mood.

Grammatical structure

Young children do not need to hear only short, simple sentences. Quality literature, including many picture books, has sentences of varied length, with some *simple* and some *compound*. Compound sentences have at least two independent clauses connected by a coordinating conjunction like *and, but, for, nor, yet*. An independent clause is one that could stand by itself as a complete sentence. (By definition, a clause contains a subject and predicate.) A complex sentence is a group of words that has a dependent clause, or one which cannot stand by itself, and one independent clause. Other sentences are compound–complex. Judy Sierra in *Wild About Books* (2004) begins with a compound–complex sentence, followed by a compound sentence.

> It started the summer of 2002,
> when the Springfield librarian, Molly McGrew,
> by mistake drove her bookmobile into the zoo.
> Molly opened the door, and she let down the stair,
> turned on the computer, and sat in her chair. (unpaged)

The rest of the story, also in rhyme, consists of compound and complex sentences. To break up the text of longer sentences, Sierra includes one page in which the insects from the zoo are writing haiku. The illustrations are displayed like a scrapbook with each picture showing one insect and its haiku, while another insect is giving its response in a single word. One frame has a walking stick with this haiku: "A cannibal twig / Silently devours a leaf— / Eating, not eaten." The other insect's response is "Pretentious." The giant hissing cockroach writes: "Hiss hiss hiss hiss hiss— / Hiss hiss hiss hiss hiss hiss hiss— / Hiss hiss hiss hiss hiss." The other insect responds with one word: "Redundant."

Literary devices

A number of literary devices used by authors make the language of a story interesting by creating or enhancing a mood. Some of these devices include *similes* and *metaphors, personification, allusion, puns, hyperbole, assonance, allitera-*

tion, onomatopoeia, and *rhyme.* Beginning in the first grade, children can learn about these devices if the teacher teaches them one at a time as they read books with each device. Drawing attention to these devices can enrich the literacy lesson. Beginning in the second grade, teachers can encourage children to use these devices themselves as they write.

Similes and metaphors. Authors often use similes or metaphors to help readers relate the unknown to the known. A simile is a comparison where an author uses the words "like" or "as" to indicate the similarity between two items. Belle Yang's main character in *Hannah Is My Name* (2004) use similes throughout the story to create vivid pictures. She describes her family's first apartment in America as a "shiny building like a lime Popsicle" and her landlady's eyes look like cats' eyes. After Hannah's friend returns to Taiwan, Hannah says, "Now that she's gone, sometimes it feels like there is a big hole inside my chest" (unpaged). When the doorman from the hotel where her father works comes to warn them that immigration men are there to check for green cards, Hannah writes, "One afternoon there is a rat-tat-tat on the glass door, and my heart jumps like a frog inside my chest" (unpaged).

Patricia McKissack uses similes to enrich the text of *The Honest-to-Goodness Truth* (2000). After Libby lies to her mother about feeding and watering their horse Ol' Boss, Libby is surprised "at how easy the lie slid out of her mouth, like it was greased with warm butter" (unpaged). When her mother asks her the second time whether she has fed and watered Ol' Boss, "Libby's stomach felt like she'd swallowed a handful of chicken feathers" (unpaged). Patricia McKissack also uses similes in *Precious and the Boo Hag* (2005). McKissack explains that Boo Hag's hair "shot out like lightning" and her voice "rumbled like rolling thunder" (unpaged). Later in the story, Boo Hag looks like a runaway rainbow, and when given clean water to drink, "one eye went to spinning like a top . . . and her tongue rolled out like a scroll" (unpaged).

A metaphor, like a simile, makes a comparison between two seemingly unrelated items; however, the words "like" or "as" are not used. Patricia McKissack uses metaphor effectively in *Precious and the Boo Hag* (2005) when she describes Boo Hag's eyes of "burning cinder." In *Goin' Someplace Special* (2001), McKissack refers repeatedly to the public library as "a doorway to freedom."

Lloyd Alexander in *How the Cat Swallowed Thunder* (2000) creates vivid images in readers' minds through the use of simile and metaphor. The goose feather from a bed floats "upward like a cloud of dandelion puffs," and the feathers floating around are "snowflakes whirled in the air." When Mother Holly hears the sound of the popcorn in Cat's stomach, she says the noises are "like my bees gathering nectar on a summer afternoon"; later she says the sounds are "like my doves, cooing together in their nest" and "like my brook, bubbling over mossy stones" (unpaged).

After explaining similes and metaphors to primary students, teachers can encourage children to find examples of them in stories that they read and write them down on a strip of paper. They can write the name of the book on the one side and the simile on the other side. Teachers can use 1" x 12" strips of paper that can be fastened together to form round, interlocking chain links. The class can be challenged throughout the year to add to the chain so that by the end of the year it wraps around the room.

Personification. Personification is another literary device used by authors to create vivid pictures. Personification is giving something nonhuman (animal, inanimate object, or abstract idea) a human characteristic. Lloyd Moss in *Zin! Zin! Zin! A Violin* (1995) describes the bassoon as a "grumpy instrument" and the oboe as an instrument that "sobs and pleads."

Some authors use personification in a subtle way and only to make a special point. For example Helen Recorvits in *My Name Is Yoon* (2003) describes the characters of her Korean name as "symbols that dance together" (unpaged). When children view the Korean symbols of the name *Yoon*, they can readily see what the author is trying to explain: the Korean symbols do look more like stick people in action than the English letters that spell her name.

Personified animals are common in children's literature. Many authors choose to use animals as characters because young children are drawn to these characters. Rosemary Wells explains that she uses animals as characters because they "are broader in range—age, time, and place—than children are. They also can do things in pictures that children cannot. They can be slapstick and still real, rough and still funny, maudlin and still touching" (Wells, 2004, p. 2). Well's animal characters such as Max, Ruby, Timothy, and Charles take on human qualities.

Sometimes personification is present in the illustrations but not in the text. Reading the first page of *Franklin Is Messy* (Bourgeois, 1994), one would not know from the words alone that Franklin is a turtle: "Franklin could count forwards and backwards. He could zip zippers and button buttons. He could tie shoes and count by twos" (unpaged). It is the illustrations, not the text, that let readers know that Franklin is a turtle instead of a child.

Think of all the many children's books in which the animals take on all the attributes of humans. Beatrix Potter used rabbits, squirrels, frogs, mice, owls, and geese. Kevin Henkes uses mice in many of his books. Mem Fox uses possums. Robert McCloskey uses ducks. There are many others besides. In all of these books, animals talk, wear clothes, and have attitudes, feelings, and emotions. Readers almost forget that the characters are animals.

Allusion. Allusion is a figure of speech that makes a casual reference to a literary or historical figure or event. It is used to associate ideas or emotions in one work with another. For example, Patricia Polacco in *Aunt Chip and the Great Triple Creek Dam Affair* (1996) uses allusion when relating to *Hans Brinker and the Silver Skates* and *Moby Dick*, two favorite novels of Aunt Charlotte. Aunt Charlotte tells Eli stories about "the little kid in Holland who held back the sea by putting his thumb in the dike or his favorite story about a great white whale that lived in the deepest, darkest part of the ocean" (unpaged).

Janet Stevens and Susan Stevens Crummel allude to two famous Jack characters—Jack, of Jack and the beanstalk, and Jack-in-the-box in *Jackalope* (2003). Later in the book the jack rabbit alludes to Snow White when he asks the mirror,

Mirror, Mirror, cracked and small
Who's the fiercest one of all? (unpaged)

Another allusion in the story is a "god rabbit" that appears and can "turn pumpkins into carriages, frogs into princes, rags into gowns . . ." (unpaged)

author sketch

Janet Stevens was born in Dallas, Texas, and lived many different places as a child. She now lives in Boulder, Colorado. As a child, she loved to draw and practiced drawing animal characters until she was satisfied with them. Today, she loves to draw animals in hilarious human situations. Many of Stevens's characters are repeated across books. For example, Hare and Bear from *Tops and Bottoms* (1995) are also seen in *Jackalope* (2003). A funny lady with a yellow hat and rose tinted, purple-rimmed glasses and high heels shoes is the main character in *To Market, To Market* (1997), *Epossumon-das* (2002), *Why Epossumondas Has No Hair on His Tail* (2004), and *Plaidypus Lost* (2004). Stevens has said that she modeled the character on Coleen Salley, who wrote *Epossumondas* and *Why Epossumondas Has No Hair on His Tail*.

Janet has both written and illustrated some of her books. Many of her recent books have been co-written with her sister Susan Stevens Crummel. In *Jackalope* (2004) and *The Dish Ran Away with the Spoon* (2001), the sister coauthors create humor through puns and by alluding to other nursery rhyme characters.

In the hilarious book *And the Dish Ran Away with the Spoon* (2001), Stevens and Crummel allude to many different nursery rhymes. The nursery rhymes are embedded in the text, so children can discuss each one as it is alluded to in the text.

> "Hmmmm." Fork thought for a moment. "Let's see. A couple of lost sheep wandered by. . . . Four and twenty blackbirds flew over . . ."
>
> "The Three Bears live one mile east and Little Boy Blue's haystack is one mile west."
>
> "Yeah," Spider interrupted. "I have the same problem with Muffet. I try to be nice, get to know her, even sit down beside her. Then pffft! Gone. Every time." (unpaged)

The map that Cat draws, which takes up the entire double page, has the following characters' homes and landmarks drawn on it: Little Miss Muffet's home, Bo Peep's home, a school with lambs around it, Jack's beanstalk, Humpty Dumpty's Wall, Three Bears' house, and Little Boy Blue's haystack. All of these nursery rhymes are mentioned in the story.

Puns. A pun is a play on words based on the similarity of sounds in words with different meanings. Stevens uses puns throughout *Jackalope* (2003):

> "Having a bad hare day?"
> "Now lettuce see, you wished for fangs . . ."
> "I see you don't carrot all about me!"
> "Beets me!"
> "Oh, Jack, I knew you'd turnip!"
> "Hare today, gone tomorrow!"
> "You butternut come any closer or I'll squash you!" (unpaged)

A book for younger children that also uses puns is Lisa Wheeler's *Farmer Dale's Red Pickup Truck* (2004); an adult reader may need to stop and muse about the puns so children can appreciate the humor, too. At one point in the

147

story Farmer Dale announces that all the animals have to get out of the truck because they weigh too much for it. Each animal has a witty reply, such as these:

"I'll pitch in," sang Woolly Sheep. "I'll ra-a-a-m it with my head."
"Don't hog the fun," said Roly Pig (unpaged). [Adults may need to explain to children that rams are male sheep and *hog* is another word for *pig*.]

Janet Stevens and Susan Stevens Crummel use puns to create humor. In *Cook-a-Doodle-Do* (1999), Iguana pulls a petunia from the garden because "flour" is the first ingredient. To measure the flour, Iguana grabs a ruler. The entire book is full of puns, and the illustrations depict four busy creatures attempting to bake a shortcake. Finally, when the first cake is brought to the table, Iguana drops it and Potbellied Pig gobbles it up. The language and illustrations create a funny, playful story.

Hyperbole. Hyperbole is a figure of speech that uses exaggeration to heighten effect or provide humor. In humorous stories, authors may use hyperbole to exaggerate the action of characters. In *Library Lil* (1997) Suzanne Williams uses hyperbole in describing the strength of Lil when a motorcycle gang will not move their motorcycles:

Lil grinned. She flexed her skinny muscles. Then she stooped down, reaching under one of the motorcycles. Straightening, she suddenly hoisted the motorcycle with one hand and tossed it into the street. It cost her little more effort than flinging an apple core. (unpaged)

Elizabeth Kennedy uses hyperbole in *The Boy Who Was Raised by Librarians* (2007). When Melvin's bugs get loose in the library, the librarians quickly take care of them: "The bugs were retrieved, identified, classified and catalogued within twenty minutes" (unpaged). Children enjoy creating their own hyperbole. Teachers can draw a man with a beard and encourage children to write hyperbole on strips of paper and add them to the beard. Each piece of paper becomes a whisker, until the man has a hyperbolic beard. See Figure 5.5 for a sample.

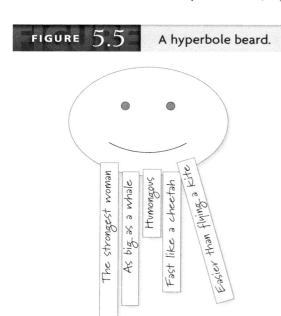

FIGURE 5.5   A hyperbole beard.

Onomatopoeia. Many young children love onomatopoeia: words that sound like what they mean. Many books for infants use onomatopoeia. David Kirk, in his board book *Miss Spider's New Car* (1999), uses it throughout. Some car noises heard in the book are *screech, growl, whine, squish, squash, Cha-Hiss, Va-Room, Ker-Plosh,* and *Ka-Boing.* Each of these words is in a different color to draw the reader's attention. Kirk also uses rhyme throughout the book:

This speedster's charged with steam
VA-ROOM—Slow down, I'm going to scream!
SQUISH, SQUASH! This snail car's much too slick.
KEER-PLOSH! Would froggy do the trick? (unpaged)

Children love to chime in with the onomatopoeic words, so teachers can reread the book, pausing whenever children can supply the words themselves.

Patricia Polacco in *Oh, Look!* (2004) also creates a whimsical tone through illustrations and the use of onomatopoeia. The goats' facial expressions, as they skip out of an unlocked gate, over a bridge, up a hill, through a pond, and beyond, are funny, exaggerated expressions. Her short sentences are filled with onomatopoeia. The gate "squeaks, squeaks, squeaks" as the goats charge through it. Their hooves "click, click, click" over the bridge. They "puff, puff, puff" as they attempt to climb the hill. They "swish, swish, swish" through the pond.

Sometimes authors use onomatopoeia to describe an event. For example, A. J. Wood in *The Little Penguin* (2001) wants children to imagine a penguin's hatching from an egg. She writes: "Suddenly a noise broke the snowy silence—a CRACK and a peep-peep-peep!" (unpaged). Because onomatopoeia words are often "noisy" words, young children enjoy repeating them. Drawing attention to words and repeating them makes reading time interactive.

Rhyme. We have talked about rhyme as it is used in poetry, but some authors use verse to tell a story in a picture book. Rhyme can enhance character and theme. Robert McCloskey, in *Make Way for Ducklings* (1941), gives each duckling a rhyming name in alphabetical order: Jack, Kack, Lack, Mack, Nack, Ouack, Pack, and Quack. The names fit the story because the ducklings walk in an orderly fashion, one after another. Richard Buckley tells a humorous story in *The Greedy Python* (1985) about a python eating everything in sight. The rhyme gives a sense of continuation, as the python continues to eat:

> when they [the swallowed animals] all begin to kick,
> The snake began to feel quite sick.
> He coughed the whole lot up again,
> Each one of them—and there were ten. (unpaged)

Still being greedy, the python begins to eat his own tail:

> He closed his jaws on his own rear,
> Then swallowed hard . . . and disappeared. (unpaged)

Sarah Stewart's poetry in *The Friend* (2004) gives the reader a sense of harmony, as Stewart writes about the strong friendship between a little girl named Belle and her housekeeper Bea. They do everything together.

> Seventh day of the week, Belle was always Bea's guest.
> They went to Bea's church, where Belle sang best.
> And Bea would say, on this most special day:
> "Hallelujah and glory be!
> I'm so lucky you're next to me." (unpaged)

Then one day when Belle ran after her ball that had bounced into the sea, Bea ran into the water to save Belle. This is how Stewart describes the bond between the two:

> Bea carried Belle toward the kitchen's warm stove
> And brought towels, hot chocolate, and cozy, clean clothes.
> Belle, all dry now, and in a safe place,
> Took another towel and dried Bea's face,
> And wanting, most of all, to cheer her up,
> Gave Bea a hug and filled up her cup. (unpaged)

In the last verse, notice how Stewart uses assonance (the short "o" in *hot* and *chocolate,* the long "o" in *stove* and *clothes,* the long "a" in *safe* and *place,* and the short "u" in *hug* and *up*) and alliteration ("cozy, clean clothes") and rhyme (*place / face, up / cup*) to give affinity to the words just as the text reveals an affinity between Belle and Bea.

Illustrations

Throughout this chapter we have made references to the ways that illustrations expand the story and complement the text. At a more basic level, illustrators must make sure that their artwork provides accurate visual information (e.g., a pink bow in a child's hair if the text states the bow is pink). Yet illustrators do much more than create a visual representation of the text. They are responsible for creating the mood of the story through color, tone, and line; for enhancing characterization by depicting facial expression and other body language; and for augmenting the plot. An illustrator takes an author's story and "clarifies and amplifies text, extending it beyond words or the reader's imagination" (Lukens, 2003, p. 44).

Creating Mood

Illustrations can create a mood for a story. Pastel colors often reflect peaceful, graceful, restful scenes or action. Bright colors often reflect happiness, bravery, or high energy. Dull tones like gray or shades of brown often reflect sadness, despair, or gloom.

Changing the colors in a book can indicate a change in mood. Don Wood in *The Napping House* (1984) begins with dark gray endpapers to suggest a dark rainy day. The opening pages have muted colors with white streaks of rain. There are no lights on in the house because everyone is sleeping. However, as a wakeful flea lands on a mouse and begins to wake everyone, Wood brightens up the color by adding some yellow. When the dog thumps a child, the right-hand page has yellow walls instead of the former blue walls. As granny wakes, all the walls are yellow; there is light outside and no more rain. The endpapers at the back of the book are blue instead of gray. Wood uses color to support the action in the story. Clement Hurd in *Goodnight, Moon* (Brown, 1947) illustrates the child's room with darker hues as night falls. David McPhail in *If You Were My Bunny* (McMullan, 1996) uses bright colors to show each animal in action with its mother, and uses dark nighttime shades for the picture that shows the mother singing a lullaby to her child.

Curvy lines and bright colors in illustrations help create a humorous and lighthearted mood. Don Wood, in *Jubal's Wish* (2000), has bright colorful pictures on pages in which Jubal is happy and exuberant; however, when he meets grumpy toadlets, the colors become darker and dull, and during a storm the two-page picture is dark, with grays and purples. Just by looking at the colors in the pictures students can tell the mood of the story on any give page. Patricia Polacco in *Aunt Chip and the Great Triple Creek Dam Affair* (1996) uses crooked houses, doorsteps, and books to set the lighthearted story of a town that no longer reads.

Janet Steven's backdrop setting for Anne Miranda's *To Market, To Market* (1997) uses some black and white photographs for the background and uses bright colors for dominant objects in the foreground. She places objects helter-skelter on the page that support the chaos of the plot and the humor of the story. Teachers and caregivers can discuss with children how the colors help create a mood. Some children may notice details such as color, while others may need to have adults point out such details.

Enhancing Characterization

The illustrations of quality picture books extend characterization by supporting and matching facial expressions and body language to the text. For example, in *The Art Lesson* (dePaola, 1989), the facial expressions of Tommy match his feelings as expressed in the text on each page. On the page that informs the readers that Tommy's favorite thing to do is draw, readers see Tommy lying on his stomach, resting his face on one hand and drawing with crayons with the other. He wears a very contented expression on his face (closed, happy eyes and a smile). Later on, readers see Tommy half tucked under the sheets, drawing on them. Again, his face shows contentment. Further on Tommy has a different expression when he is carrying home some artwork that he did in school. "If it was windy when Tommy carried his picture home, the paint blew right off the paper" (unpaged). Readers see Tommy's mouth twisted into a look of disgust, his cap flying off his head, the air full of leaves, and his body bent backwards as though the wind is blowing him over. DePaola's illustrations show the reader more about Tommy by depicting his emotions.

Augmenting Plot

In picture books, illustrations often times add suspense to the action; sometimes the suspense is not otherwise present in the text. For example, Marc Brown in *Arthur's Pet Business* (1990) creates tension in the pictures when Arthur promises to watch a neighbor's canary. Readers see Perky, a mean dog with sharp fangs, which Arthur is pet sitting, barking furiously at the canary. Arthur's facial expression indicates his fear for the canary. The text, however, merely states, "On Monday the MacMillans asked Arthur to watch their canary, Sunny" (unpaged).

Illustrations sometimes augment the plot by adding a secondary story line. For example, Kim Doner, an illustrator, depicts two stories throughout *Green Snake Ceremony*, written by Sherrin Watkins (1995). Watkins tells the story of a Shawnee custom of putting a green snake in a young girl's mouth to bring good luck and good health to her. Doner has painted two pictures on each spread. One depicts the story of Mary and her family attempting to locate a green snake for the ceremony, and the other depicts a green snake in his home, which is under the porch of Mary's house. To the reader, it appears that the dual action is happening simultaneously. For example, when Grandma Greyfeather is readying herself for the day, the green snake is also primping in front of a mirror with "Coil of Olay," "Head and Shoulderless Shampoo," and "Hissterin" mouthwash. The second set of illustrations is a wordless story by itself; it depicts how a snake feels when it realizes it will be caught and put into a girl's mouth.

Artistic Media and Techniques

Illustrators of children's literature use almost every medium in their artwork. In Chapter 1, we listed some of the media and techniques used by illustrators. Teachers can call attention to particular styles by showing children books illustrated by different artists using the same technique. Caldecott books are good for discussing medium and technique. Teachers can invite their students to create pictures using the same media and techniques. More information on the Caldecott Medal is on page 155. The author sketches throughout this chapter feature some of our favorite illustrators of children's books. They use a wide variety of artistic techniques and work in many different media. In the following sections, we discuss some media and techniques used to illustrate children's books.

Collage

Using tissue paper, construction paper, pictures from magazines, or even three-dimensional objects, an illustrator glues pieces of the chosen material on a background to create a collage. Some illustrators overlap pieces to create a unique effect. It is an

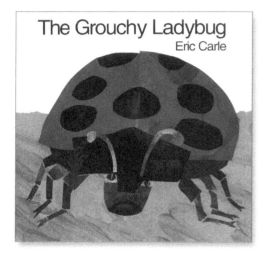

easy technique for teachers to teach young children, even as early as preschool. For example, a teacher can first discuss how Eric Carle uses tissue paper layers in *The Grouchy Ladybug* (1996) and *Pancakes, Pancakes* (1998). The teacher can demonstrate his technique by tearing red tissue paper into small pieces. He can then draw an outline of a ladybug and fill in the body with tissue paper pieces pasted with a glue stick. As a final touch the teacher can add legs and antenna with a black marker or glue segments of black pipe cleaner for a three-dimensional effect.

Lois Ehlert is another author who uses various objects to create collages in her books. After sharing *Snowballs* (1999), teachers can provide children with scraps of material—corn kernels, twigs, yarn, pasta, dried beans, and other objects—so they can create a winter scene or snowman. Lane Smith uses pictures found in magazines to create new pictures. Students can recreate this style by first looking at the illustrations in *Stinky Cheese Man and Other Fairly Stupid Tales* (Scieszka, 1992) and then using images torn from old magazines to create new pictures to illustrate their own stories.

Watercolor

Watercolor is a technique in which water-based paint is applied to paper in combination with water. This method of painting allows the artist to create a variety of styles and hues by controlling the amount of water. There are two ways to teach children how to use watercolors. The first way is the dry brush method in which a slightly damp brush dipped in pigment is dragged over dry paper. The second method is the washes method in which the paper is wetted and pigment is added by brushing across the sheet. This is another easy medium to use with young children. After discussing some of Marc Brown's "Arthur" books, a teacher can explain that Marc Brown uses watercolor to create his illustrations. First he draws the outline of his picture in pencil; he then adds watercolor. To demonstrate, the teacher can draw a picture of any object and show how to apply watercolor to the

Marc Brown grew up near Erie, Pennsylvania, and attended the Cleveland Institute of Art. He was a truck driver, cook, farmer, actor, television art director, and teacher before settling into the work of writing and illustrating children's books. He now lives in Hingham, Massachusetts, and Martha's Vineyard. He has pleasant memories of his grandmother Thora, who would take out her false teeth and tell him scary stories.

The idea for his famous character Arthur came to him as he was telling his young son Tolon a bedtime story about an aardvark. Most of his stories are about daily experiences that happened to him or one of his children. He has written and illustrated more that 20 Arthur adventure books. He later wrote stories about D. W., Arthur's little sister.

He has hidden his children's names in his books for them to find; some readers enjoy finding the hidden names themselves. He uses pen and ink and watercolor to illustrate his delightful books. Today he writes chapter books about Arthur. These are a great way to encourage young readers to read longer books. Arthur has also become a children's television program on PBS. Children can interact with Arthur at the character's PBS-sponsored website: http://pbskids.org/arthur.

paper without getting the paper too wet. Teachers can demonstrate how overlapping colors create new colors. Teachers should encourage students to draw the picture with pencil or marker first and then use watercolor to give it color.

Charcoal

Charcoal is the medium used by Kevin Henkes in *Kitten's First Full Moon* (2004). It is another medium that young children can use. Charcoal is made by burning selected woods in anaerobic (little or no oxygen) conditions. Charcoal is soft and tends to dust off paper. If artist charcoal is too expensive for the classroom budget, teachers can use colored chalk, which will provide a similar powdery appearance. Again, teachers need to demonstrate how to apply the charcoal or chalk to paper to achieve the desired effect.

Scratchboard

This technique involves etching into a piece of paper coated in black. Since scratchboards made with white China clay are rather expensive, the easiest way for young children to create scratchboard is to have them use markers to fill a piece of paper with many different colors. They then take a black crayon and totally cover the other colors with black. Using a bent paper clip or wooden skewer, they etch into the black to create their picture. The 2009 Caldecott winner *The House in the Night* (2008) by Susan Marie Swanson, and illustrated by Beth Krommes, uses this technique to illustrate the story of a young girl who walks around her cozy house at night, dreaming of flying around the world.

Paper pulp

Denise Fleming, an author and illustrator of young children's books, makes her own paper. Even though it is a process that takes a couple of days in order for the paper pulp to dry, it is a fun way to teach young children how to be resourceful by recycling paper scraps that would otherwise be discarded. Figure 5.6 has directions

FIGURE 5.6 Making paper.

MATERIALS NEEDED

- Any type of paper: newspaper, construction paper, paper towels, napkins, tissue paper, computer paper—any kind will do as long as it is not glossy.
- Sponge
- Window screen (called the "mold")
- Wood frames such as old picture frames (called "deckle")

- Plastic tub (large enough for frame to be immersed in)
- Blender (for pulping the paper)
- White felt or flannel fabric
- Staples or tacks for securing screen to frame
- Liquid starch (optional)

INSTRUCTIONS

1. Select the pieces of paper to be recycled. You can mix different types and colors to create your own unique paper.

2. Rip the paper into small bits, approximately one-inch squares, and put them in a blender (about half full). Fill the blender with warm water. Run the blender slowly at first, then increase the speed until the pulp looks smoothly blended (30 to 40 seconds).

3. The next step is to make the mold. The mold is made by stretching the window screen over the wooden picture frame and stapling or tacking screen to frame. It should be as taut as possible.

4. Fill the tub about halfway with water. Add three blender loads of pulp. The more pulp you add, the thicker the finished paper will be. Stir the mixture with your hands.

5. Stir two teaspoons of liquid starch into the pulp. This is not necessary if you are using the paper for artwork; however, if the paper is going to be used for writing, you should add some starch. The starch helps prevent ink from soaking into the paper fibers.

6. Submerge the mold in the tub of pulp, gently moving it from side to side to level off the pulp that collects on top of the screen.

7. Slowly lift the mold until it is above the level of the water. Wait until most of the water has drained from the mold. If the level of pulp is very thick, remove some pulp from the tub. If it is too thin, add more pulp and stir the mixture again.

8. When the mold stops dripping, place one edge on the side of the felt or flannel square. Lay the mold down flat, with the pulp directly on the fabric. Use a sponge to press out as much water as possible. Wring the excess water from the sponge back into the large plastic tub.

9. Now comes the tricky part. Hold the fabric square flat and slowly lift the edge of the mold. The wet sheet of paper should remain on the fabric. If it sticks to the mold, you may have pulled too fast or not pressed out enough water. It takes a little practice. You can gently press out any bubbles and loose edges at this point.

10. Repeat the steps above, and stack the fabric squares on a cookie sheet. Save one fabric square to place on the top of the stack to cover the last piece of paper. Use another cookie sheet to press the remaining water out of the stack. (Do this outside; it can make a mess.)

11. After you press the stack, gently separate the sheets. They can be dried by hanging them on a clothesline or laying them out on sheets of newspaper. When they have dried, peel them off the fabric and you have paper.

Resources

- www.pioneerthinking.com/makingpaper.html.
- http://hubpages.com/hub/How-to-Make-Paper (This website has a video in which an adult and child demonstrate each step of the process.)
- http://denisefleming.com/pages/papermaking.html (At this website Denise Fleming talks about her papermaking process.)

for making paper. Included also are the addresses of websites with additional information about paper making. After the paper is dry, children can use it to make collage pictures just as Denise Fleming has done in books such as *Buster Goes to Cowboy Camp* (2008) and *Sleepy, Oh So Sleepy* (2010).

Crosshatching

Crosshatching is usually done with pencil. One form of crosshatching is shading. To create shading, one moves a pencil back and forth down the paper. To create cross-hatching, one moves the pencil back and forth in several directions (vertically, horizontally, and diagonally). It is a technique that primary children with more developed motor skills can do. After discussing the illustrations in *Cloudy with a Chance of Meatballs* (Barrett, 1978), a teacher can demonstrate the technique by making an outline of a simple object such as an umbrella and filling it in with crosshatching.

Cutting techniques

Techniques such as paper cuts, woodcuts, and linoleum block cuts are not appropriate for young children because they require the use of blades or gouges. However, there are ways a teacher can demonstrate these techniques.

The teacher can demonstrate how David Wisniewski created his paper cuts for *Tough Cookie* (1999) by cutting out small pieces of paper with an Exacto blade and gluing them on top of one another. If the teacher would like to have children experiment with this technique, she can cut out pieces of paper in different colors and invite children to create a picture for their story.

To imitate woodcuts and linoleum cuts, a teacher can show students how to make a "potato stamp." Using a pencil, the teacher draws a simple picture on the surface of a potato cut in half, and then he chisels out the area outside the lines. The teacher then carefully dips the potato half into a shallow layer of black paint. The teacher or a student then stamps the image on a piece of paper. Once the paint has dried, the teacher or his students can fill in the outline with colored pencils.

Before reading further . . .

THE CALDECOTT MEDAL
The highest award given in the United States to an illustrator of a picture book is the Caldecott Medal. The award is named after Randolph Caldecott, a nineteenth-century illustrator. Each year since 1938 the Association for Library Service to Children, a division of the American Library Association (ALA) has awarded the medal to "the most distinguished picture book for children [preschool to 14 years] published in English in the United States" (ALA, 2005, p. 1 of 11). The award committee selects books based on the following criteria:

- Excellence of artistic technique
- Excellence of pictorial interpretation of plot, theme, or concept
- Excellence for using a style of illustration that complements the story, theme, or concept

A list of all Caldecott winners can be found on the ALA website: www.ala.org/ala/mgrps/divs/alsc/awardsgrants/bookmedia/caldecottmedal/caldecotthonors/caldecottmedal.cfm

Wordless Storybooks

We have been discussing books in which the text and the illustrations work together to tell a story. However, there are some picture books that tell a story solely through pictures or with only a few words to introduce the story. These books are called *wordless books*.

We introduced wordless books in Chapter 4, in the form of concept books that teach infants and toddlers about numbers, colors, shapes, and letters. However, there are many wordless books that portray stories; these books are appropriate for a wide range of young readers.

| FIGURE 5.7 | Creators of wordless books. |

Eric Carle	Leo Lionni	Raymond Briggs
Alexandra Day	John S. Goodall	Fernando Krahn
Peter Collington	Mercer Mayer	Eric Rohmann
Dieter Schubert	David Wiesner	Jacqueline Preiss Weitzman
Aliki	Ruth Carroll	Tomie dePaola
Pat Shories	Yoshikatsu Sugano	Nancy Tafuri
Paula Winter	Yutaka Sugita	Lena Anderson
Mitsumasa Anno	Peter Spier	Emily Arnold McCully
Brinton Turkle	Molly Bang	Quentin Blake

Websites that list wordless books:
   www.library.uiuc.edu/edx/wordless.htm
   www.weberpl.lib.ut.us/content/booklists/sort/t/31

These books help stimulate children's higher-level thinking because readers have to study each illustration to infer the story. Readers also need to supply dialogue if the illustrations suggest that characters are communicating (e.g., the detectives and townspeople in *Tuesday*, 1991, by David Wiesner). Some creators of wordless storybooks are listed in Figure 5.7 along with websites that provide more information about wordless books.

As teachers share wordless books, they can encourage children to look at the details of the pictures. Alexandra Day's *Good Dog, Carl* (1985), part of her Carl series, is a wonderful wordless book to share with toddlers because the characters are very young children and a beautiful Rottweiler named Carl. At the beginning of most Carl books, Mother leaves Carl in charge of the baby while she goes out. Once Mother is out of sight, Carl and the baby have mischievous fun! The humorous plots are easy to follow.

Emily Arnold McCully also has a series of wordless books for toddlers. Her series is about the adventures of a large mouse family. McCully's lush watercolors tell the entire story without words. In her books the adventure is always different. In *Picnic* (1984) the family is off in their truck to enjoy a family picnic in the woods. In *School* (1987), when all of Little Mouse's siblings leave for school, the house is so quiet that Little Mouse decides to go to school and slips into an empty desk at the back of the classroom. *New Baby* (1988) is a story about a family of mice welcoming a new baby to the family. Little Mouse feels left out and does not like all the attention the baby is receiving. However, when it begins to rain one day, Little Mouse gets to push the baby in the baby carriage back to the house. Feeling helpful, Little Mouse is no longer jealous of the baby.

Brinton Turkle's *Deep in the Forest* (1976) is another book that is easy for toddlers to follow. This is the reverse of the story of Goldilocks and the three bears. In this wordless book, a little bear walks into a human dwelling, where the bear finds three bowls of porridge, three chairs, and three beds. Young children who are familiar with the story of Goldilocks may recite lines from that story when they see the pictures in this book: "This porridge is too hot! This porridge is too cold! This porridge is just right!"

Two other books that are very easy for young children to follow are Tomie dePaola's *Pancakes for Breakfast* (1978) and Eric Rohmann's Caldecott winner *My Friend Rabbit* (2002). Adults can scaffold language learning by pointing to the details in the pictures and using a vocabulary that fits the story.

Many of John S. Goodall's wordless books are small, the right size for little hands. Most of his wordless books are adventures set in the 1800s. Many of the Victorian-era pictures are half pages so that the story changes as the half pages are turned. Some of his titles are *Naughty Nancy Goes to School* (1999), *The Midnight Adventure of Kelly, Dot and E. S. Meralda* (1999), *Story of a Main Street* (1987), and *Surprise Picnic* (1999).

Primary-school students will enjoy *The Flower Man* (Ludy, 2005) with its somewhat more challenging story line. The story begins with a scene of a dark, gloomy village with debris lining the streets. The only glimmer of light is cast on a little old man, who is carrying a suitcase and wearing a hat with a flower. Later, readers see the little man standing in front of a dilapidated house for sale. He buys the house and begins to restore the broken shutters. He plants flowers and gives them to the villagers. As he hands out the flowers, the pages become lighter, and readers begin to see happy villagers in a bright and clean village. Toward the end of the book, the old man leaves, finding his way to another dark, gloomy village. On the last page, readers see a little girl holding a flower that the old man has given her. She is in color and the man in the window is also in color. Teachers can use this book to elicit higher-level thinking because readers must make many inferences as they study the illustrations.

Wordless books are great sources for teachers to use the *language experience approach,* an activity in which children dictate a story to an adult, who acts as a scribe. The adult can write the text on sticky notes, which they can affix to the pages of a wordless book. Children can retell the story as they narrate it to the adult. After teachers model this type of storytelling, primary children can write their own stories on sticky notes. Some wordless books with challenging but appropriate plots for primary grades are *Where's My Monkey?* (Schubert, 1987), *Tuesday* (Wiesner, 1991), *Flotsam* (Wiesner, 2006), *The Bear and the Fly* (Winter, 1976), *Sidewalk Circus* (Fleischman & Hawkes, 2004), *Magpie Magic* (Wilson, 1999), and *My Friend Rabbit* (Rohmann, 2002).

teaching suggestions
SHARING PICTURE BOOKS

You can find a checklist of the traits of quality picture books in Appendix B.3, which you may use when selecting storybooks for use in the classroom. Once you have selected a book, there are many strategies to use when sharing the book with children. In addition to strategies we have already described, we explain some other strategies in sections to follow.

Print-Referencing Cues

Justice and Ezell (2004) suggest that when reading a book to emergent readers, an adult should use both verbal and nonverbal cues. One nonverbal cue is tracing the finger under the text while reading so that the child learns directionality (reading top to bottom, left to right). Another nonverbal cue is asking the child to point to the printed words on a page. This lets the adult determine whether the child knows the difference between print and illustrations. When the child is a little older, the adult can ask the child to find a particular word or a word repeated often in the story.

There are other cues adults can use: asking a child to find the title of the book on the cover or show the adult where to begin reading on a page. If the child gives an incorrect answer, the adult can model the correct response. For instance, the adult can find the first page, close the book again, and then ask the child to find it again. An adult might point to the word "I" on a page and ask the child to find another "I" on the same page. In all these interactions, the adult is engaging the child in the reading process.

Building Vocabulary

Beck, McKeown, and Kucan (2002) give a step-by-step strategy for helping children learn new words. This strategy can be used for both English-speaking children and English learners.

1. Choose three to five tier 1 words that are useful to children and write them on a board or on a flash card. Tier 1 words are ones that children recognize and know the common meaning of; however, these words have other meanings less familiar to children. For example, children may know what *cases* are, yet they may not understand the word when it appears in this context in *Creepy Crawlies:* "You often find cicada cases on the trunks of trees" (Davidson, 1991, p. 10).
2. Pronounce each word and ask the children to repeat it until they can pronounce it with ease.
3. Give a simple definition, using words they already know. The definition should relate to the word as it is used in the story.
4. Use the word in a context that differs from the story so they have a broader sense of the word's meaning.
5. Engage the children in using the word by having them say it to a classmate, define it in their own words, or use it in a sentence.
6. Have the children repeat the word again and praise them when you hear them use it in different context later on.

Four Types of Questioning to Use During Read-Alouds

Lane and Wright (2007) suggest four types of questions to use during a reading: *completion, recall, open-ended,* and *distancing (applied)*. A completion question should be used first. The adult begins a sentence and asks the child to complete it. For example, while reading the story of Little Red Riding Hood, the adult can begin: "When Little Red Riding Hood noticed Grandma's big eyes, Grandma said . . ." The second type of question is a recall question. Instead of beginning the sentence, the adult asks, "What did Grandma say when Little Red Riding Hood asked her about her big eyes?" An open-ended question requires higher-level thinking: "When Little Red Riding Hood first saw Grandma in bed, do you think she noticed that Grandma had fur on her face?" Finally, there are distancing questions.

In asking such a question, the adult is connecting the story to the child's life. Examples of distancing questions are the following: "Has your parent ever permitted you to walk to someone's house by yourself?" "If you were going to take a basket of food to your grandma or grandpa, what would you put in the basket?"

Using Puppets During and After Read-Alouds

Myers (2005) recommends using four puppets to engage children during and after read-alouds. The four puppets are Princess Storyteller, Clara Clarifier, Quincy Questioner, and The Wizard. Teachers can swap in a Prince Storyteller or a Clarence Clarifier puppet when needed. Four different children are given the puppets for each story. The Wizard is the one who predicts what will happen next in the story. The Princess Storyteller retells the story. Quincy Questioner asks factual questions, and Clara Clarifier asks critical thinking questions, or "why" questions. It is important that before the puppets are used, a teacher teaches children to preview a text so they can make predictions about a story and self-monitor their comprehension while they listen to the story. A teacher must also teach children how to summarize a story in the proper sequence, giving only the main points, not all the details. The teacher must also teach the children to listen carefully so they can answer factual questions, those for which answers are in the text, and open-ended questions, those for which they must think critically to answer. After the teacher teaches each of these important skills, she can give children opportunities to take a turn with the puppets.

Connecting with Math by Creating Bar Graphs

After sharing *Tikki Tikki Tembo* (Mosel, 2007) with the class, a teacher can invite students to make a class bar graph representing the number of syllables in their names. The number of syllables is plotted on the horizontal axis, and numbers one through 10 are plotted on the vertical axis. Each child states their full name (first, middle, and last) and the entire class repeats the name and claps out the number of syllables. Each student comes to the graph and colors in the square representing the number of syllables in his or her name. When all the students have done this, the class can see which bar is the highest.

Summarizing

Teaching young children to summarize stories is important. A teacher can use a white glove to teach children to be concise when retelling a story. Using an impermanent marker, so the glove can be washed often, the teacher writes one of the following words on each finger beginning with the thumb: *where/when, who, problem, main events,* and *resolution.* After reading a story together, the teacher slips on the glove, holds up her thumb and asks: "Where and when did the story take place?" The teacher should always require children to answer in complete sentences: "The story took place in a castle," not "a castle." The teacher then holds up the index finger and asks: "Who is (are) the main character(s)?" Again the teacher should require complete sentences from students. The teacher then holds up the middle finger and asks, "What was the main problem?" The teacher may need to coach children to be concise in stating the problem without also adding the main events. Usually the main problem can be stated in one sentence.

Holding up the fourth finger, the teacher asks children to list the main events in order. Again, the teacher may need to coach children to give main events only and to give them in order. Finally, the teacher holds up the last finger and asks the children how the problem was resolved.

After the teacher has demonstrated this strategy a number of times, she can invite a student to put on the glove and retell the story, using the fingers as prompts.

Conclusion

Quality picture storybooks may be short in the number of pages, but they have unity in all the literary elements, just as quality adult literature does—characters, setting, plot, theme, point of view, style, and figurative language (e.g., metaphor, onomatopoeia, alliteration). Many stories for toddlers and children in the primary grades have animals as characters. These characters may have all the qualities of human beings—emotions, feelings, needs, desires, and weaknesses. In picture books the illustrations tell much of the story and augment the text. Sometimes, with wordless books, the pictures say it all.

journeying WITH CHILDREN'S LITERATURE

1. Create a booklet (a three-ring binder works well) called "figures of speech found in fiction for young children." Create sections for simile and metaphor, personification, onomatopoeia, alliteration and assonance, and hyperbole. Add examples you come across in reading children's literature. When introducing children to these figures of speech, you will then have a list to illustrate the figures. To encourage children to be observant, have them create their own booklets.

2. Use the Internet to research different illustrators. Create a notebook that catalogs what medium or media they use and what style of art they produce.

3. Go to the websites of publishers that publish fiction picture books and find a list of their most recent publications. Go to a public library or a bookstore and read the books so that you can add them to any annotated list you have created.

4. Go to a public library and read the last 10 years of Caldecott Award and Honor books and Loretta Scott King's Picture Book Award books. Create an annotated bibliography of these award-winning books. Include in your annotations a description of the illustrations and some biographical information about the illustrators.

5. Select a number of your favorite books. Make a recording of yourself reading each one so that you have a listening library for your classroom.

6. Read the following article: Entenman, J., Murnen, T., & Hendricks, C., (2005/2006). Victims, bullies, and bystanders in K–2 literature. *The Reading Teacher, 59*(4), 352–364. It has a great matrix evaluating 25 picture books on the subject of bullying.

activities TO SHARE WITH CHILDREN

1. Read Jan Brett's *The Mitten* (1989) with preschool or kindergarten children. Review with them a number of times the order in which the animals enter the mitten. Create a "mitten" by draping a white sheet over some chairs so that there is a hole for the children to crawl into. Invite eight children to be animals (e.g., fox, bear). Reread the story and have the children crawl into the "mitten" when it is their turn.

2. Read a number of Tomie dePaola's books. End with *The Art Lesson* (1989), the one in which Tommy draws on a sheet. Purchase a cheap white cotton sheet. Divide the sheet into as many sections as you have children in your class. Assign the children a square and invite them to draw any picture they desire. Display the resulting mural in the classroom. Remind children that, while it is okay to paint on the classroom sheet, they should ask before drawing on sheets at home.

3. After sharing a number of Kevin Henkes' books, give children material to create a puppet for their favorite character. Provide white and brown paper lunch sacks, scraps of construction paper, yarn, pipe cleaners, crayons, markers, and glue sticks. Invite children to tell the story of the character as they play with their puppet.

4. Share Kim Doner's *Buffalo Dreams* (1999) with older primary students. In the back of the book, there are instructions on how to make one's own dream catcher. Provide the main materials—hoop, rawhide, waxed thread, beads, feathers and glue—and invite children to supply their favorite mementos. When the dream catchers are completed, have all the children explain what is special about the mementos they included in their dream catcher. Display them in the room.

5. After sharing a number of Eric Carle books, give each child a shoebox and other materials to create a diorama. Explain that it must be clear to all viewers what book it represents.

6. Have older primary students select their favorite picture storybook. Have them practice reading it with expression. When they are practiced, create a recording of each child reading aloud. Invite students to make a decorative jacket (a piece of paper folded like an envelope) to hold the CD or tape. The jacket should have the book's title, author, illustrator, and the reader's name. You may give these recordings to a preschool or a kindergarten class.

our favorite CHILDREN'S BOOKS

Brett, J. (2005). *Honey . . . Honey . . . Lion!* New York: Putnam Juvenile.

This story is based on a legend of the honey guide. An African bird, the honey guide leads animals to a honeycomb. However, one time a greedy badger does not share the honey with the honey guide, so the honey guide leads the greedy badger not to a honeycomb, but to the lair of a lion. Children lift a flap to find the lions hiding in the lair.

Carle, E. (2005). *10 Little Rubber Ducks*. New York: HarperCollins.

This story tells of the journey of rubber ducks from the factory assembly line to the freighter that will carry them to many countries. Ten of the rubber ducks fall off the freighter and go in every direction. The tenth one meets a real mother duck with her ducklings. Each of the ducklings says good-night with a "quack," but the rubber duck says, "squeak." Children can press the last page to hear the squeak.

Crummel, S. S., & Stevens, J. (2005). *The Great Fuzz Frenzy*. Harcourt Children's Books.

Violet the dog drops a green tennis ball down a prairie dog hole. At first the little prairie dogs are afraid, but soon they discover the ball's green fuzz. Big Bark tries to get the little prairie dogs to stop playing with the ball. He is unsuccessful until all the fuzz has come off the ball. He then declares that he is king of the fuzz. However, when an eagle comes swooping down on Big Bark, the little dogs come to his rescue. Like Crummel and Steven's *Tops and Bottoms* (1995), this book is laid out vertically to give depth to the hole.

Ehlert, L. (2001). *Waiting for Wings*. Harcourt Brace.

This is a book written in rhyme that details where the many eggs are resting before they hatch into butterflies. Readers learn about the life cycle of a butterfly. Like all of Ehlert's books, this one is illustrated with brightly colored paper collages.

McKissack, P. (2000). *The Honest-to-Goodness Truth*. Illus. Giselle Potter. New York: Aladdin.

Little Libby has been told always to tell the truth. However, when she announces in Sunday school that her best friend has a hole in her sock and later tells her neighbor that her yard looks like a jungle, her mother explains that sometimes it is better not to tell the truth.

Polacco, P. (2005). *Emma Kate*. New York: Philomel.

Emma Kate has an imaginary friend who goes and does everything with her. They go to school together, eat lots of pink ice cream, and even have their tonsils taken out together. A twist at the ending of the story will make readers laugh.

Say, A. (1999). *Tea with Milk*. Houghton Mifflin/Walter Lorraine Books.

May, a Japanese American, returns to Japan with her parents. May must repeat her high school education so that she can learn fluent Japanese. She must also learn how to be a proper lady in Japan. One of the things she must learn is to drink green tea instead of tea with milk. Readers learn as much through Say's watercolor illustrations as through his carefully chosen text.

Shannon, D. (2004). *Alice the Fairy*. New York: Blue Sky Press.

Alice is a delightful little girl who dresses up like a fairy and takes on a fairy's magical ways. Some of her magic includes making her white dress red, turning her oatmeal into cake by adding lots of "fairy dust" (sugar), and turning her dad into a horse—i.e., he gets on all fours and gives her a horseback ride. The text is simple, and the illustrations convey much of the story. The abstract pictures add to the humor.

Woodson, J. (2001). *The Other Side.* Illus. E. B. Lewis. New York: Juvenile.

> Clover, an African American girl, and Anne, a white girl, have been told by their mothers that they may not cross the fence and play with each other. Throughout the summer, each girl watches the other play. One day Anne sits on the fence; when Clover comes over with her friends, Anne invites them to sit on the fence with her. They were, after all, told not to cross the fence, but were never told they could not sit on the fence together.

children's literature IN THIS CHAPTER

Alexander, L. (2000). *How the cat swallowed thunder.* Illus. J. B. Schachner. New York: Puffin Books.

Barrett, J. (1978). *Cloudy with a chance of meatballs.* Illus. R. Barrett. New York: Aladdin.

Beard, D. B. (1999). *Twister.* Illus. N. Carpenter. New York: MacMillan.

Beaumont, K. (2008). *Doggone dogs!* Illus. D. Catrow. New York: Dial.

Bemelmans, J. M. (2008). *Madeline and the cats of Rome.* New York: Viking Juvenile.

Blume, J. (1974). *The pain and the great one.* Illus. I. Trivas. New York: Random House.

Boelts, M. (1994). *Dry days, wet nights.* Illus. K. Parkinson. Morton Grove, IL: Albert Whitman & Co.

Boelts, M. (1999). *Little Bunny's pacifier plan.* Illus. K. Parkinson. Morton Grove, IL: Albert Whitman & Co.

Bottner, B. (1996). *Nana Hannah's piano.* Illus. D. C. Bluthenthal. New York: Putnam.

Brett, J. (1981). *Fritz and the beautiful horses.* New York: Houghton Mifflin.

Brett, J. (1989). *The mitten.* New York: Putnam.

Brett, J. (1999). *Gingerbread baby.* New York: Putnam.

Brett, J. (2000). *Hedgie's surprise.* New York: Putnam.

Brett, J. (2002). *Daisy comes home.* New York: Putnam.

Brett, J. (2004). *The umbrella.* New York: Putnam.

Brown, M. W. (1942). *The runaway bunny.* New York: HarperCollins.

Brown, M. W. (1947). *Goodnight, moon.* Illus. C. Hurd. New York: HarperCollins.

Brown, M. (1990). *Arthur's pet business.* Boston: Little, Brown.

Buckley, R. (1985). *The greedy python.* Illus. E. Carle. New York: Simon & Schuster.

Bunting, E. (1994). *Smokey night.* Illus. D. Diaz. Orlando: Harcourt Brace.

Carle, E. (1996). *The grouchy ladybug.* New York: HarperCollins.

Carle, E. (1998). *Pancakes, pancakes.* New York: Aladdin.

Carlson, N. (2008). *Henry and the valentine surprise.* New York: Viking Juvenile.

Cole, R. (2004). *The story of Ruby Bridges.* Illus. G. Ford. New York: Scholastic.

Coleman, E. (1999). *White socks only.* Illus. T. Geter. New York: Albert Whitman & Co.

Cooper, F. (2008). *Willie and the all-stars.* New York: Philomel.

Creech, S. (2001). *A fine, fine school.* Illus. H. Bliss. New York: HarperCollins.

Cushman, D. (1990). *Possum stew.* New York: Dutton.

Davidson, A. (1991). *Creepy crawlies.* Photography by G. Meadows. Scarborough, Ontario: Prentice Hall Ginn.

Day, A. (1985). *Good dog, Carl.* New York: Aladdin.

Day, A. (1991). *Carl's afternoon in the park.* New York: Simon & Schuster Books for Young Readers.

dePaola, T. (1975). *Strega Nona.* New York: Simon & Schuster Books.

dePaola, T. (1978). *Pancakes for breakfast.* San Diego: Harcourt Brace.

dePaola, T. (1979). *Oliver Button is a sissy.* New York: Trumpet Club.

dePaola, T. (1989). *The art lesson.* New York: Trumpet Club.

dePaola, T. (1993). *Tom.* New York: Putnam Juvenile Books.

dePaola, T. (1996). *The baby sister.* New York: Scholastic.

dePaola, T. (2005). *Stagestruck.* Tomie dePaola. New York: Puffin.

diCammillo, K. (2008). *Louise, the adventure of a chicken.* Illus. H. Bliss. New York: HarperCollins.

DiPucchio, K. (2008). *Grace for president.* Illus. L. Pham. New York: Hyperion.

Doner, K. (1999). *Buffalo dreams.* Portland, OR: West Wind Press.

Edwards, B. (2002). *My first day at nursery school.* Illus. A. Flintoft. New York: Bloomsbury Books.

Ehlert, L. (1999). *Snowballs*. Orlando: Harcourt Brace.

Ehlert, L. (2001). *Waiting for wings*. San Diego: Harcourt Brace.

Falconer, I. (2000). *Olivia*. New York: Atheneum Books for Young Readers.

Fleischman, P., & Hawkes, K. (2003). *Sidewalk circus*. Cambridge, MA: Candlewick Press.

Fleming, D. (1994). *Barnyard banter*. New York: Henry Holt.

Fleming, D. (2003). *Buster*. Orlando: Harcourt Brace.

Fleming, D. (2007). *Beetle bop*. Orlando: Harcourt Brace.

Fleming, D. (2008). *Buster goes to cowboy camp*. New York: Henry Holt.

Fleming, D. (2010). *Sleepy, oh so sleepy*. New York: Henry Holt.

Fox, M. (1983). *Possum magic*. Illus. J. Vivas. San Diego: Gulliver.

Fox, M. (1984). *Wilfrid Gordon*. Illus. J. Vivas. New York: Scholastic.

Fox, M. (1988). *Koala Lou*. Illus. P. Lofts. New York: Trumpet Club.

Fox, M. (1992). *Night noises*. Illus. T. Denton. San Diego: Voyager Books.

Fox, M. (2005). *Hunwick's egg*. Illus. P. Lofts. San Diego: Harcourt Children's Books.

Giovanni, N. (2007). *Rosa*. Illus. B. Collier. New York: Square Fish.

Gliori, D. (1995). *The snow lambs*. New York: Scholastic.

Goodall, J. (1987). *Story of Main Street*. New York: Margaret K. McElderry Books.

Goodall, J. (1999). *Surprise picnic*. Margaret K. McElderry Books.

Goodall, J. (1999). *Naughty Nancy goes to school*. Margaret K. McElderry Books.

Goodall, J. (1999). *The midnight adventure of Kelly, Dot and E. S. Meralda*. Margaret K. McElderry Books.

Guarino, D. (1989). *Is your mama a llama?* Illus. S. Kellogg. New York: Scholastic.

Henkes, K. (1990). *Julius: The baby of the world*. New York: Scholastic.

Henkes, K. (1991). *Chrysanthemum*. New York: Trumpet Club.

Henkes, K. (1996). *Lilly's purple plastic purse*. New York: Greenwillow Books.

Henkes, K. (1997). *Chester's way*. New York: HarperCollins.

Henkes, K. (2000). *Wemberly worried*. New York: Greenwillow Books.

Henkes, K. (2004). *Kitten's first full moon*. New York: Greenwillow Books.

Henkes, K. (2006). *Lilly's big day*. New York: Greenwillow Books.

Hesse, K. (1999). *Come on, rain*. Illus. J. Muth. New York: Scholastic.

Hoffman, M. (1991). *Amazing Grace*. Illus. C. Binch. New York: Scholastic.

Holloway-Tsubakiyama, M. (1999). *Mei-Mei loves the morning*. Illus. C. Van Wright & Y. Hu. Park Ridge, IL: Albert Whitman & Co.

Hopkinson, D. (2008). *Abe Lincoln crosses a creek*. Illus. J. Hendrix. New York: Schwartz & Wade.

Hutts Aston, D. (2008). *The moon over star*. New York: Dial.

Jeffers, S. (2008). *My Chincoteague pony*. New York: Hyperion.

Jenkins, E. (2008). *The little bit scary people*. Illus. A. Boiger. New York: Hyperion.

Johnson, A. (1989). *Tell me a story, mama*. Illus. D. Soman. New York: Scholastic.

Joosse, B. (1991). *Mama, do you love me?* Illus. B. Lavallee. San Francisco: Chronicle Books.

Juster, N. (2005). *The hello, good-bye window*. Illus. C. Raschka. New York: Hyperion.

Kajikawa, K. (2009). *Tsunami!* Illus. E. Young. New York: Philomel.

Kennedy, E. (2007). *The boy who was raised by librarians*. Illus. B. Sneed. New York: Peachtree.

Kerr, J. (2002). *The other goose*. New York: HarperCollins.

Kinerk, R. (2003). *Clorinda*. Illus. S. Kellogg. New York: Aladdin Paperbacks.

Kirk, D. (1999). *Miss Spider's new car*. New York: Scholastic.

Lamb, A. (2006). *Sam's winter hat*. Illus. D. McPhail. New York: Scholastic.

Lasky, K. (1995). *She's wearing a dead bird on her head!* Illus. D. Catrow. New York: Hyperion Paperbacks for Children.

Lee, M. (2001). *Earthquake*. Illus. Y. Choi. New York: Frances Foster Books/Farrar, Straus and Giroux.

Lindbergh, R. (1990). *The day the goose got loose*. Illus. S. Kellogg. New York: Puffin.

Low, A. (1983). *The popcorn shop*. Illus. P. Hammel. New York: Scholastic.

Ludy, M. (2005). *The flower man*. Windsor, CO: Green Pastures Publishing.

MacDonald, M. R. (1995). *The old woman who lived in a vinegar bottle*. Little Rock: August House.

Marciano, J. B. (2008). *Madeline and the cats of Rome*. New York: Penguin.

Mayer, M. (1968). *There's a nightmare in my closet.* New York: Puffin.

McBratney, S. (1994). *Guess how much I love you.* Illus. A. Jeram. Cambridge, MA: Candlewick Press.

McCloskey, R. (1941). *Make way for duckling.* New York: Puffin.

McCully, E. A. (1984). *Picnic.* New York: HarperCollins.

McCully, E. A. (1987). *Space school.* New York: HarperCollins.

McCully, E. A. (1988). New Baby. Illus. New York: HarperCollins.

McCully, E. A. (1991). *Mirette on the high wire.* Illus. E. A. McCully. New York: GP Putnam's Sons.

McGovern, A. (1967). *Too much noise.* Illus. S. Taback. New York: Trumpet Club.

McKissack, P. (1986). *Flossie and the fox.* Illus. R. Isadora. New York: Penguin.

McKissack, P. (2000). *The honest-to-goodness truth.* Illus. G. Potter. New York: Aladdin.

McKissack, P. (2001). *Goin' someplace special.* Illus. J. Pinkney. New York: Atheneum.

McKissack, P. (2005). *Precious and the Boo Hag.* Illus. O. J. Mass. New York: Anne Schwartz Books.

McMullan, K. (1996). *If you were my bunny.* Illus. D. McPhail. New York: Scholastic.

McPhail, D. (1988). *Something special.* Boston: Little, Brown.

Miles, M. (1971). *Annie and the old one.* Illus. P. Parnall. New York: Trumpet Club.

Milne, A. A. (2001). *Winnie-the-Pooh and friends.* New York: Trustees of the Pooh Properties.

Miranda, A. (1997). *To market, to market.* Illus. J. Stevens. San Diego: Harcourt Brace.

Mitton, T. (2001). *Down by the cool of the pool.* Illus. G. Parker-Rees. New York: Scholastic.

Mosel, A. (2007). *Tikki tikki tembo.* Illus. B. Lent. New York: Henry Holt.

Moss, L. (1995). *Zin! Zin! Zin! A violin.* Illus. M. Priceman. New York: Scholastic.

Numeroff, L. (1985). *If you give a mouse a cookie.* Illus. F. Bond. New York: HarperCollins.

Numeroff, L. (1991). *If you give a moose a muffin.* Illus. F. Bond. New York: HarperCollins.

Numeroff, L. (1998). *If you give a pig a pancake.* Illus. F. Bond. New York: HarperCollins.

Numeroff, L. (2003). *If you take a pig to school.* Illus. F. Bond. New York: HarperCollins.

Numeroff, L. (2006). *If you give a pig a party.* Illus. F. Bond. New York: HarperCollins.

Numeroff, L. (2006). *If you give a bear a brownie.* Illus. F. Bond. New York: HarperCollins.

O'Connor, J. (2008). *Fancy Nancy: Poison ivy expert.* Illus. R. Preiss Glasser & T. Enik. New York: HarperCollins.

Perez, K. (2002). *First day in grapes.* Illus. R. Casilla. New York: Lee & Low Books.

Perez, K. (2002). *My diary from here to there.* Illus. M. C. Gonzalez. New York: Children's Press.

Pfister, M. (1997). *Hopper's treetop adventure.* Trans. R. Lannong. New York: Scholastic.

Pfister, M. (1999). *Rainbow fish and the big blue whale.* New York: North-South Books.

Polacco, P. (1990). *Thunder cake.* New York: Putnam & Grosset Group.

Polacco, P. (1991). *Some birthday.* New York: Simon & Schuster.

Polacco, P. (1992). *Picnic at mudsock meadow.* New York: Putnam Juvenile.

Polacco, P. (1996). *Aunt Chip and the great Triple Creek Dam affair.* New York: Philomel.

Polacco, P. (1999). *Luba and the wren.* New York: Philomel.

Polacco, P. (2001). *The keeping quilt.* New York: Aladdin.

Polacco, P. (2002). *Luba's wren.* New York: Putnam Juvenile.

Polacco, P. (2002). *When lightning comes in a jar.* New York: Philomel.

Polacco, P. (2004). *Oh, look!* New York: Philomel.

Polacco, P. (2007). *Ginger and Petunia.* New York: Philomel.

Potter, B. (1902). *The tale of Peter Rabbit.* New York: Fredrick Warne.

Rappaport, D. (2005). *The school is not white.* Illus. C. James. New York: Hyperion.

Recorvits, H. (2003). *My name is Yoon.* Illus. G. Swiatkowska. New York: Farrar, Straus and Giroux.

Rohmann, E. (2002). *My friend rabbit.* Brookfield, CT: Roaring Books Press.

Rylant, C. (2002). *Little Whistle's medicine.* Illus. T. Bowers. Orlando: Harcourt.

Rylant, C. (2002). *The ticky-tacky doll.* Illus. H. Stevenson. San Diego: Harcourt.

Salley, C. (2002). *Epossumondas.* Illus. J. Stevens. San Diego: Harcourt.

Salley, C. (2004). *Why Epossumondas has no hair on his tail.* Illus. J. Stevens. San Diego: Harcourt.

Salley, C. (2006). *Epossumondas saves the day.* Illus. J. Stevens. Orlando: Harcourt.

Say, A. (1996). *Emma's rug.* Boston: Houghton Mifflin.

Say, A. (1997). *Allison.* Boston: Houghton Mifflin.

Schachner, J. (2008). *Skippyjon Jones in mummy trouble.* New York: Puffin.

Schubert, D. (1987). *Where's my monkey?* Honesdale, PA: Front Street.

Scieszka, J. (1992). *The stinky cheese man and other fairly stupid tales.* Illus. L. Smith. New York: Viking.

Sendak, M. (1963). *Where the wild things are.* New York: HarperTrophy.

Seuss, Dr. (1974). *There's a wocket in my pocket.* New York: Random House for Young Readers.

Seuss, Dr. (1985). *Cat in the hat.* New York: Random House.

Shannon, D. (1998). *A bad case of stripes.* New York: Blue Sky Press.

Shannon, D. (1999). *Alice the fairy.* San Diego: Blue Sky Press.

Shannon, D. (2000). *The rain came down.* New York: Blue Sky Press.

Shannon, D. (2008). *Too many toys.* New York: Blue Sky Press.

Sheth, K. (2008). *Monsoon afternoon.* Illus. Y. Jaeggi. Atlanta: Peachtree.

Sheth, K. (2008). *My Dadima wears a sari.* Illus. Y. Jaeggi. Atlanta: Peachtree.

Sierra, J. (2004). *Wild about books.* Illus. M. Brown. New York: Knopf Books for Young Readers.

Soto, G. (1995). *Chato's kitchen.* Illus. S. Guevara. San Diego: Weston Woods.

Spiro, R. (2008). *Lester Fizz, bubble-gum artist.* Illus. T. Wiekstrom. New York: Dutton Juvenile.

Stevens, J. (1995). *Tops and bottoms.* San Diego: Harcourt.

Stevens, J., & Crummel, S. S. (1999). *Cook-a-doodle-doo!* San Diego: Harcourt.

Stevens, J., & Crummel, S. S. (2001). *And the dish ran away with the spoon.* San Diego: Harcourt.

Stevens, J., & Crummel, S. S. (2003). *Jackalope.* San Diego: Harcourt.

Stevens, J., & Crummel, S. S. (2004). *Plaidypus lost.* New York: Holiday House.

Stevens, J., & Crummel, S. S. (2008). *Help me, Mr. Mutt!* Orlando: Harcourt.

Stewart, S. (2004). *The friend.* Illus. D. Small. New York: Farrar, Straus and Giroux.

Swanson, S. M. (2008). *The house in the night.* Illus. B. Krommes. New York: Houghton Mifflin.

Thomas, J. C. (2007). *Shouting!* New York: Hyperion Books for Children.

Thompson, K. (1969). *Eloise.* Illus. H. Knight. New York: Simon & Schuster.

Turkle, B. (1976). *Deep in the forest.* New York: A Puffin Unicorn.

Van Allsburg, C. (1982). *Ben's dream.* New York: Houghton Mifflin.

Van Allsburg, C. (1995). *Bad day at Riverbend.* New York: Houghton Mifflin.

Viorst, J. (1972). *Alexander and the terrible, horrible, no good, very bad day.* New York: Aladdin.

Waddell, M. (1988). *Can't you sleep, Little Bear?* Illus. B. Firth. Cambridge, MA: Candlewick Press.

Waddell, M. (2005). *Sailor boy.* Illus. V. Austin. New York: Walker Books.

Watkins, S. (1995). *Green snake ceremony.* Illus. K. Doner. Tulsa: Council Oak Books.

Wells, R. (1995). *Max and Ruby's Midas.* New York: Dial.

Wells, R. (2000). *Timothy goes to school.* New York: Puffin.

Wheeler, L. (2004). *Farmer Dale's red pickup truck.* Illus. I. Bates. San Diego: Voyager.

White, E. B. (1973). *Stuart Little.* Illus. G. Williams. New York: HarperCollins.

Whitehead, K. (2008). *Art from her heart.* Illus. S. Evans. New York: Putnam Juvenile.

Wiesner, D. (1991). *Tuesday.* New York: Clarion.

Wiesner, D. (2006). *Flotsam.* New York: Clarion.

Wild, M. (1999). *Rosie and Tortoise.* Illus. R. Brooks. New York: DK Publishing.

Wiles, D. (2001). *Freedom summer.* Illus. J. Lagarrigue. New York: Aladdin.

Willems, M. (2004). *Knuffle Bunny.* New York: Scholastic.

Willems, M. (2008). *Naked mole rat gets dressed.* New York: Hyperion.

Willems, M. (2008). *The pigeon wants a puppy!* New York: Hyperion.

Williams, L. (2006). *The best wind.* Illus. E. Neilan. Honesdale, PA: Boyds Mills Press.

Williams, S. (1997). *Library Lil.* Illus. S. Kellogg. New York: Dial Books for Young Readers.

Wilson, A. (1999). *Magpie magic.* New York: Dial.

Winter, P. (1976). *The bear and the fly.* New York: Knopf Books.

Wisniewski, D. (1999). *Tough cookie.* New York: Lothrop, Lee & Shepard.

Wood, A. (1984). *The napping house.* Illus. D. Wood. San Diego: Harcourt Brace Jovanovich.

Wood. A. (1992). *Silly Sally.* New York: Scholastic.

Wood, A. (1993). *Rude giants.* New York: Scholastic.

Wood, A. J. (2001). *The little penguin.* Illus. S. Boey. New York: Penguin.

Wood, A. (2002). *Jubal's wish.* Illus. D. Wood. San Diego: Blue Sky Press.

Woodson, J. (2001). *The other side.* Illus. E. B. Lewis. New York: Putnam Juvenile.

Yang, B. (2004). *Hannah is my name.* Cambridge, MA: Candlewick.

Traditional and Modern Fantasy

Sharing Literature: AN EXAMPLE

Mr. Jonas teaches second grade. This week he is teaching a unit on famous fairy tales. His children love to draw and do art projects, so he has decided to add an art activity to this unit.

"Today we are going to read aloud another fairy tale," he announces to the class. "This one is called Sleeping Beauty. How many of you have heard of it?" Many hands go up, waving back and forth. "Okay, that's great," continues Mr. Jonas. "I will start reading aloud, and then I will call on you to help me read the story. Are you ready?"

Heads nod. "Now as we listen to the story of Sleeping Beauty, try and picture the different characters in your mind because afterward each of you will get to choose your favorite character to do an art project on."

Mr. Jonas starts reading the story, pausing to ask the children questions about what they think will happen next. When the story is finished he takes out paper plates, some string, glue, yarn, buttons, colored markers, and scissors. Next he holds up a finished paper plate project and explains to the children how he created a mask from a simple plate. "First, I had to imagine what my character would look like from reading and listening to the story. Then I took a pencil and drew facial features onto my plate."

"Next," he continues, "I took my colored pencils and began filling in the features. In some places I put a small dab of glue to secure button eyes and string for the hair." He pauses to make sure everyone is watching and listening, since some students are eager to start their own masks. "Okay, now clear your desks, and I will give you the materials to begin your art project."

The students go back to their seats talking about which character they have chosen and how their masks will look. Later, when all of the children have completed their masks, Mr. Jonas leads the whole class in retelling the Sleeping Beauty story wearing their masks and pantomiming the action. Everyone agrees this is a fun activity that they would like to do again.

Introduction

s far back as recorded human history, people have told stories. Oral storytelling, long before the invention of radio, television, or the Internet, was a primary form of entertainment. Families and entire communities would gather around campfires at night and listen to stories told by elder members of the group. Sometimes the stories were true: accounts of past events in the lives of families or village members. Other times the stories were made up to entertain or explain some natural phenomenon. Our modern literary labels apply to these ancient tales: the former can be seen as nonfiction, and the latter, fiction.

Fantasy, imaginative stories that conjure up unrealistic happenings such as magic spells, flying witches, and invisible elves, is a subcategory of fiction. Traditional fantasy refers to stories that are very old and have been handed down orally over generations, usually without an identifiable author. Modern fantasy, as the term implies, also involves the fantastic but has been written in more recent times and has an identifiable author (Jacobs & Tunnell, 2004).)We begin our discussion with traditional fantasy.

Traditional Fantasy

raditional fantasy includes the fairy tales and folktales that most Americans grow up with: Cinderella, Rumpelstiltskin, Goldilocks and the Three Bears, Paul Bunyan and Babe the blue ox. These and other stories have been passed down from generation to generation. They have also been the subject of scholarly research, as they provide a window into various culture traditions of the past. James Frazier, author of *The Golden Bough* (1915), studied the symbolic meaning of ancient myths, the rituals of ancient tribes, and the particular taboos within various cultures. Frazier took an anthropological view of traditional literature, using it to theorize about past cultures and to help us better understand present cultural practices. Kornei Chukovsky, in *From Two to Five* (1963), argued that for healthy development young children should hear fairy tales read aloud by their parents; in this way they begin to understand the conflicts between characters in stories and to recognize central themes in literature such as the battle between good and evil forces in the world. Today, psychologists agree that there is much value for children in listening to and reading classic fairy tales (Dundee, 1985; Haase, 2005).

In his great work, *The Uses of Enchantment* (1989), Bruno Bettelheim argued that traditional fairy tales provide children with the best opportunity to confront their innermost fears and unvoiced anxieties. Fairy tales allow youngsters to encounter characters who strive for seemingly unattainable goals yet still succeed. Good and evil, in the form of characters like a good princess and an evil witch, are clearly delineated. There are few ambiguities in fairy tales, a characteristic that initially strengthens the child's intellectual growth and understanding for later life, when ambiguities and uncertainties are commonplace.

Bettelheim's early work with psychologically and emotionally disturbed children led him to conclude that at the core of their problems was a belief that life was meaningless, that the world was unsafe and should be feared. In fairy tales, heroes are sent out into the world alone to accomplish nearly impossible tasks, to overcome great dangers, to confront primitive fears, and to encounter the unknown. The fairy tale hero's success gives hope to the child that the world can be explored and understood, that the future is not bleak, that life is worth living, and that existence is meaningful.

Of the many valuable uses of traditional fantasy, two stand out for teachers and caregivers. First, the old stories of giants, goblins, magic potions, princes, and dragons stimulate young children's imagination. These stories paint a picture in children's minds that stays with them for years and supports their own storytelling. Second, the classic themes described in traditional literature prepare children for reading and understanding other literature. For example, a major theme in traditional fairytales that also appears in other literature is the triumph of good over evil. The loyal prince saves his father from the deadly dragon. Honest, hardworking Cinderella overcomes the plotting of her wicked stepsisters. In many fairy tales courage and goodness is rewarded in the end.

In addition to theme, traditional folktales and fairy tales have other common characteristics. The plot is generally straightforward, chronological, and linear. One action leads to another, which eventually leads to a resolution. Little time is spent on such things as flashbacks, parallel plots, or multiple narrators. The characters in traditional literature are generally flat. That is, they have specific, obvious traits that make them good or evil, courageous or cowardly, clever or foolhardy. The setting and time of traditional fantasy is vaguely described as "once upon a time," or "long, long ago," in a "faraway land," rather than a particular, identifiable place. Finally, there are familiar patterns or small parts of the

FIGURE 6.1 Common fairy tale motifs.

- Wishes

  Example: *The Three Wishes: An Old Story* by Margot Zemach (1986). Magic wishes appear over and over again in fairy tales. The number three is also a common motif, as wishes, pigs, blind mice, and more come in trios.

- Spells

  Example: *Sleepless Beauty* by Frances Minters (1996), a modern day twist on a classic tale complete with a rock star prince. Spells usually come from evil witches, and they are often the catalyst for the story.

- Heroic children

  Example: *Hansel and Gretel* by James Marshall (1994). Marshall takes this classic Brothers Grimm tale and adds his own comic flare to it. Children abandoned in the woods and forced to rely on their own wits is a common motif in both traditional and modern tales.

- Enchanted animals

  Example: *The Frog Prince Continued* by Jon Scieszka (1991). What happened after the princess kissed the frog and he turned into a prince? Scieszka continues the story in a comic treatment that reveals they did not live happily ever after. Many tales have stories of humans who have been turned into animals, or who turn into animals at certain times. Other stories center around the adventures of anthropomorphic, or personified, animals.

- Good versus evil

  Example: *The Witch's Child* by Arthur Yorinks (2007). An evil witch has all the power she can wish for accept one thing, a real live child. So she creates a child from straw and leaves. But it takes real love for a child to truly come alive. Love is a powerful motif; it may be the most prevalent one in all fairy tales. Nearly every story tells of good conquering evil.

story called *motifs* that appear and reappear in story after story; some examples are tests of courage, mistaken identities, magical objects that grant the finder three wishes, or wicked stepmothers ill-disposed toward their stepchildren. Figure 6.1 identifies five motifs in picture book fantasy stories that are common to many fairy tales. Recognizing these motifs from story to story is one way young children increase their powers of listening and reading comprehension.

Folktales often have animal characters and usually teach a lesson. Fairy tales place a greater emphasis on magic: magical objects and magical spells (Trousdale, 1989). Teachers should always remember that traditional fairy tales and folktales were originally told aloud. Even when they were written down, the intent was that they be read aloud to young children. The appeal of traditional literature, at least in part, is its beautiful language, best delivered by a skillful reader. Teachers and caregivers who read fairy tales and folktales aloud to young children provide the foundation upon which all later literature will be understood.

Traditional Fantasy for Young Children

Classic fairy tales have withstood the test of time and are read over and over again by succeeding generations because they are succinctly written with an engaging storyline in language that stimulates the imagination. Quality fantasy books should have many of the characteristics of quality picture books discussed in Chapter 5 and restated below.

The story should be appropriate. First, the story content and language must be suitable for the child. The teacher or caregiver is the best person to decide what is appropriate for a particular child. Although the content of traditional fairy tales is sometimes explicitly brutal, that is not necessarily a bad thing; recall that Bruno Bettelheim (1989) sees value in traditional fairy tales as a means of helping young children confront and deal with their own fears, both real and imagined.

The story must appeal to the imagination. The essence of traditional (and modern) fantasy is that it asks readers to enter an unusual world with supernatural happenings; this requires use of the imagination. In contrast, informational (nonfiction) books are sources of real people and things in nature.

The story should be believable. The language of the stories must be crafted in such a way that the story is believable. But what constitutes believability when it comes to things like magic spells and frogs turning into princes? Consistency. The world of the fantastic has rules and an order that must be followed consistently; for example, if a spell is cast, then only a certain act can undo it. Once a listener or reader buys into this new order, the imagination takes over and the reader can enjoy the story.

The story's language can be at a higher level. In terms of the language of traditional fairy tales remember that for the most part they are intended to be read aloud by an adult, so the vocabulary does not have to be elementary enough for the children to grasp its meaning unaided.

A Global Look at Traditional Fantasy

There are many ways of grouping or categorizing traditional fantasy stories. In this text we group traditional fantasy by country of origin. Sampling a worldwide range of fantasy, children hear stories from many different countries and can be introduced to maps and globes to locate the countries. In this way young children can begin appreciating the multicultural diversity of our world. Unfortunately, most students, even older ones, lack geographical and multicultural knowledge (Kovanich, 2007). John Fahey, President of the National Geographic Society, says that most American students have little global knowledge, which isolates them from the rest of the world (Roper Survey, 2006). Thus this section on fairy tales and folktales from around the world is an excellent opportunity to introduce children to the larger world in which they live. Teachers and caregivers can test their own knowledge of world geography by going to www.northernstar.info/article.

Teachers and caregivers will also note that many popular fairy tales have similar variants from country to country. This is because the original stories were handed down from person to person orally and eventually crossed borders whereupon each culture gave its own twist to the story. Reading similar stories from various countries and having children identify the similarities and differences helps them develop comprehension abilities. In the coming sections, we look at some of the most famous tales from around the world. If you would like to explore more stories, Figure 6.2 offers some online resources.

FIGURE 6.2   Sites offering further information on fairy tales.

- http://manybooks.net/collections/Fairy_Tales.php

  This site offers free downloads of fairy tale collections. The tales are from around the world and are organized by region. Audiobook downloads are also available.

- www.cln.org

  The Community Learning Network has collected curriculum resources and instructional materials related to fairy tales. Click on "Theme Pages" and then select "[Stories], Folklore, and Fairy Tales."

- www.planetozkids.com/oban/index.htm

  Read versions of legends and fairy tales written by children from around the world. Scroll down to

"Myths, Legends and Stories sent to us by friends." These can serve as examples for children who want to write their own tales.

- www.ucis.pitt.edu/pehsc

  The University of Pittsburgh presents content enrichment strategies that use folktales to teach language arts; these strategies were developed by a group of K–2 teachers. Click on the "Lessons" link and then click on "Section 1" under the heading "When Tortoise Wins."

French Fairy Tales and the Contribution of Charles Perrault

Some of the most familiar and popular fairy tales of all time are owed to the work of one man, Charles Perrault. Perrault was born in Paris, France, in 1628. He worked in various government positions under Louis XIV. But his passion was literature, particularly the fairy tales he heard told to him as a child. And so, upon retiring from his government work, he began writing down these tales (Perrault, 1989). Among Perrault's most famous tales are the stories of Sleeping Beauty, Puss-in-Boots, Tom Thumb, Little Red Riding Hood, and Cinderella. Many children will already be familiar with some of these classic tales by the time they start school. Ask them to tell you the tale as they remember it. Then choose some of the editions listed in the following figures and read them aloud. Have the children compare them to what they had known beforehand about the tale. This would also be a good time to bring out a globe or world map to locate the country of France.

Sleeping Beauty

"Thorn Rose," collected by Perrault, was the original title for a story of Sleeping Beauty. "Once upon a time, long, long ago . . ." With this familiar opening, children recognize the beginning of a fairy tale. Perrault's version opens with a great party thrown by a king and queen to christen their infant princess. People from all over the kingdom were invited, including seven fairy godmothers. But the oldest fairy godmother was not invited, and in her anger she casts a spell that sends the princess into a deep sleep. To break the spell, a prince must find the princess and kiss her awake. Here we see the motifs of a magic spell, the battle between good and evil, and, of course, a happy ending. Teachers can choose two or three different versions of the tale from Figure 6.3 to read aloud.

Versions of Sleeping Beauty.	**FIGURE** 6.3

BOOK | **STORY**

Brooke, W. J. (1990). *A telling of the tales: Five stories.* Illus. R. Egielski. New York: Harper & Row.

A retelling of five classic tales, including Cinderella, Sleeping Beauty, Paul Bunyan, John Henry, and Jack and the Beanstalk, from a contemporary perspective.

Hutton, W. (1979). *The sleeping beauty.* Illus. J. Grimm. New York: Atheneum.

In this version the thirteenth wise woman is accidentally not invited to the King's feast. In revenge she causes the entire castle staff to fall into a deep sleep.

Mayer, M. (1984). *The sleeping beauty.* New York: Macmillan.

The author/artist tells the story of a princess who sleeps under an evil spell for 100 years, until a magical silver owl and the Star Faerie save her.

Yolen, J. (1986). *The sleeping beauty.* Illus. R. Sanderson. New York: Ariel Books/Knopf.

Enraged at not being invited to the princess's christening, the wicked fairy casts a curse on the girl that dooms her to die at age 15.

Yolen, J. (1981). *Sleeping ugly.* Illus. D. Stanley. New York: Coward McCann & Geoghegan.

When beautiful Princess Miserella, Plain Jane, and a fairy fall under a sleeping spell, a prince undoes the spell in a surprising way.

Craft, M. F. (2002). *Sleeping beauty.* Illus. K. Y. Craft. New York: SeaStar Books.

A beautifully illustrated book with classic paintings by Kinuko Craft. The storyline is a bit more complicated but will work well if read aloud by a teacher. In this version a good fairy has to use her magic to overcome the spell of an evil fairy.

Minters, F. (1996). *Sleepless beauty.* Illus. G. B. Karas. New York: Viking Press.

This is a humorous modern-day take on the classic fairy tale. Beauty is born in a big city apartment. Everyone is invited to Apartment 3D for a birthday party except the old witch who lives down the block. It takes a rock and roll star to save the day.

Perrault, C. (1977). *The sleeping beauty.* Trans. and Illus. D. Walker. New York: Thomas Y. Crowell.

This is the original, classic tale translated by David Walker in 1977. The drawings and text are a bit old-fashioned but still have the power to capture children's imagination.

Having multiple versions of the same story provides a great teaching tool for teachers and caregivers. They can ask children how the two or three versions are alike and how they are different. They can ask them how the illustrations differ from one story to the next and which ones the children prefer. The ability to compare and contrast stories is a higher-level analytical skill that can be taught early and reinforced continually with a variety of literary genres.

One version by Felix Hoffman (1960) contains simple illustrations depicting the various scenes of the story. Another by Errol Le Cain (1975) has elaborate, highly detailed pictures with the characters in gorgeous medieval costumes. Jane Yolen (1986) offers still another version of the story; here the protagonist is called Briar Rose, and the beautiful illustrations by Ruth Sanderson will captivate young and old alike. These colorful illustrations capture in great detail the interior and exterior of the castle, complete with an elaborate winding staircase, along with idyllic scenes from nature.

After looking at the different illustrations, children may want to do their own drawings. Creating their own illustrations for well-known fairy tales with pen, pencil, chalk, crayon, tempura paint, or watercolors should be an integral part of an early childhood literature program.

Puss-in-Boots

In medieval times, when parents died, only sons inherited their wealth, with the oldest son getting the most. In the story of Puss-in-Boots, this custom is a central aspect of the story. Upon the death of his father, the oldest son inherits the family flour mill, the next son receives a donkey, and the youngest son gets only what is left, a black and white cat. Of course the youngest son is upset because he doesn't know how he can make a living with only a cat. At that moment, the cat speaks up and asks his master for a sack and a pair of boots. How could one refuse a talking cat? The youngest son names him Puss-in-Boots and gives him what he asks for. In return, the clever Puss-in-Boots uses his wits to gain the favor of the king, who then rewards the youngest son (Perrault and Hague, 1989). Talking animals often play a role in fantasy. This can lead to a discussion about why animals are made to talk in some stories when they do not talk in real life. Think about the many popular children's books that personify animals: There's Peter Rabbit, Paddington Bear, and Anansi the spider. Caregivers can ask children to name other stories with animals that talk.

Oftentimes modern authors will retell a classic fairy tale. Such is the case with Lorinda Cauley's 1986 retelling of *Puss-in-Boots*. In this beautifully illustrated version the clever Puss tricks a king into providing his master with rich clothes, which in turn allow him to pursue the King's daughter. To gain a castle for his master, Puss-in-Boots tricks a nasty ogre into turning himself into a mouse, which Puss promptly pounces on and eats. In another version of this story (Perrault, 1990) Puss-in-Boots helps his master gain land, riches, a castle, and, in the end, the hand of the princess in marriage.

Tom Thumb

Many French fairy tales by Perrault deal with poor families and their struggle to survive. The story of Tom Thumb is one example. Tom, the youngest of seven boys born to a poor woodcutter and his wife, was so tiny at birth that he was no bigger than your thumb—thus his name. One night he hears his parents whispering about a famine spreading throughout the land. Because there is no food in the house, the woodcutter tells his wife that he will have to abandon the boys in the woods. The next day he takes his children deep into the woods to gather firewood. When the boys aren't looking, he slips away. But clever Tom has left a trail of pebbles to mark the way out of the forest (Perrault, 1989). In times of famine, abandoning children was not an uncommon practice in Europe, and it recurs as a theme in traditional fairy tales. Compare this story with that of Hansel and Gretel. If you share these stories with children, you can follow a read-aloud with questions like these: "Do you recall how Hansel and Gretel found their way out of the forest?" "If you were lost in the woods how would you find your way out?"

Little Red Riding Hood

In the story of Little Red Riding Hood, Perrault presents a character that has appeared in many books, such as those in Figure 6.4. Many children will be familiar with the plot of the story: Even very young children can join in on the refrain, "Why, Grandmother, what big eyes you have." This and most other classic fairy tales lend themselves to play acting, where children dress in simple costumes (a red kerchief for Little Red Riding Hood) and improvise the dialogue of the story.

Versions of Little Red Riding Hood.   FIGURE 6.4

BOOK	STORY
De Regniers, B. S. (1972). *Red Riding Hood retold in verse for boys and girls to read themselves.* Illus. E. Gorey. New York: Atheneum.	Retells in rhyming verse the adventures of a little girl who meets a wolf in the forest on her way to visit her grandmother.
Ernst, L. C. (1995). *Little Red Riding Hood: a newfangled prairie tale.* New York: Simon & Schuster Books for Young Readers.	An updated version, set on the prairie, of the familiar story about a little girl, her grandmother, and a not-so-clever wolf.
Brothers Grimm (2006). *Little Red Cap.* Illus. L. Zwerger. New York: W. Morrow.	Vivid watercolor illustrations accompany the original Grimm version of the story.
Hyman, T. S. (1983). *Little Red Riding Hood.* New York: Holiday House.	On her way to deliver a basket of food to her sick grandmother, Elisabeth encounters a sly wolf in this version created by a Caldecott-winning author.
Lowell, S. (1997). *Little Red Cowboy Hat.* Illus. R. Cecil. New York: Holt.	A Southwestern version in which Little Red rides her pony Buck to Grandma's ranch with a jar of cactus jelly in the saddlebag.
Marshall, J. (1993). *Red Riding Hood.* New York: Dial Books for Young Readers.	This version features cartoonlike drawings and humorous dialogue.
Perrault, C. (1972). *The Little Red Riding Hood.* Illus. W. Stobbs. New York: H. Z. Walck.	Not only is Grandmother eaten up in this classic Perrault version, so is Little Red Riding Hood. This may be a bit too violent for younger readers, but caregivers may want to check out Perrault's original version.
Daly, N. (2007) *Pretty Salma: A Little Red Riding Hood story from Africa.* New York: Clarion Books.	In this version set in West Africa, Pretty Selma takes a shortcut through the wild part of town as she tries to take her basket to market. Mr. Dog takes on the role of the wolf.
Young, E. (1989). *Lon Po Po: A Red-riding Hood story from China.* New York: Philomel Books.	Three Chinese sisters staying home alone are endangered by a hungry wolf disguised as their grandmother. They trick the wolf into climbing and then falling from a gingko tree.

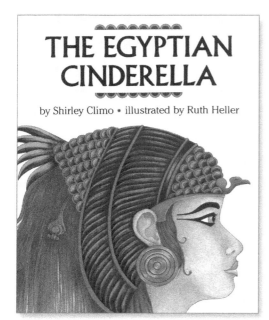

THE EGYPTIAN
CINDERELLA

by Shirley Climo • illustrated by Ruth Heller

Cinderella

Perhaps the most famous of Perrault's fairy tales is the story of Cinderella. This story has the motifs of the wicked step-mother, the wicked stepsisters, the good fairy godmother, and, of course, Cinderella herself, the epitome of goodness, generosity, and beauty. We all know how it ends with the prince fitting the slipper on Cinderella's foot and asking her to marry him. But in Perrault's version the gentle Cinderella insists that her stepsisters come and live in the palace, where eventually they are married to two noblemen. With this story Perrault presents a moral that is common in fairy tales: good people who do good things are, in the end, rewarded for their goodness. As you can see from Figure 6.5, this message has inspired numerous versions of the classic tale.

German Fairy Tales and the Brothers Grimm

Jacob Grimm (1785–1863) and Wilhelm Grimm (1786–1859) were two of six children born into a German family. They lived in a large home with servants and had a very strict classical and religious education. Their interests soon turned to the history of German literature and folklore. To support themselves, the brothers worked at the royal library researching and collecting ancient German legends. In 1816, they published their first volume of German legends and thereby acquired some fame and prosperity. Throughout their lives, their true love remained the research and collection of German folktales (Zipes, 1988).

Although the brothers Grimm are remembered primarily as collectors of German folklore, they were more than mere collectors. In 1812 and 1815, they published 156 tales of carefully edited stories aimed at appealing to the middle class. For example, they eliminated sexual references that might offend middle-class morality and added didactic lessons to appeal to parents of young children. Their goal was to present folktales and fairy tales as a way of informing people about German culture. Thus their work educates us about social injustices as much as it entertains us with magical deeds (Zipes, 1985, 1997).

The collected stories of the Brothers Grimm number in the hundreds. Here we shall review just a handful of the most famous ones readily available to teachers: Snow White and Rose Red, Hansel and Gretel, Rumpelstiltskin, and Rapunzel. In addition to exploring the Grimm's tales, children can be introduced to the country of Germany as well. For example, Bavaria is home to the real fairy tale castle of Neuschwanstein, one of the most famous castles in the world. Go to www.castlesoftheworld.com and show students pictures of this magnificent castle while you are reading German fairy tales.

Snow White and Rose Red

In *Snow White and Rose Red* (Brothers Grimm, 1964) the familiar theme of goodness rewarded is present. In the story, two sisters free an evil dwarf whose beard was caught in a fallen log. At first it does not seem that their kindness to the dwarf will be rewarded as they are confronted by a threatening bear. But the

Versions of Cinderella.

FIGURE 6.5

BOOK	STORY
Climo, S. (1992). *The Egyptian Cinderella.* Illus. R. Heller.	This version of Cinderella is set in Egypt in the sixth century B.C. Rhodopes, a slave girl, eventually comes to be chosen by the pharaoh to be his queen.
Climo, S. (2000). *The Irish Cinderlad.* Illus. L. Krupinski.	Becan, a poor boy belittled by his stepmother and stepsisters, rescues a princess in distress after meeting a magical bull.
dePaola, T. (2002). *Adelita: A Mexican Cinderella story.*	After the death of her mother and father, Adelita is badly mistreated by her stepmother and stepsisters until she finds her own true love at a grand fiesta.
Hickox, R. (1999). *The golden sandal: A Middle Eastern Cinderella.* Illus. W. Hillenbrand.	An Iraqi version of the Cinderella story in which a kind and beautiful girl mistreated by her stepmother and stepsister finds a husband with the help of a magic fish.
Huck, C. S. (1994). *Princess Furball.* Illus. A. Lobel.	A princess in a coat made of a thousand furs hides her identity from a king who falls in love with her.
Hughes, S. (2004). *Ella's big chance: A Jazz-Age Cinderella.*	In this version set in the 1920s, Ella has two men courting her—the handsome Duke of Arc and Buttons the delivery boy.
Jackson, E. B. (1998). *Cinder Edna.* Illus. K. O'Malley.	Cinderella and Cinder Edna, who live with cruel stepmothers and stepsisters, have different approaches to life; each ends up with the prince of her dreams, but one is a great deal happier than the other.
Jaffe, N. (1998). *The way meat loves salt: A Cinderella tale from the Jewish tradition.* Illus. L. August.	In this Eastern European Jewish variant of the Cinderella story, the youngest daughter of a rabbi is sent away from home in disgrace, but thanks to the help of the prophet Elijah, she marries the son of a renowned scholar and is reunited with her family.
Louie, A.-L. (1982). *Yeh-Shen: A Cinderella story from China.* Illus. E. Young.	A young girl overcomes the wickedness of her stepsister and stepmother to become the bride of a prince; this version is based on ancient Chinese manuscripts written 1,000 years before the earliest European version. Caregivers should be aware that the evil stepsisters meet an unpleasant end in this version.
Martin, R. (1998). *The rough-face girl.* Illus. D. Shannon.	In this Algonquin Indian version of the Cinderella story, the rough-face girl and her two beautiful but heartless sisters compete for the affections of the Invisible Being.
Minters, F. (1997). *Cinder-Elly.* Illus G. B. Karas.	In this rap version of the traditional fairy tale, the overworked younger sister gets to go to a basketball game and meets a star player, Prince Charming.
Pollock, P. (1996). *The Turkey Girl: A Zuni Cinderella story.* Illus. E. Young.	The turkeys make a gown of feathers for the poor girl who tends them so that she can participate in a sacred dance, but when she fails to return as promised, they desert her.
San Souci, R. D. (1989). *The talking eggs: A folktale from the American South.* Illus. J. Pinkney.	A Southern folktale in which kind Blanche, following the instructions of an old witch, gains riches, while her greedy sister makes fun of the old woman and gets her just desserts.
Schroeder, A. (1997). *Smoky Mountain Rose: An Appalachian Cinderella.* Illus. B. Sneed.	In this variation on the Cinderella story, set in the Smoky Mountains, Rose loses her glass slipper at a party given by the rich fellow on the other side of the creek.
Willard, N. (2003). *Cinderella's dress.* Illus. J. Dyer.	Although mistreated by her stepmother and stepsisters, Cinderella meets her prince with the help of two magpies and her fairy godmother.

bear reveals himself to be a handsome prince who had been put under an evil spell and robbed of his treasure by that same dwarf a long time ago.

Award-winning Caldecott author and illustrator Barbara Cooney created the picture book *Snow White and Rose Red* (1965). It provides another opportunity to ask children what similarities and differences they can identify in the two stories. Plus, having multiple versions of the same basic tale will appeal to young children, who often like to hear familiar stories told over and over again. Similarly, when they begin to read themselves, children like to reread stories multiple times. Rereading is a good strategy for developing children's comprehension skills and improving their reading fluency. Strong readers typically reread for meaning; less advanced readers may need to be told to reread as a comprehension strategy.

Hansel and Gretel

As we discussed earlier, motifs recur across fairy tales: frogs turning into princes, a poor family struggling to feed children, children getting lost in the woods, clever children outwitting ogres and witches, and magic creatures granting three wishes. In the story of Hansel and Gretel, two children are left in the woods by their poor parents, who have no way of feeding them. (Recall the story of Tom Thumb.) Also like Tom, Hansel and Gretel find their way home to safety by dropping pebbles along the way. The courage and cleverness of children is a feature of many fairy tales. Young children are not helpless in the face of danger. Bruno Bettelheim (1989) emphasized this in his writings on child development. These are qualities we want to nurture in children. Children who listen to fairy tales read aloud may see themselves as strong, brave, and heroic just like the child characters in the stories (Haase, 2005).

Rumpelstiltskin

In the story of Rumpelstiltskin a beautiful but poor girl is forced to spin straw into gold by a greedy king. She is saved from this futile labor by a strange little man who demands in return her first-born child. Later, after her child is born, the girl has a chance to guess the man's name before handing over her child. Much to Rumpelstiltskin's chagrin, she guesses correctly. Here we see some of the motifs of traditional fairy tales: magical incantations, which can change straw into gold, and good overcoming evil. Encourage children to distinguish between the real and the fantastic. Ask them, "Can you really turn straw into gold?" Perhaps bring in some straw for them to examine.

Rapunzel

In a similar story to Rumpelstiltskin, a husband and wife have long wished for a child. One day the wife becomes ill, and her husband climbs into a garden to pick a special lettuce, called "rapunzel," to help her get well. But the evil sorceress who owns the garden demands to have any child born to the couple. Fearing for his wife's health, the husband agrees. Later, when a baby girl is born, the sorceress locks her in a tower. As time passes the girl's hair grows so long that she lets it down for the sorceress to climb.

Finally, one day, a handsome prince hears the sorceress calling out, "Rapunzel, Rapunzel, let down your hair." Later, the prince climbs up Rapunzel's hair and rescues her from captivity. Children will enjoy repeating the refrains in this tale and acting out the story, where, once again, good conquers evil.

The short format of most fairy tales allows students to predict how they think the story will end before hearing the actual ending. Prediction is a major strategy to teach children to enhance their comprehension. Later this strategy can be extended to their writing new endings to familiar stories.

Scandinavian Fairy Tales and Folktales

Scandinavia is an area that includes four northern European nations: Norway, Sweden, Finland, and Denmark. Norway, Sweden, and Finland are so far north that they extend into the Arctic Circle. On the map they look like three fingers pointed downward. Denmark is a small peninsula in western Europe projecting into the North Sea.

Like traditional fantasy tales from other countries, Scandinavian tales include royalty and magic spells. However, a character unique to the folklore of Scandinavia is the troll. According to legend, trolls live for hundreds and hundreds of years. They are short and quite ugly, with long unruly hair and huge noses. They are usually mean and cause many of the troubles in Scandinavian fairy tales and folktales. Drawing trolls or making them out of modeling clay, yarn, and found objects would be a fun activity for children introduced to Scandinavian literature. Drawing and other art activities have also been shown to improve young children's later writing skills (Danko-McGhee & Slutsky, 2007; Ernst, 1998; Sidelnick & Svoboda, 2000).

Swedish tales

Irma Kaplan (1953) has retold in English the most famous collection of Swedish fairy tales. These tales date back to the early Middle Ages. Though they are referred to as Swedish in origin, they can be often traced to other countries. They include characters and motifs that children will be familiar with: witches, fairies, magic powers, and the aforementioned trolls. In the story of Cattenborg, a young brother and sister find themselves alone after their parents leave after an argument. The children decide to leave home and set out on their own. The brother takes the family cow and leaves the sister with only the cat. Later, however, the cat talks to the girl and shows her how to acquire beautiful clothes and great riches. Notice the similarities with the more famous story of Puss-in-Boots. You can have children bring in their favorite stuffed animal and create their own magical stories orally or in written form.

The Girl Who Could Spin Clay and Straw into Gold (Kaplan, 1967) is another familiar tale. Children will recognize its similarities to the story of Rumpelstiltskin and others. The protagonist of this tale is a poor farmer's daughter who is very beautiful but also very lazy. To teach her a lesson, the farmer orders her to sit on the roof and spin wool. A young prince spots the beautiful girl on the roof and hears that she can spin straw into gold. The greedy king and queen get wind of this and place her in a dungeon. They order her to spin straw into gold. Despairing of her situation, the girl is saved by the magical mothers Big Foot, Big Back, and Big

Virginia Haviland

Virginia Haviland (1911–1988) was born in Rochester, New York, and attended Cornell University. She became a children's librarian in Boston, Massachusetts, and later was asked to head the children's division of the Library of Congress in Washington, D. C. Recognized as a leading authority on children's books, she was made associate editor of *Horn Book Magazine* and served on the selection committees for the Newbery Award, Caldecott Award, and National Book Award. In the 1950s, she began compiling folktales from around the world. She wrote some of the early reference works in children's literature, including *Children's Literature: A Guide to Reference Sources; Children's Books of International Interest,* and she also edited the 16 volumes of *Favorite Fairy Tales* (1961). Today she is remembered as a great collector, translator, and author of fairy tales from traditions around the world.

Thumb, who help her on the condition that she invites them to her wedding. The girl marries the prince and later, when she becomes queen, she never asks her subjects to do more than they are capable of doing. Teachers who know how to spin thread could bring in a small spinning wheel to demonstrate how it works.

One of the more well-known Scandinavian tales is *East of the Sun and West of the Moon* (Asbjornsen and Moe, 1966). This is the story of a beautiful girl and a handsome prince, who has been turned into a bear by an evil troll. In the end, the girl overcomes the evil troll, breaks the spell, and marries the prince. Kathleen and Michael Hague (1980) have retold this ancient tale in a picture book with beautiful illustrations of the brothers of the wind, the prince-turned-bear, and female trolls. Nancy Willard (1989) has updated this same story as a play that older children can read and act out.

East of the Sun and West of the Moon, like many other fairy tales, lends itself to making predictions. When do children realize that the prince and the bear are one in the same? Can they guess how the girl overcomes the evil trolls? How does it all end? Recall Bettelheim's observation that, despite the evil, scary characters in traditional folktales, good always wins out in the end. This is an important lesson for children dealing with the normal fears of childhood. Haase (2005) similarly found that fairy tales strengthen children's belief in their own powers to overcome nightmares and deal with their fear of the dark.

Norwegian tales

Virginia Haviland (1961) has retold Norwegian tales from an 1859 translation by George Dasent. Dasent translated into English many of the tales originally collected by Asbjornsen and Moe, a duo who, in the fashion of the Brothers Grimm, published the first collection of Norwegian folktales. These tales are referred to as *pourquoi* tales or "why" stories, which explain some fact of nature, such as why birds fly, why elephants have long trunks, or why tigers have stripes. Here is a short one from Haviland that explains why the bear has a stumpy tail: A bear, who sported a fine tail, loved to eat fish. One day he asked a fox to teach him how to fish on the ice. The fox decided to trick the bear and said,

> Go out on the ice floe, cut a hole in the ice and stick your tail into the hole. Don't worry if you feel the fish biting your tail. The longer you hold it there, the more

author sketch

Judy Sierra

www.judysierra.net

Judy Sierra was born in 1945 in Washington, D. C. She received her college degree from San Jose State University in California. Early in her career she worked as a puppeteer and storyteller. She traveled around the world collecting traditional stories from many countries, which she often rewrote and adapted. She has written stories from Cameroon and other African countries, Indonesia, and Scandinavia. She is a member of the National Storytelling and American Folklore Society. Among her many writings are *The Elephant's Wrestling Match* (1992), *Wiley and the Hairy Man* (1996), *The Mean Hyena: A Folktale from Malawi* (1997), *Tasty Baby Belly Buttons: A Japanese Folktale* (1998), and *The Dancing Pig* (1999).

fish you will catch." The bear did as the fox said and held his tail in the icy water despite how much it hurt. Finally, he tried to pull it out but it was frozen stiff. He pulled and pulled until, bam! it snapped off. And that is why bear has a stumpy tail. (Haviland, 1961)

Also from Norway comes "The Pancake" (1996) as retold by Judy Sierra. In this tale, a woman is baking a sweet pancake for her children; they all want a taste, but she won't let them until it is baked to a golden brown. Just when it is nearly finished, the pancake hops out of the frying pan and scoots out the door. Along the way, it is chased by a hungry man, a hen, and a duck. Finally a pig offers the pancake a ride on its nose across a large river. When the pancake accepts, the pig gobbles it up. This tale has elements similar to the American tale of the gingerbread man. A good activity would be to ask the children to compare the two. As children encounter more fairy tales, they begin to recognize stock characters and recurrent motifs.

One of the most famous of all the Scandinavian tales is the story of the three billy goats gruff. It is a short story with repetitive language, which makes it an excellent story for children to hear, remember, and eventually read on their own. The story is about three goats all named Gruff: a little one, a medium-sized one, and a great big billy goat. One day they have to cross a bridge, but beneath the bridge lives a mean troll who won't let them pass. But big billy goat gruff, with his sharp horns and heavy hooves, proves more than a match for the ugly troll. There are many delightful picture book versions of this story, including those by Paul Galdone (1973), Janet Stevens (1995), and Glen Rounds (1993). The story lends itself to simple improvisational play-acting for young children. Children do not need to memorize the story verbatim but rather can improvise the dialogue. Have fun clopping around the classroom, imitating the goats crossing the bridge.

Danish tales

Denmark lays claim to one of the most famous storytellers of all time, Hans Christian Andersen, who wrote in the mid-1800s. He set some of his stories in Denmark. Andersen is considered by some to be the first modern fantasy author. We speak of him as a traditional author, but he certainly can be considered a transitional figure, who took very old tales and altered them to suit the tastes of nineteenth-century readers. Among his most famous tales are "The Ugly Duckling" and "The Princess and the Pea." Both of these stories will enchant young children and make them want to draw illustrations or act the stories out.

There are many picture book variations of the ugly duckling story. They all end with the same resolution: the ugly duckling, now a lovely swan, realizes that his transformation makes up for all of the early difficulties in his life. Teachers and parents should note that the modern versions take some liberties with the language and plot, but the essence of the story remains true to the original. Marianna Mayer (1987) retells this Danish tale of an awkward swan in a nest full of ducklings. Her text is accompanied by the beautiful artwork of landscape artist Thomas Locker. Troy Howell (1990) tells the story with his large colorful drawings of the country scenes. Anne Stewart's (1982) retelling has the beautiful animal illustrations of Monika Laimgruber, which arouse empathy for the ugly duckling. This classic tale should generate much discussion with children about how it feels not to fit in, how people treat those who act or look different than they do, and how everyone has things about themselves that they would like to change.

In the tale of the princess and the pea (1985), Hans Christian Andersen addresses the question "What is a real princess?" When it comes time for the prince to marry, his mother the queen insists that only a real princess will do for her son. So the royal family sets out to find a real princess.

When a bedraggled girl presents herself at the palace claiming she is a real princess, the queen devises a test for her claim. Beneath a mattress the queen slips a single pea and then piles 20 more mattresses on top of it. The next morning the Queen asks the girl how she slept; she replies that she did not get a wink of sleep. It is then that the Queen realizes the girl must indeed be a real princess.

After sharing the story with young children, teachers could ask them questions such as these: "What other tests could the Queen have contrived to test for a real princess? What qualities should a real princess have?" There are many excellent versions of this story. Janet Stevens (1995) has adapted and illustrated the story with delightful animal characters, including a bumbling, heavy-footed tiger as the princess.

Russian Folktales and Fairy Tales

Russia is a vast country, encompassing parts of Europe and Asia. It has a long history with many traditional tales told by families throughout the long Russian winters. An unusual character in traditional Russian literature is Baba Yaga, a witch, who sometimes is depicted as evil but other times as helpful. Virginia Haviland, Patricia Polacco, Judy Sierra, and Mary Hoffman have retold in English some popular fairy tales of Russia.

Vasilisa the Beautiful

"Vasilisa the Beautiful" (Haviland, 1961), should remind children of Cinderella. A beautiful young girl is left with only a magical doll to comfort her after her mother's death. When her father remarries, the girl's new stepmother and her two wicked stepsisters force her to do all of the housework, weed the gardens, and tend the fire. But with the help of her doll she performs all the tasks, which only makes her stepsisters all the more angry.

Patricia Polacco was born in 1944 in Lansing, Michigan. After her parents divorced, she divided her summers between her two sets of grandparents, who loved to tell stories. She studied art at The Ohio State University, schools in California, and later in Melbourne, Australia. She has received many awards for her picture books, which she both writes and illustrates. Many of her stories come from her early childhood experiences listening to tales told by her grandmothers (her babushkas) and reflect her Russian, Ukrainian, Irish, and Jewish heritage. Surprisingly Polacco did not become an author until 1987 at the age of 41. In addition to traditional folktales she also writes historical fiction and contemporary realistic fiction. Her books often deal with issues of race, discrimination, social justice, and her own struggles with dyslexia as a child. Among her many books are the following: *Rechenka's Eggs* (1988), *The Keeping Quilt* (1988), *Babushka's Doll* (1990), *Just Plain Fancy* (1990), *Babushkas Baba Yaga* (1993), *The Trees of the Dancing Goats* (1996), and *Luba and the Wren* (1999). An excellent video on her life and work is entitled *Dream Keeper* (1996), produced by Philomel Books.

Russian fairy tales are often more complex than other traditional tales. This is true for the tale of Vasilisa. She goes on many different adventures, moving from one to another, always proving herself with the help of her magic doll. In the end, however, like in so many other tales, Vasilisa is brought before the tsar, who falls instantly in love with her and showers her with riches.

Luba and the Wren *and* Rechenka's Eggs

As a young girl, Patricia Polacco, author and illustrator, was told many Russian folktales by her grandmother. She later featured these tales in her books, including *Luba and the Wren* (1999). In this story, a farmer lives happily with his wife and only daughter, Luba. One day Luba frees an enchanted wren caught in a hunter's net; the bird then grants her a wish. Luba's greedy parents, however, keep making her ask for bigger and bigger houses until the wren grows angry and returns them to their former cottage. The lesson of the story is that people need to be happy with what they have and take joy in the simple things of life, a common theme in folktales.

Another Russian tale told by Polacco is *Rechenka's Eggs* (1996), the story of an old babushka who lives in a tiny village in the Ukraine and whose hobby is painting eggs to enter in the Easter festival each year. One day she finds a goose that has been shot by a hunter. The old lady rescues the goose. To repay her, the goose lays beautifully colored eggs. Good deeds like this one are rewarded in many of the old folktales.

The Bun

Another favorite Russian folktale is "The Bun," retold by Judy Sierra (1996). In this story, a man asks his wife to bake him a bun. The woman mixes up flour, a cup of milk, a pinch of cinnamon, and some butter. But after the bun has baked and is sitting on the windowsill to cool, suddenly it jumps up and runs away. Close variants of this story to read and compare with children are "The Pancake" and "The Ginger Bread Man."

These stories all lend themselves to simple cooking activities such as baking cookies, pancakes, or bread. The following books include exciting cooking activities that young children can enjoy: *How to Make an Apple Pie and See the World* (2004) by Marjorie Priceman, *Everybody Bakes Bread* (1996) by Norah Dooley, *Pretend Soup and Other Real Recipes for Preschoolers and Up* (1994) by Mollie Katzen and Ann Henderson, and *Paula Deen's My First Cookbook* (2008) by Paula Deen.

Clever Katya

Another traditional tale from Russia is *Clever Katya* (Hoffman, 1998). In this story, two brothers live in a village in the Russian countryside and raise horses for a living. One brother is rich and the other poor. One night, when traveling together—the rich brother on his white stallion and the poor one on his brown mare—they stop to rest. When they later awake, they find a brown and white foal. The two brothers argue over who owns the foal. Finally, they go before the tsar to settle the matter. Since the tsar is fond of riddles, he tells the brothers that whoever can solve four riddles gets the foal. In the end, the poor brother's daughter Katya saves the day. Teachers and caregivers can make up their own riddles and have fun solving them with children. A few books of riddles to share include *Monika Beisner's Book of Riddles* (Beisner, 1983), *What Was the Wicked Witch's Real Name?* (Bernstein & Cohen, 1986), *Spooky Riddles* (Brown, 1983), and *Ribbit Riddles* (Hall & Eisenberg, 2001).

Asian Fairy Tales

Collectively, the nations of Asia, including India, Korea, Vietnam, Thailand, Cambodia, and Malaysia, have varied and ancient cultures and a long history of traditional literature. Some of the tales from Japan and China date from 500 B.C. Hearing and discussing this literature gives young children the chance to explore cultural differences in dress, customs, and language. Some children may already be familiar with eating Chinese food or the spicier cuisines of India, Korea, and Thailand.

Korean tales

Korea is a small, mountainous peninsula, lying to the east of China. Many animals live in the mountains of Korea. Fairy tales and folktales from the country often take as their subject the natural environment and the lives of animals. *The Rabbit's Judgment* (Han, 1994) is one example. One day a tiger falls into a pit. A man walking in the mountain forest sees the tiger and helps him out. But then the tiger turns on the man and threatens to eat him. The man pleads with the other animals in the forest to let him go, but the other animals know that the man cuts down trees and kills animals. Only a clever rabbit comes forward to save him.

Protecting our natural environment is a serious theme. In addition to the clever solution of the rabbit, this tale speaks to several environmental issues, like protecting our forests, and asks us to reflect on the role of humans in the natural world. It is never too early to talk to children about protecting animals and forests.

Japanese tales

Japan is a small nation made up of many islands. The country has had a history of conflicts with neighboring China and Korea. However, many of Japan's ancient folktales are similar to those of its mainland neighbors. Virginia Haviland (1967) translated "The Good Fortune Kettle." It features a poor junkman who frees a badger from a trap. To show his gratitude the badger turns himself into a beautiful teakettle to help the man earn money. The two travel from village to village together; at every stop the tea kettle dances and sings for the amazed villagers. The junkman becomes rich simply because he did a good deed. Teachers can bring in several styles of teapots for children to examine and discuss as they read the story.

Jojofu by Michael Waite (1996) is another ancient folktale from Japan. Jojofu was the favorite dog of a hunter. On numerous occasions Jojofu would stop in his tracks, refusing to go farther because he sensed danger. In this way he saves the life of his master. Many folktales and fairy tales have animals playing a central role. Modern examples are Toad, Peter Rabbit, Babar the elephant, and, of course, Winnie-the-Pooh. You can ask children about their own pets and adventures they have had with them.

Chinese tales

China is the largest and most populous nation in the world. The country contains many diverse geographic features, including mountains, plains, rivers, and deserts. It also is home to many varied ethnic groups. For a long time China was closed to outsiders, but today the country is becoming increasingly important on the world stage.

Lon Po Po, a story from China, translated and retold by Ed Young (1989), will remind children of the European Little Red Riding Hood. In this tale three children are left at home alone. A hungry wolf dresses up like the children's grandmother Lon Po Po and tries to get them to let him in, but they remember their mother's warning about not opening the door. In the end the clever children outwit the wolf.

In this and many other fairy tales, children overcome wolves and evil witches by actually killing them. As a teacher or caregiver you will want to preview these tales and decide for yourself if your children can handle the gruesome details. But remember that young children develop self-confidence by seeing their fairy tale heroes and heroines conquer evil.

Indian tales

India is a large country both geographically and demographically. The number of people living there is second only to China. It shares with China a mountainous border to the north, the Himalayas, which include some of the highest peaks in the world. It is also home to two of the great religions of the world—Hinduism and Buddhism—which are practiced widely in Asia.

From India comes the tale of *One Grain of Rice,* retold by Demi (1997). In this tale, a fair and wise raja (king) rules over many people who farm rice in the wet paddy fields. In a time of famine, when the rice crop fails, a young girl named Rani finds a small bag of rice and brings it to the raja. The only reward that she asks for is a single grain of rice and that each day for thirty days the Raja double the number of grains given the day before. Squaring the number like this raises the sum exponentially. A young heroine who shows courage in outwitting a powerful ruler is a common motif in fairy tales.

Teachers can do a variety of follow-up activities with this book. Bring in a small bag of rice and demonstrate the mathematical power of multiples that Rani used to her advantage. Also, the beautiful traditional Indian illustrations of this book make for a great comparison with the illustrations from Japanese, Chinese, and African folktales. This is an opportunity for children to make their own colored drawings in the style of a particular culture. Among the best books about the importance of art in children's education are the following: *Artful Scribbles* (Gardner, 1980), *Analyzing Children's Art* (Kellogg, 1970), *Your Child and His Art* (Lowenfeld, 1963), and *Young at Art* (Striker, 2001). David Gullatt (2008) has done an extensive review of the research on art education and found a positive correlation between the arts and later academic success. Thus it is never too early to connect literature and other subjects to arts such as drawing, painting, music, dance, and drama.

Another ancient folktale from India is *Manu and the Talking Fish* (2000), retold and illustrated with collage by Roberta Arenson. Manu was a prince in ancient India who often sat by the river Ganges wondering about all the mysteries of the world. One day a fish popped out of the river and asked Manu to help him. Manu did, and the fish continued to grow and grow. Eventually the oceans flooded the land, but Manu was saved because the fish warned him of the flood. Manu gathered together plant seeds, birds, and animals and escaped with them on his boat. Recall from the motifs of traditional fairy tales and folktales that magical talking animals with special powers are common in such tales. Moreover, the story of a catastrophic flood is found in many cultures. Christian cultures, for instance, have the story of Noah's ark from the Old Testament. Using colored paper, scissors, and paste, teachers and caregivers can recreate the collage-like illustrations from this story with children.

A tale from Indonesia

Indonesia is a country in southeast Asia made up of many islands, including Java and Borneo. Its capital is Jakarta. Indonesia is not well-known to most Americans. But a story like *The Gift of the Crocodile: A Cinderella Story* (Sierra, 2000) shows that Americans may be familiar with some of its stories that share cross-cultural themes. In *The Gift of the Crocodile,* a young girl named Damara suffers under the cruelty of her stepmother. However, Damara is a good and honest girl who never complains. For this, Grandmother Crocodile, the great spirit of the jungle river, rewards Damara with a beautiful native dress, the sarong. With this, Damara can now go to the great ball hosted by the handsome prince. A sarong is a vibrantly colored cloth seven feet by five feet in length and worn as a wraparound dress. Throughout Southeast Asia it is worn by both men and women. To see pictures of the colorful batik patterns visit BatikSarong.com.

Folktales from the Middle East

The Middle East includes parts of North Africa, southern Europe, and countries west of India, including Egypt, Iran, Iraq, Saudi Arabia, Turkey, Israel, and others. Much of the land is hot and dry. The region is home to both big cities and nomadic tribes. For some old tribes of the Middle East a popular traditional tale featured wisemen known as the Sufi. Sufi tales are often clever and witty; they teach a lesson as they entertain the listener.

What About Me?

In one tale called *What About Me?* (2002), retold by Ed Young, a little boy goes to Grand Master Sufi to ask for knowledge. In response the grand master says, "First you must bring me a small carpet to sit on." After fulfilling this request, the boy is asked to meet other requests. As the boy meets each subsequent request, he gains knowledge for himself. Master illustrator Ed Young enhances the retelling of this story with simple, colorful pictures depicting the boy and all the people he meets dressed in robes and headscarves of Middle Eastern style. You might want to bring in your own "magic carpet" for telling this and other stories in your classroom.

Agib and the Honey Cakes

Perhaps the most famous collection of stories from the Middle East are the tales of the Arabian nights. Most are complex stories not suitable for very young children. However, some of the stories have been reworked, modified, and illustrated to appeal to younger readers. Kathleen Lines's *Agib and the Honey Cakes* (1972) is one such story. Once in ancient Egypt there lived a wise man who worked as advisor to the sultan of Egypt. This man had a beautiful daughter named Babura. Hassan, a baker of honey cakes, is in love with Babura, but the greedy sultan wants her for himself. As in most folktales things work out in the end, and parents are reunited with their children.

Two Pairs of Shoes

P. L. Travers, known for her classic work *Mary Poppins,* has retold a story from ancient Baghdad in *Two Pairs of Shoes* (1980). It tells the tale of Abu Kassem, a rich merchant who is very stingy and will not part with his slippers, even though they are worn and dirty. But when the ruler of Baghdad's slippers get mixed up with Abu's slippers, trouble begins. From then on it is one adventure after another for Abu and his slippers. Leo and Diane Dillon have beautifully illustrated the colorful and exotic dress of ancient Baghdad. Teachers can ask children to bring their bedroom slippers to school and compare them to those of their classmates. Teachers can also bring in pictures of the pointed leather sandals of Morocco and other Middle Eastern countries.

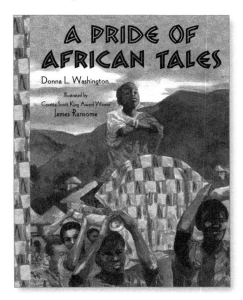

African Tales

Sharing folktales of Africa with young children is a first step to broadening their vision and understanding of a continent filled with diverse countries, geographic features, languages, peoples, and animals.

Donna Washington (2004) has collected a number of tales from different African countries in *A Pride of African Tales,* which has beautiful colorful illustrations by James Ransome, winner of the Coretta Scott King Award. Washington tells us that African

Adwoa Badoe was born and raised in Ghana, a country on the West African coast. She studied medicine in Ghana and eventually became a doctor. However, she always remembered the stories of her childhood and loved to tell them to others. Eventually she became a famous storyteller and dancer who travels the world participating in cultural festivals. Her books include *Crabs for Dinner* (1995), *The Queen's New Shoes* (1998), *The Pot of Wisdom* (2001), and *Nana's Cold Days* (2002).

In one of her stories, Ananse, this time portrayed as a spider, is thinking about how he wants to be remembered when he dies. He thinks of gathering all of the stories in the world to make him famous. But the king tells him he has to do something great first. Thus the king assigns Ananse three difficult tasks: capture alive a hive of honey bees; capture one of the evil forest dwarfs; and, finally, capture the great python. Clever Ananse finds a way to do all of these things and is rewarded by the king.

folktales are meant to be told, not read. Teachers may want to learn the stories and tell them extemporaneously. Identifying the various African nations on a world map or a globe is a great way to introduce young children to the geography of this continent.

Anansi tales

One of the most famous characters in African folklore is Anansi (sometimes Ananse). Anansi is by nature a trickster, and a clever one, too. Stories of Anansi are humorous. At the end of many, Anansi's tricks backfire on him. Children enjoy these stories and also learn valuable lessons about morality.

In many tales Anansi is depicted as a spider, though in the following tale he is a man. Adwoa Badoe's (2001) "Anansi's Fishing Expedition" is a trickster tale from Ghana where the trickster is the one who gets tricked. One day Anansi decides to go fishing. But in order to fish, he has to do a lot of work building and setting fish traps. Anansi is very lazy, so he finds a friendly but simple man in the village who agrees to help him. Anansi intends to trick the man into doing all of the work, but in the end, Anansi himself is tricked and loses all the fish.

If you share Badoe's story of Anansi with children, you can ask them how they might perform the tasks differently. For example, how might you capture a giant python? Such exercises develop critical thinking.

Gerald McDermott has adapted and colorfully illustrated another of Anansi's many adventures in *Anansi the Spider: A Tale from the Ashanti* (1972). Anansi is a trickster but also a hero to the Ashanti people of Ghana. In this tale, Anansi the spider has six sons: See Trouble, Road Builder, River Drinker, Game Skinner, Stone Thrower, and Cushion. One time Anansi travels far away and is swallowed by a fish. Each son helps to rescue Anansi in his own way. For example, See Trouble sees that something is wrong and calls his brothers to help. Road Builder builds a path to follow. Since a fish has swallowed Anansi, River Drinker drinks the river dry. Then Game Skinner cuts open the fish. But all of a sudden a huge bird appears and grabs Anansi. Stone Thrower then flings a stone and hits the bird, and Anansi falls from the sky. At this point in the story, teachers can ask children to make a prediction: "Who do you think caught him?" This

author sketch

Gerald McDermott

Gerald McDermott, an American author and illustrator, was born in 1941 in Detroit, Michigan. From an early age he loved to draw, and he later attended the Detroit Institute of the Arts and New York's Pratt Institute of Art. He collects and adapts folktales from all over the world. McDermott began his career as a maker of animated films. Later he met and was influenced by folklore scholar Joseph Campbell, the author of *The Power of Myth*. This led him to explore traditional art and storytelling from many different countries. He has received awards for both his artwork and his writing. In 1974 he won the Caldecott Medal for *Arrow to the Sun*. He has also produced and directed animated films for Public Television's Channel 13. These films include *The Stonecutter, Anansi the Spider, The Magic Tree,* and *Arrow to the Sun*. Among his many books are the following: *Anansi the Spider: A Tale from the Ashanti* (1972), *The Magic Tree: A Tale from the Congo* (1973), *Arrow to the Sun: A Pueblo Indian Tale* (1974), *The Stonecutter: A Japanese Folktale* (1975), *Papagayo the Mischief Maker* (1978), *Tim O'Toole and the Wee Folk: An Irish Tale* (1990), *Zomo the Rabbit: A Trickster Tale from West Africa* (1992), and *Raven: A Trickster Tale from the Pacific Northwest.*

story also lends itself to having the children role-play the characters, improvising their own dialogue as they act out the story.

Author Eric Kimmel and illustrator Janet Stevens have collaborated on an Anansi tale called *Anansi and the Talking Melon* (1994). One day Anansi sees Elephant working in his melon patch. He decides to fool Elephant by burrowing into the fruit and pretending to be a talking melon. All of the other animals are amazed by this. However, in the end the king revealed it is Anansi's trick. A teacher might ask students what makes a trickster character loveable despite the bad things he does to others. Since Anansi is discovered and punished at the end, children can learn a lesson from this story while being entertained by Anansi's antics.

Eric Kimmel (1990) has also retold the story of *Anansi and the Moss-Covered Rock*, which has great illustrations by Janet Stevens. Stevens is well known for her large, colorful and comic drawings of animals. This book is no exception. In this tale Anansi the spider discovers a magic rock that causes people to fall fast asleep. Anansi tricks Lion into visiting the rock; and while Lion sleeps, Anansi steals Lion's yams. Next he tricks Elephant and steals Elephant's bananas. In the end, though, Anansi himself is tricked by Little Bush Deer, who all along had been watching Anansi make his mischief. The lesson to be learned here is, again, that tricking others often backfires on the trickster.

Verna Aardema, an American author who has retold many traditional African tales, tells yet another tale of Ananse in *Oh, Kojo, How Could You!* (1984). Kojo is a lazy boy who lives with his mother by the side of a river. He loves to spend money on things, often foolishly so. Ananse, who also lives by the river, turns himself into an old man and tricks Kojo many times into buying things he doesn't really need. But in the end Kojo finally tricks Ananse and pleases his mother. He is given a magic ring to make him rich. A common motif in many folktales is a trickster who can magically transform himself into something else. Encourage your children to tell and write their own trickster tales. Illustrating such tales with colored pencils, chalk, or paint is another excellent activity.

author sketch

Eric Kimmel was born in 1946 in Brooklyn, New York. He holds many degrees, including a Ph.D. from the University of Illinois. From 1973 to 1994, he taught at Portland State University in Oregon, where he also wrote and illustrated children's books. In 1994 he decided to become a full-time writer and professional storyteller. He is well known for his adaptations and retellings of folktales from around the world, especially Yiddish tales from his Jewish heritage. Many of the stories come from Russia and eastern Europe, tales he had heard from his grandmother as a child. Some of the books he has written are the following: *Anansi and the Moss-Covered Rock* (1988), *The Chanukkah Tree* (1988), *Hershel and the Hanukkah Goblins* (1989), *The Greatest of All: A Japanese Folktale* (1991), *Boots and His Brothers: A Norwegian Tale* (1992), *Three Sacks of Truth: A Story from France* (1993), *Rimonah of the Flashing Sword: A North African Tale* (1995), *Sirko and the Wolf: A Ukrainian Tale* (1997), *The Runaway Tortilla* (2000), and *Zigazak! A Magical Hanukkah Night* (2001).

Tales from Liberia and Central Africa

Koi and the Kola Nuts (2003) is another traditional African tale from Liberia by Verna Aardema. Koi is the youngest son of a great chief. After Koi's father dies, the new chief suspects that Koi wants to marry his daughter, the beautiful princess. So the chief sets some impossible tasks for Koi to do, a motif common to many European fairy tales and folktales. With the help of the animals he befriends, Koi performs the tasks successfully and wins the hand of the princess. Doing good deeds is rewarded once again. The beautiful color illustrations by Joe Cepeda will enthrall children and make them want to do their own drawings.

Verna Aardema has also collected many tales from central Africa, just south of the great Sahara Desert. *Misoso: Once Upon a Time Tales from Africa* (1994) is a collection of 12 such tales with a beautiful color map illustration of the continent of Africa showing where the different stories came from. One tale from Zambia is "Toad's Trick." In this tale, Toad tells Rat that he can do something that Rat can't. "I shall pass right through that group of men without being harmed." Rat scoffs and says, "You can't even run fast." So Toad hops over to the group of men, who say, "Toads eat bugs. Let him go." But when Rat races toward the same group of men, they shout, "Get that ugly rat." And they chase after him with sticks. When the rat finally escapes, he says to Toad, "You were right." All of us have things we can do better than others. After reading this story, teachers can encourage children to talk about the special things they can do.

Africa is filled with many different kinds of animals that fascinate young children. In *Rabbit Makes a Monkey out of Lion* (1989), Verna Aardema tells how Lion, king of the jungle, gets tricked by the other animals. This story also introduces children to animals such as Honey Bird and Bush Rat. After hearing this tale, children can make up their own animal stories. A good follow-up to this story is to have the children make up their own animal stories to fool Lion.

"The Boy Who Wanted the Moon" (Washington, 2004) is a pourquoi tale from the Congo, in west central Africa, that explains why there are monkeys in the world and why they can be so silly. Pourquoi tales, tales that explain the wherefore of something in the natural world, appear in many cultures. In this

Verna Aardema

Verna Aardema was born in Michigan in 1911. As a young girl she loved to read and make up stories. Later she graduated from Michigan State University, married, and became a school teacher. While teaching and raising a family, she also wrote many children's books. Her most famous ones are retellings of African tales, such as *Why Mosquitoes Buzz in People's Ears* (2004), *Rabbit Makes a Monkey out of Lion* (1989), and *Anansi Does the Impossible* (2000).

story, a king has many wives and many daughters but only one son. The king loves his son so much that he spoils him by giving him everything he asks for. But nothing satisfies the young prince. Finally, the son demands that he be given the moon. The king then orders his workers to build a tower tall enough so that his son can reach the moon. But the disastrous consequences to follow are predictable. Pourquoi tales lend themselves to writing and drawing activities, where children make up their own stories to explain something in nature, such as why zebras have stripes, why the lion roars, or why giraffes have long necks.

"A Talking Skull" (Washington, 2004) is a tale from Cameroon, located on the west coast of Africa. The story's protagonist is a man who thinks only deep, important thoughts. He talks and talks to anyone who will listen. One day he finds a talking skull. But when he brings it back to his village, the skull refused to talk. As the tale continues, he learns that having a talking skull brings more problems than benefits. Compare this story with the one where Anansi animates Elephant's melon. This story leads naturally to a discussion of when talking is appropriate in class and at home. Children can be asked to think of times when talking got them in trouble. Most African folktales have a moral that can spark good discussions with the children.

Like so many other folktales, African tales also reward the good and punish the bad. John Steptoe's (1987) beautifully illustrated picture book *Mufaro's Beautiful Daughters* is one such tale. Mufaro had two daughters. The older daughter has a bad temper and liked to tease the younger daughter. One day the two girls hear that the king is looking to marry, so they both set out on the long trip to the king's palace. The ill-tempered older sister does her best to keep the younger girl from reaching the king. Of course, in the end, the kindness of the younger sister is rewarded. You can compare this story to the story of Cinderella and her evil stepsisters.

From the central African nation once known as Zaire (now called the Democratic Republic of Congo) comes the folktale of "The Boy Who Tried to Fool His Father" (Sierra, 1996). One day a boy decides to hide from his father by crawling inside a peanut. But a series of animals come along, gobbling up the peanut first and then one another. The father comes along and sees a python with a big bulge in its belly. He finds each animal inside the snake, and when he finally gets to the peanut, the boy jumps out of it. With its simple sequential plot, this is a good story for having children predict what will happen next at points in the story. Ask them to guess who will jump out when the father finally breaks open the peanut.

Native American Tales

Native Americans have a long tradition of oral storytelling. Reading these folktales aloud is a first step toward appreciating the cultures and customs of the many varied tribes of Native Americans. Many Native American tales show respect for the environment and for what nature has provided to humanity. An excellent website with educational resources for Native American folklore is www.americanfolklore.net/ee.html.

Iroquois tales

In *Skywoman*, Joanne Shenandoah and Douglas George (1998) have collected tales of the Iroquois, who lived in the northeastern region of the United States when the first European settlers arrived. "The Star Dancers" tells of how the Iroquois came to settle in the fertile lands of what is now the state New York, where they raised crops and hunted and foraged in the forest. In the story the Iroquois parents spend more and more time tending their bounteous gardens and begin to ignore their children. The children begin to play by themselves farther and farther away from the settlement. This angers the gods of the Iroquois, who turn the children into the stars of the heavens. Angering the gods and suffering the consequences is a motif found in many folktales. You can have children discuss how they think the parents might have handled things differently.

How the Bear Clan Became Healers tells of the life of the Iroquois living along the shores of Lake Ontario in their longhouses. Families had organized themselves into clans, each named after a special animal: beaver, wolf, bear, deer, etc. Over time each clan begins to think it is the best clan and need not share crops with other clans.

One night an old man who had come to the village becomes ill. The woman of the bear clan does not know what to do. The old man tells her to gather the ivy plant that grows in the forest and boil it in water to make a tea. When the old man drinks the tea, he gets feeling better. Later the old man reveals that he is Creator, who had come to earth in disguise. He is upset that the people are no longer kind and generous and respectful of the elderly. Because the bear clan had cared for the old man, he rewards them with the knowledge of healing.

Many art and drama projects could follow naturally from these tales. Children can learn to build simple longhouses from paper, cardboard, and sticks. They can paint forest scenes with all of the wild animals and plants that the Iroquois respected. Role-playing scenes from these tales and learning native dances also enhance children's understanding of the stories. Recall Howard Gardner's theory of multiple intelligences and the importance of various activities to enhance comprehension skills.

Cherokee tales

Cherokee Animal Tales (Scheer, 1992) is a collection of stories from the Cherokee, who originally lived in the southern Appalachian Mountains. As they grew in number, they spread to what are now the states of Virginia, North Carolina, South Carolina, Tennessee, Georgia, and Alabama. They hunted for game and also planted crops. They built their homes from logs, bark, and mud. In the center of each village was a large council house that served the entire community. Beginning in the 1600s, Europeans began to arrive in the Cherokee land. Although the Cherokee were known as fierce warriors, they tried to live in peace with the European settlers. In the 1700s they signed a treaty with the king of England that ceded land to the English colonists. In the early 1800s Sequoyah invented the Cherokee alphabet so that the Cherokee could read and write their own language. In 1837 the Cherokee people were forced off their land and made to walk 800 miles to the west in the middle of winter, to settle in Indian territory, which is in present-day Oklahoma. Many people died on that walk, which the Cherokee call the Trail of Tears.

Many Cherokee tales are pourquoi tales that explain how the various animals of the forest came to be. George Scheer (1992) has collected some of them. In "How the Groundhog Lost His Tail" we learn that seven wolves caught Groundhog and threatened to eat him. Clever Groundhog manages to fool the wolves and escape, but he loses his tail in the process. In "How the Deer Got His Horns," the animals of the forest decide to have a race. Rabbit decides to cheat, but in the end, the prize is awarded to Deer, who receives a pair of beautiful horns. Many folktales teach that cheating never pays. You can have children discuss incidents of cheating from their own lives. Playing fairly is an ethical concept for all children to learn.

Inuit tales

Inuit tales come from a people of the Pacific northwest—what is today northern Canada and Alaska. *Amorak* (Jessel, 1994) is an Inuit creation story. In this tale the Great Being in the Sky cuts a hole in the ice from which, one by one, all the animals come forth. But human hunters gradually kill off the most valuable animals like the caribou herds. This story emphasizes the need for humans to live in harmony with animals, a valuable lesson for children to learn.

Stories like this lend themselves to drawing activities, soap and balsa wood carving, and three-dimensional constructions of igloos, kayaks, glaciers, wolves, seals, and polar bears. Teachers and caregivers may also want to have children experiment with making a three-dimensional topographical map out of different colors of clay. Or they can visit the site www.alaskatrekker.com/natives.htm to learn more about the Alaskan Eskimo and Inuit tribes.

Coyote tales

Many Native American tribes have stories about the coyote. The Pueblo of northern New Mexico tell one called *Coyote and the Laughing Butterflies* (Taylor, 1995). One day Coyote's wife asks him to gather salt for her to cook with. But the Great Salt Lake is a long way away, and Coyote is lazy. He decides to take a nap before heading home with his salt. While he naps, some butterflies trick Coyote by taking him home without the salt he had gathered. After reading this story to students, you can ask them if they have ever fallen asleep and had a dream that seemed very real.

Traditional fantasy, which we have just surveyed, was originally an oral tradition going back many hundreds of years; often the originator of the tales is unknown. There are modern-day authors who write in the fantasy genre; their stories include witches, goblins, fairies, magic spells, and talking animals. The next section discusses these authors and their work.

Modern Fantasy for Young Children

Many modern writers today write in the fantasy genre; their exciting stories capture the imagination of children. These stories have many of the characteristics described in the section on traditional fantasy, but they do not come from an oral tradition that can be traced back hundreds of years. Instead, they reflect a more contemporary society, albeit with traditional elements of the fantastic. The key thing to remember is that fantasy contains elements that are supernatural, such as talking animals, flying people, imaginary creatures, and magical spells.

Writers of modern fantasy combine the fantastic with elements of realistic fiction. Sometimes the writer creates an entire imaginary world that could have existed in the past or might take place in the future; science fiction is considered a subgenre of modern fantasy. Above all else, modern fantasy must appeal to the imagination (Alexander, 1988).

As with all good writing quality modern fantasy must have a vivid setting; strong, interesting characters; a plot that is easy to follow; and a theme appropriate for children, such as those that delineate right from wrong or have good overcome evil.

Many of the best-known modern fantasies are chapter books with complicated plots, a multitude of characters, and sophisticated themes beyond the grasp of the very young child. C. S. Lewis's *The Lion, the Witch and the Wardrobe* (1970), Roald Dahl's *James and the Giant Peach* (1962), and J. K. Rowlings' Harry Potter series are beautifully written and excellent examples of the modern fantasy genre. But they are too long and difficult for very young children. Therefore we focus on picture books in the modern fantasy genre that would appeal to preschoolers and children in the primary grades. The following categories of modern fantasy could be the basis for teaching units in the classroom. A unit should include not only reading and listening to books, but related activities in art, music, drama, writing, and other types of reader response.

Talking Animal Tales

For young children, a popular type of modern fantasy features talking animals. The plots are generally simple, having only a few characters, and are often humorous. Laura Backes, publisher of *Children's Book Insider* (2006), notes that talking animal stories remain the most popular kind of modern fantasy for young children.

Elephants

In 1931 Jean de Brunhoff wrote *The Story of Babar the Little Elephant*. Originally published in French, one of its greatest fans was the author A. A. Milne, of Winnie-the-Pooh fame, who convinced his American publishers to translate it into English and publish it, which they did in 1933. The story and its sequels tell of an elephant in a green suit who drives a car, goes to school, and becomes king of the elephants. Today, Babar, dressed up in his fancy suit of clothes, remains a favorite of children all over the world. Another modern elephant story is *When*

An Elephant Comes to School (Ormerod, 2005). The elephant in this story does all the things that ordinary kids do at school: brings his lunch box, plays games, paints, splashes water, and loves to read during quiet time.

Reading these stories could lead to a unit on elephants. On a world map or globe find Africa, India, and other countries in Southeast Asia where elephants live. From issues of *National Geographic* cut out pictures of real elephants. Children may want to draw elephants of their own.

Crocodiles

Children may think that an elephant going to school is strange, but they will find a crocodile living in a Manhattan apartment stranger still. Lyle in *Lyle, Lyle, Crocodile* (Waber, 1965) lives in the Primm family's bathtub in an apartment on East 88th Street. This is a cute modern fantasy story that mixes real events in an apartment building with the fantastic life of a crocodile. This book would present a good opportunity to have students list in parallel columns what things are real in the story and what things could not happen. Distinguishing real from make-believe is an important comprehension skill.

Monkeys

In 1941 H. A. Rey wrote a modern fantasy book about a character who remains popular with children today: Curious George. George is always getting into trouble because he is so curious. For example, one time he gets trapped under a hat and taken far away to a distant city. He lives there with the man in the yellow hat and gets into all sorts of mischief. Some of the Curious George books that children have enjoyed for many years are listed in Figure 6.6. Curious George puppets are available to bring to class. Also, teachers and caregivers might compare George's fantastic adventures with books about real monkeys and apes. Some informational books to consult are *Tracking Wild Chimpanzees* (Powzyk, 1988), *Koko's Story* (Patterson, 1987), *Chimpanzees* (Donovan, 2002), *Monkeys: The Japanese Macaques* (Overbeck, 1981), *In the Wild Chimpanzees* (Robinson, 1997). This last book contains excellent photographs to stimulate class discussion.

Pigs

Another talking animal book is Ian Falconer's *Olivia and the Missing Toy* (2003). Olivia is a very modern pig. She wants to wear her favorite soccer outfit before going out to play with her toys. But she can't find her favorite toy. She

---

Curious George books by H. A. Rey.   **FIGURE** 6.6

Curious George Takes a Job (1947)	*Curious George Rides a Bike* (1957)
Curious George Flies a Kite (1957)	*Curious George Learns the Alphabet* (1963)
Curious George Gets a Medal (1957)	*Curious George Goes to the Hospital* (1966)

wonders whether brother Ian or baby brother William took it. At night she hears a strange noise in the house. She takes her flashlight and goes in search of whoever or whatever has taken her toy. After reading this book, teachers and caregivers can ask children to tell about a time they lost something and whether or not they found it.

In David McPhail's *Pig Pig Grows Up* (1992) Pig Pig doesn't want to grow up. He loves sleeping in his baby crib, though it has become too small for him. He loves eating baby food from a high chair and being pushed in a stroller by his mother. Teachers and caregivers can ask children what they think it will take to get Pig Pig to grow up.

Dumpy La Rue (Winthrop, 2001) is a pig with a strange passion; he wants to dance. "But pigs don't dance," says his father. "Pigs snort and grovel, and wallow in the mud." But Dumpy La Rue dances away to the delight of the other farm animals. This book is written in rhyme that will appeal to young children. After reading this book, teachers may want to dance around the room with their students.

Mice

Frederick (1967) by Leo Lionni is a simple story with beautiful collage illustrations. It has been a favorite of children year after year. A family of field mice begin to gather corn and wheat and straw to get ready for the long winter. But Frederick gathers things like colors and words. The other mice wonder what use they will be. But when the cold winter sets in and snow covers the wall, everyone loves to hear Frederick's stories of the warmth of the sun and his description of the colors of spring flowers.

Horace and Morris but Mostly Dolores (Howe, 1999) is a story of three mice who are great friends and do all sorts of things together. One day Horace and Morris build a club house just for boys. Excluded, Dolores builds her own club house. Soon, however, the three friends realize that they miss one another. This story could start a conversation about boys and girls playing together or playing separately.

Birds

Duck on a Bike (Shannon, 2002) is a funny story about a duck who decides to go for a ride on a bicycle all around the farmyard. Even though the children will recognize this story is fantasy, it can lead to interesting discussions about their own lives. For example, teachers may ask "Can you ride a bike?" "Do you know someone who rides a bike?" "Do you use trainer wheels or only two wheels like the duck in the story?" After these questions, teachers may suggest, "Let's all sit back in our chairs and pretend to ride our bikes."

Can a caterpillar and a gosling be friends? That's the question in Holly Keller's *Farfallina and Marcel* (2002). Farfallina the caterpillar and a young gosling named Marcel become friends. One day, however, Farfallina doesn't feel like coming out to play. She feels different because she is ready to spin a cocoon. Marcel is also growing and changing. The story raises the question of whether the two can remain friends despite their changes. Teachers can raise a caterpillar in their classrooms and invite children to watch as it changes into a beautiful butterfly.

Mercer Mayer was born in 1943 in Little Rock, Arkansas. As a child he moved around a lot, as his father was in the U.S. Navy. He graduated from high school in Hawaii and attended the Honolulu Academy of Art. Later he attended the Art Students League in New York City. His first job was as an art director for an advertising agency, but he soon quit to devote himself to writing and illustrating children's books. He is best known for his Little Monster series, Little Critter series, and Frog series. Mercer was one of the first artists to produce wordless books with interesting and humorous plots. Some of his books include *A Boy, a Dog and a Frog* (1967), *Frog, Where Are You?* (1969), *A Frog and a Friend* (1974), *Herbert the Timid Dragon* (1980), *Little Critter's Camp Out* (1993), and *Little Monster's Moving Day* (1995).

Earthworms

Doreen Cronin's *Diary of a Worm* (2003) tells about an earthworm who keeps a diary of his adventures above and below ground. This humorous book, with only a single sentence per page, has illustrations by Harry Bliss that make children giggle. For instance, the earthworm tries to teach his friend the spider how to dig under the ground and form tunnels to live in. But the poor spider gets stuck and even twists one of his eight ankles. On another day, the spider tries to teach the earthworm to walk upside down on a tree branch, with disastrous results. The earthworms even go to the school dance and do the "Hokey Pokey," even though their head and their bottom look the same. Teachers can bring in real earthworms for the children to examine and teach them how to dance the "Hokey Pokey."

Dragons, Monsters, and the Supernatural

Dragons and monsters appear in many modern fantasies. Often the stories are humorous or have young heroes who conquer huge dragons. Researchers Frazier (1915), Chukovsky (1963), Dundee (1985), Bettelheim (1989), and Haase (2005) all found that reading fantasy tales and allowing young children to talk about their normal fears promote their psychological development. The stories we describe are humorous and appropriate for young children.

Mercer Mayer, of Frog and Toad fame, has beautifully illustrated *Everyone Knows What a Dragon Looks Like* (Williams, 1976). Before reading the story, let children draw what they think a dragon looks like, and then read them this tale. In this story the city of Wu is being threatened by the wild horsemen from the north. A tiny old man approaches the city gates and proclaims that he can save the city because he is a dragon. The leaders of the city laugh at the thought because they know what dragons look like. Or do they? In modern fantasy, as in traditional fairy tales, people often change themselves into fantastic creatures and vice versa.

The Dragon Nanny (Martin, 1988) tells the story of Nanny Nell Hannah, who has just been fired by the king after spending her entire life caring for the royal children. As she wanders alone in the woods, she meets a fierce dragon who prepares to eat her up. But Nanny Nell thinks quickly and offers to be a nanny to the dragon's crying children. You can have students draw a picture of a dragon and make up their own dragon story.

Elvira (Shannon, 1993) is a baby dragon who doesn't like fighting or breathing fire or eating princesses. Her mother and father are worried about her. The other dragons make fun of her. So Elvira packs her bags one day and heads off on her own. She becomes a princess and learns about fancy dresses and how to paint her nails. When eventually her parents bring her back to the dragons, Elvira is able to share with them what she learned from living as a princess.

The Knight and the Dragon (1998) by Tomie dePaola tells the story of a young knight who has never fought a dragon and a dragon who has never fought a knight. Fortunately, they both can read books and learn how to fight. But will they? This story could start a discussion about how to resolve conflicts without fighting.

In *If I Had a Dragon* (Ellery & Ellery, 2006) Morton's mother tells him to play with his younger brother. But poor Morton wishes his baby brother could turn into something else, like a dragon. Then they could have lots of fun. This book is fun and easy to follow. It's also written in both English and Spanish, which provides an opportunity to talk about different languages. Walton (2007) and many others have shown that the best time to introduce children to a foreign language is when they are very young. Children as young as 4 can learn another language. See also www.LittlePim.com/Foreign Language for videos designed to teach young children various foreign languages.

Reading all of these stories over a period of time and doing related activities such as drawing dragons, recording original dragon stories, or play-acting will make for a unit on dragons that the children will remember more than a single, isolated story.

While dragons are a common sight in the world of fantasy, many other supernatural creatures and places also interest young children. Anthony Browne tells the story of a brother and a sister who find a dark and mysterious tunnel in *The Tunnel* (1989). The brother crawls in and dares his sister to follow. Although she is frightened, she crawls through the tunnel and comes out in a mysterious forest. But where is her brother? After reading this story, ask children to talk about other stories they know where love restores a loved one.

In *Leonardo the Terrible Monster* (Willems, 2005) we meet Leonardo, a monster with a real problem—no one is afraid of little Leonardo. He isn't big or scary, nor does he have huge teeth and claws. So Leonardo goes in search of a timid kid to scare. After reading this book, children will want to draw and talk about their own ideas of what makes a monster scary.

teaching suggestions
SHARING FANTASY BOOKS

Author Study Units

Fantasy authors such as Marc Brown, who created the Arthur books, and Kevin Henkes, whose books include characters such as Olivia and Wemberly, have created books that lend themselves to grouping as author study units. Reading multiple stories by the same author is an excellent way of teaching children to recognize similarities and differences across characters, setting, plot, and even

author sketch

Helen Lester was born in 1936 in Evanston, Illinois. Upon graduating from Wheelock College she taught primary school in Lexington, Massachusetts. After marrying she moved to Chicago, Illinois, and later San Francisco, California, all the while continuing to teach school. Once her two children were grown, she began her writing career, focusing on humorous animal fantasy stories. Among her most famous are those featuring Tacky the penguin.

Tacky, dressed in his Hawaiian shirt, is a nonconformist who battles the odds to do the right thing, like a modern-day Don Quixote. Lester's themes include cooperation, feelings of guilt, and clumsiness, all of which children can relate to. Some other titles of hers not already mentioned are *Tacky the Penguin* (1988), *Wuzzy Takes Off* (1995), *Wrong Way Reggie* (1996), *Tacky In Trouble* (1998), and *Tacky and the Emperor* (2000).

theme. Doing a variety of art, writing, and dramatic activities inspired by the books results in an author study unit that children will long remember.

A Marc Brown unit might include the following:

- Reading as many Arthur books as possible to the children
- Collaborating on a letter to Marc Brown that asks him to come to your school for a book talk
- Making Arthur posters
- Acting out favorite scenes from the books
- Having an Arthur dress-up party with Arthur's favorite snack, homemade cookies and milk.

Another writer who would make for a good author study is Helen Lester, who has written many quality picture books featuring talking animals. Most of Lester's books were illustrated by Lynn Munsinger. *Hooway for Wodney Wat* (1999) features a rat named Rodney who cannot pronounce his *R* properly. *Me First* (1992) focuses on Pinkerton, a pig who has to be first at everything. *Three Cheers for Tacky* (1994) introduces us to Tacky, a penguin who wants to be like all the other penguins.

A Helen Lester unit would include:

- Each day, read a different Helen Lester book aloud.
- After each day's reading and discussion, have children create a puppet for a character in that day's book. Rodney the rat can be created from a paper bag, with string for hair and buttons for eyes. For Pinkerton the pig, a sock puppet pig can be made using colored yarn and glued on paper eyes and ears. For Tacky the penguin, make a stick puppet or cloth puppet stuffed with batting to represent Tacky. Color or paint him in his black and white tuxedo.
- Create a puppet stage by draping a blanket over a table behind which the children can crouch. Paint scenery on stiff cardboard to display behind the stage.
- At the end of the week, once the puppets have been completed, the class can act out their own puppet show using all of the Helen Lester characters.

Scenery Backdrop Construction

For both traditional and modern fantasy, setting plays a major role—exotic or unusual settings like a dark, scary forest; a magical wonderland; an imaginary island home of wild things; or a grand castle for a mighty king and queen. You can first discuss with children the role that setting plays. Remind them that authors select specific settings to enhance their story and create a particular atmosphere. Next, using large pieces of butcher paper and watercolor, tempera paint, or crayons and magic markers, create a backdrop of a magical forest or castle that can be taped to a wall. Once children know traditional and modern fantasy tales from multiple readings, have them act out a story or favorite scene from a story, improvising the dialogue, in front of the scenery they created.

For this and other large-scale projects, you may want to invite parents or grandparents to volunteer to help out in the classroom. Another great source of volunteers is high school students earning service learning credits toward graduation. Contact the high school in your area and speak to the guidance counselor about having students volunteer for an hour a week at the local elementary grade school to assist with various art projects. Some high schools make earning service learning credits a requirement for graduation. Visit www.service-learningpartnership. org, www.nylc.org, www.servicelearning.cps.k12.il.us, or www.nationalservice resources.org to learn more about service learning in high school.

Fantasy Dress-up

Children love to dress up and act as different characters. In preparation for this activity, teachers need to gather many different types of materials that can be used for constructing costumes. Materials such as large paper bags, cardboard boxes, colored construction paper, magic markers, watercolor paints, yarn and colored string, cellophane and aluminum foil can all be used creatively. Weekend garage sales are a source for materials and found objects. Soliciting families to donate old or unused clothing is another source of costume-making items. Local community businesses and organizations also often have materials to donate that would otherwise be discarded. Your local recycling plant is another great source. Finally, searching online for "Free and Inexpensive Materials for Teachers" in your state can provide leads to free or inexpensive supplies to use in your classroom. Other useful websites for obtaining classroom materials are www.iLoveSchools.com, www.TeachersCount.org, www.Merlot.org, and www. education-world.com.

Once you have gathered all the necessary materials, read aloud some traditional and modern fantasy picture book stories, showing children the pictures and explaining that the illustrator had to imagine what the characters would look like. Tell them that they can use their own imaginations to decide how characters should look. Have the children sketch their character and costume on drawing paper. Then help them to decide what materials they will want to use. Sketching, cutting, and pasting are all important fine motor skills that can be developed through costume construction. After the costumes are complete, have children form groups to act out a scene from the book. Use a digital camera to take a picture of each student and have them write a short description of their character's appearance.

Some books that would adapt well as theater are Steven Kellogg's *The Christmas Witch* (2000), Michael Tunnell's *Halloween Pie* (1999), Scott Franson's *Un-brella* (2007), and Pat McKissack's *Precious and the Boo Hag* (2005).

Fantasy versus Reality Chart

All fantasy, be it modern or traditional, contains elements of the fantastic, things that could not really happen in real life, like witches flying on broomsticks or dragons breathing fire. But these same books refer to other things that could happen, like children getting lost in the woods, farmers raising crops, fishermen going to sea to catch fish, or pets doing heroic deeds. Oftentimes young children have a difficult time distinguishing the impossible from the possible. To help them, make up a class chart with one column labeled "FANTASY: things that could not happen in real life." Label a second column "REALITY: things that could really happen." As you read various fantasy picture books, stop and ask children, "Could this really happen?" Then decide in which column to enter circumstances from the story. Continue adding to your chart throughout the school year as you read more books.

Conclusion

Traditional and modern fantasy are popular with readers of all ages. With fantasy's emphasis on imagination—exploring the unknown, magic spells, and good and evil characters—it contains many elements that appeal to young children. Traditional fantasy originated as oral stories that go back hundreds of years. Often these stories contain serious messages or morals. Comparing similar traditional tales from different countries can be one of the lessons teachers and caregivers use to develop children's critical comprehension skills. Modern fantasy continues this genre into the present time. Talking animals, humorous and ridiculous characters, and impossible adventures give pleasure to young and old alike.

journeying WITH CHILDREN'S LITERATURE

1. Design a unit around the traditional tales of a particular country or region (e.g., Africa or Germany). Do background library and Internet research on the country or region in terms of its geography, foods, clothing, languages, and customs. Create activities for children that enhance their understanding, not only of the stories themselves, but of the culture they come from.
2. Select one or more authors mentioned in this chapter. Go to their websites and find out more interesting information about them to share with your students. You can also create an author poster complete with photographs of the author taken from their websites.

3. Visit your local library and discovery what DVDs, CDs, films, and audio cassettes they have of traditional and modern fantasy. Build your reading and special units around these multimedia experiences.
4. Read Steven Friedson's *Dancing Prophets: Musical Experiences in Tumbuka* (1996) for an ethnographer's fascinating account of life in contemporary Malawi, Africa. Share what you have learned about African music with the children, who may want to make their own music using household items.

activities TO SHARE WITH CHILDREN

1. Talk about the different types of illustrations found in various books. Then have children practice imitating these illustration types using crayon, paints, water colors, collage, cut colored tissue paper, etc.
2. Have children make up their own versions of favorite fairy tales and folktales. Then, using a digital or tape recorder, have the children record their tales. Emphasize speaking slowly, clearly, and with feeling.
3. With found materials you have gathered, help children create their favorite characters from traditional and modern fantasy. Then do simple play acting sketches of scenes from favorite books.
4. Have children write letters to favorite authors about favorite characters, books, scenes. Many author and publisher websites have staff members who will respond to fan letters.

our favorite CHILDREN'S BOOKS

dePaola, Tomie (1981). *Fin M'Coul the Giant of Knoockmany Hill*. New York: Holiday House.

This modern-day Irish tale is about Fin M'Coul, a good giant. As big as he was, Fin M'Coul was afraid of the bad giant Cucullin, who'd beaten up everyone in the country. It's up to Fin's wife, the lovely Oonagh, to trick Cucullin and save the day.

Falconer, Ian (2003). *Olivia and the Missing Toy*. New York: Atheneum Books for Young Readers.

Olivia, a talking pig, has all sorts of silly adventures. In this book, her mother makes her a special outfit to play soccer in. But when she returns from the big game, her favorite toy is missing. Olivia whines and cries and then sets out to discover who took it.

Fox, Mem (1999). *Sleepy Bears*. Illus. Kerry Argent. New York: Harcourt Brace.

It's wintertime, the time for bears to hibernate. But the baby bear cubs aren't sleepy. Momma bear has to tell them each a bedtime story before they fall asleep.

Kimmel, Eric (1990). *The Chanukkah Guest.* New York: Holiday House.

> A hilarious book about a nearsighted woman and the celebration of Chanukkah, the Jewish festival of lights. The woman mistakes a hairy bear for a rabbi and welcomes him to the family celebration.

Kimmel, Eric (2000). *The Jar of Fools: Eight Hanukkah Stories from Chelm.* New York: Holiday House.

> The town of Chelm is famous in Yiddish literature for its foolish people always doing downright silly things. Here, many of the Hanukkah stories are retold, but with a funny twist by the silly people of Chelm.

Levy, Elizabeth (1996). *Cleo and the Coyote.* Illus. Diana Bryer. New York: HarperCollins.

> This story is told in first person by Cleo the dog, who is found by a little boy in Queens, New York, and brought to the wilds of Utah. There he makes friends with a wild coyote. Cleo tells the coyote funny stories about life in New York, like riding the subway, and the coyote tells Cleo about life in the desert.

Sierra, Judy (1992). *The Elephant's Wrestling Match.* New York: Lodestar Publishers.

> This story comes from Cameroon, Africa. The elephant challenges all of the animals to a wrestling match to determine who is the strongest. One after the other he defeats a leopard, a lion, and others. When he meets a tiny clever bat, however, something unexpected happens.

children's literature IN THIS CHAPTER

Aardema, V. (1984). *Oh, Kujo! how could you!: An Ashanti tale.* Illus. M. Brown. New York: Dial.

Aardema, V. (1989). *Rabbit makes a monkey of lion.* Illus. J. Pinkney. New York: Penguin Books.

Aardema, V. (1994). *Misoso: Once upon a time tales from Africa.* Illus. R. Ruffins. New York: Knopf.

Aardema, V. (2000). *Anansi does the impossible.* Illus. L. Desimini. New York: Aladdin.

Aardema, V. (2003). *Kio and the kola nuts.* Illus. J. Cepeda. New York: Aladdin.

Aardema, V. (2004). *Why mosquitoes buzz in people's ears.* Illus. L. Dillon & D. Dillon. New York: Puffin.

Andersen, H. C. (1985). *The princess and the pea.* Illus. D. Duntze. New York: Holt, Rinehart & Winston.

Andersen, H. C. (1986). *The ugly duckling.* Illus. R. Van Nutt. New York: Knopf.

Arenson, R. (2000). *Mano and the talking fish.* New York: Barefoot Books.

Asbjornsen, P. C., & Moe, J. E. (1986). *East of the sun and west of the moon and other tales.* New York: MacMillan.

Badoe, A. (1995). *Crabs for dinner.* Illus. B. Ageda. Toronto, ON: Sister Vision Press.

Badoe, A. (2001). *The pot of wisdom: Ananse stories.* Illus. B. W. Diakite. Toronto: Douglas and McIntyre.

Badoe, A. (2002). *Nana's cold days.* Illus. B. Junaid. Toronto, ON: Groundwood Books.

Beisner, M. (1983). *Monika Beisner's book of riddles.* New York: Farrar Publishers.

Bernstein, J., & Cohen, P. (1988). *What was the wicked witch's real name?* Illus. A. Iosa. New York: Albert Whitman & Co.

Brooke, W. J. (1990). *A telling of the tales: Five stories.* Illus. R. Egielski. New York: HarperCollins.

Brothers Grimm (1964). *Snow White and Rose Red.* Illus. A. Adams. New York: Charles Scribner's Sons.

Brothers Grimm (1965). *Snow White and Rose Red.* Illus. B. Cooney. New York: Delacorte Press.

Brothers Grimm. (1987). *Little Red Cap.* Illus. L. Zwerger. New York: W. Morrow.

Brown, M. (1983). *Spooky riddles*. New York: Random House.

Browne, A. (1989). *The tunnel*. New York: Knopf.

Cauley, L. (1986). *Puss-in-boots*. San Diego: Harcourt Brace Jovanovich.

Climo, S. (1992). *The Egyptian Cinderella*. Illus. R. Heller. New York: HarperCollins.

Climo, S. (2000). *The Irish Cinderlad*. Illus. L. Krupinksi. New York: HarperCollins.

Cooney, B. (1965). *Snow White and Rose Red*. Illus. G. Spirin. New York: Delacorte.

Craft, M. F. (2002). *Sleeping beauty*. Illus. K. Craft. New York: SeaStar Books.

Cronin, D. (2003). *Diary of a worm*. Illus. H. Bliss. New York: Joanna Cotter books.

Dahl, R. (1962). *James and the giant peach*. Illus. N. Burkett. New York: Knopf.

Daly, N. (2007). *Pretty Salma: A little red riding hood story from Africa*. New York: Clarion Books.

De Brunhoff, J. (1933). *The story of Babar the little elephant*. New York: Random House.

De Regniers, B. S. (1972). *Red Riding Hood retold in verse for boys and girls to read themselves*. Illus. E. Gorey. New York: Atheneum.

Deen, P. (2008). *Paula Deen's my first cookbook*. New York: Simon & Schuster.

Demi. (1997). *One grain of rice*. New York: Scholastic.

dePaola, T. (1998). *The knight and the dragon*. New York: Penguin.

dePaola, T. (2002). *Adelita: A Mexican Cinderella story*. New York: G. P. Putnam's Sons.

Donovan, S. (2002). *Chimpanzees*. New York: Raintree Steck-Vaughn.

Dooley, N. (1996). *Everybody bakes bread*. Illus. P. J. Thornton. Minneapolis: Carolrhoda Books.

Ellery, T., & Ellery, A. (2006). *If I had a dragon / Si yo tuviera un dragon*. New York: Simon & Schuster.

Ernst, L. C. (1995). *Little Red Riding Hood: A newfangled prairie tale*. New York: Simon & Schuster.

Falconer, I. (2003). *Olivia and the missing toy*. New York: Atheneum Books for Young Readers.

Galdone, P. (1973). *The three billy goats gruff*. New York: Clarion Books.

Hague, K., & Hague, M. (1980). *East of the sun and west of the moon*. New York: Harcourt Brace Jovanovich.

Hall, K., & Eisenberg, L. (2001). *Ribbit riddles*. Illus. R. Bender. New York: Puffin.

Han, S. (1994). *The rabbit's judgment*. Illus. Y. Heo. New York: Henry Holt.

Haviland, V. (1961). *Favorite fairy tales told in Norway*. Illus. L. Weisgard. Boston: Little, Brown.

Haviland, V. (1961). *Favorite fairy tales told in Russia*. Illus. H. Danska. Boston: Little, Brown.

Haviland, V. (1967). *Favorite fairy tales told in Japan*. Illus. G. Suyeoka. Boston: Little, Brown.

Hickox, R. (1999). *The golden sandal: A Middle Eastern Cinderella*. Illus. W. Hillenbrand. New York: Holiday House.

Hoffman, M. (1998). *Clever Katya: A fairy tale from old Russia*. New York: Barefoot Books.

Howe, J. (1999). *Horace and Morris but mostly Dolores*. New York: Atheneum.

Howell, T. (1990). *The ugly ducking*. New York: Greenwillow.

Huck, C. (1994). *Princess Furball*. Illus. A. Lobel. New York: Greenwillow Books.

Hughes, S. (2004). *Ella's big change: A jazz-age Cinderella*. New York: Simon & Schuster.

Hutton, W. (1979). *The sleeping beauty*. Illus. J. Grimm. New York: Penguin.

Hyman, T. S. (1977). *The sleeping beauty*. Boston: Little, Brown.

Jackson, E. (1998). *Cinder Edna*. Illus. K. O'Malley. New York: Lothrop, Lee & Shepard.

Jaffe, N. (1998). *The way meat loves salt: A Cinderella tale from the Jewish tradition*. Illus. L. August. New York: Holt.

Jessell, T. (1994). *Amorak*. Mankato, MN: Creative Editions.

Kaplan, I. (1967). *The girl who could spin clay and straw into gold*. Illus. C. Calder. Chicago: Follett.

Kaplan, I. (1953). *Swedish fairy tales*. Illus. C. Calder. New York: Follett.

Katzen, M., & Henderson, A. (1994). *Pretend soup and other read recipes*. Berkeley: Tricycle Press.

Keller, H. (2002). *Farfallina and Marcel*. New York: Greenwillow.

Kimmel, E. (1988). *The Chanukkah tree*. Illus. G. Carmi. New York: Holiday House.

Kimmel, E. (1989). *Hershel and the Hanukkah goblins*. Illus. T. S. Hyman. New York: Holiday House.

Kimmel, E. (1990). *Anansi and the moss-covered rock*. Illus. J. Stevens. New York: Holiday House.

Kimmel, E. (1991). *The greatest of all: A Japanese folktale*. Illus. G. Carmi. New York: Holiday House.

Kimmel, E. (1992). *Boots and his brothers: A Norwegian tale*. Illus. K. B. Root. New York: Holiday House.

Kimmel, E. (1993). *Three sacks of truth: A story from France*. Illus. R. Rayevsky. New York: Holiday House.

Kimmel, E. (1994). *Anansi and the talking melon*. Illus. J. Stevens. New York: Holiday House.

Kimmel, E. (1995). *Rimonah of the flashing sword: A North African tale.* Illus. O. Rayyan. New York: Holiday House.

Kimmel, E. (1997). *Sirko and the wolf: A Ukrainian tale.* Illus. R. Sauber. New York: Holiday House.

Kimmel, E. (2000). *The runaway tortilla.* Illus. R. Cecil. New York: Winslow Press.

Kimmel, E. (2001). *Zigazak!: A magical Hanukkah night.* Illus. J. Goodell. New York: Doubleday.

Lester, H. (1999). *Hooway for Wodney Wat.* Illus. L. Musgrave. Boston: Houghton Mifflin.

Lester, H. (2000). *Tacky and the emperor.* Illus. L. Musgrave. Boston: Houghton Mifflin.

Lester, H. (1998). *Tacky in trouble.* Illus. L. Musgrave. Boston: Houghton Mifflin.

Lester, H. (1988). *Tacky the penguin.* Illus. L. Musgrave. Boston: Houghton Mifflin.

Lester, H. (1996). *Wrong way Reggie.* Illus. T. Foley. Parsippany, NJ: Celebration Press.

Lester, L. (1994). *Three cheers for Tacky.* Illus. L. Musgrave. Boston: Houghton Mifflin.

Lester, R., & Lester, H. (1995). *Wuzzy takes off.* Illus. M. Imai. Cambridge, MA: Candlewick.

Lewin, T., & Lewin, B. (1999). *Gorilla walk.* New York: Lothrop, Lee & Shepard.

Lewis, C. S. (1970). *The lion, the witch and the wardrobe.* Illus. P. Baynes. New York: Collier.

Lines, K. (1972). *Agib and the honey cakes.* Illus. by B. Wilkinson. New York: Henry W. Walck.

Lionni, L. (1967). *Frederick.* New York: Pantheon Books.

Louie, A. -L. (1982). *Yeh-Shen: A Cinderella story from China.* Illus. E. Young. New York: Philomel.

Lowell, S. (1997). *Little red cowboy hat.* Illus. R. Cecil. New York: Holt.

Marshall, J. (1990). *Hansel and Gretel.* New York: Dial Books for Young Readers.

Marshall, J. (1997). *Red riding hood.* New York: Dial.

Martin, C. L. G. (1988). *The dragon nanny.* Illus. R. Rayevsky. New York: MacMillan.

Martin, R. (1998). *The rough-face girl.* Illus. D. Shannon. New York: G. P. Putnam's Sons.

Mayer, M. (1967). *A boy, a dog, and a frog.* New York: Dial.

Mayer, M. (1974). *A boy, a dog, a frog and a friend.* New York: Dial.

Mayer, M. (1969). *Frog, where are you?* New York: Dial.

Mayer, M. (1980). *Herbert the timid dragon.* New York: Golden Books.

Mayer, M. (1993). *Little Critter's camp out.* Greensboro, NC: Carson-Dellosa.

Mayer, M. (1995). *Little Monster's moving day.* New York: Scholastic.

Mayer, M. (1984). *The sleeping beauty.* New York: Macmillan.

Mayer, M. (1987). *The ugly duckling.* Illus. T. Locker. New York: MacMillan.

McDermott, G. (1972). *Anansi the spider: A tale from the Ashanti.* New York: Henry Holt.

McDermott, G. (1974). *Arrow to the sun.* New York: Viking Press.

McPhail, D. (1992). *Pig Pig grows up.* New York: Puffin.

Minters, F. (1997). *Cinder-Elly.* Illus. G. B. Karas. New York: Viking Press.

Minters, F. (1996). *Sleepless beauty.* Illus. G. B. Karas. New York: Viking.

Ormerod, J. (2005). *When an elephant comes to school.* New York: Orchard Books.

Patterson, F. (1987). *Koko's story.* Photographer R. Cohn. New York: Scholastic.

Perrault, C. (1972). *The little red riding hood.* Illus. W. Stobbs. New York: H. Z. Walck.

Perrault, C. (1977). *The sleeping beauty.* Trans. & Illus. D. Walker. New York: Thomas Y. Crowell.

Perrault, C. (1989). *Cinderella and other tales from Perrault.* Illus. M. Hague. New York: Henry Holt.

Perrault, C. (1990). *Puss-in-boots.* Illus. F. Marcellino. New York: Farrar, Straus and Giroux.

Polacco, P. (1990). *Babushka's doll.* New York: Aladdin.

Polacco, P. (1990). *Just plain fancy.* New York: Dragonfly Books.

Polacco, P. (1993). *Babushka baba yaga.* New York: Penguin.

Polacco, P. (2001). *The keeping quilt.* New York: Aladdin.

Polacco, P. (1996). *Rechenka's eggs.* New York: Putnam Juvenile.

Polacco, P. (1996). *The trees of the dancing goats.* New York: Simon & Schuster.

Polacco, P. (1999). *Luba and the wren.* New York: Philomel.

Pollock, P. (1996). *The turkey girl: A Zuni Cinderella story.* Illus. E. Young. Boston: Little, Brown.

Powzyk, J. (1988). *Tracking wild chimpanzees.* New York: Lothrop, Lee & Shepard.

Priceman, M. (1996). *How to make an apple pie and see the world.* New York: Dragonfly Books.

Rey, H. A. (1975). *Curious George takes a job.* Boston: Houghton Mifflin.

Rey, H. A. (1980). *Curious George rides a bike.* Boston: Houghton Mifflin.

Rey, H. A. (1985). *Curious George gets a medal.* Boston: Houghton Mifflin.

Rey, H. A. (1991). *Curious George learns the alphabet.* Boston: Houghton Mifflin.

Rey, H. A., & Rey, M. (1994). *Curious George goes to the hospital.* Boston: Houghton Mifflin.

Rey, M. (1986). *Curious George flies a kite.* Boston: Houghton Mifflin.

Robinson, C. (1997). *In the wild chimpanzees.* Chicago: Heinemann.

Rounds, G. (1993). *The three billy goats gruff.* New York: Holiday House.

San Souci, R. D. (1989). *The talking eggs: A folktale from the American South.* Illus. J. Pinkney. New York: Dial.

Scheer, G. (1992). *Cherokee animal tales.* Illus. R. Frankenberg. Tulsa, OK: Council Oaks Books/Holiday House.

Schroeder, A. (1997). *Smoky mountain rose: An Appalachian Cinderella.* Illus. B. Sneed. New York: Dial.

Scieszka, J. (1991). *The frog prince continued.* Illus. S. Johnson. New York: Penguin.

Shannon, D. (2002). *Duck on a bike.* New York: Blue Sky Press.

Shannon, M. (1993). *Elvira.* New York: Tickner & Fields Publishers.

Shenandoah, J., & George, D. (1998). *Skywoman: Legends of the Iroquois.* Santa Fe, NM: Clear Light.

Sierra, J. (1999). *The dancing pig.* Illus. J. Sweetwater. San Diego: Gulliver.

Sierra, J. (1992). *The elephants wrestling match.* New York: Dutton Juvenile.

Sierra, J. (2000). *The gift of the crocodile: A Cinderella story.* Illus. R. Ruffins. New York: Simon & Schuster Children's Publishing.

Sierra, J. (1997). *The mean hyena: A folktale from Malawi.* Illus. M. Bryant. New York: Dutton Juvenile.

Sierra, J. (1996). *Nursery tales around the world: Selected and retold by Judy Sierra.* Illus. S. Vitale. New York: Clarion.

Sierra, J. (1998). *Tasty baby belly buttons: A Japanese folktale.* Illus. M. So. New York: Knopf.

Sierra, J. (1996). *Wiley and the hairy man.* Illus. B. Pinkney. New York: Dutton Juvenile.

Steptoe, J. (1987). *Mufaro's beautiful daughters: An African tale.* New York: Lothrop, Lee & Shepard.

Stevens, J. (1995). *The three billy goats gruff.* San Diego: Harcourt Brace Jovanovich.

Taylor, H. (1995). *Coyote and the laughing butterflies.* New York: Macmillan Books for Young Children.

Travers, P. L. (1980). *Two pairs of shoes.* Illus. L. Dillon & D. Dillon. New York: Viking.

Waber, B. (1965). *Lyle, Lyle, crocodile.* Boston: Houghton Mifflin.

Waite, M. (1996). *Jojofu.* New York: Lothrop, Lee & Shepard.

Washington, D. (2004). *A pride of African tales.* Illus. J. Ransome. New York: HarperCollins.

Willard, N. (2003). *Cinderella's dress.* Illus. J. Dyer. New York: Blue Sky Press.

Willard, N. (1989). *East of the sun and west of the moon.* Illus. B. Moser. New York: Harcourt Children's Books.

Willems, M. (2005). *Leonardo the terrible monster.* New York: Hyperion.

Williams, J. (1976). *Everyone knows what a dragon looks like.* Illus. M. Mayer. New York: Four Winds Press.

Winthrop, E. (2001). *Dumpy La Rue.* Illus. B. Lewin. New York: Henry Holt.

Yolen, J. (1986). *The sleeping beauty.* Illus. R. Sanderson. New York: Knopf.

Yolen, J. (1981). *Sleeping ugly.* Illus. D. Stanley. New York: PaperStar Books.

Yorinks, A. (2007). *The witch's child.* Illus. J. A. Smith. New York: Abrams Books for Young Readers.

Young, E. (1989). *Lon Po Po.* New York: Philomel.

Young, E. (2002). *What about me?* New York: Philomel.

Zemach, M. (1986). *The three wishes: An old tale.* New York: Farrar, Straus & Giroux.

Realistic and Historical Fiction

Sharing Literature: AN EXAMPLE

Ms. Steinberg teaches second grade. Yesterday she read to her children the picture book *Rosa* by Nikki Giovanni (2007), the story of Rosa Parks and the beginning of the Civil Rights movement.

"Class, who remembers the book I read to you yesterday?" A number of hands go up. "Yes, that's right, it was called *Rosa*."

"It was about the lady who wouldn't get off the bus," offers Sheldon from the back of the room.

"That's right, Sheldon, but why did the bus driver make her leave the bus?"

"Because she didn't pay?" offers Allyson.

"No, it was something else. Who remembers?" Ms. Steinberg can see that the children are puzzled. "I'm going to read the book again, and this time afterward we are going to act it out. But first let's rearrange our chairs to make them look like a bus. Okay, everyone take their seats in the bus. Who wants to be the bus driver?" A few hands wave wildly, "Me, me, me."

After Ms. Steinberg has read the book a second time, a few of the children wave their hands indicating that they now understand what happened to Rosa Parks on that fateful day. One little girl plays Rosa Parks, with her arms full of stuff after a long day at work.

"I'm so tired after work," says Rosa, "I'll just sit up here in this empty seat." The other boys and girls on the bus stare at her angrily. They mumble things about her not being able to sit in the front of the bus because she is black.

"Rosa, go to the back of the bus where the black people sit," says the boy playing the bus driver. The other children nod and chant, "Back of the bus. Back of the bus."

"No, I won't leave this seat. Go ahead and arrest me. I'm not moving."

The last scene has two boys (the policemen) coming on to the imaginary bus to arrest Rosa Parks. Then Ms. Steinberg gathers the children around to discuss the story and what happened next. She explains about the protests that followed Rosa Parks's arrest. Afterward, the class decides they want to make protest signs. Ms. Steinberg hands out paper and crayons and helps the children spell out words for their signs such as, "NOT FAIR," "LET ROSA GO," and "DON'T RIDE THE BUS."

Introduction

The single factor that ties all fiction together is that it consists of made-up stories. That is, the story has been created from the imagination of a writer. It may include real elements such as real places, people, and past events. However, the story itself is a creation of the author. For very young children the line between fiction and nonfiction (true stories, informational books, autobiographies, and biographies) is often confusing and blurry. Children view the world and process it differently than do adults. Well-written realistic and historical fiction can seem very real to young children, and they often believe that these are true stories. Teachers and caregivers must help explain that such stories could have happened, but they did not.

Under the general heading of "fiction" we have realistic fiction and historical fiction. Though both genres consist of made-up stories from the imagination of an author, they have some fundamental differences. Realistic fiction deals with contemporary, real-life problems that young children might encounter in their own lives; the plot will most likely be familiar to them. So too will many of the characters be familiar. Historical fiction, on the other hand, though still a made-up story from an author's imagination, is based on a real event that happened in the past or on the lives of real people who lived in the past. Children may not be aware of the situations or may not know the details of the historical event. Authors who write historical fiction, like Jean Fritz and Ann Rinaldi, take great pains to do careful research and present accurate information but do so within the context of a story that they have created.

Let's begin our discussion with realistic fiction. These are picture book stories that plausibly could happen, even though they are the creation of an author. The characters in these stories seem real. Their problems are ones that children could encounter in the real world. Sometimes the stories deal with themes that are hard for young children to explore (like the death of a pet) or controversial themes such as racial discrimination in a school yard. Teachers, parents, and caregivers will have to use their own judgment as to how they approach such books and the discussions that may follow.

Realistic Fiction

Realistic fiction, also called contemporary realistic fiction, is the largest and most popular genre of literature (Monson & Sebesta, 1991; Hancock, 1996). Its popularity with young children and adolescents lies in its subject matter: realistic people with realistic problems. That is what makes the stories so believable. The stories have events that could actually happen to children and adults, and they raise issues and pose conflicts that children recognize.

Realistic fiction may deal with topics that are often controversial or difficult, such as death, divorce, family relationships, gender roles, disabilities, and the like (Lehr, 1995). Since much of contemporary realistic fiction is explicit in its story content, some writers feel it is more suited for the upper elementary grades and older (Giblin, 1987). Well-known child psychologist David Elkind (1981) warns that asking young children to respond to very serious problems and issues may be too much for them to handle. Others disagree, arguing that it depicts the real world in all its dimensions, good and bad, and allows young people to reflect on important issues (Alexander, 1981). Picture books such as Eve Bunting's *Fly Away Home* (1991) and *Smokey Night* (1994), about homelessness and race issues respectively, should stimulate many questions and great discussions among young listeners and readers. Furthermore, contemporary realistic fiction is often a child's first introduction to multicultural literature.

Teachers and caregivers will have to decide if a particular topic in a book is appropriate for an individual child or group of children. Thoughtful choices by a caring adult are at the heart of good teaching. Some guidelines for selecting realistic fiction for young children are provided in the next section.

Selecting Realistic Fiction

As with any genre, teachers, parents, and caregivers must select stories carefully for their young audience. The checklist in Appendix B.3 lists the characteristics that all quality fiction books should have and also includes guidelines specific to realistic and historical fiction. Quality realistic fiction is well written and should hold the attention of the audience. The literary elements of plot, setting, character, and theme should be carefully considered. The plot should be one that is easily followed by children and believable. The events are sequenced often in a linear fashion and move at a lively pace. A good example of this is *Twister* (Beard, 1999). Lucille and Natt love to sit on the porch swing watching the sky and clouds on their Oklahoma farm. But one day a tornado roars up, and they have to hide in the tornado shelter.

The setting, or time and place of the story, should be authentic and vividly described. For instance, Jane Yolen's *Owl Moon* (1987) takes readers through the woods at night with a father and young child in search of owls. Main characters should be fully developed without stereotyping; this is achieved through their dialogue and actions. Barbara Park's Junie B. Jones series presents a memorable and humorous character who deals with school, friends, and parents. In *Junie B. Jones and That Meanie Jim's Birthday* (1996) Junie B. finds that everyone in her class except her has been invited to Meanie Jim's birthday party and she must face being left out.

The theme or underlying message of the story should be an integral part of the plot and not just a moralistic message added at the end of the story. In the example above, Junie B. Jones struggles at school and with her friends over the fact that she has not been invited to Jim's birthday party. She does not handle the situation well. Her feelings have been hurt, and she wants to get back at Jim. A savvy teacher would ask her class questions such as, "How else could Junie have handled this situation?" "What might Jim have done differently?" Another example is *Ira Sleeps Over* (1972) by Bernard Waber. In this classic picture book a young boy is afraid to go on his first sleepover. A teacher can start with basic discussion starters such as, "Do you think the other boys will make fun of him?" and "What if he gets scared and wants to go home?" Then, young children can be encouraged to talk about their own fears of being away from home. Not being invited to a class party or a first time away from their parents or caregivers are serious issues for young children and make for important class discussions.

Categories of Realistic Fiction

Categorizing contemporary realistic fiction books is never easy. Often realistic fiction books will have multiple themes, which makes them difficult to fit easily into firm categories. In this chapter we group books using categories for young children suggested by leading authorities such as Charlotte Huck (Huck et al., 1997). If a teacher or caregiver decides to read aloud a number of books from a single category, then they have taken the first step in creating a unit for the children. The next step is to come up with simple activities for the children to do with each book. For example, for one book, a teacher could have children draw a favorite scene. For another book children could write a single sentence or short paragraph about the book. For a third book they could make a hand puppet for one of the characters and act out a scene. Some units might also lend themselves to listening to music or viewing a video related to that theme.

Family relationships

Families and family relationships are a basic part of contemporary realistic fiction, and young children can learn many important lessons from literature. A teacher or caregiver should begin by asking the children to share, either orally or by drawing pictures, things about their own families. Then as they listen to

author sketch

Beverly Cleary   www.beverlycleary.com

Beverly Cleary was born in 1916 and raised on a farm in Yamhill, Oregon. Later her family moved to Portland, Oregon. She received a degree in librarianship from the University of Washington and became a librarian in Yakima, Washington. In 1940 she married and moved to California where she worked as a librarian and in a bookstore. In 1948 she began writing her first children's book featuring Henry Huggins and his dog Ribsy. This series and others like Ramona and Beezus were based on her own school days in Portland, Oregon. Cleary is a prolific author and the winner of many awards, including the 2000 Library of Congress selection as one of the United States's Living Legends. In her autobiography, *A Girl from Yamhill,* she tells about her first six years growing up on a farm established by her pioneering great grandparents. Some of her books include *Henry Huggins* (1950), *Henry and Ribsy* (1954), *Beezus and Ramona* (1955), *Ramona the Pest* (1968), and *Ramona Quimby, Age 8* (1981).

or read books about other families, they can identify similarities and differences with their own families. Such comparisons are the basis for critical thinking and higher-order mental operations.

Daddy Makes the Best Spaghetti (Hines, 1986) is a simple but significant picture book that discusses the many and varied roles of mommies and daddies in a household where both parents work. In this book, Corey's Dad picks him up at day care, then they go shopping for dinner. They fix dinner together and set the table just before Mommy gets home from work. You can ask students what their favorite food is and who in their family makes it.

Jenna has a new baby brother and Mama has her hands full. In *Mama, Coming and Going* (1994), Judith Caseley tells about all the funny and forgetful things Mama does as she tries to care for newborn Mickey and Jenna at the same time. For example, she accidently leaves the keys in her car, with the door locked, and poor Mickey inside. Children may discuss the funny things they remember their parents doing, and teachers can talk about why busy days can make parents forgetful.

A favorite author of both younger children and older children is Beverly Cleary. She has written almost 50 books in various genres. Her Ramona series, about family relationships, is an example of contemporary realistic fiction. In *Ramona Quimby, Age 8* (1981), Ramona is about to enter third grade and she is excited because now that she is 8 years old, she thinks she knows everything. This is also the year her father decides to go back to college so he can become a teacher. In this chapter book given to reading aloud, Ramona has to deal with those nasty boys in the schoolyard, learn to write in cursive, and take care of her younger sister Willa Jean, while listening to her older sister Beezus brag about junior high school.

The small chapter books of Peggy Parish are similar in writing style to Cleary's. Parish is the author of the very popular Amelia Bedelia series and offers young children a natural transition from picture books to chapter books. Her books contain simple vocabulary and short sentences but a fast-paced and very humorous plot. They all recount the silly antics of Amelia Bedelia, who works as a maid for the Rogers family and gets in constant predicaments

Peggy Parish was born in 1927 in Manning, South Carolina. She graduated from the University of South Carolina and was a teacher for many years. She taught English and creative dance in Texas, Oklahoma, and finally at the Dalton School, a well-known private school in New York City. It was only after she retired from teaching in 1967 that she turned to writing full time. Her Amelia Bedelia series about a wacky maid who takes everything literally became an instant hit, and she continued writing until her death in 1988. Her books include *Amelia Bedelia* (1963), *Thank you, Amelia Bedelia* (1964), and *Amelia Bedelia Goes Camping* (1985).

because she interprets everything literally. For example, in *Amelia Bedelia*, when she is asked to "dust" the furniture, Amelia sprinkles powder over the furniture (Parish, 1963). Even so, the Rogers family loves her in spite of the crazy things she does. Series books like those by Cleary and Parish have been popular with young children generation after generation. Their humor, memorable characters, and easy to follow plots make them a good transition from picture books to short chapter books.

S. E. Hinton is the well-known author of young adult novels such as *The Outsiders* and *Tex*, but she has also written a book for younger children. *Big David, Little David* (1995) is a humorous account of little Nick's first day in kindergarten. Nick's Dad's name is David, and in kindergarten there's a little boy also named David. Could this be his Dad, only a smaller version? Nick's confusion grows when his Dad pretends that he is both Little David and Big David. To figure out who is who, Nick tests his father with questions about what went on in school that day. Teachers may ask the children in class if they know their parents' names or what they do for a living. Many young children know their parents only as Mom and Dad. A follow-up activity would be to ask children to bring in something for show and tell that represents what Mom or Dad does during the day; perhaps Mom works in a bank, so the child brings in some play money.

Many children have a favorite piece of clothing or a blanket they carry with them. In *Aaron's Shirt* (Gould, 1989), Aaron goes clothes shopping with his mother and finds the perfect shirt: short sleeves with red and white stripes. He loves his new shirt and wears it to dinner and to school and outside to play. When winter comes, Aaron can't wait for spring when he can wear his favorite shirt again. Children may tell teachers and caregivers about or draw their favorite piece of clothing or blanket.

Cynthia Rylant is the author of a series for young children that features Henry and his dog Mudge. In *Henry and Mudge and the Careful Cousin* (1994), Henry can't wait for a visit from his cousin Annie, whom he's never met before. But when Annie arrives in her little white dress with perfect ruffles, she's greeted by a slobbering Mudge and Henry's messy room. Teachers and caregivers can ask the children to talk about visits from their cousins.

In *Oscar's Half Birthday* (Graham, 2005), young Millie and her Mom and Dad decide to celebrate baby Oscar's six-month birthday by going on a picnic. When they get to the hillside park across from their apartment building, they meet lots of other people there. The illustrations make clear that the parents are an interracial couple. Ask the children to identify the different people they see in the pictures to open a discussion about different races.

Lauren Child has written about a memorable little girl named Clarice Bean and her wacky family. In *Clarice Bean Guess Who's Babysitting* (Child, 2000) Mom and Dad have to go out on important business so Clarice and little brother Minal are babysat by Uncle Ted, the firefighter. In *Clarice Bean That's Me* (1999) we meet Clarice's entire family, including her older sister Marcie, who has a room to herself; older brother Kurt, who shuts his door when Clarice wants to play; and Grandad, who spends most of his time sleeping in his favorite chair. Have the children tell about some of their babysitters or other members of their family. Then have them draw pictures of their families.

Not all families spend their days in the same way. Rachel Isadora has written and illustrated two beautiful multicultural picture books depicting authentic everyday life for many South Africans. In *Over the Green Hills* (1992), Zolani and his mother are going to visit Grandma Zindzi. First Zolani gathers mussels from the sea, and he ties them to his goat. His mother balances a box of dried fish on her head. Then off they go. Along the way they meet many people, trade for firewood, and see an ostrich running across the Transkei. Teachers and caregivers can ask children to tell about visits to their grandparents and compare their travels to Zolani's. In *At the Crossroads* (1988) Rachel Isadora tells the story of young children living in South Africa's shantytowns. They are waiting at the crossroads on the special day that their fathers return from working in the mines. The colorful scenes from Africa, with its different animals, introduce children to a world they may not know exists.

South Africa is also the setting for *Jamela's Dress* (1999) by Niki Daly. Mama has bought some beautiful, colorful fabric to make a dress to wear to a wedding. And Jamela is in charge of watching the material while it dries in the sun. Beautiful color illustrations reveal everyday life in Cape Town's black community. You can try your hand at some of the African arts and crafts described in the "Africa" section of www.kinderart.com/multic/. Remember that art activities enhance learning for all subjects (Gullatt, 2008).

American children are familiar with the customs associated with birthday parties. However, families celebrate birthdays in different ways. *Henry's First-Moon Birthday* (Look, 2001) is a fictional account of a Chinese birthday custom. Jenny is excited. She's the older sister and gets to help out in the upcoming celebration for baby Henry. His one-month-old birthday, or "first-moon" as it is called in Chinese, is coming up, and the whole family will celebrate. They'll write Henry's name in Chinese characters using a special ink pad, eat pig's feet and ginger soup, and dye eggs red for good luck. This story lends itself to comparing this Chinese tradition with American birthdays.

Nontraditional families. Today, the nuclear family of mother, father, and children living together is not necessarily the norm. More and more children grow up in families with one parent, or they are raised by a grandparent, an aunt or uncle, or even by an older sibling. Mary Hoffman has written *Boundless Grace* (1995) with this in mind. Grace lives with her mother and Nana but never knew her father. Her father separated from her mother and moved to Gambia, Africa. One day a letter arrives from her father inviting Grace and Nana to visit him in Africa. And so begins a great cultural and personal adventure for Grace, as she reconnects with her father in a strange and exciting country. You can ask children who they live with: a mom or a dad or perhaps a grandparent. A family is defined by the love it provides a child, not who its members are.

Juan lives in *The Most Beautiful Place in the World* (Cameron, 1988), which is a village on a great lake in the mountains of Guatemala. But things are changing for Juan. First, his father leaves. Then, his mother remarries, but her new husband does not want to care for Juan. So Juan must go live with his grandmother. Life is hard for Juan and his grandmother, but still he decides he would like to go to school. This will not be easy without money to buy books or new clothes. Many children take school and nice clothes to wear for granted. Teachers and caregivers can help explain that this is not true for all children. They can also show students where Guatemala is located on a map or talk about some of the cultural traditions of the country.

Siblings. Brothers and sisters and their relationships with one another provide a constant source for stories that young children like to hear and talk about. Whether readers are the youngest, the oldest, or in the middle, having brothers and sisters makes life interesting for children.

A new baby in the house can be a wonderful experience, but sometimes an older brother or sister may think otherwise. *I Love My Baby Sister (Most of the Time)* (Edelman, 1984) is a story about a big sister and her new baby sister. Baby sister is fun to play with, but sometimes she cries and pulls the big sister's hair. But the big sister realizes that when the baby grows older she will have fun teaching her all the things she knows. Teachers and caregivers can invite children to tell about their younger or older brothers and sisters, conflicts they have, and how they were or could be resolved.

Julian and his little brother Huey are always getting into some sort of mischief; their adventures are presented as short stories in *The Stories Julian Tells* (1981) by Ann Cameron. For example, in one story, Julian's father decides to make a lemon pudding for mother before she comes home. But Julian and Huey can't wait and eat the entire pudding themselves while their father naps. In another story Julian gets a fig tree for his fourth birthday and is supposed to care for it. This multi-chapter book is meant to be read aloud to children.

When you are the youngest and smallest in the family, life can sometimes be difficult. In *Keep Running, Allen!* (1978), by Clyde Bulla, Allen's older sister and two older brothers do everything together. But Allen's legs are just too short, and he can't keep up with their adventures. Teachers and caregivers may ask children to talk about what it might be like to be the youngest sibling in the family.

In *Jamaica Tag Along* (1989) by Juanita Havill, little Jamaica wants to hang out with her older brother Ossie and play basketball with the boys. But she's too little and has to find her own playmates. Then, when baby Berto wants to play with Jamaica, she won't let him because he's too little. The watercolor illustrations bring these African American siblings to life on the page and raise issues of fairness and responsibility toward younger siblings.

A similar problem is described in *Dance, Tanya* (1989) by Patricia Gauch. Tanya loves to follow along when her older sister Elise goes to ballet practice. But Tanya is too young for ballet lessons. All she can do is watch Elise's recitals. But she can dance around the living room and outside garden. Dance and movement have many benefits for young children, including developing motor coordination, balance, flexibility, strength, stamina, and discipline. Teachers can have children practice standing on their toes and doing pirouettes like Tanya. The following website has instructions and videos for performing basic ballet moves: www.ehow.com/videos-on_2664_neoclassical-ballet-steps-beginners.html.

In a small village in Tanzania, Elizabeti watches her mother care for her new baby brother. She wishes she had a doll to care for just like her mother cares for baby brother. In *Elizabeti's Doll* (1998), by Stephanie Stuve-Bodeen, Elizabeti's mother finds the perfectly shaped rock to be a baby doll. Elizabeti washes her rock and wraps it in cloth and calls it Eva. The illustrations show life in an African village and the universal qualities of mother and child. Teachers and caregivers may have children bring their favorite doll or toy to class to share with others while they talk about how to properly care for infants.

In *Con Mi Hermano/With My Brother* (1991), a simple picture book by Eileen Roe, a little boy can't wait for his older brother to come home from school each day so that they can play together. Told in both English and Spanish, this book could be a first introduction to another language for children. Teachers may use this book to help children understand and appreciate our multilingual and multicultural world.

Grandparents. Prior to the 1960s elderly people rarely appeared in children's stories. If they did, they were often depicted as ailing and feeble. Older adults have much to offer the very young and many lead active, exciting lives. Children's books now include such characters frequently in stories about grandparents.

The Hello, Goodbye Window (2005) by Norton Juster tells of a little girl who loves to visit her Nana and Poppy in their big house. She loves just to hang out in the kitchen and examine all the stuff on the shelves. She hears Poppy playing "Oh, Susannah" on his harmonica. Poppy also makes the best breakfast in the mornings: oatmeal with raisins and bananas. Sometimes the little girl just likes to sit by the kitchen window and wonder who will come by. Teachers may let the children take turns telling stories about their grandparents.

Karen Ackerman's *Song and Dance Man* (1988) won the Caldecott Medal for its outstanding illustrations. Three grandchildren get to visit their grandpa and explore the attic where he keeps his old clothes, shoes, hats, and cane from the days when he sang and danced and told jokes on the vaudeville stage. This is a great book for getting children to act out, pretending they are on a vaudeville stage. Teachers can explain what vaudeville is and how entertainment has changed over generations.

A book with a similar theme is *Papa Lucky's Shadow* (Daly, 1992). Papa Lucky is retired from his moving job and lives with his daughter and granddaughter Sugar. He tells stories about how he used to love to dance. One day Papa Lucky gets the idea that maybe he can earn some extra money in the city dancing in the streets for people's entertainment. He takes Sugar along as his "hat girl." Teachers can help children enjoy the book by letting them try tap dancing on the floor in the classroom or out in the hallway. Also, discuss with them what it means to retire from work.

In *Babu's Song* (2003), author Stephanie Stuve-Bodeen tells of the relationship between a boy and his grandfather in modern day Africa. Bernardi lives with his grandfather, Babu, in a poor village in Tanzania. Babu works hard making toys out of found objects that Bernardi sells in the market place. Bernardi wishes he could go to school and play soccer like the other boys, but he is too poor.

Another story about a boy and his grandfather comes from Tomie dePaola. Bobby and Bob, his grandfather, are best friends. They do all sorts of things together like play with wooden block letters under the old staircase. But one day Bob has a stroke, and Bobby must now help his granddad. Tomie dePaola tells this simple but thoughtful story in *Now One Foot, Now the Other* (1981).

Adoption. There are many children waiting to be adopted by loving families. Children who are adopted often have mixed, confused feelings about their new situation. Parents, caregivers, and teachers should discuss these issues, when appropriate, with young children.

Kathryn Miller has written *Did My First Mother Love Me?* (1994) to answer one of the most common questions that young adoptees have about their birth parents. In this simply written story, young Morgan asks her adopted mother this question. In response her mom reads a letter from Morgan's birth mother explaining how much she loved her and what she wished for her daughter. For children in a similar situation or with similar questions, this book could be the starting point for an honest discussion about a difficult topic.

Jeannette Caines's *Abby* (1973) is an early book about what it means to be adopted. Little Abby loves to look at her baby book from the time she was adopted. But older brother Kevin isn't interested. Abby asks her mother to explain why they adopted her. Children who are adopted may have many questions to ask.

In *Through Moon and Stars and Night Skies* (Turner, 1990), a little boy from a faraway country tells how he took a long plane ride and came to a new country where he met his new parents. He was afraid during his first plane ride, and everything seemed strange in his new country and new home. But gradually he came to love his new momma and poppa and his new life in the United States. This simple story touches on the fears of all adopted children, especially those going to a new country.

Jin Woo (Bunting, 2001) tells the story of an American family who adopt a child from Korea. This is a big adjustment for everyone, not only is a new member entering the family but cultural differences make it even more complicated. Cultural differences in language, food, and dress should be seen as a strength in a classroom. We all have something to learn from one another.

In *Emma's Yucky Brother* (Little, 2001) Emma is excited that she'll be getting a new brother. But when Max arrives he's not what she expected. First of all, he's not so little for a four-year-old. And he doesn't like the cookies Emma baked. And he cries for his foster mom, Ann. This easy to read chapter book is a nice transition from picture books and raises the issues of the conflicts faced by established siblings in homes when an adopted child arrives.

Death and dying

Death and dying are a natural part of life, but dying is something that most young children don't understand and consequently fear. Realistic fiction books about death and dying allow children to talk about these issues without feeling personally threatened.

Grandpa Abe (Russo, 1996) tells of the loving relationship between young Sarah and her Grandpa Abe. They love to eat spaghetti together, and they love to dance in the living room. But when Sarah turns nine, Abe dies. Afterward, at the funeral, Sarah and her grandmother share their favorite stories of Abe while Sarah gets to keep one of her grandfather's sweaters so that she will never forget him. Teachers and caregivers may ask if any children have lost a grandparent or a loved one. If so, what do they remember best about that person?

In *Everett Anderson's Goodbye* (Clifton, 1983) young Everett is having a very hard time accepting the death of his father. Told in simple language with black and white drawings, this book leads you through the five stages of grieving: denial, anger, bargaining, depression, and acceptance. Eventually, Everett learns that love doesn't stop even with death.

Sophie (1994) by Mem Fox tells of Sophie, who is born into a loving family. When she grows older, she can help her Grandpa. But then Grandpa begins to grow feeble. Although a book about dying and death, this is an uplifting, easy-to-read story about the cycles of life. At the end, Sophie gets a new baby sister.

Other books tell about the death of beloved pets. *The Forever Dog* (Cochran, 2007) tells about Mike and his dog Corky. Mike and Corky go everywhere and do everything together. When Mom tells Mike that Corky is very sick, it's a sad time in the household. You can have children share stories, happy and sad, about their own pets.

Finally, in *I Remember Miss Perry* (Brisson, 2006), little Stevie and his classmates are saddened by the death of their favorite teacher in a car accident. Eventually the children deal with their grief by sharing their favorite memories about Miss Perry.

School and friends

Young children often love their teachers. Next to their parents and their caregivers these are the adults they interact with the most in terms of number of hours per day. School is also the place where children meet other children beyond their home and neighborhood. It is the primary environment for making friends and dealing with kids who are not so friendly.

Mickey and Jack used to be best friends, but then Jack changed. In *Bully* (Caseley, 2001) Mickey has his lunch cookies stolen by Jack. The next day he sits far away from Jack. But on the school field trip Jack takes Mickey's cap and plays "keep away" until the teacher stops the game, confiscates the cap, and bans Mickey from recess the next day. Bullying is a very serious issue in our schools today and needs to be discussed (Olweus, 2002). Other realistic fiction picture books on bullying for young children include *Fat, Fat Rose Marie* (Passen, 1991) and *Bootsie Barker Bites* (Bottner, 1992). Teachers and caregivers may ask children how they would deal with a bully in their class and explain that the teacher is there to help and protect them. Adults can also use the resources at www.stopbullyingnow.com to discuss with children what to do if they are being bullied.

For many children school is also the first place where they get to play a musical instrument in a real band. In *Ada Potato* (Caseley, 1989) Ada can't wait to learn the violin and practice with Mr. Lenny, the band teacher. But walking

author sketch

Ezra Jack Keats

Ezra Jack Keats was born in 1916 in a poor section of Brooklyn, New York. His parents had emigrated from Poland a few years earlier. As a young boy he loved to draw, but his father felt an artist could not make a living. His mother however encouraged his drawing. Living in New York City, his family visited the Metropolitan Museum of Art, where he saw the great art masters of the world. During the Depression he loaded trucks to make money while studying at the Art Students League. During World War II he served in the Air Force. After the war he began writing and illustrating children's books. In 1963 he won the Caldecott Award for *Snowy Day*. Some of his picture books have been made into filmstrips. Some of his titles are *Whistle for Willie* (1964), *John Henry, An American Legend* (1965), *Peter's Chair* (1967), *Pet Show* (1972), *Louie's Search* (1980), and *Clementina's Cactus* (1982).

to school with her violin case is a problem when some kids call her names and make fun of her violin. Ada solves her problem in a clever way. Teachers and caregivers can make this a lesson about both music and self-confidence. They can ask what musical instruments young children would like to play. Let the children listen to the different instruments in an orchestra. They can also role-play other ways to deal with mean children calling others names.

In *My Teacher for President* (Winters, 2004) young Oliver thinks his teacher would make a great president of the United States. After all, the kids follow her around just like the press corps follows the president, she goes to lots of meetings, she's great at handling emergencies (like the day the pet snake got loose), and she listens to everyone's problems. Teachers and caregivers may include children in a discussion about who is currently the president of the United States, how a president gets elected, and what duties the office has.

School can also be a scary time for some children. Young Ben, in *I Don't Want to Go Back to School* (Russo, 1994), is just winding up the summer after his first year in school. He'll have a new teacher, who might be mean, and maybe the bus driver won't know which stop to let him off at. The first day of a new school year, whatever grade, is always filled with apprehensions. Questions that teachers may ask children include the following: "What do you worry about on the first day of school?" "What are you looking forward to?"

Ezra Jack Keats has written some of the finest picture books for young children. He was also among the earliest author/illustrators to have multiracial children as the central characters. *A Letter to Amy* (Keats, 1968) is such a book. Peter is going to have a birthday party and he is inviting all his friends from school, including Amy, even though he knows the other boys would never invite a girl to their party. He decides to send Amy a real letter invitation. You can have students create an invitation to a party and send it to a friend in the class. Remember that writing activities strengthen reading abilities.

Getting held back a grade in school is a fear for every child (and parent). In *The Beast in Ms. Rooney's Room* (Giff, 1984) Richard "Beast" Best has to repeat third grade at the Polk Street School. The new kids in his class don't like him. His old friends now in fourth grade won't play with him. But when Mrs. Paris, the new reading teacher arrives, things begin to change for the better for Richard. Patricia Reilly Giff has written many realistic stories about the Polk

Street School kids. These short easy-to-read chapter books are great for those children ready to read something other than picture books.

In *Once Upon a Time* (2003), author/illustrator Niki Daly, who lives in Cape Town, South Africa, tells the story of how one little child learns to read and experiences the joys of literature. Sarie hates reading aloud in class. The other kids laugh. She even feels sick to her stomach. After school she sits in the old rusted car of Aunt Anna and tells her how the children make fun of her because she can't read. Wise Aunt Anna has an idea. Teachers may use the book as a starting point to have children vocalize their own concerns about learning to read.

As we mentioned earlier, Barbara Park has authored a series of books for young readers that feature the memorable Junie B. Jones. Strong-willed and outspoken, Junie B. Jones has one misadventure after another at school. In *Junie B. Jones and the Stupid Smelly Bus* (1992) the first day of kindergarten does not go at all well for Juni B. And besides, she's scared of riding the school bus that smells. In *Junie B. Jones Loves Handsome Warren* (1996) Junie B. and her best friends Lucille and Grace love kindergarten. They play all sorts of games and get into all sorts of mischief. Then Lucille meets Warren, the new boy from room eight. And is he handsome! But Junie B. decides that Warren will be her boyfriend and not Lucille's. After reading a number of these books, ask your students to tell about or make up some of the adventures they have had or imagine they had at school. After telling these stories in a circle, have students write them down or draw them.

Another series of easy-to-read chapter books features the irrepressible Amber Brown. In *Get Ready for Second Grade, Amber Brown* (2002), author Paula Danziger shows Amber Brown, her stuffed toy Bear Lee, and her knee scab Scabulous heading off to school. But what if the new teacher, Ms. Light, is mean and gives seven hours of homework and won't allow her to go to the bathroom? Children may want to talk about what kinds of things they are worried about when they go to a new grade.

Friendships also develop outside of school. In *Gregory Cool* (1994) by Carline Binch, Gregory thinks he's cool with his baseball cap, sneakers, and matching pants and shirts. But what's he going to do for four weeks on the Caribbean island of Tobago with his grandparents? His younger cousin, Lennox, goes barefoot but knows how to climb coconut trees and swims with the dolphins. A new friendship develops on this hot island where they eat bread and saltfish for breakfast and drink milk from a coconut. This multicultural book should stimulate discussions about other lands, and the gorgeous color illustrations will get children wanting to use their watercolor paints.

Racial issues

Today many children are likely to interact with children of different races and from different countries. More children have mixed-race ancestry and cross-cultural identities. In Hawaii, for example, one quarter of citizens check two different racial boxes on all forms (Goodman, 2008). Early childhood experts agree that parents should discuss issues of race when their children are young. Racial prejudices begin between the ages of 8 and 12. By the time children are in junior high school, peers, television, and music have already shaped their attitudes toward race. Experts agree that by high school it is often too late to change attitudes of racial prejudice (Thompson & Aldridge, 2001). Thus parents, caregivers, and teachers of preschool and primary-grade children have a unique opportunity to teach tolerance.

An early book for young children that deals with race and interracial marriage is Arnold Adoff's *Black Is Brown Is Tan* (1973). In this simple and easy to read book, a little boy enjoys the colors of his mother and father and all the colors of the world around him. This book would make a good starting point to talk about skin color and why we are the way we are.

In *My Name Was Hussein* (Kyuchukov, 2004) a young Roma boy lives in Bulgaria. People in Europe refer to the Roma as gypsies and often discriminate against them. Hussein's family is Muslim, and they have lived in a farming village with aunts, uncles, and cousins for many generations. One day police come with guns, dogs, and tanks. They tell Hussein's parents not to speak their native Roma language or pray at the mosque. They also must change their names to Christian names. Based on actual events in the 1980s this story raises serious issues worth discussing. Some discussion questions can include, "What freedoms do we take for granted?" and "Why do you think the police did not like the gypsies?"

Sound of Sunshine, Sound of Rain (Heide, 1970) is a beautifully written story about a young black boy who is blind. Each morning he listens to the sounds of the house and sounds outside his apartment window. He hopes his big sister can take him to the park. One day while shopping together they encounter prejudice. The little boy is confused about what happened, but his sister is only angry. Comparing and contrasting the boy's positive attitude with his sister's negative feelings should be a good discussion starter. You might also introduce the children to using a Venn diagram for comparison.

Immigration

The United States is a land of immigrants, who include the early pilgrims, colonists from England; later immigrants from Italy, Germany, the Netherlands, China, Japan; and recent immigrants from Latin America and the Caribbean. The United States was settled by people from many different lands who brought with them their languages, customs, food, and dress, which all add to the colorful mosaic that is the United States today.

During the Vietnam War (1965–1973) many Vietnamese fled their country and came to the United States, sponsored by American families, civic organizations, and churches. Vietnamese families were often separated during the journey and had a long waiting period to enter the United States. In Michele Surat's *Angel Child, Dragon Child* (1983) we meet one such family. Ut and her older sisters came to the United States with their father. But they still are waiting for their mother to arrive. In their American school the children make fun of Ut's way of speaking and the pajama-like outfit she wears. It's difficult starting over in a new land. Teachers may discuss whether any children or their parents or their grandparents came from another land.

In *How Many Days to America?* (1988) author Eve Bunting tells the story of one Caribbean family escaping the harsh rule on their island. Their wooden boat is small and crowded and dangerous on the open seas. The days pass and the people are hungry; some are sick. Not everyone will make it. Teachers and caregivers may ask children why would people risk their lives to leave their homes to journey to a strange land.

In *Yang the Youngest and His Terrible Ear* (1992) Lensey Namioka tells of a Chinese family who move to Seattle, Washington. In the Yang family everyone is a musician: the father plays the violin in an orchestra, the mother plays the piano, and all the Yang children play violin. But the youngest Yang just can't seem to get it right; his older sisters make fun of him. Then, at school, he discovers baseball. This short novel gives insights into how a family from another country and culture has to adjust to its new life in the United States.

Gender roles

Early children's literature books and basal reader series like Dick and Jane stereotyped boys and girls as occupying fixed roles with certain behaviors (Enciso & Rogers, 1999; Nodelman, 1999). Even today adults and children alike often view various occupations, sports, and activities as being either for boys or girls. Child psychologists make clear that gender role stereotyping is as negative and harmful as any other type of stereotyping (Hughes & Seta, 2003). As an antidote to older ways, contemporary realistic fiction picture books tend to present boys and girls in many varied roles.

An excellent book by Charlotte Zolotow is *William's Doll* (1972). Little William can shoot the basketball through the hoop and play with the train set that his father bought him, but what he really wants is a doll with blue eyes and curly lashes. His father and older brothers are horrified. Only sissies play with dolls. Teachers and caregivers can discuss with children how William's problem might be solved. Name calling like "sissy" is an issue that many young children have to deal with and discussing this first with an adult may help some children deal with their hurt feelings.

In *Max* (1984) by Rachel Isadora, young Max is the star of his baseball team. His sister Lisa takes ballet lessons while Max plays baseball on Saturdays. One day Max goes with Lisa to watch the girls do their stretches and warm-ups. The teacher asks Max to join in. Teachers may ask children if they think ballet dancing and baseball are compatible. Do they have anything in common? What do the children think Max will do?

Gender stereotyping and racial discrimination often go hand in hand. In *Amazing Grace* (1991) by Mary Hoffman we meet Grace, who loves to act out stories and dress up as her favorite characters from books. When the teacher announces tryouts for the play Peter Pan, Grace knows that she can be a great Peter. But Grace's feelings are hurt when the other children tell her she can't be Peter because Peter is a boy and not black. The beautiful illustrations of this multicultural book will help young children follow the storyline. Teachers and caregivers can use questions to stimulate discussion: What do you think about boy and girl roles? Are there things that girls shouldn't do? That boys shouldn't do?

Individuals with disabilities

We have many labels for children who for various reasons (physical, emotional, social, or cognitive) don't fit the norm: e.g., "children with special needs." Many years ago some of these children either did not attend our public schools or were placed in special classrooms, isolated from the rest of the school community. That is no longer the case. Primarily through the efforts of parents, classrooms are more integrated, mixes of children of various abilities and disabilities. Parents realized, before educators did, that one of the primary purposes of school is to socialize children to one another. The following books should encourage critical thinking and much discussion among teachers and students. You can also find resources about children with disabilities and special needs at www.comeunity.com.

The most common disability teachers will encounter among school children is a learning disability. In *One Little Girl* (Fassler, 1969), Laurie can do many things. She was the first child on her block to run outside, she can brush her own hair, and she can jump rope without missing once. But at school Laurie is slow in math and slow in writing her name. A kind teacher helps Laurie and her parents understand that even though she may be slow in some things, she is fast in others.

Eddie Lee has Down syndrome. Christy and JimBud go off to wade in the creek and don't want Eddie Lee tagging along. *Be Good to Eddie Lee* (Fleming, 1993) is a beautifully written and illustrated book with a simple but poignant message: children with Down syndrome and other special needs children can enjoy the same activities as other children but may need a little more help to do so.

In *Rachel* (1975), by Elizabeth Fanshawe, Rachel does all the things other children do at school: she draws and writes and helps feed the gerbil. She goes to Brownies and plays games, even though she is in a wheelchair. She goes on vacations with her parents and dreams of all the things she might be when she grows up. Ask children if they know anyone in a wheelchair and how he or she manages to do everyday things. Children sometimes fear what they do not know or understand. Having a person with a disability speak to your class is a good way to overcome this.

Howie lives in an apartment building with his mother, father, and sister. But Howie needs help in doing things; he has cerebral palsy. His legs are weak, so he can't run. His hands are weak, so he can't write with a pencil. He rides a special school bus that has a lift for his wheelchair. In *Howie Helps Himself* (Fassler, 1975), children can read how, despite his handicap, Howie learns to do things for himself. Teachers and caregivers can use this book to help children understand that everyone needs to develop a sense of self-esteem and independence.

Lisa Rowe Fraustino tells the story of Louis and his Gran in *The Hickory Chair* (2001). Louis loves his Gran. Even though he is blind, Louis can do most everything other kids do. But one day Gran dies. The strong relationship between a grandfather and a grandson who is dealing with the handicap of blindness is beautifully portrayed in this book. Discussing issues like blindness and deafness with young children before they enter school will help them better accept children with these differences.

Goose's Story (2002), by Cari Best, is told by a little girl who lives in the country with her family. Each spring she watches for the brilliant black and white Canada geese to arrive on the nearby pond. But one goose is by herself. She has only one good leg. She can't fly or swim or feed with the other geese. Animals as well as humans must learn to cope with their disabilities. Brilliant collage illustrations enhance this heartwarming story.

- The Global Ideas Bank at www.globalideasbank.org encourages children to write letters about environmental issues that affect their lives, like the pollution of a local stream or overwhelming garbage disposal in large cities.
- The United Nations Volunteer website at www.unv.org provides ways for young people to get involved in environmental issues locally and around the world.
- The Institute for Children's Environmental Health (ICEH) is a nonprofit educational organization concerned specifically with environmental issues that affect children's health. For example, they provide a database for parents on toxic toys. Their website is www.iceh.org.

Environmental issues

Environmental issues concern adults and children alike. It is never too early to educate children about the importance of protecting our natural environment. Parents, caregivers, and teachers may want to investigate websites, such as those in Figure 7.1, with ideas for educating children about the environment.

In *Judy Moody Saves the World* (McDonald, 2002) Judy gets really serious about protecting the environment. Not everyone agrees with her, but in the end she motivates her entire class to get involved in an environmental school project. This short chapter book could be read aloud to young children.

In *Trash Trouble* (Brimner, 2003) a second grade class goes on a field trip to a nature center. They decide to pick up all the trash they can after they find a bird caught in some discarded plastic bags. Picking up trash around school would be a good instructional lesson for young children.

In Lauren Child's *What Planet Are You from Clarice Bean?* (2002) saving a tree on their street from being cut becomes a real challenge for Clarice and her family. Not everyone at school understands what she is doing. This book shows that sometimes, you have to just do what is right.

Five-year-old Eli decides to save the planet by recycling, everything! Soon his room fills up with more and more junk that he intends to recycle some day. *Mr. Garbage* (Hooks, 1997) is a humorous picture book that gets a serious message across to young children: having good intentions is not enough, you also have to act on them. This story could lead to a small-scale recycling effort in a classroom.

Taken together these books could form the foundation for a unit on cleaning up the environment. Children could write stories about the environment, write letters to their local newspaper, help with a clean-up project around their school and neighborhood, and encourage their parents to get involved in keeping the environment clean.

The Year of the Panda (1990) by Miriam Schlein is a short chapter book that deals with protecting the animals in our environment. Lu Yi and his family are wheat farmers in rural China. When he is not helping his family around the farm, Lu Yi goes to school in the town. One day when returning with his father from gathering firewood in the mountains, they come across a baby panda bear. Some one has killed its mother, and Lu Yi takes it home with him. This book would make for an excellent discussion of the need to protect endangered animals.

Historical Fiction

istorical fiction, as mentioned earlier, is a subcategory of fiction. Historical fiction books are stories that come from an author's imagination but are based on real events and real people from the past. Historical fiction deals with the past, sometimes the very distant past. Time is an abstract concept difficult for very young children to grasp. Long ago could be a month, a year, or any time before they were born. Events that took place hundreds of years ago may be difficult for young children to fathom. But they can still understand and relate to a powerful story that took place "a long time ago." Thus historical fiction becomes an introduction to both the concept of and the events of the past.

Once children enter school, many classes are dominated by textbooks that have been adopted by the school district. The latter have a number of weaknesses as vehicles for teaching and exciting children about history, particularly young children (McGowan & Guzzetti, 1991). Textbooks, even in the early grades, often cover too much material, and, consequently, serious topics are dealt with briefly. Textbooks also focus on facts: names of people and places and dates. What's missing is the story behind those facts, the real people and real settings that make history come alive (Lasky, 1990). The advantages of historical fiction children's books are that

- They cover a single topic, person, or event in some detail
- They focus on interesting facts, anecdotes, and descriptions that make the person, event, or period come alive for the reader
- The writer's creative style makes for an exciting story that allows the child's imagination to soar.

A good story captures the imagination of children so that they can sail the wooden ships with Columbus, exult in a slave's escape to freedom via the Underground Railroad, feel the frightening aspects of the Civil War, be repelled by the horrors of the Holocaust. This is what quality historical fiction is about. When children respond to literature with strong feelings, we say they have a vicarious experience. For a moment, they are in the story, feeling the wind against their faces, smelling the smoke, experiencing the anguish of real people at war. Placing oneself in the historical moment or the shoes of a historical character is a key step to a critical understanding of history. Historical fiction also reveals the mistakes of the past, allows us to learn from those mistakes, and maybe avoid making them again.

Selecting Historical Fiction

In evaluating the quality books available for young children in the historical fiction genre, we still need to make sure there is a realistic plot, believable characters, a memorable setting, and significant theme, as discussed in Chapter 5 and in Appendix B.3. On top of this, the plot, setting, characters, and their dialogue must be historically authentic. In good historical fiction, the author has researched the time period thoroughly and presents the reader not only with a believable story, but one that is based on historical facts. The details must be authentic. The place descriptions must be authentic. The time period, with its special dress, food, technology, etc., must be authentic. Authenticity is the hallmark for historical fiction (Collier, 1982).

Categories of Historical Fiction

Historical fiction can be a large and intimidating genre, but breaking it into categories can help make the genre less intimidating. We have chosen to organize this section chronologically, beginning with the distant past and leading up to the more recent past. We do not intend to cover every time period or every significant event in American or world history. Rather we present a selection of books meant to engage the hearts and minds of young children with the people, places, and events of the past.

Early history

Roman chariots, Egyptian mummies, the great pyramids, early discoverers and explorers have all long captured the minds of young children. A few books dealing with ancient history have been written for the very young child. One of these is *Zekmet the Stone Carver* (1988) by Mary Stolz. It tells the story of how the great stone Sphinx, part lion and part human, came to be. This well-written story with excellent illustrations is a great introduction to a time long past. In *Nefertari, Princess of Egypt* (Angeletti, 1998) a young girl follows a cat into the tomb of Nefertari, daughter of the Queen of Egypt. There she learns about hieroglyphic writing, Egyptian burial practices, and many other things. Teachers and caregivers may take children to the library to find other picture and art books on Egyptian pyramids, tombs, and mummies.

Most children know of Christopher Columbus and the discovery of the New World. In Jane Yolen's picture book, *Encounter* (1992), another side to the story is told. Native American tribes who lived in the New World were often treated harshly by the Europeans, who saw them as savages. In this book a young Taino boy first welcomes the Europeans with gifts; later when he is captured into slavery he realizes their true intent and tries to warn his people.

American Colonial and Revolutionary periods

Jean Fritz is an outstanding writer of historical fiction for young children. In *The Lost Colony of Roanoke* (1975) Fritz tells the fascinating story of one of the great mysteries of the early American colonies. Sir Walter Raleigh helped to found the first colony on Roanoke Island off the coast of what today is North Carolina. He left settlers there, but when he returned from England the colony had vanished without a trace. Ask your children what they think happened to the colony and why. Was it attacked by Indians and destroyed? Did the crops fail and the colonists left without a trace?

Molly Bannaky (McGill, 1999) is based on the true story of young Molly, who was sent to the United States in 1683 as an indentured servant, and who eventually won her freedom. Unable to run a farm by herself, she buys an African slave to help her. Later they fall in love, marry, and have four daughters. A son of one of the daughters, Benjamin Banneker, grew up to be a respected scientist and mathematician in the new country of the United States, and corresponded with Thomas Jefferson about the injustices of slavery. Discuss with the children what life would be like on a farm in the seventeenth century where all work was done by hand.

In *Sleds on Boston Common* (2000) Louise Borden tells of the rising tensions between the British redcoats and the people of Boston through the eyes of a 9-year-old boy. It's winter time, 1774, and England's King George III has closed Boston Harbor and stationed British troops in the city to punish the colonists who opposed his newest restrictive laws. But young Henry Price and his friends are determined to take advantage of the snowy hills for sledding. This story lends itself to dramatic role-playing with one group of children pretending to be the colonists and another the British soldiers. Dramatic role-playing is a way for children to explore the emotional side of past events and increase their understanding of history (Mynard, 2005).

Six Silver Spoons (Lowrey, 1971) is set in Concord, Massachusetts, a small town outside of Boston in the year 1775. There, the colonists have hidden their guns for the upcoming fight with the British. Debby and her brother Tim have gone to Boston to buy silver spoons from Mr. Paul Revere to take to their grandmother's farm in Lexington. The road they have taken will soon be the site of the first battle of the American Revolution. This is an easy-to-read chapter book for children who are making the transition from picture books. The exciting scenes lend themselves to role-playing.

In 1777, British soldiers captured Fort Ticonderoga and were headed to Bennington, Vermont, where the colonists had their supplies. Little did they know that the colonists were hiding in wait on the Green Mountains of Vermont. In *Aaron and the Green Mountain Boys* (Gauch, 1972), a young boy wants to join in the fight for freedom, but his pa tells him he's too young. But Aaron is determined to help in some way. This is another easy-to-read chapter book. You might want to step outside your classroom and recreate the Green Mountain Boys' attack on the British soldiers.

In *George Washington's Breakfast* (1969), Jean Fritz takes you on a journey with modern-day student George Allen, who wants to know what our first president ate for his daily breakfast. So after school he heads to the public library and begins his search. He learns that George Washington was six feet tall, that the name of his favorite horse was Nelson, but finding out what the president had for breakfast was harder than he realized. This would be a great book to introduce young children to the library. Teachers can ask children: What questions do you want to find an answer for?

The Civil War era

The Civil War divided the United States like no other event in our history: North against South, freemen against slaveholders, industrialism versus agrarianism. History texts will tell you when the Battle of Gettysburg was fought and who Robert E. Lee was. But there is much more to this period, particularly the human story, that needs to be known to understand the racial and regional differences that still divide America today.

Deborah Hopkinson has carefully researched and vividly written about the period before the Civil War. In Hopkinson's *Sweet Clara and the Freedom Quilt*

Jean Fritz

Jean Fritz was born in 1915 in Hankow, China, where her parents were missionaries. She moved back to the United States with her family in 1928. In 1937 she graduated from Wheaton College in Norton, Massachusetts. But it was not until around 1951 when she moved with her husband Michael to Dobbs Ferry, New York, that she began writing seriously. Today she is considered an outstanding writer of children's historical fiction and biographies. She has won many awards for her work, including the National Humanities Medal. Her autobiography *Homesick: My Own Story* tells what it was like to be an American child growing up in China. Among her most notable picture books for children are *And Then What Happened, Paul Revere?* (1973), *Traitor: The Case of Benedict Arnold* (1981), and *You Want Women to Vote, Lizzie Stanton?* (1995).

(1993), the story follows young Sweet Clara as she is torn from her mother and sent to work the fields on another plantation in the South. But then she gets a chance to work in the big house sewing dresses. As time passes and she hears more stories of the Underground Railroad, she longs to escape to the North to freedom. Her skills as a seamstress hold the key. Based on a true incident, this story and its colorful illustrations by James Ransome should raise many thoughtful questions about the nature of slavery in the South and the desire for all people to live free.

In *Under the Quilt of Night* (2002), Hopkinson and Ransome collaborated again to tell the journey of slaves escaping plantations and their slave owners, hiding in the woods by day and traveling north by night. Along the way they find safe homes that hide them for a day, and kindly farmers who pack them in their wagons under sacks of grain. This book provides a good introduction for children to the Underground Railroad of the 1850s that led all the way to Canada.

Another picture book story of the Underground Railroad is *Journey to Freedom* (1994) by Courtni C. Wright. Eight-year-old Joshua and his family have escaped their tobacco plantation in Kentucky and, with other slaves, travel the Underground Railroad toward Canada. The group is led by Harriet Tubman, a former slave herself who returns to the South to lead other slaves to freedom. But as they travel farther north in winter, the snows come, something barefoot Joshua did not expect. The hardships of traveling on foot for 20 days bring authenticity to this exciting story.

Ten-year-old Nettie is excited to be taking her first train ride from Albany, New York, to Richmond, Virginia. Set in the pre–Civil War years, *Nettie's Trip South* (Turner, 1987) opens her eyes to a world she could have never imagined: the slaves who work in the hotel where she stays, the shacks where slaves live on the plantation, but most of all the slave auction where families are split up and sold. This story is based on the real diary of the author's great-grandmother.

During the Civil War, thousands of boys (some as young as 12) fought on the Confederate and Union sides. *Pink and Say* (Polacco, 1994) is a story of two boys, one African American, one European American, fighting for the Union. During a fierce battle the two boy soldiers are separated from their units. One is wounded. Patricia Polacco shows readers how two boys of different races depend on each other to survive this man's war. It is beautifully written and illustrated to show the serious themes of the horrors of war and issues of race and to stimulate critical thinking and discussion.

In *A Band of Angels* (1999), author Deborah Hopkinson tells the true story of how the Jubilee Singers of Fisk College came to be. After the Civil War ended, Ella, a former slave girl of 14, was free to attend school. But most schools still would not accept blacks. The Fisk School of Nashville, Tennessee, was one of the first schools founded for the newly freed slaves and that's where Ella headed. There she studied, played the piano, and sang in the choir. The news that Fisk School might close came as a shock to her and the other students. Then she got the idea of taking the school choir on the road singing the old songs they all knew. Teachers may want to teach children the gospel song, "Swing Low, Sweet Chariot," first made popular by the Jubilee Singers.

Not everyone was directly involved in fighting or the issues of slavery during the mid-nineteenth century. In the town of Amherst, Massachusetts, lived a woman who rarely left her house. Across the street a little girl wonders who this strange person could be. *Emily* (Bedard, 1992) describes the everyday life in a small town whose residents include the reclusive poet, Emily Dickinson (who lived from 1830 to 1886). The beautiful illustrations by Barbara Cooney capture the time period well.

The move westward across the United States

The westward movement by pioneers from the middle until the end of the nineteenth century was one of the most significant factors in the establishment of the United States as a great country on the world stage. In *Apples to Oregon* (Hopkinson, 2004), one pioneer family sets out from Iowa in their wagon headed west to Oregon. They carry with them little plants and sapling trees of apple, peach, pear, grapes, and cherry. The journey is difficult, but when they make it safely to Oregon they raise and sell the fruit that would make them wealthy. Told tongue-in-cheek as a "tallish" tale, this story is nevertheless based on the true beginnings of the fruit industry around Portland, Oregon. A map on the inside cover allows you to track the family's journey westward. If children have not tasted the different fruits mentioned in this story, teachers may consider having a little fruit picnic.

Working a farm on the Great Plains was difficult. There's plowing by horse and milking by hand. And when her mama dies, there's just the young girl narrator and her pa to keep things going in *The Giant* (2003) by Claire Ewart. Told in simple, poetic language, this story captures the hard work and beauty of life on a small farm.

Elvirey and her family live in South Carolina. But when her mother dies, Pap decides to move the family to Michigan, where there's more land to farm and game to hunt. In *Log Cabin Quilt* (Howard, 1996) Elvirey, her brother, sister, and Granny help Pap build a cabin for shelter against the winter's first storm. But it still doesn't feel like a real home until they all create a single family quilt to keep them warm. Teachers can have children color paper squares, add personal information, and "quilt" them together with yarn as they listen to this story of a pioneer family. This makes for a great class display.

In 1850, Faith and her family loaded their covered wagon and headed west to California. The wagon can't hold all their belongings and certainly not Josefina, Faith's pet hen. *The Josefina Story Quilt* (Coerr, 1986) is an easy-to-read chapter book about Faith and Josefina's many adventures heading westward. Teachers can help students imagine the difficulties that children like Faith experienced while making the 6-month journey by wagon: riding in the bumpy wagon crowded with people and animals, enduring the heat of the desert and the cold winds of the mountains. Ask children what they think they could do to find food and water to sustain themselves.

It is two thousand miles from St. Joseph, Missouri, to Sacramento, California. In 1860, the mail was carried by horseback along that route. Young Bill Cody signed up to ride one of the toughest stretches in the West as a rider for the Pony Express. Eleanor Coerr's *Buffalo Bill and the Pony Express* (1995) tells of Bill's adventure carrying the mail, his encounters with the Indians, bandits, and wolves along the trail. The actual Pony Express lasted only 18 months and ended with the completion of telegraph lines from East to West, but its legends live on today. The story can lead to a discussion about how long it took mail to get across the country and how it would affect people's knowledge of distant events. With students, make a list of all the ways we can communicate today: mail, e-mail, cell phones, and so on.

Journeying by oxcart from the hills of Illinois to the vast plains of the Nebraska Territory is a frightening experience for Zoe and her younger sister Rebecca. But this is where her papa has staked his claim for free land. They have to dig their own well for water, build a house from sod bricks made by hand. The nearest neighbors are a three hour oxcart ride away. This is the story told in *Dandelions* (1995) by the well-known author Eve Bunting. Read the story aloud to students, without showing them the pictures. As you read, have students draw pictures of what they think the plains of Nebraska and a sod house would look like. Then compare their drawings with the illustrations in the book.

The history of the orphan trains is often forgotten. It began around 1850 on the streets of New York City and continued into the early twentieth century. There were many orphaned and homeless children in New York in need of homes. Out West there were couples and families who needed another hand on the farm or help in the store. In *Train to Somewhere* (1996) Eve Bunting tells the story of Marianne and her younger sister, Nora, two among 14 orphans headed cross-country by train to an unknown destination. Where will the sisters eventually wind up? What happens if they get separated? Brainstorm with the class possible scenarios before reading the end of this story.

Early twentieth century

The beginning of the twentieth century in the United States was a period of great industrial development, marked by the spread of the automobile, cross-country trains, scientific developments, and the growth of the modern city.

In 1900, many poor immigrants from Europe had settled in New York City. They lived in crowded apartment buildings called tenements. In *Peppe the Lamplighter* (1993), author Elisa Bartone tells the story of one Italian family

Eve Bunting was born in 1928 in Maghera, Northern Ireland. Her father was a merchant who traveled often, and at age 9 Eve was placed in a boarding school. Eventually she graduated from Methodist College in Belfast, Ireland. She married, and she and her husband moved first to Scotland and then to the United States, settling first in San Francisco and eventually Pasadena, California, where they became American citizens. In 1969 she began freelance writing and taught writing at UCLA. Her first picture book was published in 1972. Since then Bunting has proven to be a prolific writer (over 200 titles), who writes in a variety of genres, including historical fiction, contemporary realistic fiction, mysteries, and science fiction. Some of her books include *One More Flight* (1976), *Goose Dinner* (1981), *The Wall* (1990), *Fly Away Home* (1991), *Sunshine Home* (1991), and *Rudi's Pond* (1999).

struggling to make ends meet in the United States. Peppe lives with his father and seven sisters. When his father becomes ill Peppe sets out to find work to help the family. But who would hire a young boy? The colorful paintings of Ted Lewin take the reader back to the time of lower Manhattan's Little Italy before there was electricity and where vendors used horses to pull carts of fruits and vegetables to sell to the people.

In the early 1900s it took about three weeks by boat for European immigrants to reach New York City and settle in the Lower East Side of Manhattan. They came with few possessions and not knowing the language of their new home. *Watch the Stars Come Out* (1985) by Riki Levinson tells what it was like for one little girl and her 10-year-old brother to make this sea voyage alone. Ask students to try to imagine this sea voyage, with the ship rolling and with no sight of land day after day. How would they feel if they were this little girl?

Another story about immigrating across the ocean is *The Long Way to a New Land* (Sandin, 1981), a simple chapter book about a family from Sweden. Life in rural Sweden in the early 1900s was hard. When the rains failed, the crops died. Many Swedes thought of emigrating to the United States where the soil was rich. Carl Erick's father must sell their farmhouse and land to get money to travel to the seaport of Gothenborg. There they must sell their horse and cart to pay for the sea voyage to England. The people are tired and many get sick. Then there is another long and difficult sea voyage to the United States. You can ask children this: Why do you think people would leave their homes in Europe to come to a new and unknown land? Write the children's ideas on a poster.

In British Columbia (Canada) the transcontinental railroad links west coast to east coast. In 1927, silk from China was sent by train across Canada to New York City to be fashioned into clothing. In *Emma and the Silk Train* (Lawson, 1997) Emma and her brother Charlie love to watch the silk train roar by their tiny town. But one day, early in the school year, the children hear about a serious accident; the silk train flipped over and all the valuable silk is floating away in the river. Based on a true incident, this story captures the excitement of the early railroad years and one child's adventures. Bring in some toy trains and talk about how goods are still being distributed across the country via trains.

Many young children like to cook or help their parents around the kitchen. But how many of them know the story of the young girl who invented the modern recipe? Fannie Farmer worked as a teenager in the home of a wealthy family in Boston, Massachusetts. There she enthralled family and guests alike with her superb cooking. Eventually, she wrote down these recipes and went on to publish the first famous cookbook in the United States. Deborah Hopkinson tells her story in *Fannie in the Kitchen* (2001), along with tips for baking fluffy light biscuits and a recipe for her famous pancakes. Teachers can demonstrate how to make pancakes to the class or students can try writing out their own unique recipes for pancakes.

World War I and the Great Depression

World War I was also known as the Great War or, ironically, the War to End All Wars, and lasted from 1914 to 1918. The immediate cause of the war was the assassination on June 28, 1914, of Archduke Ferdinand, the heir to the Austro-Hungarian throne. This set off a chain of events throughout Europe involving various entangling alliances among the nations. By 1917 the United States entered the war on the side of France, Great Britain, and Russia against Germany, Austro-Hungary, and the Ottoman Empire. The war was fought mainly in Europe and featured trench warfare and hand-to-hand combat. In the end, 40 million people died.

The period between the end of World War I and the start of World War II was a difficult one, not only in the United States, but throughout the world. The Great Depression began in 1929 when businesses failed, workers lost their jobs, and foreclosed homes were seized by banks. This time in the United States coincided with the severest drought ever to hit the Great Plains, turning the land into what was called the great Dust Bowl.

Waiting for the Evening Star (1993) by Rosemary Wells tells the story of Berty, age 6, who is growing up on a small Vermont farm during the early twentieth century. In the rural United States, life was simple. Small farms dotted the landscape. People worked hard just to make ends meet. In the winter the men cut ice from the lake for keeping butter and eggs cool in the summer. With the milk from their cows, they made butter and cheese. They also tapped the trees for maple syrup. In August they ate tomatoes, squash, corn, and wild huckleberries for breakfast. Berty's older brother Luke watches the trains go by and dreams of leaving for the big city. Years pass by slowly. Then, in 1917, war breaks out in Europe and Luke joined the Navy. The world has changed and life for Berty will never be the same again. You can talk to students about some of the things we take for granted, like going to the supermarket and buying fresh foods. Then talk about all the food that had to be raised by hand in the early 1900s. Bring in some Vermont maple syrup for the children to taste or try making butter by shaking cream in a jar.

In *The Dust Bowl* (Booth, 1997) Matthew's Grandpa tells him about life on the farm in the 1930s when the rains stopped, the wind blew, and enormous dust clouds swept over the Great Plains. Things were so hot and dry that the crops struggled to survive. And then the grasshoppers arrived, millions of them, blackening the skies. The illustrations by Karen Reczuch capture both the bleakness of the land and the hardiness of the people. Visit http://memory.loc.gov/fsowhome.html to search the Library of Congress' database of documentary photos from the Dust Bowl.

In 1929 the New York stock market crashed. Overnight, businesses collapsed, banks failed, and people lost their entire savings. Over the preceding years, in New York City's Lower East Side, thousands of immigrants from Europe had settled in and were struggling to make a living. Delancey Street was the heart of activity for the Lower East Side. In *What Zeesie Saw on Delancey Street* (1996), Elsa Rael tells the story of 7-year-old Zeesie, who is going to her first "package party." These were fund-raising parties organized to help new arrivals from Europe adjust to life in New York City. It was a time when movies cost a dime, where pushcarts sold pickled herring on the street, and people baked bread in a woodstove. During these days poor people pulled together to help one another, like with the package party that Zeesie attends. Ask children what they might do to help those in need, something such as donating old clothes that have gotten too small to wear.

A similar story of immigrants living in the Lower East Side during the 1930s is *The Dream Jar* (1996) by Bonnie Pryor. Little Valentina and her family have come from Russia to live in one of the many tenement apartments in lower Manhattan. Finding work is hard for Papa because he doesn't speak English yet. His dream is to save up enough money some day to buy his own store. Everyone contributes to the dream jar. Valentina wishes she was older and could work so that she too could help the family. The lovely pictures by Mark Graham capture life inside the tenements and on the streets of the Lower East Side. You could bring a piggy bank to class and talk to the children about saving pennies, nickels, and dimes. What do students want to save for?

World War II

World War II or the Second World War was fought between the Allied nations headed by Great Britain, Russia, the United States, and France and the Axis powers of Germany, Italy, and Japan. It began in Europe in 1939 when the German Army invaded Poland. Shortly thereafter Germany invaded Austria, Holland, and France. In Asia, Japan attacked China and then, in 1941, attacked Pearl Harbor, Hawaii, bringing the United States into the war. Four long years later the war ended with the Allies' defeat of Italy, Germany, and Japan. Over 70 million people, most of them civilians, died in the war. Immediately after the war, the United Nations was founded in an attempt to maintain peace in the world.

In *Grandfather's Journey* (1993), Allen Say tells the story of his grandfather's journey from Japan to California and then back again to Japan, where the author was born. His grandfather told him many stories of California and all that he had seen in the United States. And then came the war. Japanese cities and countryside were bombed. Parents and teachers can lead children to understand that war is real and affects real people on both sides.

One of the great moral tragedies of World War II was the illegal forced removal of Japanese American citizens from their homes and internment in remote camps in Arizona, Montana, Idaho, and Utah for the duration of the war. In *The Bracelet* (1993), by Yoshiko Uchida, 7-year-old Emi and her family are forced to leave their home in San Francisco and live behind barbwire fences in a prison camp, just because they are Japanese Americans. Her best friend Laurie gives her a bracelet to remember her by and keep until the war ends and they can be neighbors once again. Find Arizona, Montana, Idaho, and Utah on a map of the United States and talk about what it might have been like to live behind barbwire. The internment of Japanese Americans during World War II is not a pleasant part of our history, but it is one that all children should learn about so that it is not repeated again (Mukai, 2000).

In *Baseball Saved Us* (1993) Ken Mochizuki describes one Japanese family's experience in an internment camp from 1942 through 1945. The desert land was barren, dust blew everywhere, the wooden barracks were sparse, and a barbwire fence kept everyone inside. The food was bad, people were restless, and children were not obeying their parents. This is an experience few of us can understand, but children can relate to the saving power of baseball to lift the spirits of all. After reading the story, ask students to explain the meaning of the title. Mochizuki's story is based on authentic research and depicts the actual conditions that Japanese Americans suffered under during World War II.

John, Tonky, and Wanly were performing elephants at the Ueno Zoo in Tokyo, Japan. Families came to see the elephants do their tricks and they were known throughout Japan. When the war came to Japan and bombs started falling on Tokyo, the Japanese Army ordered the zookeepers to poison all the wild animals so they would not escape and be a danger to the people of the city. But the elephant handlers could not bear to destroy their giant friends. *Faithful Elephants* (1988) by Yukio Tsuchiya tells this true story with emotional detail. This is a powerful story, based on authentic research. Teachers should preview this book before sharing it with young and impressionable children. However, the message it contains about the horrors of war is an important one.

In *The Greatest Skating Race* (2004), Louis Borden tells the story of young Piet Janssen who must guide his friends to safety by skating the frozen canals of Holland to Brugge, Belgium. It's a long, cold, and dangerous journey as the German troops are everywhere. Find Holland and Brugge, Belgium, on a world map and explain how in that part of Europe the canals freeze over, making them ice roads for transportation. The Netherlands (Holland) is a flat land of rivers and canals that was overrun by the German armies in 1941. Ask students how they think Piet felt on his journey?

Civil Rights

The Civil Rights movement in the United States has a long and varied history. Long before the sit-ins and boycotts of the 1960s, people tried to bring equality to an unequal country. Discrimination and prejudice are, unfortunately, a very real part of the history of the United States. Today students may be familiar with the names of Dr. Martin Luther King, Jr., or Rosa Parks. Teachers can help students learn more about this important part of American history.

In the 1920s, throughout the segregated South, many African Americans worked as rural sharecroppers, rarely venturing into towns. *Uncle Jed's Barbershop* (Mitchell, 1993) tells the story of Uncle Jed who travels from farm to farm cutting people's hair. His dream is to one day open his own barbershop. But along the way he helps others less fortunate than himself, and then the Great Depression comes. James Ransome's beautiful paintings illustrate this story. Separate, segregated hospitals, water fountains, schools, and stores for blacks and whites is an important concept for young children to understand and one that should raise serious questions.

In 1947, Jackie Robinson became the first African American to play in the Major Leagues for the Brooklyn Dodgers. Before that, however, there was a flourishing Negro Baseball League with stars of their own, like Satchel Paige and Josh Gibson. In *The Bat Boy and His Violin* (Curtis, 1998) Reginald loves to play his violin. But his Papa, the manager of the Dukes, the worst team in the Negro National League in 1948, is in no mood for music. It's time for Reginald to help out the team as the bat boy. Traveling around the country, in places where many hotels won't accept colored people, is hard on Reginald. And he struggles to find time to practice the violin. As true of all historical fiction this story will hold children's interest as they relate to Reginald while at the same time they learn important facts about a time in history.

teaching suggestions
SHARING REALISTIC AND HISTORICAL BOOKS

Let's Have a Grand Conversation

Grand Conversations: Literature Groups in Action (Peterson & Eeds, 2007) describes how to get children talking about books beyond the superficial description of plot, setting, and characters. A grand conversation is similar to the literature response groups used with older children. Here are the steps:

1. First have children read copies of the same book or books on a similar theme; in the case of historical fiction one might choose a unit on the American colonial period or the American Revolutionary period or slavery and the Civil War period, for example.
2. Every child reads her book on her own in class and at home. Get parents involved in helping the children to understand the book they have selected by reading it along with them.
3. Assign children to groups of four or five and set a date for the grand conversation.
4. On the given day, have the children come prepared with their books, including notes they have taken or sticky notes placed in the book to help them remember important scenes or details.
5. The teacher could guide the initial discussion by asking each child to briefly tell about the book he or she read.
6. Next encourage each child to share something interesting learned from the book about the particular historical period (colonial, Revolutionary, or slavery/Civil War).
7. Let the grand conversation continue with the children now taking the lead and sharing things they learned and found interesting.
8. At the conclusion, the teacher can create a large chart entitled "Things We Have Learned from Our Grand Conversation About [historic era]."

Here are some books that would make from great conversations: *Sweet Clara and the Freedom Quilt* (Hopkinson, 1993), *Under the Quilt of Night* (Hopkinson, 2001), *A Good Night for Freedom* (Morrow, 2004), *The Blue and the*

Gray (Bunting, 1996), *Oh, What a Thanksgiving!* (Kroll, 1988), *Sleds on Boston Common* (Borden, 2000), *The 18 Penny Goose* (Walker, 1998), and *Pink and Say* (Polacco, 1994).

We All Have Feelings

Contemporary realistic fiction often deals with problems that evoke strong feelings or emotions in young children: for example, parents in the midst of a divorce, the recent loss of a favorite pet, relocation to a new school, or the complex issue of adoption. Gather up picture books on these and other themes and read them aloud to the class. Encourage the children to discuss their own feelings or experiences with these serious issues.

After reading aloud the books and having a class discussion on the topics, break the class into two groups. One group will be given writing paper and pencils and asked to write down their own feelings about the topics discussed. The other group will be given drawing paper, markers, and crayons and asked to draw about the feelings. After about 15 minutes alternate activities. After another 15 minutes ask the class how they would like to share their writings and drawings. They can do it one at a time in a whole-class setting. Or get into small groups to share with classmates. Or perhaps the children would like to take clear tape or pushpins and hang their drawings and writings around the room for everyone to examine.

Let's Share About It

Children love to share their work with other children, their parents, and their grandparents. Sharing can be done in many ways following many different projects. Start by reading aloud or having the children read silently historical fiction books on a particular period, say the American Revolution. Next have the class decide on how they want to decorate the room for their American Revolutionary theme. The class could draw or paint houses and street scenes from the 1776 period, battle scenes of the patriots and the redcoats, or portraits of famous people like Paul Revere, Benjamin Franklin, and George Washington. Continue the unit by having the children audio- or video-record the historical stories that they know about each of the scenes. Set up recorders along with constructed or collected props in front of each illustrated scene. Rehearse with the students what they will record. When everything is ready, invite in parents, grandparents, or other classes to see, hear, and experience the final production.

Letters to the Author

For this activity, you will first need to teach some of the basic letter writing skills to your class by modeling how to begin a letter with an appropriate greeting, how to develop the body of the letter, and how to end a letter with a closing. Then let the children read some books by authors such as Jean Fritz, Eve Bunting, Patricia Polacco, and Allen Say. These and other authors have websites that explain how you can contact them, usually at the publisher's address. Once you have the actual addresses, practice addressing the envelopes.

Then it is time to write the actual letters. Brainstorm with the children the things they might want to say in their letters. For example, suggest that children might tell the author some of the books they have read. What did they like best about those books? Do they have any questions they want to ask the authors? For example, what gave Allen Say the idea to write about his grandfather's journey to America? Finally, once the letters have been written, encourage the children to take them home to share with their parents. Parents might want to make some final corrections in spelling or grammar. Then bring the letters back to the classroom where the class can place them in envelopes and mail them out. It will be exciting to wait for return responses from the authors.

Conclusion

Contemporary realistic fiction and historical fiction are two genres that can turn children into lifelong readers. Realistic fiction deals with probable and often serious issues for children, such as divorce, the elderly, disabilities, and sibling rivalry. Historical fiction is rooted in the past and focuses on real people and true events. It is based on authentic research but told as stories imagined by a skilled author. Young children can enjoy reading and listening to exciting stories while at the same time learning about world and American history, geography, and cultures from other lands.

journeying WITH CHILDREN'S LITERATURE

Use the following activities to prepare for sharing contemporary realistic fiction or historical fiction with children.

1. Select a serious topic that children may be interested in, such as divorce or adoption or a particular disability. Research that topic using the encyclopedia. What did you find? Now find some realistic fiction books on the same topic and read them. What more did you learn? Did the realistic fiction books change your thinking about the issue?

2. Sibling rivalry is a real issue for many children. What do child psychologists say about this topic? What about birth order? Do you think there are advantages to being born first, last, or in the middle? What children's books can you find on this topic?

3. Select a historical period from American or world history, such as the American Revolution or World War II. Do library research on this period. Next find some adolescent fiction books on the same period. Then find some children's picture books on the same period. How do they differ? How are they alike?

4. Some historical periods seem to have less written about them for children than others. World War I is such a period. Visit your public library and find some adolescent fiction books and children's picture books on this important era in history. What specific events or results would you want your children to remember about World War I?

activities TO SHARE WITH CHILDREN

1. Select a favorite contemporary realistic fiction picture book. Read the book aloud and ask the children to draw their own illustration of a favorite scene. You can use colored chalk, watercolor, colored pencil, or a combination of media.

2. Select a favorite historical fiction picture book. Do some more research on that particular historical period, say pioneer days, using the Internet and other resources. Then have a dress-up day where the children dress in a particular period (e.g., long skirts and bonnets for the girls, ruffled sleeve and collared shirts for the boys). Many states still have historical old one-room schoolhouses that you can visit on a field trip. One such pioneer school that hosts classroom visits is located in Stillwater, Oklahoma. Visit the website for one-room schoolhouses (http://oneroomschoolhouses center.weebly.com) to find those in your state.

3. As a follow-up to the preceding activity, have a penny arcade day at school. Children dress as a favorite historical figure (John Adams, Clara Barton, Benjamin Franklin, Robert E. Lee). They draw or paint an appropriate historical background panel. Adults drop a penny into their jar and the children, in character, perform a brief speech.

4. For either a favorite contemporary realistic fiction picture book or historical fiction book select a favorite scene. Then using a shoebox, found materials, crayons, and paint, design a three-dimensional diorama.

our favorite CHILDREN'S BOOKS

Addy, S. H. (2007). *Lucky Jake*. Illus. W. Zahares. Boston: Houghton, Mifflin.

Young Jake and his pa work hard panning for gold. One day Pa finds a gold nugget, worth enough to buy some real food and maybe a dog for Jake. But at the store there's no dog, only a pig. So Pa buys the pig for Jake who names him Dog. Dog the pig turns out to be really good luck for the Jake and his pa. Modernistic watercolors enhance this delightful story.

Bunting, E. (2006). *One Green Apple*. Illus. T. Lewin. New York: Clarion Books.

Farah has come to the United States from a faraway country. With her head scarf, she doesn't look like the other girls. She doesn't speak or understand English. But on the second day of school the class goes on a field trip to an apple orchard to pick apples and make cider. Farah makes her first friend and feels better about her new home.

Johnson, A. (2003). *I Dream of Trains*. Illus. L. Long. New York: Simon & Schuster.

A young boy and his father work the cotton fields of the Mississippi Delta. But as he works, the boy dream of trains taking him far away, like the one Casey Jones drove from Canton, Mississippi, to Memphis, Tennessee. The real Casey Jones died in a train wreck in 1900, but his legend lives on, especially among the people of Mississippi.

Kessler, C. (2000). *My Great-Grandmother's Gourd*. Illus. W. L. Krudop. New York: Orchard Books.

In the Sudan, Africa, young Fatima is excited because a water pump has been installed for the first time in her small village and she will no longer have to haul water every day. But her grandmother is not so excited and insists that the old way of storing water, in the hollow trunk of the huge baobab tree, is still the best way. This is a beautifully written and illustrated book about the clash between modern and old values.

Littlesugar, A. (2001). *Freedom School, Yes*. Illus. F. Cooper. New York: Philomel Books.

This inspiring story is based on the true events of the 1964 Mississippi Freedom School Summer Project to teach reading, writing, and to register voters. Young Jolie's mother has offered her home to Annie, a white teacher from up North who has volunteered to conduct Freedom School for the children of rural Mississippi. But there are still many people in Mississippi who don't like the thought of a school for blacks.

children's literature IN THIS CHAPTER

Ackerman, K. (1992). *Song and dance man*. New York: Dragonfly Books.

Adoff, A. (1973). *Black is brown is tan*. Illus. E. A. McCully. New York: Amistad.

Angeletti, R. (1998). *Nefertari, Princess of Egypt*. Oxford, UK: Oxford University Press.

Appelt, K. (2003). *Bubba and Beau go night-night*. Illus. A. Howard. New York: Harcourt.

Bartone, E. (1993). *Peppe the lamplighter*. Illus. T. Lewin. New York: Lothrop, Lee & Shepard.

Beard, D. (1999). *Twister*. New York: Farrar, Straus and Giroux.

Bedard, M. (1992). *Emily*. New York: Doubleday.

Best, C. (2002). *Goose's story*. Illus. H. Meade. New York: Farrar, Straus and Giroux.

Binch, C. (2002). *Gregory Cool*. New York: Frances Lincoln Children's Books.

Booth, D. (1997). *The Dust Bowl*. Illus. L. Reczuch. Buffalo, NY: Kids Can Press.

Borden, L. (2000). *Sleds on Boston Common*. New York: Simon & Schuster.

Borden, L. (2004). *The greatest skating race*. New York: Simon & Schuster.

Bottner, B. (1992). *Bootsie Barker bites*. Illus. P. Rathymann. New York: G. P. Putnam's Sons.

Brimner, L. D. (2003). *Trash trouble*. Illus. C. Tripp. New York: Children's Press.

Brisson, P. (2006). *I remember Miss Perry*. Illus. S. Jorisch. New York: Dial Books.

Bulla, C. (1978). *Keep running, Allen!* Illus. S. Ichikawa. New York: Thomas Y. Crowell.

Bunting, E. (1976). *One more flight*. Illus. D. de Groat. New York: Penguin.

Bunting, E. (1981). *Goose dinner*. Illus. H. Knotts. San Diego: Harcourt.

Bunting, E. (1988). *How many days to America? A Thanksgiving story*. Illus. B. Peck. New York: Clarion / Houghton Mifflin.

Bunting, E. (1988). *How many days to America?* Illus. B. Peck. New York: Clarion Books.

Bunting, E. (1990). *The wall*. Illus. R. Himler. New York: Clarion Books.

Bunting, E. (1991). *Sunshine home*. Illus. D. de Groat. New York: Clarion Books.

Bunting, E. (1991). *Fly away home*. Illus. R. Himler. New York: Clarion Books.

Bunting, E. (1993). *Fly away home*. Illus. R. Himler. New York: Clarion.

Bunting, E. (1995). *Dandelions*. Illus. G. Shed. San Diego: Voyager Books.

Bunting, E. (1996). *The blue and the gray*. Illus. N. Bittinger. New York: Scholastic.

Bunting, E. (1996). *Train to somewhere*. Illus. R. Himler. New York: Clarion Books.

Bunting, E. (1999). *Rudi's pond*. Illus. R. Himler. New York: Clarion Books.

Bunting, E. (1999). *Smokey night*. Illus. D. Diaz. New York: Voyager Books.

Bunting, E. (2000). *Train to somewhere*. Illus: R. Himler. New York: Clarion.

Bunting, E. (2001). *Jin Woo*. Illus. C. K. Soentpiest. New York: Clarion.

Caines, J. (1973). *Abby*. New York: Harper & Row.

Cameron, A. (1981). *The stories Julian tells*. Illus. A. Strugnell. New York: Pantheon Books.

Cameron, A. (1988). *The most beautiful place in the world*. Illus. T. B. Allen. New York: Yearling.

Caseley, J. (1989). *Ada Potato*. New York: Greenwillow Books.

Caseley, J. (1994). *Mama, coming and going*. New York: Greenwillow Books.

Caseley, J. (2001). *Bully*. New York: Greenwillow Books.

Child, L. (1999). *Clarice Bean that's me*. Cambridge, MA: Candlewick Press.

Child, L. (2000). *Clarice Bean guess who's babysitting?* Cambridge, MA: Candlewick Press.

Child, L. (2002). *What planet are you from, Clarice Bean?* Cambridge, MA: Candlewick Press.

Cleary, B. (1950). *Henry Huggins*. Illus. L. Darling. New York: HarperTrophy.

Cleary, B. (1954). *Henry and Ribsy*. Illus. T. Dockray. New York: HarperTrophy.

Cleary, B. (1955). *Beezus and Ramona*. Illus. T. Dockray. New York: Avon Camelot.

Cleary, B. (1968). *Ramona the pest*. Illus. T. Dockray. New York: HarperTrophy.

Cleary, B. (1981). *Ramona Quimby, age 8*. Illus. T. Dockray. New York: HarperTrophy.

Cleary, B. (1992). *Ramona Quimby, age 8*. Illus. T. Dockray. New York: William Morrow Junior Books.

Clifton, L. (1993). *Everett Anderson's goodbye*. Illus. A. Grifalconi. New York: Holt, Rinehart and Winston.

Cochran, B. (2007). *The forever dog*. Illus. D. Andreasen. New York: HarperCollins.

Coerr, E. (1986). *The Josefina story quilt*. Illus. B. Degan. New York: Harper & Row.

Coerr, E. (1995). *Buffalo Bill and the Pony Express*. New York: HarperCollins.

Curtis, G. (2001). *The bat boy and his violin*. Illus. E. Lewis. New York: Simon & Schuster.

Daly, N. (1999). *Papa Lucky's shadow*. New York: Aladdin.

Daly, N. (2004). *Jamela's dress*. New York: Farrar, Straus and Giroux.

Daly, N. (2003). *Once upon a time*. New York: Farrar, Straus and Giroux.

Danziger, P. (2003). *Get ready for second grade, Amber Brown*. New York: G. P. Putnam's Sons.

dePaola, T. (1981). *Now one foot, now the other*. New York: G. P. Putnam's Sons.

Edelman, E. (1985). *I love my baby sister (most of the time)*. New York: Puffin.

Ewart, C. (2003). *The giant*. New York: Walker & Company.

Fanshawe, E. (1975). *Rachel*. Illus. M. Charlton. Scarsdale, New York: Bradbury Press.

Fassler, J. (1975). *Howie helps himself*. Illus. J. Lasker. Morton Grove, IL: Albert Whitman & Co.

Fassler, J. (1969). *One little girl*. Illus. M. J. Smyth. New York: Behavioral Publications.

Fleming, V. (1963). *Be good to Eddie Lee*. Illus. F. Cooper. New York: Philomel.

Fox, M. (1994). *Sophie*. Illus. B. Robinson. New York: Harcourt Brace.

Fraustino, L. (2001). *The hickory chair*. Illus. B. Andrews. New York: Scholastic.

Fritz, J. (1969). *George Washington's breakfast*. Illus. P. Galdone. New York: Coward-McCann.

Fritz, J. (1973). *And then what happened, Paul Revere?* Illus. M. Tomes. New York: G. P. Putnam's Sons.

Fritz, J. (1975). *The lost colony of Roanoke*. New York: G. P. Putnam's Sons.

Fritz, J. (1981). *Traitor: The case of Benedict Arnold*. New York: Putnam Juvenile.

Fritz, J. (1995). *You want women to vote, Lizzie Stanton?* Illus. D. DiSalvo-Ryan. New York: PaperStar.

Gauch, P. (1972). *Aaron and the Green Mountain Boys*. Illus. M. Tomes. New York: Coward, McCann, & Geoghegan.

Gauch, P. (1989). *Dance, Tanya*. New York: Philomel.

Giff, P. R. (1984). *The beast in Ms. Rooney's room*. New York: Dell Yearling Book.

Gould, D. (1989). *Aaron's shirt*. Illus. C. Harness. New York: Bradbury Press.

Graham, B. (2005). *Oscar's half birthday*. Cambridge, MA: Candlewick Press.

Havill, J. (1989). *Jamaica tag-along*. Illus. A. S. O'Brien. Boston: Houghton Mifflin.

Heide, F. P. (1970). *Sound of sunshine, sound of rain*. Illus. K. Longtemps. New York: Atheneum.

Hines, A. (1988). *Daddy makes the best spaghetti*. New York: Clarion Books.

Hinton, S. E. (1995). *Big David, Little David*. Illus. A. Daniel. New York: Delacorte Press.

Hoffman, M. (1991). *Amazing Grace*. Illus. C. Binch. New York: Dial Books.

Hoffman, M. (1995). *Boundless Grace*. New York: Dial Books.

Hooks, W. (1997). *Mr. Garbage*. Illus. K. Duke. New York: Bantam Books.

Hopkinson, D. (1993). *Sweet Clara and the freedom quilt*. New York: Knopf.

Hopkinson, D. (1999). *A band of angels*. New York: Simon & Schuster.

Hopkinson, D. (2001). *Fannie in the kitchen*. New York: Simon & Schuster.

Hopkinson, D. (2002). *Under the night of quilt*. New York: Simon & Schuster.

Hopkinson, D. (2004). *Apples to Oregon*. Illus. N. Carpenter. New York: Simon & Schuster.

Howard, E. (1999). *The log cabin quilt*. Illus. R. Himler. New York: Holiday House.

Hurwitz, J. (2001). *Busybody Nora*. Illus. L. Hoban. New York: HarperCollins.

Isadora, R. (1984). *Max*. New York: Aladdin.

Isadora, R. (1981). *Jesse and Abe*. New York: Greenwillow Books.

Isadora, R. (1991). *At the crossroads*. New York: Greenwillow Books.

Isadora, R. (1992). *Over the green hills*. New York: Greenwillow Books.

Juster, N. (2005). *The hello goodbye window*. Illus. C. Raschka. New York: Hyperion Books for Children.

Keats, E. J. (1962). *The snowy day*. New York: Viking.

Keats, E. J. (1964). *Whistle for Willie*. New York: Viking Juvenile.

Keats, E. J. (1965). *John Henry, an American legend*. New York: Dragonfly Books.

Keats, E. J. (1967). *Peter's chair*. New York: Harper & Row.

Keats, E. J. (1968). *A letter to Amy*. New York: Harper & Row.

Keats, E. J. (1972). *Pet show*. New York: Viking Juvenile.

Keats, E. J. (1980). *Louie's search*. New York: Viking Juvenile.

Keats, E. J. (1982). *Clementina's cactus*. New York: Viking Juvenile.

Kroll, S. (1988). *Oh, what a Thanksgiving!* Illus. S. D. Schindler. New York: Scholastic.

Kyuchukov, H. (2004). *My name was Hussein*. Illus. A. Eitzen. Honesdale, PA: Boyds Mills Press.

Levinson, R. (1995). *Watch the stars come out*. Illus. D. Goode. New York: Puffin.

Lawson, J. (1997). *Emma and the silk train*. Buffalo, NY: Kids Can Press.

Little, J. (2001). *Emma's yucky brother*. Illus. J. Plecas. New York: HarperCollins.

Look, L. (2001). *Henry's first-moon birthday*. Illus. Y. Heo. New York: Atheneum.

Lowery, J. (1971). *Six silver spoons*. New York: Harper & Row.

McDonald, M. (2002). *Judy Moody saves the world!* Illus. P. H. Reynolds. Cambridge, MA: Candlewick Press.

McGill, A. (1999). *Molly Bannaky*. Illus. C. K. Soentpiet. Boston: Houghton Mifflin.

Miller, K. A. (1994). *Did my first mother love me?* Illus. J. Moffett. Buena Park, CA: Morning Glory Press.

Mitchell, M. (1998). *Uncle Jed's barbershop*. Illus. J. Ransome. New York: Aladdin.

Mochizuki, K. (1993). *Baseball saved us*. Illus. D. Lee. New York: Lee & Low Books.

Morrow, B. (2004). *A good night for freedom*. Illus. L. Jenkins. New York: Holiday House.

Namioka, L. (1992). *Yang the youngest and his terrible ear*. Illus. K. de Kiefte. Boston: Houghton Mifflin Harcourt.

Parish, P. (1963). *Amelia Bedelia*. Illus. F. Siebel. New York: HarperCollins.

Parish, P. (1985). *Amelia Bedelia goes camping*. Illus. L. Sweat. New York: Greenwillow Books.

Parish, P. (1964). *Thank you, Amelia Bedelia*. Illus. B. S. Thomas. New York: HarperTrophy.

Park, B. (1992). *Junie B. Jones and the stupid smelly bus*. Illus. D. Brunkus. New York: Random House.

Park, B. (1996). *Junie B. Jones loves handsome Warren*. Illus. D. Brunkus. New York: Random House.

Park, B. (1996). *Junie B. Jones and that Meanie Jim's birthday*. New York: Scholastic.

Passen, L. (1991). *Fat, fat, Rose Marie*. New York: Henry Holt and Co.

Polacco, P. (1994). *Pink and Say*. New York: Philomel.

Pryor, B. (1996). *The dream jar*. Illus. M. Graham. New York: HarperCollins.

Rael, E. (2000). *What Zeesie saw on Delancey street*. Illus. M. Priceman. New York: Aladdin.

Roe, E. (1991). *Con mi hermano / With my brother*. Illus. R. Casilla. New York: Aladdin.

Russo, M. (1996). *Grandpa Abe*. New York: HarperCollins.

Russo, M. (1994). *I don't want to go back to school*. New York: Greenwillow Books.

Rylant, C. (1994). *Henry and Mudge and the careful cousin*. Illus. S. Stevenson. New York: Scholastic.

Sandin, J. (1986). *The long way to a new land*. New York: HarperTrophy.

Say, A. (1993). *Grandfather's journey.* New York: Houghton Mifflin.

Schlein, M. (1990). *The year of the panda.* Illus. K. Mak. New York: HarperCollins.

Stolz, M. (1988). *Zekmet, the stone carver: A tale of ancient Egypt.* Illus. D. Lattimore. Orlando: Harcourt Brace Jovanovich.

Stuve-Bodeen, S. (2003). *Babu's song.* Illus. A. Boyd. New York: Lee & Low Books.

Stuve-Bodeen, S. (1998). *Elizabeti's doll.* Illus. C. Hale. New York: Lee & Low Books.

Surat, M. (1983). *Angel child, dragon child.* Illus. V. D. Mai. New York: Scholastic.

Surat, M. (1989). *Angel child, dragon child.* Illus. V. May. New York: Scholastic.

Tsuchiya, Y. (1997). *Faithful elephants.* Illus. T. Lewin. Boston: Houghton Mifflin.

Uchida, Y. (1996). *The bracelet.* New York: Putnam Juvenile.

Turner, A. (1987). *Nettie's trip south.* Illus. R. Himler. New York: Aladdin.

Turner, A. (1990). *Through moon and stars and night skies.* Illus. J. G. Hale. New York: HarperCollins.

Waber, B. (1972). *Ira sleeps over.* Illus. B. Waber. Boston: Houghton Mifflin.

Walker, S. M. (1998). *The 18 penny goose.* Illus. E. Beier. New York: HarperCollins.

Wells, R., & Jeffers, S. (1997). *Waiting for the evening star.* New York: Puffin.

Winters, K. (2004). *My teacher for president.* Illus. D. Brunkus. New York: Dutton.

Wright, C. C. (1994). *Journey to freedom.* Illus. G. Griffith. New York: Holiday House.

Yolen, J. (1992). *Encounter.* Illus. D. Shannon. Boston: Houghton Mifflin Harcourt.

Yolen, J. (1987). *Owl moon.* Illus. J. Schoenherr. New York: Philomel.

Zolotow, C. (1972). *William's doll.* Illus. W. P. Du Bois. New York: HarperCollins.

Informational Texts

Sharing Literature: AN EXAMPLE

Mrs. Johnston is anticipating a good report on Alex during the spring parent–teacher conference. Alex, a first grader, always comes home happy, talking about things he learned, and is eager to leave each morning for school.

Mrs. Johnston is therefore shocked when during the conference Ms. Hughes says, "I recommend additional reading assessment for Alex by a specialist."

"What? Why?" Mrs. Johnston asks.

"Because we suspect he can't read. Alex never volunteers to read. When I ask him to read, he never knows where we are. In fact, he actually avoids reading time by asking to be excused to get a drink or go to the bathroom."

"Alex is waiting for me in the hallway. May I ask him to come and join us?"

Surprised, Ms. Hughes agrees to have Alex join them.

Mrs. Johnston calls Alex into the room, goes over to the encyclopedias, and pulls one out. She says to Alex, "Ms. Hughes would like to hear you read. Why don't you find a page, any page, and read something for her."

Alex turns to a page and begins to read fluently. Ms. Hughes is shocked. "Alex, why don't you read when the class is reading?"

"Oh, those are such silly stories and they're so easy. I like reading stuff that lets me learn new stuff like fly-fishing or building bridges or different kinds of bugs."

Needless to say, Alex does not undergo testing by a specialist; and for the rest of the school year, he is permitted to bring his informational books from home to read during reading time.

Introduction

"Mommy, why did that snowball melt?"

"Daddy, why is the sky blue? Why is the grass green?"

"Grandma, what makes it rain?"

"Teacher, what will happen if I mix this food coloring with Play-Doh?"

Many of us have been inundated with these types of questions from children. Children are naturally curious about their world, and they want to know how things work and what causes things to happen (Yopp & Yopp, 2004). Because of this curiosity, parents, caregivers, preschool teachers, and primary teachers should expose children, beginning at a young age, to expository (informational) texts (Gambrell, Morrow, & Pennington, 2002; Kamil & Lane, 1997; Duke & Kays, 1998; Clay, 1993; Harste, Woodward, & Burke, 1984).

Informational Texts Defined

Informational texts are "texts written with the primary purpose of conveying information about the natural and social world . . . and having particular text features to accomplish this purpose" (Duke, 2003, p. 14). They cover a broad range of areas and topics—animals, plants, outer space, countries and cultures, geographical wonders, people and occupations, math, science, physics, cooking, and more—and many are written specifically for young children. The information is presented in one of three ways:

1. reflecting the familiar
2. revealing the unfamiliar
3. making the familiar unfamiliar (DeDroff, 1990)

In the first type of presentation, authors reveal only one or two new facts about a familiar topic. For example, Margaret Wise Brown in *Big Red Barn* (1989) tells what barn animals do during the day, evening, and nighttime, but she doesn't overwhelm readers with details about the animals. In the second type of presentation, obscure topics are explored or narrow, in-depth information on familiar topics is given. For example, *Sam Goes Trucking* (Horenstein, 1990) explains how a reefer trucker hauls fish. In the third type of presentation, authors take familiar information and present it in an unusual manner, such as through detailed photographs or with poetry. Jerry Pallota uses the alphabet to organize information about insects in *The Icky Bug Alphabet Book* (1993), dinosaurs in *The Dinosaur Alphabet Book* (1990), and ocean creatures in *The Underwater Alphabet Book* (1991). Likewise, in *Earthquakes* (2006), Simon uses photographs to show the devastation of the San Francisco earthquake. In all three types of presentation, authors of quality informational books "use vocabulary appropriate to the topic rather than easy words that don't convey the facts as well" (Doralek, 2003, p. 22).

There are a number of reasons why teachers may be hesitant to use informational books in the primary grades. Some teachers believe that children are not interested in nonfiction. Other teachers believe that there is a lack of quality informational books. Still others believe that these books are too dense with technical concepts or terms that are not clearly explained. Some schools do not buy informational texts; therefore, there are not enough of these books available for each grade level (Palmer & Stewart, 2003). However, in this chapter we explain that there is a wide range of quality nonfiction books written for different age groups.

We believe that quality informational books answer many of the questions of curious young children. Previously, in Chapter 5, we discussed the importance of engaging infants, toddlers, and young children in concept books—books that teach readers about numbers, colors, shapes, and the alphabet. In this chapter we discuss (1) what research says about exposing children to informational books; (2) what are the traits of quality informational text; (3) what are the strategies caregivers and teachers can use as they share informational books with children; and (4) what are some of the many different categories of informational texts.

What Research Tells Us About Informational Texts

The International Reading Association (IRA) and the National Association for Education of Young Children (NAEYC) (1998), in a joint statement, agree that kindergartners "need to be exposed to vocabulary from a wide variety of genres, including informational text as well as narratives" (p. 203). We agree and believe there are a number of reasons why information books should be read to and shared with young children:

- Exposing children to informational books promotes their interest in and positive attitude toward learning while reading (Gambrell, Morrow, & Pennington, 2002). Research indicates that some children in the primary grades actually prefer informational books to fiction books (Caswell & Duke, 1998; Duke, 1998; Pappas, 1993). Informational books can be springboards to engaging children in critical thinking and thus lead to more reading (McMath, King, & Smith, 1998).

- As the IRA/NAEYC statement suggests, informational books enrich young children's vocabulary as they learn the technical terms associated with unfamiliar concepts (McMath et al., 1998). Not only does children's vocabulary increase, their world knowledge increases while reading and discussing these texts, especially when adults choose books that are age-appropriate (Oyler & Barry, 1993).

- Reading informational books can integrate science and social studies to enhance intrinsic motivation in multiple content areas (Guthrie et al., 1996). Brassell (2006) found that there is a strong positive relationship between children reading nonfiction books and their academic achievement in reading, writing, and science.

- When adults stop and read the captions under pictures, diagrams, and charts, children become aware that reading can be nonlinear (e.g., pausing, skipping around, rereading) (Oyler & Barry, 1996). Adults can also demonstrate to children how to use features like the table of contents and the glossary (Clay, 1993; Harste, Woodward, & Burke, 1984).

- Children understand that they can learn about their world through books (Yopp & Yopp, 2004).

Sometimes adults believe that young children cannot comprehend informational texts; they believe that young children can only comprehend narrative texts. However, Maduram (2000), Oyler, Barry, Moss, Leone, and Dipillo (1997), Duke and Kays (1998), and Pappas (1993) found that children as young as 3 can comprehend informational texts. They demonstrate their comprehension through their ability to respond to, discuss, reproduce, or reenact these texts when assisted by more mature readers. Through exposure to informational texts, children begin to internalize typical text structures (e.g., chronological, cause/effect, problem/solution) just like they internalize narrative structure (Heller, 2006). Therefore, it is important for caregivers and teachers to share informational books like they do narrative books.

Oyler and Barry (1996) found that young children are not only able to comprehend informational texts, they can make intertextual connections during read-alouds. Intertextual connections are links among all kinds of information (books, videos, television, movies, video games, the Internet). For example, young children have the ability to recall what they learned about dinosaurs from a video when they later encounter more information about dinosaurs in a nonfiction picture book.

Even though infants and preschoolers cannot read the books themselves, adults can read these books to them and engage them in discussions. Adults can, for instance, give children an opportunity to ask the questions, a first step in critical reading (Oyler & Barry, 1996; Kletzein & Szabo, 1998; Harste, Burke, & Woodward, 1984). Just like adults, when children are exposed to new information, they need time to ponder, look at the illustrations, think through the facts, make mental images of the information, and ask questions. During this social interaction with adults, cognitive growth occurs (Heller, 2006).

Selecting Informational Books

Because a child's world is small, a child tends to choose books on familiar subjects. It is the adult's responsibility to expand a child's world by introducing unfamiliar topics. For example, if a child loves to read about snakes, an adult may introduce books about other reptiles, thus building on the child's established interest while expanding the boundaries of the child's knowledge. After an adult has interested the child in informational books, the adult can constantly encourage the child to select from a variety of books that continually build on the base of what intrigues the child. These books should also present various perspectives on the topic (Akerson & Young, 2004). For example, authors of nonfiction may discuss possible misconceptions readers have about a concept and then offer factual information. In *Chameleons Are Cool* (1998), Martin Jenkins states, "Lots of people think chameleons change color to match their surroundings. They don't. They change color when they're angry, or when they're too cold or too hot, or when they're sick" (p. 18).

After considering interest, caregivers and teachers should select quality nonfiction books that meet a set of standards. One list of quality books to consider is the list of winners of the Orbis Pictus Award for Outstanding Nonfiction for Children, an award presented each November at the annual convention for the National Council of Teachers of English. One book is selected as the winner and five other books are recognized as honor books. A list of award winners is provided in Appendix A.18. While the winners are all excellent books for children, teachers should preview any book to make sure its content is age-appropriate. The selection committee looks at accuracy, organization, design, and style (the criteria in Appendix B.4). These criteria are good guides for selecting nonfiction for young children. One last consideration teachers should keep in mind when selecting books for a classroom is that they have on hand books that cater to a wide range of reading levels so that, on any particular topic, all children can read books by themselves.

Accuracy

As noted by NCTE, the information in nonfiction must be accurate. Authors should be either experts in the field or should have researched the topic and checked the information with an expert (McMath, King, & Smith, 1998). Books published in recent years often state the author's level of expertise or the author's research sources in a biography or on the back cover of the book. For example, if an author writing about the rainforest travels to one with a biologist along as a guide, that author's information will be more accurate than another author who goes to a rainforest alone.

Also, since new facts are always being discovered, teachers need to be sure they are sharing the most recent information. For example, on a recent trip to Swaziland, Africa, one of the authors of this text learned that there is no such animal as a white rhino. Instead the animal is called a "wide-mouth rhino." It seems that English-speaking researchers in the middle of the twentieth century misunderstood Swazi speakers. Yet many books published in the early twenty-first century identify two types of rhinos as black and white. When teachers learn

Joanna Cole is the author of the beloved "magic school bus" series. Her favorite part of school was explaining things in written reports. One of her teachers was much like her character Mrs. Fizzle, who loves science. Each week this teacher would permit one child to do a science experiment in front of the class. Joanna loved doing this. Her favorite books were about insects and other science topics. Joanna Cole was herself once a teacher, a librarian, and an editor of children's books. All these experiences gave her the inspiration to write her own books. Her first book was about cockroaches. She now has written over 90 fiction and nonfiction books.

She wanted to make science fun for children, so she decided to use humorous stories to convey scientific information. She makes Mrs. Fizzle zealous about science because she wants her readers to "catch the science bug." However, before any of her zany books makes it into print, she does extensive research to ensure the facts are accurate. She visits museums and talks with experts to check that all the details are correct. The illustrator of her books, Bruce Degen, has said that his favorite part of the illustrations is selecting the weird outfits for Mrs. Fizzle. Readers may realize that the outfit Mrs. Fizzle wears at the end of the book foreshadows the subject for the next book. Joanna Cole has won the Washington Post/Children's Book Club Nonfiction award and the American Library Association's Notable Children's Book award.

information firsthand, they can share the correct information with children. If teachers know that the rest of the book's information is accurate, they can still use the book, updating the students on the most recent findings.

When discussing science topics, teachers need to explain to students the difference between fact and theory. A fact is a statement that can be backed up with evidence, while a theory is formulated after much research has been conducted on a topic. A theory is an informed but still provisional best guess as to how or why something occurs. Teachers can share books with both facts and theories, engaging students in a discussion on why something is a fact or a theory. For example, our knowledge about the behavior of dinosaurs is mostly theorized from archaeological findings. Quality books on dinosaurs will let readers know that the information about dinosaurs is based partly on theory, not entirely on fact. Facts may include information about bones that archaeologists find in a particular region. Theories may explain how dinosaurs tended to their young for formed social groups.

The depth of information should be appropriate for the intended reader's age. Books written for second and third graders can have more details than books for toddlers and kindergarten children. Returning to the rhino example, *Rhinoceroses* (Stewart, 2002) gives basic information intended for children who know very little about rhinos; however, a book about rhinos for older children, *Black Rhino* (Penny, 2001) gives information about breeding and shows graphic pictures of hyenas killing a black rhino. The breeding details may be incomprehensible and the killing scenes too upsetting for toddlers and preschoolers. Teachers should preview information books so they know the information is appropriate for the age of the children they teach.

Authors that build on basic facts help young children connect their background knowledge to new facts. For example, most young children know simple facts about butterflies; but when they read *Butterflies* (Neye, 2000), they can build on their previous knowledge by learning that butterflies suck nectar from flowers instead of eating leaves like caterpillars. This new and interesting information keeps children reading and wanting to find out more.

Organization

Information organized in a logical manner helps readers comprehend the material (DeDroff, 1990; Cote & Goldman, 2004; Meyer & Poon, 2004). Logical organization of nonfiction material can take many forms: chronological order (sequencing), compare/contrast (similarities/differences), question/answer (author states a question and then answers it), cause/effect (events bring about change), problem/solution (the author states a problem and then gives one solution or possible solutions), description/enumeration (the topic is described as to its composition, color, and other characteristics), or persuasion (the author attempts to change the thoughts of readers through reason).

The organization that is easiest to understand, and thus appropriate for preschool children, is description/enumeration because only one concept is being explained. The second easiest organizational format for children to follow is comparison/contrast. Most authors will explain two concepts by comparing how they are alike and how they are different from each other. Sequencing and question/answer formats are also easy to follow. What is key here is that the logic of organization be a good fit for the topic.

Sequential organization works well in books that show how things grow or how things are made. Life cycles, for example, are best told in chronological order. In *Grub to Ladybug* (Berger & Berger, 2004), a book for beginning readers, the authors clearly explain the life cycle of ladybugs—from egg to grub to pupa to ladybug. In *The Life Cycle of a Flower* (Aloian, 2004) readers can follow the life of a flower from a seed to a plant that produces seeds of its own. Aloian explains how seeds are formed, what different seeds look like, and what plants require to germinate. *The Life Cycle of an Owl* (Bailey, 1990) explains the life cycle of an owl from mating to the time that young are driven from the parents' nest. The last page reviews the cycle through a circular diagram.

The compare/contrast organizational pattern is used when authors want to compare an unfamiliar subject to another subject that the child already knows. They can also contrast a subject with something else that children may mistakenly think is the same. One such book is Barbara Juster Esbensen's *Baby Whales Drink Milk* (1994). In the beginning of the book, Esbensen makes a comparison: she explains that whales are mammals like humans, dogs, horses, and pigs because their babies are all born alive and they drink the milk of their mothers. Later in the book, Esbensen contrasts whales with fish because many young children have the misconception that whales are fish.

Some authors choose to use the question/answer format. The question is the heading or subheading, and the answer comes in the following paragraph or section. Melvin and Gilda Berger use this organizational format in *What Makes an Ocean Wave?* (2000). Each page has one or two questions, followed by a concise answer. Some of the questions answered are "Do any deep-sea fish make their own light?" "Do fish sleep?" "What is the largest ocean?" Two other books that use this format effectively are . . . *If You Traveled West in a Covered Wagon* (Levine, 1986) and . . . *If You Sailed on the Mayflower in 1620* (McGovern, 1969).

Design

Photographs, illustrations, diagrams, and maps should support and augment the text, just as they do in fiction. The NCTE also recommends that the design should be attractive, since young children often make a quick judgment about a book merely by thumbing through the pages. The "nature book" series published by Child's World, the "true book" series published by Children's Press, and the "animals animals" series published by Benchmark Books are all accurate and appealing. The photographs show animals such as rhinos, hippos, zebras, and armadillos living in their natural settings and performing the actions described on the facing page.

The detailed illustrations and vivid photographs of Kathryn Smithyman in the *Life Cycle of a Tree* (Kalman, 2002) show readers how a seed is produced, how it sprouts, and how the sprout becomes a mature plant. Margaret Reich's bordered photographs and detailed illustrations aid young readers to understand the scientific life stages of a butterfly. The photographs in *Pillbug* (St. Pierre, 2008) reveal the vivid details of the insect's shell, underside, eggs, and larvae. Since pillbugs (often called "roly-polies") are found almost everywhere, children can turn over stones on the playground to observe them after they have read this book.

Diagrams can be simple, such as the several drawings that show the life cycle of a plant in *From Bulb to Daffodil* (Weiss, 2008). This book depicts it in a sequence of illustrations. Readers see a bulb being planted, watch the roots grow, see the daffodil forming inside the bulb, observe the sprout coming up, see the first signs of a bloom, and finally observe the cup unfolding into a beautiful full-blown flower.

Step-by-step drawings are especially important in how-to books in order to help readers execute science experiments. *Awesome Ocean Science* (Littlefield, 2003), for example, has clear illustrations for children to follow as they do experiments on the water cycle, seawater salinity, and the function of whale blubber. Science projects in *Super Science Projects About Earth's Soil and Water* (Gardner, 2008) has experiments about how water is polluted, how water moves soil, how water evaporates, and how rain passes through the different layers of soil. The step-by-step process, the labeled illustrations, and the explanation in the text make the information clear for young children.

Maps help readers understand where in the world something may be found. Young children have limited sense of distance, but with the help of an adult and a clear map, their understanding of geography (mountains, deserts, prairies) can increase (Hannibal, Vasiliev, & Lin, 2002). For example, in the back of *Wild Cats: Cougars, Bobcats and Lynx* (Hodge, 1996) a world map shows pictures of all the wild cats found on each continent.

Other aids such as the table of contents, glossary, index, headings, and subheadings also help readers locate information. Highlighting, boldface, and italics draw attention to a word. The word may be the main topic of the paragraph, or it may be an unfamiliar or technical term. An easy pronunciation guide for unfamiliar or technical vocabulary aids the reader when introduced to new terms. Some authors will put phonetic spelling in parentheses in the running text, often with the accented syllable in all capital letters so the reader can continue reading without stopping to look the word up in a dictionary or even the glossary. Teachers should look for books that do not mix highlighting, boldface, and italics but

author sketch

Gail Gibbons   www.gailgibbons.com

As a young child, Gail Gibbons had all the traits needed to become a famous author and illustrator of information books. She was very curious about how things worked and how things are made; she also loved to draw, paint, and write.

Gibbons has written and illustrated over 135 non-fiction books. She does her research by traveling to remote places, visiting with scientists, and observing the topic firsthand. She visited the rain forest in two Caribbean Islands to write *Nature's Green Umbrella and Tropical Rain Forest* (1994). She has been on the seventeenth floor of an unfinished skyscraper to understand how skyscrapers are constructed, has visited with truck drivers to understand the mechanical parts of a truck, and has dismantled clocks to see how their gears work. Through illustrations and text, she explains phenomena that captivate young children. When she writes, Gail Gibbons uses a technical vocabulary that conveys the facts rather than choosing easy words. She says she gets her ideas from talking to teachers and students while on school visits and while traveling with her husband.

rather consistently use one method of drawing readers' attention to new words. A few titles with useful aids are *Clown Fish* (Sexton, 2007), *Easy Paper Crafts in 5 Steps* (Llimos, 2005), *Projects About Colonial Life* (Broida, 2004), and *Prairie Food Chains* (Kalman, 2005).

Gail Gibbons uses many of these reader aids in her nonfiction books. The illustrations are neat, with labels clearly marking each part of an object. In *Penguins!* (1998), she illustrates the many kinds of penguins so that young children can see the differences among them. She labels the parts of a penguin so children can understand what part of its body the penguin uses for different purposes. Her map indicates where each of the different penguins lives in the southern hemisphere. She often also gives a phonetic spelling for new terms. The illustrations throughout the book complement the text. Some pages may have two or three smaller pictures because the text on the page describes two or three different things, while on other pages there is one large illustration to depict what the text refers to. In this particular book, the text is typed on a white background at the bottom of the page; this gives an uncluttered appearance to the book.

Style

As we mentioned in Chapter 1, the writing style of children's books should be interesting and age-appropriate. Authors who use vivid language pull in young readers. Consider how the following passage in *Fancy Nancy: Explorer Extraordinare!* uses and explains technical terms in a way that sounds as though the author is talking to the readers: "Birds are the only animals with feathers. (The fancy word for feathers is plume.) They also have light, hollow bones. One of the reasons we can't fly is because our bones are too heavy—and we don't have wings" (O'Connor, 2009, unpaged). By not being afraid of using technical terms, authors acknowledge readers' intelligence instead of "dumbing down" the text (Doralek, 2003). Children are never too young to learn new terms. Think of the long names toddlers can rattle off when talking about their plastic dinosaurs. Using the technical terms increases young children's vocabulary.

When considering style, teachers should also look at the author's verb usage. Authors should use timeless verbs (Duke, 2003). For example, "Birds eat insects" is timeless, while "The bird is eating the insect" is not. In the second sentence the author is talking about a particular bird and a particular insect. This phrasing does not convey that the information applies to all birds.

Often young children like only to look at pictures and not read the text. Authors realize that fact, so in order to get children to listen to or to read the text they use a writing style that intrigues readers. An excellent example is Caroline Arnold's *A Penguin's World* (2006). Arnold uses onomatopoeia such as the wind WHOOSHES, the penguin PLOPS on the ground, the egg CRACKS, and the chick CHEEPS. Such language keeps the attention of young children.

Books that have varying sentence length instead of having only simple sentences are often clearer because complex sentences show relationships, such as cause and effect, between things. Having a catchy title and a catchy lead will also entice readers to read.

Consider the intriguing language of the opening paragraph of *Baby Koala* (Lang, 2004):

> When the baby koala is born she is no bigger than a jellybean and weighs less than a penny. She looks like a tiny, pink, wiggly worm. Like a mother kangaroo, the mother koala has a pouch on her belly. The baby koala crawls inside the warm pouch and hides there for six months, drinking her mother's milk and growing big and furry. One day she wriggles out of the pouch for the first time. (p. 7)

Children can identify with the size of a jellybean and the weight of a penny. Comparing the baby to a wiggly worm evokes a concrete picture in the readers' minds. Lang uses "hides" instead of a simple verb such as "stays." "Wriggles" is also a vivid verb that creates a specific image in readers' minds. After reading this opening page, children will want to read on or listen to an adult read.

Some authors choose to use a bit of fiction to make information more interesting. Eric Carle's *The Very Hungry Caterpillar* (1989) mixes nonfiction with fiction, but the overall purpose of the book is still to convey information. Of course, teachers need to make sure that children understand that caterpillars do not actually eat cake, pickles, ice cream, and all the other human food that this particular caterpillar eats on the seventh day. One way to do this would be to pair Carle's book with another book on caterpillars such as *From Caterpillar to Butterfly* (1996) by Deborah Heiligman, which looks at the life cycle of the creature from a nonfiction perspective. Students can then compare the two books, a teaching strategy discussed in detail later in the chapter.

Similes in both text and illustrations can also help young children connect new information to existing knowledge. For example, in *Tropical Fish* (2008) Megan Duhamel compares the physical appearance of a lionfish to a lion: "The fins looks like a lion's mane" (p. 15). The illustration has a photograph of a lionfish with an inset picture of a lion's head. The caption by the lion asks the reader to compare the two by asking, "Do you think the lionfish looks like a lion?" (p. 15). In the same book, Duhamel (2008) describes the starry balloonfish by saying it "is shaped like a balloon" (p. 16), and she describes the white spotted boxfish by saying it "is shaped like a box" (p. 16). The two fish are angled in the photograph such that children can easily see their shapes.

Types and Topics of Nonfiction Books

In this next section, we discuss books focused on specific topic areas. There are many categories of nonfiction, so we group them by subject matter for easier discussion. As you read more nonfiction, you can add categories and books of your own.

Science Experiments

What child doesn't enjoy watching something explode or seeing some other "magic trick"? There are many science experiment books written for children that will cause them to ooh and ah when they see the results of the experiments. The best books are ones where children can follow the step-by-step instructions. These books also have illustrations accompanying each step to supplement written instructions. Teachers should always look for experiments that use inexpensive household materials because, as we have experienced, once teachers get children interested in reading science experiment books and doing experiments, they will want to do them every day. Teachers should note that even the simplest experiments need to be done with some adult supervision.

Fortunately, there are a number of excellent science experiment books that call for common, inexpensive materials. Janice VanCleave, a former public school science teacher, has written a number of science experiment books for children. Each has easy-to-follow instructions with illustrations. She poses critical thinking questions about why things happen in the experiments and then offers the scientific reason behind them. *Janice VanCleave's 201 Awesome, Magical, Bizarre, and Incredible Experiments* (1994) is a book that permits children to stir common things like water, glue, and laundry soap to make slimy, gooey globs, thereby demonstrating chemical reactions among common household ingredients. *Janice VanCleave's Help! My Science Project Is Due Tomorrow! Easy Experiments You Can Do Overnight* (2001) focuses on stars, telescopes, cells, spiders, and chemical change. *Janice VanCleave's Play and Find Out About Science: Easy Experiments for Young Children* (1996) focuses on force, air, magnets, and sound. Notice how her titles can capture the attention of children.

Some other science experiment books intended for young children are *Slimy Science and Awesome Experiments* (Martineau, 2000), *Everything Kids Magical Science Experiments Book* (Robinson, 2007), *730 Easy Science Experiments with Everyday Materials* (Churchill & Loesching, 1997), *365 Simple Science Experiments with Everyday Materials* (Churchill, Loesching, Mandell, & Zweifel, 1997), and *Easy Science Experiments* (Molleson, Savage, & Petach, 1993). All of these books have illustrations that make the experiments easy to do.

Craft Projects

Many young children enjoy constructing things like bird feeders, musical instruments, and other objects made from household items. Just like the science experiment books, these books should be written with step-by-step instructions and accompanying illustrations. Many of the craft books are written for teachers: *Art and Crafts with Children* (Wright, 2001) and *Make Your Own Playdough,*

Paint, and Other Craft Materials (Caskey, 2007). However, teachers can easily rewrite the instructions and create their own illustrations so that primary-age children can read and follow along themselves.

Three books written for young children are *The Little Hands Big Fun Craft Book* (Press, 2008), *Easy Paper Crafts in 5 Steps* (Llimos, 2008), and *Jumbo Book of Easy Crafts* (Sadler, 2001). To make these books easier for students to use, teachers can tear out the pages, laminate them, and put the laminated sheets in a box (one book per box). Teachers can then teach children to place the pages back in the correct order by looking at the page numbers. For teachers who organize their curriculum around centers, they can have one center for crafts with one or two crafts per week. All of these books use inexpensive household items that are readily available. All crafts are appropriate for kindergarten through second grade.

Cookbooks

Many young children love to cook or bake alongside an adult in the kitchen. To further this interest, teachers, with the support of the school principal and the school kitchen staff, can teach children how to make healthy dishes. Recipe books intended for children have step-by-step instructions and drawings that illustrate how to measure, stir, fold, toss, cream, and other cooking procedures.

Three visually appealing, kid-friendly cookbooks are *Simply in Season Children's Cookbook* (Beach, 2006), *The Toddler Cookbook* (Karmel, 2008), and *Emeril's There's a Chef in My Soup!* (Lagasse, 2005). The first one is organized around foods that are in season. The recipes are easy to follow, with vivid colors and large photographs. The second cookbook first shows photographs of all the kitchen utensils the children will need, and then it has step-by-step photographs of children making such foods as a mini Caesar salad, lettuce boats, pita pizzas, corn quesadillas, and easy party foods. The third cookbook features kitchen rules, tools, and safety. The recipes, with zany titles such as "Gone Fishin' Fish Sticks" and "Pokey Brownies," are organized around the three meals of the day. The recipes include eggs, pizza, pasta, vegetables, salads, and desserts.

There are also some cookbooks that are based on children's favorite books— *The Boxcar Children Cookbook* (Blain, 1992), *The Little House on the Prairie Cookbook* (Walker, 1989), and *The Chronicles of Narnia Cookbook* (Gresham, 1998). *The Boxcar Cookbook* features recipes related to incidents in the stories that inspired it: baker's bread in a bag, food for campfire cooking, beverages, and desserts. *The Little House on the Prairie Cookbook* features Ma's stewed blackberries, pie dough, and one hundred others. *The Chronicles of Narnia Cookbook* features foods mentioned in the books such as Edmund's Turkish delight, Mr. Tumnus's sugar-topped cake, and Lucy's roasted apples.

Animals

Young children are interested in dinosaurs and they are intrigued by living animals found in the zoo and in the wild. Books for infants and toddlers teach how to identify animals, and books intended for kindergarten and primary children offer additional information.

Dinosaurs

Toddlers, preschool, and primary-school children are often attracted to dinosaurs. Because dinosaurs have unusual names, reading books about dinosaurs is a wonderful way to increase young children's oral vocabulary. Books about dinosaurs are written for many age levels. Those written for infants and toddlers introduce them to different kinds of dinosaurs. Usually one page features a picture of one or two dinosaurs and their names, usually accompanied by phonetic spellings. The Smithsonian Institute has created board books for infants and toddlers with one object on each page and open-ended questions to engage caregivers and toddlers. The illustrations are very bright and colorful. *My Dinosaur Book* (Carr, 2007) and *Lone Star Dinosaurs* (Jacobs, 2007) are two of these books created by the Smithsonian Institute. They feature such dinosaurs as the stegosaurus, parasaurolophus, and triceratops. *My Big Dinosaur Book* (Priddy, 2004) is another board book with one or two dinosaurs per page. *My First Jumbo Book of Dinosaurs* (Scholastic, 2007) has six or seven dinosaurs per page and invites infants and toddlers to feel the bumps. This book also has phonetic spelling. *Dinosaurs* (Jeunesse, 2007), also written for toddlers, has transparent plastic sheets that lay over pages to transform one image into another. Two books that feature many dinosaurs are *National Geographic Dinosaurs* (Barrett, 2001) and *Big Book of Dinosaurs* (DK Publishing, 1994).

Once children get into kindergarten and primary grades, they want to learn more specific facts about each dinosaur. Five books that give basic information about a number of different dinosaurs are *Centrosaurus and Other Dinosaurs of Cold Places* (Dixon, 2005), *My Favorite Dinosaurs* (Ashby, 2005), *Beyond the Dinosaurs: Monsters of the Air and Sea* (Brown, 2007), *Neovenator and Other Dinosaurs of Europe* (Dixon, 2007) and *Dinosaurs! Strange and Wonderful* (Pringle, 1996). One book by Gail Gibbons has a different focus. *Dinosaurs Discoveries* (Gibbons, 2006) shows how scientists have pieced together information about dinosaurs by studying fossils. The illustrations show the paleontologists at work labeling parts of dinosaurs. This book shows young children how so much information about dinosaurs has been collected. Gibbons also describes the three geological periods of the dinosaur age with illustrations of many different kinds of dinosaurs from each era.

In *New Questions and Answers About Dinosaurs* (1993), Seymour Simon organizes the information around questions that many children may have, such as "Were all dinosaurs giants?" "How were they named?" and "Which was the largest meat-eater?" The answers are concise so that primary school children can easily understand the information.

Zoo animals

Many books written for infants and toddlers are board books with an illustration or photograph and the name of one animal per page. The purpose of these books is to introduce infants and toddlers to different animals. Most of these books show the zoo as the animals' environment. Like its dinosaur books, The Smithsonian Institute created *My Baby Animal Book* (Levine, 2007), a board book with one animal on each page and a question to encourage interaction between the caregiver and an infant or toddler. Some other titles intended

Seymour Simon has written over 200 science books. He writes about topics that intrigue children: space, animals, weather, natural disasters, rocks and minerals, stars, mirrors, optical illusions, and the human body. In each of his books he gives accurate and detailed information about the topic. His books go beyond the general information found in encyclopedias; he loves to include interesting tidbits that will spark children's curiosity and desire to read further on the subject. He was a teacher and understands the curiosity of elementary children and the need to give them accurate information about topics not found in textbooks. Over 100 of his books have been recognized as outstanding science trade books for children by the National Science Teachers Association.

for infants are *Dear Zoo* (Campbell, 2007), *Animals at the Zoo* (Lilly, 1982), and *Zoo Animals* (Ingle, 1992). One simple zoo book, available in English or in Spanish, is *Zoo Animals* by Brian Wildsmith (2003).

Zoo Keepers (Community Helpers) (Deedrick, 1998) gives young readers information about what zoo keepers do, what they wear, and what equipment they use. *My Visit to the Zoo* (Aliki, 1999) explains the natural habitat and the physical and social characteristics of each animal. *Going to the Zoo* (Paxton, 1996) has engaging language and a musical score at the end of the book. In the singsong text, the "monkeys are scritch, scritch scratchin" and the "Big Black Bear is a-huff, huff-a-puffin." This language helps draw young children's attention.

Wild animals

Once children enter kindergarten and the primary grades, they want to learn about animals in their natural environments. There are many wonderful books that describe animals in their natural habitats. Most of the books have photographs, which help children see what the environment looks like in other parts of the world. Many books focus on only one animal, describing its physical appearance, diet, prey, predators, and life cycle. Some titles written for children in the early grades are *Gorillas* (Stewart, 2003), which describes their life cycle, habitat, mannerisms, and predators. Seymour Simon's *Gorillas* (2000) is another book that describes the animal's appearance, habitats, diet, and daily habits and behaviors. The oversized photographs complement the text. Melissa Stewart has written many books about African animals: *Elephants* (2002), *Rhinoceroses* (2002), *Hippopotamuses* (2002), *Zebras* (2002), and others. All of her books have photographs showing the animals in their natural habitat. Ann Squire also has a number of books about zoo animals in their natural surroundings. Two of her titles are *Jaguar* (2005) and *Leopard* (2005). A short annotated list of these and other books appears at the end of this chapter. Primary students can read some of these books and then give book club presentations (discussed later in this chapter), or the books can be shared by the teacher and students can write their favorite facts on a card that is then posted

author sketch

Melissa Stewart   **www.melissa-stewart.com**

Melissa Stewart has written many wonderful books about our natural world. Her love of observing the natural world began when her father took her for long walks through the fields and woods near their rural New England home. Her father always asked her what she saw and helped her focus on details. Biology was her favorite subject in high school, and she majored in biology at college, where she also studied journalism. Both of these subjects have helped her in writing over 100 books for young readers.

Like all scientists, she must do a lot of research. To gather her information, she explores the places about which she writes. When writing her books about African animals, she traveled to East Africa and went on a number of safaris so that she fully understood the habitats and habits of the animals. To write about rainforests, she explored tropical forests in Costa Rica. To write about sea lions, she swam with them off the Galapagos Islands. Her books are written so that beginning readers can read them by themselves. The photographs in each book bring the information to life. Stewart's website is worth a visit because she offers a readers' theatre selection on her recent book *When Rain Falls* (2008) and a curriculum guide for K–3. The curriculum covers science, art, and geography.

on a bulletin board entitled "True Facts About Zoo Animals!" More books on zoo animals are presented in Appendix A.19.

Primary children's curiosity is also aroused when they learn about woodland animals that may be wandering around their neighborhoods or roaming in woods they have visited. *Where Are the Night Animals?* (Fraser, 1999) is a great book for arousing students' curiosity about animals that roam in their neighborhoods while they are sleeping. The book explains the habits of a number of nocturnal animals—coyotes, skunks, owls, opossums, frogs, raccoons, and bats. This book may prompt children to find more information about a particular animal that intrigues them. *A Time for Sleeping* (Hirschi, 1993) explains where animals sleep. A unique feature of this book is that one animal is featured on each double page with both a box of concise facts and a poem about that animal.

If students live in one of the southwestern states, they may wake up in the morning and see evidence of armadillos. Even those outside the area will be curious about the funny-looking creatures. There are a number of books that give intriguing information about these armored animals: *Digging Armadillos* (Jango-Cohen, 1999), *Armadillos* (Jango-Cohen, 2004), and *It's an Armadillo!* (Lavies, 1989). The photographs in each of these books give close-up views of their armor, claws, dens, and digging habits.

Children love to play detective, and books about the footprints of birds and animals encourage children to be observant in nature. One excellent book that shows animal tracks at their actual size is *Wild Tracks!* (Arnosky, 2008). The book gives children information about where to find the different tracks. It shows the difference among many different bird tracks, dog and cat prints, and other animals that may be found in the woods. Arnosky writes in a manner likely to interest the less curious child. Another book about animal tracks is *Tracks in the Wild* (Bowen, 1993). This book includes animals that may be unfamiliar to some children, but the information is presented in such a way that readers will feel like they can still be detectives. Some of the animals are white-footed mice, bears, wolves, moose, otters, ermines, and other wild animals. *Animal Tracks and Traces* (Kudlinski, 1991) encourages readers to look for clues such as tracks, shedding, scents, nests, and "dirty dishes" of animals. Some specific creatures are birds, snakes, deer, dogs, horses, cats, pigeons, sparrows, and geese. All these books are wonderful books that encourage children to become detectives in their own backyards. Since many urban areas lack trees and grassy areas, children may need to visit a local park to observe the footprints of dogs, cats, and birds.

Infants and toddlers are intrigued by baby animals, but primary children also are curious about care and growth of the young. Pamela Hickman and Pat Stephens in *Animals and Their Young: How Animals Produce and Care for Their Babies* (2003) divide their discussion of animals into two categories: those that come from eggs and those born live. Technical terms are given, for example, "cubs" instead of "baby bears." Because this book covers a number of animals, it can be used as a springboard for primary students to research the animal that most intrigues them.

Two other books that may pique the curiosity of young children are *I Wonder Why Camels Have Humps and Other Questions* (Ganeri, 1993) and *Animal Groups* (Kaner, 2004). Many of the questions posed in *I Wonder Why Camels Have Humps and Other Questions* are questions that children and even adults may have about animals. Each question is followed by a concise answer. In *Animal Groups,* readers learn how animals live together in herds so they can protect one another. Both books encourage readers to research the animals in greater detail.

Two books that explain the hardships of animals as they encounter predators and humans are *Vanishing from Grasslands and Deserts* (Radley, 2001) and *The Big Caribou Herd* (Hiscock, 2003). *Vanishing from Grasslands and Deserts* explains how humans have become the enemy of many animals as they build suburbs in prairies and in deserts. It is a thought-provoking book for children. *The Big Caribou Herd* explains that caribou herds are shrinking because the animals encounter ice, snow, wolves, grizzly bears, and wolverines as they migrate across the Arctic National Wildlife Refuge. This book gets readers to realize that animals are constantly fighting for survival. Both of these books should pique the curiosity of children to read more about animals.

Oceans

Many books have been written about the ocean, sea creatures, and plant life. Children are intrigued with ocean life because it is beyond their personal world; life in the ocean appears to be a life of adventure. Caregivers and teachers can build many different types of thematic units around marine life. Many authors, for example, have written about penguins, so a thematic unit, discussed later in this chapter, can be centered around them. Children and adults are fascinated by these creatures that waddle on sheets of ice and dive through icy waters. Some books that give readers basic facts, but facts that may still surprise them, are *Penguins! Strange and Wonderful* (Pringle, 2007), *Penguins: Watch Me Grow* (DK Publishing, 2004), *Plenty of Penguins* (Black, 2000), and *Penguins* (Fromental, 2006). Each one has vivid illustrations or photographs. The rhyming text in *Plenty of Penguins* captivates young children.

While some books discuss many sea creatures in one book (such as the sea animals of the Antarctic), others feature only one kind of sea creature (such as sharks, seals, octopuses, and so on). Often, books about a single group of creatures will describe the general characteristics of that group and then compare and contrast different members within that group. For example, the beginning reader book *Sharks* (Berger & Berger, 2003) gives some basic facts about all sharks and then explains some differences among sharks. *Sharks* by Martin (2008) also describes the skills and senses of all sharks and then describes some differences across various species. Both of these books can be springboards for students to read more about a specific kind of shark such as hammerheads, tiger sharks, and pygmy sharks. Martin's book includes a table of contents, glossary, and boxed fact sheets that help readers locate specific information.

Deep-Sea Creatures* (Bennett, 2008) also gives general information about many different types of fish. Teachers can use this book along with Gail Gibbon's books *Exploring the Deep, Dark Sea* (2002) and *Sunken Treasure* (1990) to encourage children to read more about marine life at different depths of the ocean. *Safari Beneath the Sea* (Swanson, 1996) gives readers information about the inhabitants of the North Pacific coastal waters. Through photographs, Swanson explains specific things about coastal life such as wind currents, jellyfish, octopuses, and the curious habits of sea otters who use rocks as tools. Readers also learn about a species of shark that can lose and replace 30,000 teeth in a lifetime.

In its science vocabulary readers series, Scholastic Publishing has created books on single topics about 24 pages long. Many of these are about the sea. Each book has a table of contents, a glossary, and comprehension questions. Many of the pictures are photographs with small inset "fast fact" boxes. Some titles in this series are *Whales* (Prager, 2008), *Sharks* (Martin, 2008), *Tropical Fish* (Duhamel, 2008), *Deep-Sea Creatures* (Bennett, 2008), *Dolphins* (Martin, 2008), and *Sea Turtles* (Carlin, 2008). Each of these books gives enough information to encourage readers to explore more about each topic.

Weather and Natural Disasters

Many young children have experienced a thunderstorm, flood, blizzard, ice storm, tornado, hurricane, or earthquake. They may wonder what causes these events. Books that give scientific facts about thunder may alleviate children's fear of thunder when they learn what causes it. Books with information about counting the seconds between lightning and thunder to determine how close a storm is may make children more curious about than fearful of thunder. Appropriate books about tornadoes would be books that not only explain what happens in a tornado but what children can do to remain safe when they hear tornado warnings.

It is possible for teachers to create an entire unit around weather and natural disasters, using one author—Seymour Simon. His books are easy to comprehend, and the photographs make the events come alive. Two of his books that give general information about different kinds of weather are *Storms* (1992) and *Weather* (2006). *Lightning* (2006) focuses on this specific act of nature. It explains the three different kinds of lightning and then gives precautions about its dangers. *Tornadoes* (2001) explains all different types of windstorms: twisters, whirlwinds, water spouts, cyclones, and dust devils. *Earthquakes* (2006) explains how the earth is always moving and shifting. It describes the different faults, the Richter scale, seismographs, the Pacific Ring of Fire, and other details of earthquakes. The photographs also show the destruction caused by the 1906 San Francisco earthquake.

Volcanoes (2006) has beautiful photographs of volcanoes erupting and spilling lava over the earth. Simon explains in the text and through the photographs what causes volcanoes to erupt and the destruction that may ensue. Teachers can also share two books about hurricanes. *Oceans* (2006) explains how Earth differs from all other planets because it has water on its surface and then explains the different oceans and how the water is warmed near the equator and moves to colder waters; this movement makes the conditions needed to form hurricanes. *Hurricanes* (2007) tells how hurricanes are formed, how they move over water, and what happens as they cross over land. Some photographs are satellite photographs taken as a hurricane forms over the water and intensifies. The photographs show the force of hurricanes and the destruction that they leave behind.

After sharing Simon's books with students, teachers can encourage students to check out other books to compare the information found in them. When they have compiled a list of facts about hurricanes, they can write their own information books about hurricanes and share them with classmates.

Holidays and Festivals

Children love to celebrate their own birthday, attend birthday parties of cousins and friends, and delight in opening presents at Christmas or spinning the dreidel at Hanukkah. The books in this section cover holidays familiar to many American students and festivals from other cultures that may be unfamiliar to most. Though some of the books have a more narrative quality to them than traditional informational books, the main intent of the author is still to convey information to the reader.

Thanksgiving by David Marx (2002) is one of a series of easy-to-read books with pictures and photographs that help tell the history of Thanksgiving. The single words beneath colorful photographs—of a turkey, for instance—is one way to get children started reading sight words on their own.

Kwanzaa is a seven-day holiday celebrated during December by many African Americans. In *Seven Candles for Kwanzaa* (Pinkney, 1993), children can experience the holiday through one African American family. The seven candles represent the seven principles of family life that can be traced back to Africa. A number of simple African words are introduced along with activities that children do to celebrate the holiday. Today, in some urban schools, Kwanzaa is celebrated along with Christmas and Hanukkah.

In Mary D. Lankford's *Christmas Around the World* (1995), children learn about how Christmas is celebrated in Australia, Germany, Guatemala, the Philippines, and many more places. In Australia, for instance, Christmas dinner ends with a flaming plum pudding, made from suet, apples, spices, and raisins. It is steamed for six hours but contains no plums! In Northern British Columbia, Canada, smoked salmon accompanies the traditional turkey dinner. In the red-roofed stalls of Nuremberg, Germany, at Christmastime people buy figurines of men and women, about 10 inches high, made from prunes, dried figs, and walnuts; these edible figurines are thought to bring good luck. In Guatemala, Christmas is celebrated with a combination of Christian ceremonies and ancient rituals. This book lends itself to studying a map of the world and perhaps making some of the different dishes described in it.

Many children may also be familiar with wedding ceremonies if they have ever attended one; perhaps they have even been a ringbearer or flower girl. *Navajo Wedding Day: A Dine Marriage Ceremony* (Schick, 1999) tells how Navajo Indians celebrate a wedding through the eyes of a young Navajo girl. The wedding ceremony, for example, takes place in a hogan, the traditional six-sided house of the Navajo. The bride and groom stay there for four days, during which time the groom is expected to herd the sheep of his new mother-in-law. Instead of a long white gown and wedding veil, the bride wears a velvet and satin skirt, silver and turquoise jewelry, and moccasins. Although many of the details of this book may seem strange to children, there is much that is familiar, such as the arrival of relatives and friends bringing food and gifts.

Among many Native American tribes the powwow is a special ceremony for celebrating a variety of events; often there are different types of dances performed. George Ancona in *Powwow* (1993) describes a modern powwow, with its grand entry and other dances. Children can identify the details of the costumes that include eagle feathers, deerskins, beads, sequins, and ribbons, which make for a spectacular display of color. Susan Braine in *Drumbeat . . . Heartbeat* (1995) also describes typical dances performed at modern powwows. She shares her personal feelings about each dance.

Gorgeous color photographs help to illustrate George Ancona's *Fiesta U.S.A.* (1995). Hispanic people have migrated from many countries and settled across the United States. Their fiestas are one way they celebrate holidays and maintain customs from their native lands. On November 2, many cities with large Hispanic populations celebrate El Dia de los Muertos, the Day of the Dead. It is a festival to honor and celebrate those who have died. Children are given colorful candy skulls made of crystallized sugar. Families build altars in their home where they display photographs and other objects to honor their deceased friends and relatives. A grand parade through the streets of the barrio with people dressed in wild costumes and playing musical instruments culminates the fiesta. Other Hispanic festivals include the lighting of thousands of luminaries (brown paper bags filled with sand that hold lit candles) at Christmastime on the streets of Albuquerque, New Mexico. In Spanish Harlem in New York City giant puppets representing the three wise kings are carried through the streets as part of a great parade on January 6 called Three Kings Day.

Another beautifully photographed book by George Ancona is *Carnival* (1999). For five days in February, the people of Olinda, Brazil, celebrate with music, dance, giant puppets, and great food. February is summer in Brazil and it's hot. But the three main cultures of Brazil—indigenous Indian, European, and African—all get together to dance and celebrate carnival. Unlike the larger carnival in Rio de Janeiro, the small town of Olinda has no stands for viewing the parade through the narrow streets; instead, tourists are encouraged to join the parade.

Mardi Gras: A Cajun Country Celebration (Hoyt-Goldsmith, 1995) takes you to a small town in the bayou country of Louisiana, where young Joel, his family, relatives, and friends celebrate Mardi Gras, or Fat Tuesday, just the way their Cajun ancestors did hundreds of years ago. Joel helps with the harvest of rice and crawfish, which go into gumbo and boudin sausage—both traditional Cajun dishes. For Mardi Gras Joel dresses in a mask and costume he has made himself, and the streets are filled with fiddle, guitar, and accordion music. This book features colorful photographs and Cajun recipes.

Biographies and Autobiographies

Biographies are stories written about people who are usually famous for their accomplishments. Autobiographies are accounts people write of their own lives. Many of us have enjoyed reading biographies and autobiographies of famous presidents, war heroes, sports figures, film stars, opera singers, and others. Biographies and autobiographies not only satisfy our curiosity about famous people's lives but also help us understand historical periods (Abraham Lincoln and the Civil War era) or modern times (George W. Bush and the conflicts in the Middle East). Many children find it easier to learn about historical periods from books that focus on one person. As such, biographies and autobiographies are an important genre for readers.

Biographies and autobiographies belong to the category of informational books because their primary purpose is to convey information about a person's life. One way to get young children interested in this genre is to encourage them to create their own simple autobiographies known as "All About Me" books. Children are asked by teachers or caregivers to tell about themselves: their favorite foods, a favorite TV show, favorite games to play, the names of their best friends, their parents' occupation, and so on. An adult writes their statements down and collects them in a simple book form that the child can then illustrate. Reading the book together is an early way to start preschool children or kindergarteners reading biographies and autobiographies.

We begin by describing some books that deal with people of color and the prejudices they faced. As noted child psychologist Alvin Poussaint (Poussaint & Linn, 2008) tells us, parents, caregivers, and teachers of young children have the responsibility of raising children to understand and accept racial diversity. No child is born with prejudices toward others; such attitudes are learned from adults around them and society at large. Adults need to demonstrate, by their own actions, positive ways to interact with others. Reading and sharing the following books can encourage children's understanding of and positive outlook toward others.

Moses by Carol Weatherford (2006) tells the story of Harriet Tubman, who, though born into slavery, escaped and later returned to the South to lead other slaves northward to freedom. This book won both the Caldecott Award for the gorgeous illustrations by Kadir Nelson and the Coretta Scott King Award for furthering nonviolent social change.

Nikki Giovanni is a well-known African American poet and author of books for both children and adults. Her children's picture book *Rosa* (2005) introduces young people to Rosa Parks, one of the heroines of the Civil Rights movement of the 1950s and 1960s. Beautiful colored illustrations depict the life of this humble woman and her simple but courageous refusal to give up her seat on a bus in Alabama. The book also tells of the other women who rallied to her support after her arrest. Even young children can appreciate the injustices toward African Americans in the 1950s and 1960s.

Unfortunately prejudice comes in many forms and is deeply tied to the history of our nation. Long before Martin Luther King, Jr., made his famous speeches, Marian Anderson also influenced the United States to change its policies toward blacks, but did so in a very different way. *When Marian Sang* (Ryan, 2002) tells how, when only 10 years old, Anderson was recognized as truly gifted in church choirs in Philadelphia, Pennsylvania. Yet when she applied to music school in 1915, she was rejected because "colored" girls were not allowed to mix with whites. So she practiced on her own at home. Soon she traveled throughout the country performing for audiences of blacks and whites alike. Later, she would become the toast of Europe. But when she returned to America in 1939, concert managers refused to book her, until Eleanor Roosevelt, wife of President Franklin D. Roosevelt, insisted she be allowed to sing on the steps of the Lincoln Memorial.

All children, boys and girls alike, enjoy sports. Sports mean physical exercise, competition, and winning or losing. Sports also mean learning to respect your opponent, playing by the rules, and displaying good sportsmanship. Sports have proved to be a social leveler of sorts, allowing poor children to rise to greatness and riches and break down racial barriers still in place elsewhere in society. *Louis Sockalexis* (Wise, 2007) tells the true story of baseball's first Native American star. Raised in the late 1800s, Sockalexis grew up on the Penobscot Indian Reservation in Maine at a time when Indians did not mix or play with whites. But Louis's skills later led him to be noticed by colleges. He was offered a baseball scholarship to attend Holy Cross College in Massachusetts. His father knew of the discrimination that he would face and urged Louis to remain on the reservation. But Louis had a dream. In 1897, he became the first Native American to play in a professional baseball game against the New York Giants in the Polo Grounds.

Another sports biography that deals with the issues of discrimination is *Teammates* (Goldenbock, 1990). This is the story of how Jackie Robinson, in 1947, became the first African American to play professional baseball at a time in America when African Americans were not allowed to play in the major leagues. It is also the story of Pee Wee Reese, the shortstop and captain of the Brooklyn Dodgers who had grown up in the South, where discrimination against blacks was common. Illustrated with drawings and era photographs, this is a heartwarming story of the triumph of teammates over prejudice. *Teammates* is also what we call a partial biography because it tells only a portion of a person's life and does not attempt to cover Robinson's entire life from birth to death.

Less well known than Jackie Robinson is the story of Isaac Murphy, a son of slaves who grew up free in Lexington, Kentucky. In 1873, a chance encounter with a wealthy owner of thoroughbred race horses would propel Isaac, at age 12, into a career as a jockey that earned him fame and fortune. Illustrated with beautiful watercolor paintings, *Perfect Timing* (Trollinger, 2006) captures Isaac's story along with the thrill of horse racing.

Clara Barton was the youngest of seven children. As a child growing up in Massachusetts she was afraid of animals and was shy around strangers. Yet she cared deeply for others less fortunate than her and anguished over the major issue of her day—slavery. In *Clara Barton: I Want to Help* (Dubowski, 2006), young children can learn about the many things Clara did in her life and see real photographs of the Civil War. While she was working as a clerk in Washington, D. C., the Civil War broke out, and she soon found herself tending to the wounded soldiers that were brought to the city. Later she would care for soldiers on the battlefields and earned the nickname "the angel of the battlefield." Discussing the acts of famous people such as Clara Barton can help children realize that the actions of one person can really impact history.

The history of early America comes alive for young children through the stories of real people. Two easy-to-read books for young children—*A Picture Book of Davy Crockett* (1996) and *A Picture Book of Benjamin Franklin* (1990), both by David Adler—tell of the story of different but equally famous Americans. For example, in *A Picture Book of Davy Crockett,* children learn about life in the West in the eighteenth century. Born in 1786, in Tennessee, Davy Crockett was taught to hunt and fish and live off the land at an early age. He became a guide, a soldier, and was later elected to the United States House of Representatives. In *A Picture Book of Benjamin Franklin,* Adler makes Benjamin Franklin come alive by telling how he, who was the youngest of 17 children, started his career in his brother's print shop in Philadelphia. He later became a well-known writer, scientist, and inventor in the colonial days of America before the American Revolution. Franklin also helped to write the Declaration of Independence, and after the Revolution he was our ambassador to England and France. Adler has written many other historical biographies of famous Americans such as George Washington, Abraham Lincoln, Paul Revere, and Patrick Henry. In each of these books, Adler gives information in chronological order.

A different type of discovery and exploration is told in the autobiography *Buzz Aldrin: Reaching for the Moon* (Aldrin, 2005). This autobiography details the extensive education and training that Aldrin went through and also his disappointment over not being selected for the astronaut program the first time he applied. This is a great book to begin a class discussion about perseverance—if something does not work out the first time, continue to work so that you can accomplish your goals. Robert Burleigh and Mike Wimmer have captured the first walk on the moon in *One Giant Leap* (2009). This book describes Armstrong's and Aldrin's amazement as the moon came "rushing up toward them," with its colors of gray, brown, and blue along the edges. "Like a battlefield from some ancient war," the surface was "cracked," "scarred," "gouged," "cratered," and "pitted with tiny holes" (unpaged).

teaching suggestions
Sharing Informational Books

Children should be encouraged to respond freely: asking questions, giving interpretations, making suggestions for additional reading, sharing their personal experiences linked to the topic, relating personal feelings evoked by the topic, and sharing expertise on the topic (Oyler, 1996). However, there are a number of particular strategies that preschool teachers and primary teachers can use to facilitate children's engagement as they read nonfiction. Research indicates that children as young as three years can discuss and respond to informational texts (Maduram, 2000). Thus, when choosing a strategy, teachers should consider what is age-appropriate and what best fits the chosen book (Duke, 2003). While we provide one book as an example for each strategy, a good strategy can be used with many other ones as well.

Interactive Read-Alouds

The interactive read-aloud strategy is very popular with narrative texts, and can also be very effective when sharing nonfiction with toddlers and primary school students. When using this strategy, adults encourage children to look at the cover and title of a book and ask them to make predictions by telling what they think they will learn from the book. Making predictions is an important part of the metacognitive process. As teachers read the text, they stop periodically so that the children can confirm a prediction or make a new one. Some questions the adult can ask are "Why?" "How do you think X will turn out?" "What if Y had done something different?" or "Have you ever done Z yourself?" Figure 8.1 shows how one teacher engages her students during a read-aloud.

Ms. Hernandez leads a read-aloud. FIGURE 8.1

Ms. Hernandez: Boys and girls, this book is called *Dogs.* It was written and illustrated by Gail Gibbons. Look closely at the cover and tell me what you think you will learn as we read this book.

Olivia: Different types of dogs. There's all kinds in the picture.

Eric: What they eat. That dog is looking at a bone.

Anthony: Which ones are mean. We have a mean dog by our house.

Ms. Hernandez: *[turning the page]* Let's look at the title page and see if we can make some more predictions about what we'll learn. What do you think now?

Eric: Why they wear that thing around their neck.

Anthony: I see these words by the dogs. I bet that tells us their names.

Ms. Hernandez: Good, you noticed the labels that Gail Gibbons uses in many of her books that we have read. That is not their own name, but the kind of dog they are. This one is a mongrel. This one is a fox terrier. Does anyone know what kind this one is?

Olivia: A poodle because they have curly fur.

Ms. Hernandez: Correct. Do any of you have any of these types of dogs at home?

Camilla: No, but my grandma has one like this *[pointing to the fox terrier].*

Ms. Hernandez: Wonderful! Let's turn the page and continue.

[Ms. Hernandez reads the first page and gives time for the children to study the four pictures.]

Anthony: That one is a firehouse dog.

Ms. Hernandez: Yes, it is. Does anyone know what those white dogs with black spots are called?

Olivia: Damnation.

Ms. Hernandez: Very close. It's called a Dalmatian. Can we all say that together—*Dalmatian.*

[The class says the name four times, with Ms. Hernandez not saying it with them on the fourth time.]

Ms. Hernandez: Let's turn the page and continue.

Eric: Oh, that's a wolf! *[pointing to a husky]*

Ms. Hernandez: Yes, this wolflike looking dog is a husky.

Camilla: That is a wiener dog *[pointing to a dachshund].*

Ms. Hernandez: That is one name for them; the real name is *dachshund.* Why do you think we call them wiener dogs.

Camilla: Because it's long like a hot dog.

Anthony: That is like my dog *[pointing to the beagle].* It likes to bark up trees at squirrels. And it goes like this *[getting on all floors and sniffing the floor and whining].*

Ms. Hernandez: Why do you think it sniffs like that?

Anthony: It's trying to hunt for animals.

[After the teacher reads the page about dogs being the descendents of wolves, the following discussion continues.]

Anthony: Wolves are mean.

Ms. Hernandez: Yes, wolves are wild animals. How do you think they became pets?

Anthony: Someone started to pet them.

Olivia: People fed them.

[The studying of pictures and reading continues. Throughout the reading and discussion Ms. Hernandez asks many more questions that get the children to think about possible answers.]

Book Clubs

Book clubs have become a very popular way of bringing adults together over books, and a variation on that arrangement can be used to engage young children as a group. Based on constructivism theory, the book club strategy (Heller, 2006) invites students beginning as early as kindergarten to select a book on their own, share it with the class, and lead a group discussion. During the talk, students may have a prop that represents their book. Figure 8.2 gives the steps for leading a

---

FIGURE 8.2   **Steps to use during book club sharing.**

1. The student first activates classmates' prior knowledge by asking what they know about the topic.
2. The student tells what he learned.
3. The student shares the special message or main idea of the book.
4. The student discusses what he thought about the book.
5. The student discusses how it made him feel.
6. The student reads his favorite part.
7. The student gives ideas for writing in response or drawing an illustration.

AN ARMADILLO BOOK CLUB

Nick, a second grade student, stands in front of his class and holds up a book for everyone to see.

Nick: I read *Digging Armadillos* by Judith Jango-Cohen. Photographs are by a bunch of different people. I selected this book because we had an armadillo digging in my mother's flower bed. Do any of you know anything about armadillos?

Darnell: They have hard skin.

Madison: Their skin is a shell like a turtle.

Briana: They live in Texas because I saw one by Granddad's house. They have really long tails that are pointed at the end. I think they are hard too.

Nick: Anything else?

Scott: I think they bite people.

Nick: Here is what I learned. *[He pulls out a poster board with the following written on it:]*

1. They dig in the ground to get bugs, to hide from their predators, and to sleep.
2. Their hard shell is called a carapace. It protects them. The carapace has bands in the middle so they can bend.
3. They can swim.
4. A baby armadillo is a pup. It drinks milk from its mother.

(continued)

| Steps to use during book club sharing, *continued.* | FIGURE 8.2 |

Nick: Here is my one special thing I learned. They are diggers. These are my thoughts about the book: I liked to read about its carapace because I did not know that word and did not know they had them. This is how the book made me feel: I learned a lot from this book and

I liked the photographs; they made everything look real. But my favorite part in on page 20. [*He opens the book to page 20 and reads.*] "An armadillo holds its breath as it digs to keep dirt out of its nose." I drew an outline of an armadillo and wrote facts on its back.

book club and demonstrates its use in the classroom. As you can see, book club presentations not only promote interest in informational texts, they also facilitate students' oral language, reading, writing, and listening skills (Heller, 2006).

Author Studies

Duthie (1994) suggests teachers use author studies to teach children about nonfiction books, just as teachers do author studies on those who write fiction, as was discussed in Chapter 6. During an author study, teachers show students that authors and illustrators must research their topic and gather information from many sources before they write an informational book. They teach that authors of nonfiction "can have [a] strong voice, be creative and use techniques from other genres" (Duthie, 1994, p. 588). They highlight the technique that different authors and illustrators use to convey their message. For example, during an author study of Gail Gibbons, teachers can have students look through a wide selection of her books and discover that she often uses more than one illustration per page, either to show a cycle (*Gulls . . . Gulls . . . Gulls . . .,* 2001) or a progression (*From Seed to Plant,* 1991) or to show the differences between types of animals and things. Students may discover that Jerry Pallatto uses the alphabet to organize the information found in his many books, that Caroline Arnold uses die-cuts for her illustrations, and that Ann McGovern uses the question/answer format for many of her books.

During author studies, Duthie (1994) suggests that teachers explain to students that many different authors write about the same topic, and they can read many different books to gather a lot of information. Author websites can also be used to further enhance unit studies. Figure 8.3 gives an example of how one teacher made the bridge from fiction author studies to nonfiction author studies.

FIGURE 8.3 Mr. Armstrong introduces nonfiction author studies.

Mr. Armstrong loves nature and tries to instill a love of nature in his third graders. He knows his class enjoys informational books about animals. Some students can't read enough about snakes, some are intrigued with penguins, and others are fascinated with bats.

Each year he does at least four author studies with his students because he wants to get them interested in the person who wrote the book, and he hopes to pique one or two students' interest in writing. With each author studied, he attempts to offer a glimpse into the life of the author so students understand how authors are real people with real passions. He wants to share with his students how authors get ideas for their books. However, he always ends up focusing only on authors who write fiction.

One day in early fall, Josh comes to Mr. Armstrong with *An Extraordinary Life: The Story of a Monarch Butterfly* by Laurence Pringle and asks, "Mr. Armstrong, have you ever read this book? I think you would like it because you are always talking about how you like to watch and study animals and bugs. This book explains how this monarch was born in Massachusetts and goes to Mexico. It even has a map that shows how it went from one state to another. And the book also tells me how to raise a monarch butterfly. I am going to ask my dad if I can buy an egg. Do you want to read it?"

Mr. Armstrong is intrigued with Josh's enthusiasm, especially since he has never shown any strong interest in reading. Mr. Armstrong stops to look at the book and agrees with Josh that it is truly fascinating.

Mr. Armstrong asks, "Do you mind if I read this to the class today during our shared reading?"

Josh considers for a moment. "It's okay by me. But don't tell the class I chose it because what if they don't like the book? Oh, my dad and I found other books by this author that are really good too. Do you want me to bring them to school?"

Mr. Armstrong agrees not to tell the class and says he would love to read more of Mr. Pringle's books. When he reads it to the class, they too are fascinated that one butterfly can fly so far and not get lost. Afterward they want to read more about monarch butterflies.

Mr. Armstrong has not read other books by Laurence Pringle, so after school he searches the name on the Internet and finds that Pringle has written over 100 books. Many are books about animals and insects. Since he always does an animal unit with his class, he decides to incorporate an author study on Pringle in the unit.

Mr. Armstrong visits the public library to get as many of Pringle's books as possible, and online he finds some fascinating facts about Pringle. Mr. Armstrong also likes the way the facts are presented in sidebars and diagrams and plans to use a similar format for his presentation.

Through his research, Mr. Armstrong also discovers that Pringle does school visits. Mr. Armstrong contacts the district's central office and talks with Mrs. Reid, the director who arranges such visits for the district. He suggests Pringle, and Mrs. Reid contacts the author and arranges for a spring visit. Because Pringle is coming, the district purchases as many of his books as possible, and the elementary schools in the district rotate his books throughout the year so that children have the opportunity to read his books before he comes. The visit is a success, and now Mr. Armstrong does an author study every year on Laurence Pringle.

Thematic Units

Thematic units are a way for teachers to encourage children to research a topic, using many different books, as shown in Figure 8.4. Students will learn that sometimes many different people write about the same subject and that, while some information may overlap from one book to another, some information is unique to one book. This facilitates students' ability to analyze and synthesize information from different sources.

There are many possibilities for thematic units—animals, places, events, inventions, and others. We encourage you to search your own public library and curriculum library and develop units on different topics.

A mammal thematic unit in the classroom.	**FIGURE** 8.4

Mr. Cho found during a previous unit on oceans that his students are very interested in whales and dolphins. He wants to encourage the students to learn more so he visits the school library and the local public library to find as many books as he can about these ocean mammals. He then covers a bulletin board with blue paper. He keeps 4" x 6" index cards in his pocket, and as students read and learn new facts they are encouraged to write one fact on each card and include the reference at the bottom so that other students can read the book if they find that fact intriguing. Mr. Cho encourages the students to read the posted fact cards and to post new facts frequently. Mr. Cho also teaches his students the correct format for providing a reference. He explains the importance of giving all the information because many books have similar or identical titles. He shows the student where to find the copyright date, the publisher, and the publisher's city. Following are a few of the students' cards.

1. The biggest animal is the blue whale. It is longer than a giraffe is tall. It is heavier than the heaviest hippo. Its heart is the size of a small car.
   Source: Greenberg, D. (2001). Whales.

2. A whale has only one baby at a time, and the calf stays with its mother for about a year.
   Source: Landau, E. (1996). Ocean Mammals.

3. There are 37 different kinds of dolphins. Most are gray or black and white, but two kinds are pink.
   Source: Thomson, S. (2006). Amazing Dolphins!

4. The killer whale is also called an orca. A baby can swim when it is born.
   Source: Arnold, C. (2006). A Killer Whale's World.

5. The orca is the largest dolphin. It can weigh up to nine tons and can be over 30 feet long. Orcas are found in all the oceans in the world.
   Source: Simon, S. (1989). Whales.

6. A dolphin hunts using echolocation. An echo tells the dolphin if something is near or far. Humans cannot hear a dolphin's echo because the sound is so high pitched.
   Source: Taylor, L. (1999). Dolphins.

3-2-1

Welmer (2007) has developed the 3-2-1 strategy to keep students organized and focused when writing summaries. After reading and sharing a book, the children write about what they discovered following this format:

3. Three things they never knew before they heard or read the book.
2. Two things they found interesting. These may be facts they knew before they read the book or things they learned. Teachers should encourage children to list two things that are not in their first list of three things they learned.
1. One question they still have about the topic.

For example, after reading Gail Gibbon's *Ducks!* (2001), Miss Wilson shared the 3-2-1 chart in Figure 8.5 with her first graders. By sharing the strategy, she lets her students know that even though she is an adult, she does not know everything about all subjects and makes her learning explicit. A blank chart for use in your class is available in Appendix C.5.

FIGURE 8.5   A 3-2-1 chart for *Ducks!*

Name of the book: Ducks! (2001)

Author: Gail Gibbons

3

Three things I never knew before I read the book:

1. A duck makes its own feathers waterproof by rubbing the feathers with a waxy oil from a gland near its tail.
2. Ducks live on every continent except Antarctica.
3. Some ducks dive 10 to 25 feet underwater to get their food—fish, clams, and snails.

2

Two things I found interesting.

1. The male duck is called a drake; a female duck is called a hen.
2. After a hen lays about 10 to 12 eggs, the eggs hatch in about 3 to 4 weeks.

1

One question I still have about ducks.

1. How do down feathers differ from surface feathers?

K-T-W-L

Based on Ogle's (1986) K-W-L strategy, the K-T-W-L (Akerson & Young, 2004) adds one additional column. For this strategy, the teacher makes four columns: K for "things I know," T for "things I think I know," W for "things I want to learn," and L for "things I learned." The first three columns are completed *before* children hear or read the text, and the last column is completed *after* reading. The T column is used because many times children think they know something about a topic, but they are not sure. The T column permits them to record those ideas. Figure 8.6 is a sample of Ms. West's kindergarten class's K-T-W-L on penguins. The L column was added after reading *Penguins* (Gibbons, 1998). A blank chart is provided in Appendix C.6.

FIGURE 8.6   A K-T-W-L chart for the book *Penguins*.

Name of the book: Penguins

Author: Gail Gibbons

K	T	W	L
• They live where it's cold.	• They live at the North Pole.	• How do they stay warm?	• The male penguin protects the egg.
• They can swim.	• They eat fish.	• How long do they live?	• They are found in the southern hemisphere.
• They are black and white.			

Compare Facts with Fiction

After reading a fictional story that has an animal as the main character, such as the dinosaur in *Edwina* (Willems, 2006), who can do all types of extraordinary feats, teachers can share some nonfiction books about dinosaurs and have the students create a class chart like the one found in Figure 8.7. The chart would be completed after the teacher shared Willems's *Edwina*, Gibbons's *Dinosaurs Are Extinct* (2005), and Brown's *Beyond the Dinosaurs: Monsters of the Air and Sea* (2007). Appendix C.7 includes a blank version of the chart.

Table of Contents Prediction

To further help students make predictions, teachers can select an informational book with a table of contents and read through it with children, asking them to predict what new information they will encounter in the book. Teachers can record the children's responses, and after they read the chapter or section, they can discuss if the predictions were correct. For example, using *Deep-Sea Creature* (Bennett, 2008), Mr. Whitebear turned to the table of contents and asked his first graders to predict what they would learn from each of the chapters. Figure 8.8 has the students' responses to some of the chapter titles.

Fiction versus facts chart.   **FIGURE** 8.7

Subject: Dinosaurs

FICTION

Book: Edwina

- They played with children
- They did favors for people
- They baked cookies
- They talked
- They walked through a brick wall

FACT

Books: Dinosaurs Are Extinct and Beyond the Dinosaurs: Monsters of the Air and Sea

- 65 million years ago a cataclysmic event killed many plants and animals
- They are extinct
- Some were gentle
- Some were attackers
- First dinosaur fossils were found in England in 1820
- There were over 1,000 different kinds
- Some ate plants; some ate animals
- Some had long tails or thick plates and spikes
- Some of their names are pteranodon, ichthyosaurus, mosasaurus, pterodaustro, hainosaurus.

FIGURE 8.8 Using the table of contents to predict learning.

Mr. Whitebear: The first chapter is "Way Down Deep." What do you think you will learn while listening to this chapter?

Ethan: About fish on the bottom of the ocean.

Teresa: About plants on the bottom.

Aileen: I bet there is a shipwreck down there and there will be money and jewels.

Mr. Whitebear: Great guesses! We will have to see if you are correct. The next chapter is called "Exploration." What do you think you will learn in this chapter?

Sam: About the people who wear those black suits and goggles so they can find things.

Teresa: They are going to explore the shipwreck.

Kyle: I think they're going to look for sharks and whales and octopus.

Mr. Whitebear: Again, you have great guesses! Now the next chapter is called "Fascinating Fish." What do you think you will learn when we read this chapter.

Kyle: They will tell us about those pretty colored fish like rainbow fish.

Teresa: We will learn about fish that don't look like fish.

Mr. Whitebear: Do you know about fish that don't look like fish?

Teresa: Yeah. Those flat fish with big stingers in them.

Mr. Whitebear: Do you mean stingrays?

Teresa: Yeah, that's what they're called.

Notice that Mr. Whitebear never tells a child her response was right, wrong, or silly. At times he expands the discussions by asking a student to clarify a response. When teachers engage students in this type of discussion before they read, they are more likely to listen to see if their predictions are correct or incorrect.

Detective Work

James Hymes (1981) suggests that when teachers introduce a nonfiction book, they can encourage children to become detectives by attempting to find answers to the following questions about the topic of the book.

- What is it?
- Where does it come from?
- What is it made of?
- What is it for?

Figure 8.9 has a sample sheet that an adult and children can complete together as they read the book. A blank version is available in Appendix C.8.

Dramatizing the Topic

Children love to act out stories, and teachers can also encourage children to act out nonfiction by becoming anyone or anything they are studying—volcanoes,

Detective worksheet.   **FIGURE** 8.9

Name of the book: Projects About Colonial Life

Author: Marian Broida

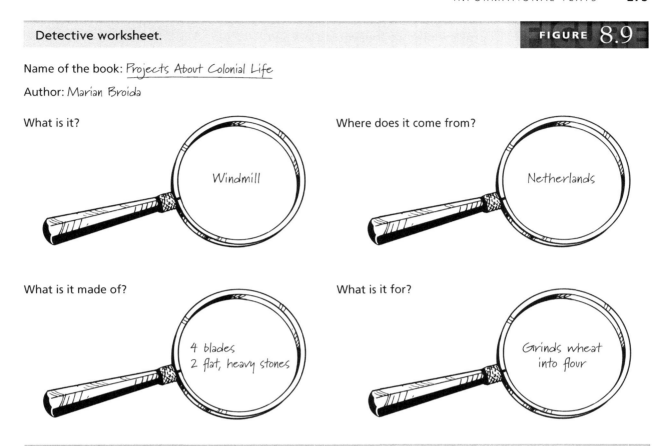

What is it?

Windmill

Where does it come from?

Netherlands

What is it made of?

4 blades
2 flat, heavy stones

What is it for?

Grinds wheat
into flour

thunderstorms, dinosaurs, snowflakes, mountains, and roaring oceans. Putnam (1991) suggests that children dramatize *The Pilgrims' First Thanksgiving* (McGovern, 1984) by getting the children into a small crowded spot to show how crowded the pilgrims were on the ship. They can rock back and forth to get the feeling of the ship. They can pretend that they are running out of food and water. After dramatizing the book, children can discuss how they felt and then imagine how the pilgrims must have felt after weeks on the ship.

Preview-Predict-Confirm

Yopp and Yopp (2004) suggest teachers use the preview-predict-confirm strategy to encourage oral language, foster social learning, increase self-directed learning, and stimulate deliberation over differing interpretations. Before reading a book, teacher and students preview the pictures together. Children can discuss what they see. They then can predict what they think the book is about and what they will learn based on the pictures they have viewed. During reading and after reading, the teacher can confirm their predictions with students. In Figure 8.10 Ms. Logan engaged her third grade class in a Preview-Predict-Confirm while sharing *Exploring the Deep, Dark Sea* (Gibbons, 1999). Figure 8.10 follows the students' responses as Ms. Logan does a picture preview.

FIGURE 8.10 A preview-predict-confirm of *Dark Sea*.

Ms. Logan is showing the illustrations of *Dark Sea* to the class. To keep an appropriate pace, she permits one response per page. She begins with the frontispiece, which often gives the setting for the book. For this book, it is a picture of an ocean liner out at sea.

Gabe: It looks like the story will happen from a ship.

Alyssa: Looks like they are going to study fish from the ship.

[The teacher then flips to other pictures.]

Maya: The little picture looks like there are mountains in the ocean.

Lucas: It looks like they are lowering this thing with people in it. The people lower it with the use of buttons.

Gabe: Look, the water is getting darker and the fish are different from the other ones. It looks like this thing has headlights on.

Lucas: It's black water now and look how some fish swim toward the light and others swim away like they are scared.

Gabe: Oh, man! They touched the bottom of the ocean. Look at all those weird-looking fish.

Alyssa: Look! The machine is picking up things from the ocean and it looks like it puts the stuff in cans on the outside of their machine.

Ms. Logan: All of you are seeing many things. When I read it to you, we can learn about this machine and how it picks up things from the ocean floor. You also have noticed that the water became darker as they went lower. I wonder whether these ocean layers have specific names.

After piquing the students' interest, she is ready to read so they can learn the particulars of what they saw in the pictures.

Conclusion

Teachers can make reading nonfiction as exciting as reading fiction. Obviously, teachers may already know much of the information that is in informational books intended for young children. But in order to get children excited about nonfiction, teachers must marvel with children as they learn about the wonderful world in which they live. Teachers should not shy away from topics that may be unfamiliar to children because children have a natural curiosity about what they don't know. It is important that teachers build on information that the children already know to increase their knowledge about different topics. We have touched on only a few of the many topics addressed in nonfiction. Teachers should seek books that interest them or listen to their children's *why, how,* and *how come* questions. New topics of interest may come up as teachers listen to their students.

journeying WITH CHILDREN'S LITERATURE

1. Select a favorite nonfiction author, such as Gail Gibbons or Seymour Simon, and create a PowerPoint presentation about the author that you can show to your students to get them excited about that author.

2. Create a thematic unit that interests you or your students. Using your local public library, your curriculum library, or websites such as www.amazon.com, create an annotated bibliography on that topic.

3. Go to your university's curriculum library or local public library with your annotated bibliography and search the nonfiction shelves to see which books are available.

4. If you teach in the primary grades, you will experience a wide range of reading abilities. Select a topic such as planets, weather, animals, or any other topic that interests you. Go to your curriculum library or local library to find books on that topic. Using www.renlearn.org, find the reading levels of the books so you will have books for a wide range of reading abilities.

5. Browse through some back issues of *The Reading Teacher, Language Arts,* and other educational journals to find reading and writing strategies to use with nonfiction. Keep a file of the strategies you find.

activities TO SHARE WITH CHILDREN

1. After sharing Gail Gibbons's *Exploring the Deep, Dark Sea* (1999), create a class mural in three layers to represent the three layers of the sea. Make the top part of light blue paper, the next of dark blue, and the bottom part of black to represent the abyss. Have children look at the type of life found in each layer and let them choose a plant or creature they want to research. Permit them to draw or create a 3-D representation of the plant or creature and affix it to the appropriate layer of the mural. Then have them write some basic facts on a 3" x 5" index card that they place under their drawing.

2. After reading about the size of some large sea creatures, have students mark the length of each creature with a yardstick with chalk outside on the sidewalk or with markers on a long piece of butcher paper.

3. After studying African animals, invite your second or third graders to make papier-mâché replicas of their favorite animal. Invite children to research their chosen animals in multiple books and then have them present their information to the class.

4. After reading books about famous people, invite your students to dress like the character and deliver a monologue in character.

5. Create a "Nonfiction Books You Should Read" poster near your classroom library. Invite students to write the title, author, and a few reasons why they recommend the books to others.

6. After reading Gail Gibbons's *The Pumpkin Book* (1999), bring a large pumpkin to school and scoop out the pulp. Permit the children to separate the seeds from the pulp. Rinse the seeds under cold water. Then, as Gibbons suggests at the end of the book, spread the seeds on a screen or cookie sheet and have them dry in the sun for a week. Once they are completely dry, put them in a jar for future snacks.

our favorite CHILDREN'S BOOKS

Arnold, C. (2006). *A Penguin's World*. Minneapolis: Picture Window Books.

Arnold's die-cut illustrations depict the life of a penguin, beginning with the egg. Phonetic spellings are given for technical terms. Arnold uses onomatopoeia throughout the book to give cadence to his text.

Ashby, R. (2005). *My Favorite Dinosaurs*. Illus. J. Sibbick. New York: Milk & Cookies Press/Simon & Schuster.

This book is a survey of the many types of dinosaurs—Tyrannosaurus Rex, Coelophysis, Ceratosauraus, Brachiosaurus, and many others. Sibbick's illustrations show groups of each type in their natural setting. Each page features one type with a small box with information about the dinosaurs' habitat, body structure, and prey.

Berger, M., & Berger, G. (2000). *What Makes an Ocean Wave? Questions and answers about oceans and ocean life*. Illus. J. Rice. New York: Scholastic.

The format of this book is to ask questions, followed by concise answers. Some questions include "What are tsunamis?" "Are oceans, seas, gulfs, and bays the same or different?" "What causes high tides?' "Are whales fish?"

Gibbons, G. (1991). *From Seed to Plant*. New York: Holiday House.

The illustrations complement the text so that children can easily understand the concepts. At the end of the book is a "From Seed to Plant" project with step-by-step instructions and illustrations.

Heller, R. (1999). *Color*. New York: Putnam Juvenile.

Through brilliant, detailed illustrations and rhyming text of vivid language, Heller describes primary colors, secondary colors, tints, and hues. She also explains how color is added to print.

Johnston, T. (2005). *The Harmonica*. New York: Charlesbridge Publishing.

A boy is separated from his parents and sent to a Nazi concentration camp in Poland. The only thing he has to keep his hopes alive is the harmonica his father gave him.

Lang, A. (2004). *Baby Koala*. Photographer W. Lynch. Allston, MA: Fitzhenry and Whiteside.

The book gives the happenings of a first year of a koala's life as it lives with it mother. Physical features, habitat, food, and predators are discussed. The table of contents and index help readers find specific information.

Littlefield, C. A. (2003). *Awesome Ocean Science: Investigating the secrets of the underwater world*. Illus. S. Rakitin. Charlotte, VT: Williamson Publishing.

> This is a book of science experiments for young children to do with a caregiver or teacher. The reading level is too difficult for primary children. But because the experiments are easy and appropriate, it makes for a great read-aloud project.

Markle, S. (2007). *Zebras*. Minneapolis: First Avenue Editions.

> The photographs show zebras in their natural surroundings. The text also explains how herds stay together and how they help protect each other. The text is intriguing, as it tells about attacks from many different types of predators.

Simon, S. (2002). *Destination: Space*. New York: HarperCollins.

> The information in this book is about what has been seen through the Hubble Space Telescope as it has orbited Earth since April 1990. The in-depth information is great for children who are really enthusiastic about space.

Taylor, L. (1999). *Dolphins*. Photographer N. Wu. Minneapolis: Lerner Publications.

> Physical descriptions of dolphins are given along with descriptions of the sounds they make, the schools they form. The book also explains how babies and their mothers relate and how dolphins interact with humans. A table of contents, glossary, and index are helpful features for locating specific information.

VanCleave, J. (1994). *Janice VanCleave's 201 Awesome, Magical, Bizarre and Incredible Experiments*. Hoboken, NJ: John Wiley.

> These experiments are easy to follow and call for inexpensive materials. The results will amaze children and teachers.

Woodson, J. (2005). *Show Way*. Illus. H. Talbott. New York: Putnam.

> Author Woodson's great-grandmother was taken from her parents and sold as a slave at age 7. The "Show Way" quilt weaves one generation into the next, right up to Woodson's own daughters.

children's literature IN THIS CHAPTER

Adler, D. (1990). *A picture book of Benjamin Franklin*. Illus. A. Wallner & A. Wallner. New York: Holiday House.

Adler, D. (1996). *A picture book of Davy Crockett*. Illus. A. Wallner & A. Wallner. New York: Holiday House.

Aldrin, B. (2005). *Buzz Aldrin: Reaching the moon*. Illus. W. Minor. New York: HarperCollins.

Aliki. (1999). *My visit to the zoo*. New York: HarperTrophy.

Aloian, M. (2004). *Life cycle of a flower*. New York: Crabtree Publishing.

Ancona, G. (1995). *Fiesta U.S.A.* New York: Lodestar.

Ancona, G. (1993). *Powwow*. New York: Harcourt Brace.

Ancona, G. (1999). *Carnival*. New York: Harcourt Brace.

Andersen, W. (2005). *M is for Mount Rushmore: A South Dakota alphabet book*. Illus. C. Harsese. Chelsea, MI: Sleeping Bear Press.

Arnold, C. (2006). *A penguin's world*. Minneapolis: Picture Window Books.

Arnold, C. (2006). *A killer whale's world*. Minneapolis: Picture Window Books.

Arnold, K. (2005). *Elephants can paint too*. Photographer K. Arnold. New York: An Anne Schwartz Book/ Atheneum.

Arnosky, J. (2008). *Wild tracks!* Illus. K. Horel. New York: Sterling.

Ashby, R. (2005). *My favorite dinosaurs*. Illus. J. Sibbick. New York: Milk & Cookie Press/Simon & Schuster.

Bailey, J. (1990). *The life cycle of an owl.* Illus. J. Harland. New York: Bookwright Press.

Barrett, P. (2001). *National Geographic dinosaurs.* Illus. R. Martin. Washington, DC: National Geographic Children's Books.

Beach, M. (2006). *Simply in season children's cookbook.* Illus. J. Kauffman. Scottdale, PA: Herald Press.

Bennett, E. (2008). *Deep-sea creatures.* New York: Scholastic.

Berger, M., & Berger, G. (2001). *What makes an ocean wave?* Illus. J. Rice. New York: Scholastic.

Berger, M., & Berger, G. (2003). *Sharks.* New York: Scholastic.

Berger, M., & Berger, G. (2004). *Grub to ladybug.* Photo Researcher S. Longacre. New York: Scholastic.

Biddle, M. (1998). *Origami: Inspired by Japanese prints from the Metropolitan Museum of Art.* Illus. S. Biddle. New York: Viking Juvenile.

Black, S. (2000). *Plenty of penguins.* Illus. T. Maccombie. New York: Cartwheel.

Blain, D. (1992). *The boxcar children cookbook.* New York: Scholastic.

Bowen, B. (1993). *Tracks in the wild.* Boston: Little, Brown.

Braine, S. (1995). *Drumbeat . . . Heartbeat.* Minneapolis: Lerner Publishing Group.

Broida, M. (2004). *Projects about colonial life.* New York: Benchmark Books.

Brown, C. L. (2007). *Beyond the dinosaurs: Monsters of the air and sea.* Illus. P. Wilson. New York: HarperCollins.

Brown, M. W. (1989). *Big red barn.* Illus. F. Bond. New York: Harper.

Bull, J. (2006). *The best craft book ever.* New York: Dorling Kindersley Publishing.

Burleigh, R. (2009). *One giant leap.* Illus. M. Wimmer. New York: Philomel.

Campbell, R. (2007). *Dear zoo.* New York: Little Simon.

Carle, E. (1981). *The very hungry caterpillar.* New York: Philomel.

Carlin, L. (2008). *Sea turtles.* New York: Scholastic.

Carr, K. (2007). *My dinosaur book.* New York: HarperCollins.

Caskey, P. (2007). *Make your own playdough, paint and other craft materials.* St. Paul: Red Leaf Press.

Churchill, E. R., & Loesching, L. (1997). *730 easy science experiments with everyday materials.* Illus. M. Mandell. New York: Tess Press.

Churchill, E. R., Loesching, L., Mandell, M., & Zweifel, F. (1997). *365 easy science experiments with everyday materials.* New York: Sterling Publishing.

Esbensen, B. J. (1994). *Baby whales drink milk.* Illus. L. Davis. New York: HarperCollins.

Deedrick, T. (1998). *Zoo keepers (community helpers).* Mankato, MN: Capstone Press.

DK Publishing. (1994). *Big book of dinosaurs.* New York: Dorling Kindersley Publishing.

DK Publishing. (2004). *Penguins: Watch me grow.* New York: Dorling Kindersley Publishing.

Dixon, D. (2005). *Centrosaurus and other dinosaurs of cold places.* Illus. S. Weston & J. Field. Minneapolis: Picture Window Books.

Dixon, D. (2007). *Neovenator and other dinosaurs of Europe.* Illus. S. Weston & J. Field. Minneapolis: Picture Window Books.

Dubowski, C. (2006). *Clara Barton: I want to help.* New York: Bearpoint Publishing.

Duhamel, M. (2008). *Tropical fish.* New York: Scholastic.

Fraser, M. S. (1999). *Where are the night animals?* Illus. M. A. Fraser. New York: HarperCollins.

Fromental, J. L. (2006). *Penguins.* Illus. J. Jolivet. London: Abrams Books for Young Children.

Ganeri, A. (1993). *I wonder why camels have humps and other questions about animals.* Illus. S. Holmes. New York: Kingfisher/Houghton Mifflin.

Gardner, R. (2008). *Super science projects about earth's soil and water.* Illus. T. Labaff. Berkley Heights, NJ: Enslow Publishers.

Gibbons, G. (1987). *The pottery place.* New York: Holiday House.

Gibbons, G. (1989). *Whales.* New York: Holiday House.

Gibbons, G. (1989). *From seed to plant.* New York: Holiday House.

Gibbons, G. (1991). *Sunken treasure.* New York: Holiday House.

Gibbons, G. (1991). *The puffins are back.* New York: Holiday House.

Gibbons, G. (1991). *Zoo.* New York: Holiday House.

Gibbons, G. (1998). *Penguins!* New York: Holiday House.

Gibbons, G. (1999). *Exploring the deep, dark sea.* New York: Holiday House.

Gibbons, G. (1999). *Sea turtles.* New York: Holiday House.

Gibbons, G. (1999). *Penguins!* New York: Holiday House.

Gibbons, G. (1999). *The pumpkin book.* New York: Holiday House.

Gibbons, G. (2001). *Ducks!* New York: Holiday House.

Gibbons, G. (2001). *Gulls gulls gulls.* New York: Holiday House.

Gibbons, G. (2001). *Dogs.* New York: Holiday House.

Gibbons, G. (2005). *Dinosaur discoveries.* New York: Holiday House.

Gibbons, G. (2005). *Dinosaurs are extinct.* New York: Holiday House.

Gibbons, G. (2006). *Dinosaurs!* New York: Holiday House.

Gibbons, G. (2006). *Surrounded by the sea.* New York: Holiday House.

Gibbons, G. (2007). *Coral reefs.* New York: Holiday House.

Gibbons, G. (2007). *Penguins!* New York: Holiday House.

Giovanni, N. (2005). *Rosa.* Illus. B. Collier. New York: Henry Holt.

Goldenbock, P. (1990). *Teammates.* Illus. P. Bacon. New York: Gulliver Books.

Gresham, D. (1998). *The chronicles of Narnia cookbook.* Illus. P. Baynes. New York: HarperCollins.

Greenberg, C. (2001). *Whales.* Photographer Z. Leszczynski. New York: Benchmark Books.

Heale, J. (1993). *Baby's book of animals.* New York: Dorling Kindersley Publishing.

Heiligman, D. (1996). *From caterpillar to butterfly.* Illus. B. Weissman. New York: HarperCollins.

Heller, R. (1995). *Color.* New York: Scholastic.

Heller, R. (1998). *Merry-go-round: A book about nouns.* New York: Putnam Juvenile.

Heller, R. (1998). *Behind the mask: A book about prepositions.* New York: Putnam Juvenile.

Heller, R. (1998). *Kites sail high: A book about verbs.* New York: Putnam Juvenile.

Heller, R. (1998). *Up, up and away: A book about adverbs.* New York: Putnam Juvenile.

Heller, R. (1998). *A cache of jewels and other collective nouns.* New York: Putnam Juvenile.

Heller, R. (1999). *Animals born alive and well.* New York: Putnam Juvenile.

Heller, R. (1999). *Plants that never bloom.* New York: Putnam Juvenile.

Heller, R. (1999). *The reason for a flower.* New York: Putnam Juvenile.

Heller, R. (1999). *Mine, all mine: A book about pronouns.* New York: Putnam Juvenile.

Heller, R. (2000). *Fantastic! Wow! And unreal!: A book about interjections.* New York: Putnam Juvenile.

Hickman, P. (2003). *Animals and their young: How animals produce and care for their babies.* Illus. P. Stephens. Toronto: Kids Can Press.

Hirschi, R. (1993). *A time for sleeping.* Photographer T. D. Mangelsen. New York: Cobblehill Books/Dutton.

Hiscock, B. (2003). *The big caribou herd: Life in the Arctic National Wildlife Refuge.* Honesdale, PA: Boyds Mills Press.

Hodge, D. (1996). *Wild cats: Cougars, bobcats and lynx.* Illus. N. G. Ogle. Tonawanda, NY: Kids Can Press.

Horenstein, H. (1990). *Sam goes trucking.* Photographer H. Horenstein. Boston: Houghton Mifflin.

Hoyt-Goldsmith, D. (1995). *Mardi Gras: A Cajun country celebration.* Photographer L. Migdale. New York: Holiday House.

Ingle, A. (1992). *Zoo animals.* New York: Random House.

Jacobs, L. (2007). *My dinosaur book.* Illus. K. Carr. New York: Smithsonian Institute & HarperCollins.

Jacobs, L. (2007). *Lone star dinosaur.* Illus. K. Carr. New York: Smithsonian Institute & HarperCollins.

Jango-Cohen, J. (1999). *Digging armadillos.* Photographers J. Dunlap, J. Foorr, R. Goff, & D. Marzbaugh. Minneapolis: Lerner Publications.

Jango-Cohen, J. (2004). *Armadillos.* New York: Benchmark Books.

Jenkins, M. (1998). *Chameleons are cool.* Illus. S. Shields. New York: Scholastic.

Jeunesse, G. (2007). *Dinosaurs.* Illus. J. Prumier & H. Galeron. New York: Scholastic.

Kalman, B. (2002). *The life cycle of a tree.* Illus. K. Smithyman. New York: Crabtree Publishing.

Kalman, B. (2005). *Prairie food chains.* New York: Crabtree Publishing.

Kaner, E. (2004). *Animal groups: How animals live together.* Illus. P. Stephens. Tonawanda, NY: Kids Can Press.

Karmel, A. (2008). *The toddler cookbook.* Photographer D. King. New York: Dorling Kindersley Publishing.

Kudlinski, K. V. (1991). *Animal tracks and traces.* Illus. M. Morgan. New York: Franklin Watts.

Lagasse, E. (2005). *Emeril's there's a chef in my soup!* Illus. C. Yuen. New York: HarperCollins.

Landau, E. (1996). *Ocean mammals.* New York: Children's Press.

Lang, A. (2004). *Baby koala.* Photographer W. Lynch. Allston, MA: Fitzhenry & Whiteside.

Lankford, M. (1995). *Christmas around the world.* Illus. K. Dugan. New York: Morrow Junior Books.

Lavies, B. (1989). *It's an armadillo!* New York: Puffin.

Levine, E. (1986). *. . . . If you traveled west in a covered wagon.* Illus. E. Freem. New York: Scholastic.

Levine, S. P. (2007). *My baby animal book.* New York: HarperCollins.

Littlefield, C. (2003). *Awesome ocean science!* Illus. S. Rakitin. Charlotte, VT: Williamson Publishing.

Lilly, K. (1982). *Animals at the zoo.* New York: Little Simon.

McGovern, A. (1969). *. . . . If you sailed on the Mayflower in 1620.* Illus. A. DiVito. New York: Scholastic.

Llimos, A. (2008). *Easy paper crafts in 5 steps.* Berkley Heights, NJ: Enslow.

Look, L. (2001). *Henry's first-moon birthday*. Illus. Y. Heo. New York: Atheneum.

Look, L. (2006). *Uncle Peter's amazing Chinese wedding*. Illus. Y. Heo. New York: Atheneum.

Marx, D. (2002). *Thanksgiving*. New York: Children's Press.

McGovern, A. (1969). . . . *If you sailed on the Mayflower in 1620*. Illus. A. DiVito. New York: Scholastic.

McGovern, A. (1984). *The Pilgrims' first Thanksgiving*. Illus. E. Freem. New York: Scholastic.

Martin, J. M. (2008). *Dolphins*. New York: Scholastic.

Martin, J. M. (2008). *Sharks*. New York: Scholastic.

Martineau, S. (2000). *Slimy science and awesome experiments*. Illus. M. Ursell. Los Angeles: Roxbury Park.

Molleson, D., Savage, S., & Petach, H. (1993). *Easy science experiments*. New York: Scholastic.

Nakano, D. (1994). *Easy origami*. Illus. E. Kenneway. New York: Puffin.

Neye, E. (2000). *Butterflies*. Illus. R. Broda. New York: Scholastic.

O'Connor, J. (2009). *Fancy Nancy explorer extraordinaire!* Illus. R. P. Glasser. New York: HarperCollins.

Olexiewicz, C. (2000). *50 nifty super more origami crafts*. Los Angeles: Lowell House.

Ono, M. (2008). *Origami for children*. Illus. R. Ono. New York: Cico/HarperCollins.

Pallotta, J. (1990). *The dinosaur alphabet book*. Illus. R. Masiello. Watertown, MA: Charlesbridge.

Pallotta, J. (1991). *The underwater alphabet book*. Illus. E. Stewart. Watertown, MA: Charlesbridge.

Pallotta, J. (1993). *The icky bug alphabet book*. Illus. R. Masiello. Watertown, MA: Charlesbridge.

Paxton, T. (1996). *Going to the zoo*. Illus. K. L. Schmidt. New York: HarperCollins.

Penny, M. (2001). *Black rhino*. Austin, TX: Raintree Steck-Vaughn Publishers.

Pinkney, A. (1993). *Seven candles for Kwanzaa*. Illus. B. Pinkney. New York: Puffin.

Prager, J. (2008). *Whales*. New York: Scholastic.

Press, J. (2008). *The little hands big fun craft book: Creative fun for 2-to-6-year-olds*. Illus. L. T. Braren. Charlotte, VT: Williamson Publishing.

Priddy, R. (2004). *My big dinosaur book*. Cincinnati: Priddy Books.

Pringle, L. (1996). *Dinosaurs! Strange and wonderful*. Illus. C. Heyer. Honesdale, PA: Boyds Mills Press.

Pringle, L. (2000). *An extraordinary life: The story of a monarch butterfly*. Illus. B. Marstall. New York: Scholastic.

Pringle, L. (2007). *Penguins! Strange and wonderful*. Illus. M. Henderson. Honesdale, PA: Boyds Mills Press.

Raczek, L. T. (1999). *Rainy's powwow*. Illus. G. Bennett. Flagstaff, AZ: Rising Moon Publishers.

Radley, G. (2001). *Vanishing from grasslands and deserts*. Illus. J. Sherlock. Minneapolis: Carolrhoda Books.

Robinson, T. (2001). *The everything kids' science experiments book: Boil ice, float water, measure gravity—challenging the world around you*. Cincinnati: Adams Media.

Robinson, T. (2007). *Everything kids magical science experiment book*. Cincinnati: Adams Media.

Ryan, P. A. (2002). *When Marian sang*. Illus. B. Selznick. New York: Scholastic.

St. Pierre, S. (2008). *Pillbug*. Chicago: Heinemann Library.

Sadler, J. (2001). *Jumbo book of easy crafts*. Illus. C. Price. Toronto: Kid's Can Press.

Sarasas, C. (2002). *The ABC's of origami: Paper folding for children* (2nd ed.). North Clarendon, VT: Tuttle Publishing.

Schick, E. (1999). *Navajo wedding day: A Dine marriage ceremony*. New York: Marshall Cavendish Publishers.

Scholastic. (2007). *My first jumbo book of dinosaurs*. New York: Scholastic.

Saville, L. (1988). *Horses in the circus ring*. New York: Dutton.

Scillian, D. (2003). *S is for Sooner: An Oklahoma alphabet book*. Chelsea, MI: Sleeping Bear Press.

Sexton, C. (2007). *Clown fish*. New York: Scholastic.

Shachtman, T. (1986). *America's birthday: A Fourth of July*. Photographer C. Saaf. New York: MacMillan.

Sheldon, D. (2006). *Barnum Brown: Dinosaur hunter*. New York: Walker & Co.

Shepherd, R. (2004). *C is for Cornhusker: A Nebraska alphabet book*. Illus. S. Appleoff. Chelsea, MI: Sleeping Bear Press.

Simon, S. (1989). *Whales*. New York: HarperCollins.

Simon, S. (1992). *Storms*. New York: HarperTrophy.

Simon, S. (1993). *New questions and answers about dinosaurs*. Illus. J. Dewey. New York: Mulberry Books.

Simon, S. (1998). *Wild babies*. New York: HarperTrophy.

Simon, S. (2000). *Gorillas*. New York: HarperTrophy.

Simon, S. (2001). *Tornadoes*. New York: HarperTrophy.

Simon, S. (2002). *Baby animals*. San Francisco: Chronicle Books.

Simon, S. (2006). *Earthquakes*. New York: HarperCollins.

Simon, S. (2006). *Lightning*. New York: HarperCollins.

Simon, S. (2006). *Oceans*. New York: HarperTrophy.

Simon, S. (2006). *Volcanoes*. New York: HarperCollins.

Simon, S. (2006). *Weather*. New York: HarperCollins.

Simon, S. (2006). *Whales*. New York: HarperCollins.

Simon, S. (2007). *Hurricanes.* New York: HarperCollins.

Skrepnick, M. (2005). *Diplodocus: Gigantic long-necked dinosaurs.* Berkley Heights, NJ: Enslow.

Squire, A. (2005). *Leopards.* Photographer B. Coleman. New York: Children's Press/Scholastic.

Squire, A. (2005). *Jaguars.* Photographer B. Coleman. New York: Children's Press/Scholastic.

Stevens, C. (2002). *Origami: Step-by-step children's crafts.* Illus. C. Stevens. Petaluma, CA: Search Press.

Stewart, M. (2002). *Elephants.* New York: Children's Press/Scholastic.

Stewart, K. J. (2003). *Gorillas.* New York: Voyageur Press.

Stewart, M. (2002). *Hippopotamuses.* New York: Children's Press/Scholastic.

Stewart, M. (2002). *Rhinoceroses.* New York: Children's Press/Scholastic.

Stewart, M. (2002). *Zebras.* New York: Children's Press/Scholastic.

Stewart, M. (2003). *Gorillas.* New York: Children's Press/Scholastic.

Stewart, M. (2008). *When rain falls.* Illus. C. Bergum. Atlanta: Peachtree Publishers.

St. Pierre, S. (2008). *Pill Bug.* Chicago: Heinemann-Raintree Library.

Swanson, D. (1996). *Safari beneath the sea.* San Francisco: Sierra Club Books for Children.

Taylor, L. (1999). *Dolphins.* Photographer N. Wu. Minneapolis: Lerner Publications.

Thomson, S. (2006). *Amazing dolphins!* Photographer Wildlife Conservation Society. New York: HarperCollins.

Trollinger, P. (2006). *Perfect timing.* Illus. J. LaGarrique. New York: Viking Juvenile.

VanCleave, J. (1989). *Janice VanCleave's chemistry for every kid.* Hoboken, NJ: John Wiley.

VanCleave, J. (1990). *Janice VanCleave's biology for every kid.* Hoboken, NJ: John Wiley.

VanCleave, J. (1991). *Janice VanCleave's physics for every kid.* Hoboken, NJ: John Wiley.

VanCleave, J. (1991). *Janice VanCleave's earth science for every kid.* Hoboken, NJ: John Wiley.

VanCleave, J. (1994). *Janice VanCleave's 201 awesome, magical, bizarre and incredible experiments.* Hoboken, NJ: John Wiley.

VanCleave, J. (1996). *Janice VanCleave's play and find out about science: Easy experiments for young children.* Hoboken, NJ: John Wiley.

VanCleave, J. (1999). *Biology for every kid: 101 easy experiments that work.* Topeka, KS: Topeka Bindery.

VanCleave, J. (2001). *Janice VanCleave's Help! My science project is due tomorrow! Easy experiments you can do overnight.* Hoboken, NJ: John Wiley.

Walker, B. (1989). *The little house on the prairie cookbook.* Illus. G. Williams. New York: HarperTrophy.

Weatherford, C. (2006). *Moses.* Illus. K. Nelson. New York: Hyperion.

Weiss, E. (2008). *From bulb to daffodil.* New York: Scholastic.

Wildsmith, B. (2003). *Brian Wildsmith's zoo animals.* Long Island City, NY: Star Bright Books.

Willems, M. (2006). *Edwina, the dinosaur who didn't know she was extinct.* New York: Hyperion.

Wise, B. (2007). *Louis Sockalexis: Native American baseball pioneer.* Illus. B. Farnsworth. New York Lee & Low Books.

Wright, A. (2001). *Art and crafts with children.* New York: Oxford University Press.

Appendices

Book Lists

A.1   Ten Timeless Favorites

1. Bridwell, N. (1985). *Clifford the big red dog.* New York: Scholastic. Emily Elizabeth experiences the dilemmas and delights of owning a really big red dog.
2. Brown, M. W. (1991). *Big red barn.* Illus. F. Bond. New York: HarperCollins. Through rhymed text, infants and toddlers are introduced to animals that live in the barn.
3. Brown, M. W. (1975). *Goodnight moon.* Illus. C. Hurd. New York: HarperTrophy. Lying in bed, the young child says goodnight to all the objects in the room.
4. Brown, M. W. (1972). *The runaway bunny.* Illus. C. Hurd. New York: HarperCollins. A young bunny plays an imaginary game of hide-and-seek to "test" the depth of his mother's love.
5. Freeman, D. (1968). *Corduroy.* New York: Viking Penguin. A little girl wants her mother to buy her a cute stuffed bear. Her mother refuses. Corduroy, a stuffed bear, decides during the night to explore the big department store. The night watchman finds Corduroy and returns him to the shelf, leading to a surprise the next morning.
6. Martin, Jr., B., & Archambault, J. (1989). *Chicka chicka boom boom.* Illus. L. Ehlert. New York: Scholastic. The rhyme is the adventure of the alphabet climbing a tree.
7. McCloskey, R. (1976). *Blueberries for Sal.* New York: Viking Penguin. A bear cub and a little girl each mistake the other's mother for her own.
8. McDermott, G. (1987). *Anansi the spider: A tale from the Ashanti.* New York: Henry Holt. Six sons of Anansi the spider combine their talents to save their father's life.
9. Numeroff, L. (1985). *If you give a mouse a cookie.* Illus. F. Bond. New York: HarperCollins. The first "If You . . ." story plays out the logical sequence of satisfying a mouse once he is given a cookie.
10. Piper, W. (1976). *The little engine that could.* New York: Grosset & Dunlap. Little blue engine thought she could pull a heavy train. Of course, she succeeds.

A.2   Authors Writing About Their Native Culture

Balgassi, H. (1996). *Peacebound trains.* Illus C. K. Soentpiet. New York: Clarion Books. Sumi misses her mother, who is serving in the army. She sits with Harmuny, her grandmother, and together they recall Sumi's mother's escape from Seoul on top of a peacebound train (a train that transported Koreans from North to South Korea).

Cheng, A. (2000). *Grandfather counts.* Illus. A. Zhang. New York: Lee & Low Books. This is a bilingual story of Helen and Gong Gong, Helen's grandfather, who count train cars; his counting is in Chinese and hers is in English. Readers are introduced to Chinese words and characters. A glossary with the Chinese words, characters, and pronunciations are located at the beginning of the book.

Herrera, J. F. (2006). *The upside down boy / El niño de cabeza.* Illus. E. Gomez. San Francisco: Children's Books Press. This book depicts the emotions of Juanito as he adjusts to an Anglo school. The narrative, written in both Spanish and English, uses rhythmic, flowing language.

Herrera, J. F. (2001). *Calling the dove / El canto de las palomas*. Illus. E. Simmons. San Francisco: Children's Books Press. A personal narrative about growing up as a migrant farm worker. The prose is lyrical, and the colored pencil and acrylic illustrations are bright.

Lee, H. V. (1994). *At the beach*. Illus. H. V. Lee. Topeka, KS: Topeka Bindery. Xiao Ming writes Mandarin in the sand and compares it to the English alphabet that she sees around her.

Lee, J. M. (1989) *Toad is the Uncle of Heaven: A Vietnamese folktale*. New York: Henry Holt. A Vietnamese folktale that has a toad as a trickster main character.

Lee, M. (2001). *Earthquake*. Illus. Y. Choi. Boston: Farrar, Straus & Giroux. A historical fiction picture book that relates the story of a Chinese American family's ordeal during the 1906 San Francisco earthquake.

Pak, S. (2001). *Dear Juno*. Illus. S. K. Hartung. New York: Puffin. Juno cannot read Korean, and his grandmother in Korea cannot read English. When Juno receives a letter from his grandmother, he cannot read it; however, he gets her message from little clues tucked inside

the letter. Then Juno must figure out how to respond to his grandmother.

Stroud, V. A. (1994). *Doesn't Fall Off His Horse*. New York: Dial Books. Stroud relates how her Navajo grandfather got his warrior name, Doesn't Fall Off His Horse.

Watkins, S. (1996, 1997). *Green Snake Ceremony* and *White Bead Ceremony*. Illus. K. Doner. Tulsa, OK: Council Oak Books. Both are stories about Shawnee traditions.

Williams, L. E. (2006). *The best winds*. Illus. K. N. Eujin. Honesdale, PA: Boyd Mills. Jinho does not understand his grandfather's love of making and flying a *bangpae-yeon* (a shield kite) until the day comes when Jinho attempts but fails to fly his kite by himself. It is his grandfather's strong hands that teach Jinho to pull the line tightly so the kite will soar.

Wong, J. S. (2002). *Apple pie 4th of July*. Illus. M. Chodos-Irvine. New York: Voyager. A Chinese family who runs a Chinese restaurant must decide if apple pie or Chinese food is appropriate for the Fourth of July.

Yang, B. (2004). *Hannah is my name*. New York: Candlewick. This story relates the worry and optimism of a Chinese family as they wait to see if they will receive their green cards.

Yin. (2001). *Coolies*. Illus. C. K. Soentpiet. New York: Philomel. This story relates how Chinese immigrants played a part in building the railroad across the United States.

A.3   Poetry with Rhythm

Agell, C. (1994). *Dancing feet*. San Diego: Gulliver Books. This book, for ages 3 to 7, describes ethnic similarities and differences with beautiful watercolor illustrations and rhyming text. It is a text the makes children want to dance.

Andrews, S. (1997). *Rattlebone rock*. Illus. J. Plecas. New York: HarperCollins. This is a humorous book for ages 3 to 7 about Halloween set in a small town. It has spooky illustrations, a carefree beat, and a surprise ending.

Axtell, D. (1999). *We're going on a lion hunt*. New York: Henry Holt. This book is an African adventure for children ages 4 to 8. It is a musical

chant about an animal hunt set in a beautiful savanna landscape. Children enjoy the sequential building of suspense.

Baer, G. (1989). *Thump, thump, rat-a-tat-tat*. Illus. L. Ehlert. New York: Harper & Row. March along with the band in this book for ages 2 to 6. Words gradually increase and decrease as the text progresses. This book is both a visual and an auditory treat.

Fleming, D. (1991). *In the tall, tall grass*. New York: Henry Holt. Read from a caterpillar's point of view to learn about daytime and nighttime creatures. Children from 2 to 6 explore numbers, rowdy rhyme, and rhythm.

Fleming, D. (1993). *In the small, small pond.* New York: Henry Holt. The pulp-dyed, brightly colored paper illustrations in this book are the perfect introduction to nature for ages 2 to 6. It is a sequel to Fleming's book on the inhabitants of the tall, tall grass.

Sturges, P. (1995). *Rainsong / snowsong.* Illus. S. Halpern. New York: North–South Books. This book's cheerful illustrations and brief text, for ages 2 to 5, express a child's joy at dancing in the rain and later in the snow.

<h2>A.4   Poetry That Rhymes</h2>

Alarcon, F. X. (2005). *Poems to dream together / Poemas para soñar juntos.* Illus. P. Barragan. New York: Lee & Low. This collection of poems for ages 4 to 8 celebrates the power of children's dreams.

Andreae, G. (2001). *Giraffes can't dance.* Illus. G. Parker-Rees. New York: Scholastic. The story of how Gerald, the uncoordinated giraffe, shows the rest of the jungle that he, too, has rhythm will appeal to many children ages 4 to 8.

Brown, C. (2008). *Soup for breakfast.* New York: Houghton Mifflin Books for Children. Four- to 8-year-olds will love this nonsense verse about food.

Brown, M. W. (2002). *Give yourself to the rain: Poems for the very young.* Illus. T. L. Weidner. New York: Simon & Schuster Children's Publishing. This is another of Margaret Wise Brown's wonderful books about the things that children love. It is intended for children ages 4 to 8.

Cabrera, J. (2004). *Over in the meadow.* New York: Holiday House. Preschool children are introduced to animals and their young, while exploring numbers 1 through 10 in this old nursery poem set in a thriving meadow.

dePaola, T. (2004). *Tomie's little book of poems.* New York: Penguin Group. This is a board book about nature, parents, and bedtimes for infants and preschoolers.

Dewdney, A. (2005). *Llama llama red pajama.* New York: Penguin Group. This Llama drama about bedtime fears is brought to life with four-line rhymes. It works best with infants and preschool children.

Dotlich, R. K. (2004). *Over in the pink house: New jump-rope rhymes.* Illus. M. W. Hall. Honesdale, PA: Boyds Mills Press. The topics for these rhymes include jam, gingerbread, and teddy bears. They are perfect for children from ages 4 to 8.

Hamanaka, S. (1997). *The hokey pokey.* New York: Simon & Schuster. In this book for ages 3 to 8, children sing along with multicultural children and animals. The pace goes from normal to frenzied as they learn about body parts. The illustrator has made dynamic drawings in an assortment of colors and print sizes.

Hoberman, M. A., & Westcott, N. B. (2003). *Skip to my Lou.* Boston: Little, Brown. Farm animals take over a house in a vision of energetic watercolors intended for children ages 4 to 8.

Johnson, P. B. (2006). *On top of spaghetti.* New York: Scholastic. In this variation on a folk song, intended for toddlers and preschoolers, children follow a meatball on a humorous adventure.

Keats, E. J. (1999). *Over in the meadow.* New York: Scholastic. This original version of the song is every bit as enjoyable as more recent editions.

Kuskin, K. (2005). *Toots the cat.* Illus. L. Bechtold. New York: Henry Holt. Children from ages 4 to 8 will love this rhyming story of Toots, a beloved feline who does whatever she wants.

Marshall, J. (2003). *Pocketful of nonsense.* New York: Houghton Mifflin Books for Children. These nonsense rhymes appeal to children ages 4 to 8. They are especially good for reading aloud.

O'Neill, M. (2003). *The sound of day / The sound of night.* Illus. C. Jabar. New York: Farrar, Straus & Giroux. The two rhyming poems in this book describe the bustle of the day and the silence of the night. It is intended for infants and preschool children.

Peek, M. (2006). *Mary wore her red dress and Henry wore his green sneakers.* Boston: Houghton Mifflin. In this Texas folk song, children see drawings go from black and white to full color. Preschool children experience a birthday party and sing along with this easy musical arrangement.

Phinn, G. (2006). *What I like!: Poems for the very young*. Illus. J. Eccles. Swindon, UK: Child's Play International. This book is filled with hilarious rhymes and pictures. It captures the world of the very young child and is most appropriate for children ages 4 to 8.

Prelutsky, J. (2008). *Awful ogre running wild*. Illus. P. O. Zelinsky. New York: HarperCollins. Awful ogre is a hit on his summer vacation. Prelutsky's humorous rhymes about the ogre's adventures are suitable for children ages 4 to 8.

Raffi. (1996). *Spider on the floor*. Illus. T. Kelly. New York: Crown Publishers. This interactive book is about a silly song children ages 4 to 8 are sure to enjoy. The familiar repetition and rhythm make it easy to sing along as the busy spider goes from the floor, up your body, and back down again.

Rounds, G. (1990). *Old MacDonald had a farm*. New York: Holiday House. The bold printed words and pictures leap out in this book for ages 4 to 8. Children sing along with the flashy musical beat as the farmyard animals and their sounds are introduced one at a time.

Ryder, J. (2007). *Toad by the road: A year in the life of these amazing amphibians*. Illus. M. Kneen. New York: Henry Holt. The rhyming poems in this book are devoted entirely to the life cycle of toads. It is a delightful source of information for ages 4 to 8.

Spier, P. (2007). *The fox went out on a chilly night: An old song*. New York: Doubleday. In this timeless folk song, the fox is searching for food in a small town. Children ages 4 to 8 will enjoy the funny, bright drawings, waiting to see what happens next.

Spier, P. (1992). *The star-spangled banner*. New York: Doubleday. Children ages 4 to 8 will enjoy the beautifully detailed illustrations as they celebrate our nation's history.

Taback, S. (1999). *There was an old lady who swallowed a fly*. New York: Viking Press. In this really silly book for ages 4 to 8, children engage in rhyme and play with language as they follow the sequence of animals, small to large, that the old woman swallows.

Trapani, I. (1998). *I'm a little teapot*. Boston: Whispering Coyote Press. For infants up to 5-year-olds, this text has beautiful full-color illustrations of a playful little teapot engaged in adventure.

Trapani, I. (2004). *The itsy bitsy spider*. Danvers, MA: Whispering Coyote Press. For preschool children, this story of a spider who travels to the top of a tree is written in rhyme. It also features a variety of critters.

Trapani, I. (1997). *Twinkle, twinkle little star*. Danvers, MA: Whispering Coyote Press. For preschool children, this traditional childhood rhyme takes them, imaginatively, on an enchanted ride through beautiful scenery.

Westcott, N. B. (1997). *I've been working on the railroad: An American classic*. New York: Hyperion Books for Children. This American folktale of a train journey illustrated in pastels is suitable for ages 4 to 8.

Yolen, J., & Peteres, A. F. (2007). *Here's a little poem: A very first book of poetry*. Illus. P. Dunbar. Cambridge MA: Candlewick Press. This book captures the experiences of the young child. It can be read to children from age 6 months to 5 years.

A.5   Recommended Mother Goose

Anglund, J. (1960). *In a pumpkin shell: A Mother Goose ABC*. New York: Harcourt, Brace. For babies and preschoolers, this is an older but really wonderful rhyming alphabet book in which each letter has its very own rhyme.

Crews, N. (2004). *The neighborhood Mother Goose*. New York: Greenwillow Books. This is a modern Mother Goose, which uses color photos and digital graphics to portray urban youngsters role-playing the rhymes.

Hale, S. J. (1993). *Mary had a little lamb*. Illus. B. McMillan. New York: Scholastic. This version of the story has Mary as a young African American girl who wears glasses and has a male teacher. The pictures and effective layout will appeal to children ages 4 to 8.

Hale, S. J. (2000). *Mary had a little lamb*. Illus. by S. Mavor. New York: Orchard Books. This book is truly a work of art, made using a fabric relief technique that creates tactile pictures. This book will engage babies and preschoolers.

Hoberman, M. A. (2006). *You read to me, I'll read to you: Very short Mother Goose tales to read together.* Illus. M. Emberley. New York: Megan Tingley. The fractured tales in this book retell and elaborate on Mother Goose rhymes, giving some of them very new endings.

Lobel, A. (2003). *The Arnold Lobel book of Mother Goose.* New York: Knopf Books for Young Readers. Originally published as the *Random House Book of Mother Goose*, this version pairs rhymes with appropriate illustrations.

Moore, R. (Ed.) (2006). *The tall book of Mother Goose.* Illus. A. Ivanov. New York: Harper Festival. This is a collection of 51 well-known rhymes with lively illustrations.

Rackham, A. (1998). *Mother Goose: Old nursery rhymes.* New York: NTC Contemporary Publishing. These are traditional rhymes and stories, a wonderful collection of old favorites for children ages 4 to 8.

Sabuda, R. (1999). *The movable Mother Goose.* New York: Little Simon. This is a lavish pop-up book, in which animals portray the nursery rhyme characters; it has a sturdy three-dimensional design.

Smith, J. W. (2004). *Mother Goose for kids.* Gretna, LA: Pelican Publishing Company. This is a board book edition with big glorious full-color pictures.

Tudor, T. (1989). *Mother Goose.* New York: Random House. Tudor illustrates 76 traditional nursery rhymes for ages 4 to 8.

Wright, B. F. (2007). *The real Mother Goose* (illustrated edition). New York: Cartwheel. This is a touch and feel, scratch and sniff version of the poems. The actual verses are on the left, and Edwardian-style pictures are on the right.

A.6 Humorous Poetry

Dahl, R. (2003). *Roald Dahl's revolting rhymes.* Illus. Q. Blake. London: Puffin. For ages 4 to 8, this text features colorful illustrations of original Dahl characters.

Florian, D. (1998). *Beast feast: Poems.* New York: Voyager Books. For ages 4 to 8, this is a cheerful collection of bouncy poems to surprise you.

Florian, D. (2001). *In the swim.* New York: Voyager Books. This is a whimsical collection of intelligent and funny rhymes for ages 4 to 8.

Florian, D. (2005). *Lizards, frogs and polliwogs.* New York: Harcourt Children's Books. For ages 4 to 8, this is an amusing collection with fun word play.

Nash, O. (2008). *The adventures of Isabel.* Illus. B. Taylor. Boston: Little, Brown. This is a lively yet stylish work featuring silly scoundrels.

Nash, O. (1998). *The tale of Custard the Dragon.* Illus. L. Munsinger. Boston: Little, Brown. This book has glorious illustrations that will make readers want to laugh out loud.

Prelutsky, J. (1984). *The new kid on the block.* Illus. by J. Stevenson. New York: Greenwillow Books. This book has vivid sketches in pen and ink. No one can resist "Bleezer's Ice Cream," with its 28 flavors.

Prelutsky, J. (1990). *Something big has been here.* Illus. J. Stevenson. New York: Greenwillow Books. This book of silly verses has funny monologues.

Prelutsky, J. (2000). *It's raining pigs and noodles.* Illus. J. Stevenson. New York: Greenwillow Books. This text has skillful wordplay and lively line drawings.

Prelutsky, J. (2002). *Scranimals.* Illus. P. Sis. New York: Greenwillow Books. This book has outlandish wordplay and muted ink and watercolor illustrations.

Seuss, Dr. (1960). *One fish, two fish, red fish, blue fish.* New York: Random House. This adored text is a delightfully silly treat involving rhymes, colors, and numbers.

Seuss, Dr. (1974). *There's a wocket in my pocket!* New York: Random House. For babies to preschoolers, this is a silly and imaginative board book.

Seuss, Dr. (1957). *The cat in the hat.* New York: Random House. This is a beloved and amusing tale of a cat and the misadventures of a rainy afternoon.

Seuss, Dr. (1960). *Green eggs and ham.* New York: Random House. This text is a timeless, wonderfully silly tale of Sam-I-Am, who does not like green eggs and ham.

Sierra, J. (1998). *Antarctic antics: A book of penguin poems.* Illus. J. Aruego & A. Dewey. New York: Gulliver Books. Funny cartoonish paintings represent the lives and habitats of emperor penguins in Antarctica.

Silverstein, S. (1981). *A light in the attic.* New York: Harper & Row Publishers. This is an adored collection of silly and imaginative poems.

Young J. (2006). *R is for rhyme: A poetry alphabet.* Illus. V. Juhasz. Ann Arbor, MI: Sleeping Bear Press. For ages 6 to 10, this is a wonderfully funny twist on factual information.

A.7   More Books for Infants and Toddlers

Awdry, W. R. (1999). *Thomas the tank engine's hidden surprises (Let's go lift-and-peek book).* Illus. J. Yee. New York: Random House. Thomas, a little engine, goes to the circus and on the way sees a hot air balloon, a dolphin, a barrel of monkeys, and many other intriguing sights.

Cousin, L. (1999). *Where is Maisy? A lift the flap book.* New York: Candlewick. Readers lift flaps to see where Maisy is on each page.

Cousin, L. (2001). *Maisy's big flap book.* New York: Candlewick. This books has 36 flaps for readers to lift to see what Maisy and her friends see throughout the day. The books teachers numbers, colors, shapes, and opposites.

Cousin, L. (2001). *Maisy's morning on the farm.* New York: Candlewick. Maisy milks cows, feeds pigs and chickens, and then has her own breakfast. Readers lift flaps to see what Maisy is doing.

Katz, K. (2004). *What does baby say? A lift-the-flap book.* New York: Little Simon. A cranky baby says, "Waah-Waah!" a cuddly baby says, "Ma-Ma!" Readers lift flaps to see what hungry, happy, and other babies say.

Katz, K. (2002). *Grandma and me.* New York: Little Simon. Grandma arrives for a visit. Readers lift flaps to see what is in her suitcase and what she is doing around the house while visiting.

Katz, K. (2004). *Grandpa and me: A lift-the-flap book.* New York: Little Simon. Grandpa and baby make a pizza. Readers lift flaps to see what they need to make one.

Kunhardt, E. (2000). *Pat the pony.* New York: Golden Books. This book is similar to *Pat the Bunny,* written by the author's mother, Dorothy Kunhardt. The text is simple, and there is a white pony for readers to pet.

Kunhardt, E. (2001). *Pat the puppy.* New York: Golden Books. Readers can scratch and sniff warm brownies, pull a tab to make a rocking chair move, and turn a wheel to watch a video.

Santoro, C. (1993). *Open the barn door, find a cow (a chunky flap book).* New York: Random House. Infants can lift flaps to see what animals are found in a barn.

A.8   Books with Repetitive Text

Adams, P. (2007). *Old MacDonald had a farm.* Swindon, UK: Child's Play International. This book has holes to reveal each animal on Old MacDonald's farm.

Adams, P. (2007). *This is the house that Jack built.* Swindon, UK: Child's Play International. This book has holes to reveal all the objects Jack needs to build his house.

Cameron, P. (1961). *"I can't" said the ant.* New York: Scholastic. This story is about friends encouraging one another. The little ant does not believe he can do anything; however, his friends tell him he can. The response of each friend is in rhyme; for example: "'Don't be dumb,' said the crumb."

Carle, E. (1993). *Today is Monday.* New York: Scholastic. Each day, a different animal eats a different food. Each day, Carle repeats all the previous days and the foods eaten. On the last page, the days are listed backwards, and children are encouraged to remember each food as the adult reads the day of the week.

Christelow, E. (2007). *Five little monkeys sitting in a tree.* New York: Trumpet Club. These five little monkeys do not heed the warning of their mother not to sit in the tree. One by one they fall out of the tree.

Guarino, D. (1989). *Is your mama a llama?* Illus. S. Kellogg. New York: Scholastic. Little llama asks many of his friends, "Is your mama a llama?" Readers get to predict what animal is being described as each animal answers little llama's question. The text is in rhyme.

Hoban, T. (1997). *Look book.* New York: Greenwillow. The reader looks through holes to discover photographs of ordinary things: a dog, pretzels, and so on.

Kalan, R. (2003). *Jump frog, jump!* Illus. B. Barton. New York: Greenwillow. A fly is attempting to escape a frog's tongue. The frog is encouraged to keep jumping. The text is cumulative with "Jump, frog, jump!" on every other page.

McGovern, A. (1992). *Too much noise.* Illus. S. Taback. New York: Trumpet Club. An old farmer is annoyed by the swishing of the leaves and the hissing of the teakettle. A wise man teaches the farmer that the sounds of his house can be enjoyed in comparison to the din of the outside world.

Rosen, M. (1990). *Little Rabbit Foo Foo.* Illus. A. Robins. New York: Aladdin. Little Rabbit Foo Foo hops through the forest, picking up creatures and bopping them on his head. The fairy warns him to stop. When Little Rabbit Foo Foo does not heed the warning, the fairy turns him into a goon.

Rosen, M. (2003). *We're going on a bear hunt.* Illus. H. Oxenbury. New York: Macmillan. Brave bear hunters go through grass, a river, mud, and other obstacles before they encounter a bear. Then they retreat through all the obstacles in reverse order.

Seuss, Dr. (1970). *Mr. Brown can moo! Can you?* New York: Random House. Mr. Brown, an expert at imitating all noises, encourages readers to do the same.

Shaw, C. G. (1988). *It looked like spilt milk.* New York: Harper Festival. Readers look at cloud shapes to decide what object the cloud looks like.

Williams, L. (1988). *The little old lady who was not afraid of anything.* Illus. M. Lloyd. New York: Scholastic. The little lady who is not afraid of anything encounters two shoes, pants, a shirt, two gloves, a hat, and a big pumpkin head on her way back through the forest. The text is cumulative.

A.9 Alphabet Books

Baker, A. (1999). *Black and White Rabbit's ABC.* London: Kingfisher. Each letter is written in upper and lowercase. Each letter has an item beginning with that letter. Black and White Rabbit is also on each page.

Baldus, P. (2002). *The amazing alphabet maze book.* Emeryville, CA: Price Stern Sloan. Each upper and lower case letter is a large black and white maze for children aged 4 to 8 to solve.

Base, G. (1996). *Animalia.* New York: Harry N. Abrams. Each page of this wordless book is filled with detailed illustrations of a wide array of animals and objects that begin with the featured letter.

Carter, D. (2006). *Alpha bugs: A pop-up alphabet.* New York: Little Simon. Each letter has a short sentence of alliteration. Some letters have pop-ups, while other letters require children to pull tabs or lift flaps or turn dials to make something happen.

Crowther, R. (1999). *Robert Crowther's most amazing hide-and-seek alphabet book.* New York: Candlewick. This is an interactive pop-up book. The child pulls a tab with a letter printed on it and out pops an object that begins with that letter.

Degezelle, T. (2000). *Bugs A to Z.* Mankato, MN: Capstone Press. Each letter of the alphabet features one bug. There is a little information about each bug. This is especially good for young children who are fascinated with bugs and love to learn about them.

Eastman, P. D. (1974). *The alphabet book.* New York: Random House. Each page features one letter. The zany pictures are unique for each letter. For example, the A page has a long line of ants, carrying American flags up a hill. The text states, "American ants."

Fleming, D. (2006). *Alphabet under construction.* New York: Henry Holt. Letter by letter and page by page a mouse creates the alphabet. Verbs and nouns are given for each letter, such as *airbrushing, carving, scaffolding, ladders.*

Gag, W. (2004). *The ABC bunny.* Illus. H. Gag. Minneapolis: University of Minnesota Press. The illustrations, in black and white, are of a bunny's day as he encounters objects that begin with each letter of the alphabet.

Hobbie, H. (2000). *Puddle's ABC (Toot & Puddle).* Boston: Little, Brown. Puddle wants to teach Toot how to write his name, but Toot first needs to learn his letters. So Puddle first teaches Toot the letters and then how to write his name.

Hood, S. (1997). *Animal ABC's.* Illus. L. McCue. New York: Troll Communications. Each page has a short poem that corresponds with a picture. For example, on the first page there is an ant on an apple held by an ape. The text states, "My name is ant / I know I'm very small / Tell me, friend, what did you eat / To grow so very tall?"

Howland, N. (1994). *ABC drive! A car trip alphabet.* New York: Clarion Books. Each letter is written in black in a bright yellow box, with one word that begins with that letter. All the illustrations are objects one would find while riding in a car. For example, "A" is paired with "ambulance" and "Y" with "yield sign."

Inches, A. (2004). *Barney's super-dee-duper ABCs.* New York: Scholastic. The letters in this board book are followed by a phrase of alliteration. Example: "Adding Apples." Readers see Barney adding one apple plus one apple on the chalk board.

Inkpen, M. (2001). *Kipper's A to Z: An alphabet adventure.* New York: Red Wagon Books. This is a story about cute Kipper, a dog, and his friend Arnold. Each page features a letter in a short sentence that advances the story. For example, on the R page, the text says: "It started to rain. R is for rainbow." The illustration shows Kipper and Arnold standing in the rain under a rainbow.

Jordan, M. (1996). *Amazon alphabet.* London: Kingfisher. Each letter of the alphabet is represented by some creature or plant found in the Amazon. There is a simple phrase explaining what the creature or plant is. The oil painting pictures are beautiful.

Lionni, L. (2004). *The alphabet tree.* New York: Alfred A. Knopf. The letters of the alphabet live in a tree until one day a storm comes and they huddle deep in the branches. An insect comes along and tells the letters how to make words. Another storm comes and the words huddle in the branches. Then a caterpillar arrives and shows the words how to make sentences.

Martin, B., & Archambault, J. (1989). *Chicka chicka boom boom.* Illus. L. Ehlert. New York: Scholastic. A rhyming book of the alphabet. The text has the letters in uppercase, but the letters climbing the coconut tree are lowercase. The rhythmic text also has words to increase phonemic awareness: *skit, skat, skoodle; flip, flop, flee.*

Milne, A. A. (2001). *Winnie-the-Pooh's ABC.* Illus. E. H. Shepard. New York: Dutton Children's Books. A larger board book where each letter of the alphabet is featured in a scene taken from the original stories of Winnie-the-Pooh. The letter is in large, bold print along with one word that begins with the letter. For example, *P* has a picture of Piglet puffing the seeds from a dandelion. The word Piglet is in large print at the bottom of the picture.

Napier, M. (2002). *Z is for zamboni: A hockey alphabet.* Ann Arbor: Sleeping Bear Press. In this book objects from hockey are featured for each letter. Zamboni is the machine that smoothes the ice. The text is simple enough for toddlers.

Pratt, K. J. (1992). *A walk in the rainforest.* Nevada City, CA: Dawn Publications. Each letter is featured with a plant or animal from the rainforest. Children learn about different species found in the rainforest.

Pratt, K. J. (1994). *A swim through the sea.* Nevada City, CA: Dawn Publications. Each letter is paired with a plant or fish from the sea. Young children are introduced to sea life.

Polacco, P. (2003). *G is for goat.* New York: Philomel. Each page has a delightful Polacco illustration. There is one letter per page. Each letter has a short sentence with one word that begins with the letter. For example, "A is for Apple, the best treat of all." The illustration has a little girl reaching for an apple in the tree. Little goats are also on each page.

Rau, D. M. (1998). *The secret code.* Illus. B. Weissman. Danbury, CT: Children's Press. A blind boy explains each letter of Braille to his friends. Each letter is also written in Braille.

Rosen, M. (1995). *Michael Rosen's ABC.* Brookfield, CT: The Millbrook Press. Each letter is a poem based on a character that children may recognize. The illustrations have vivid colors, and there is one letter per page. The J page has the following rhyme: "Jack and Jill went up the hill / Juggling a jug of jelly. / A passing bug jumped in the jug / which made the jelly smelly."

Scarry, R. (2002). *Mr. Paint Pig's ABC.* New York: Random House. Huckle and Lowly search for objects in Busytown. On each page readers lift flaps to find objects starting with the featured letter.

Seuss, Dr. (1963). *Dr. Seuss's ABC.* New York: Random House. Each page has letters with zany pictures and a short text. For example, the H page states, "Big H little h Hungry horse. Hay. Hen in a hat. Hooray! Hooray!"

Shannon, G. (1999). *Tomorrow's alphabet.* Illus. D. Crews. New York: HarperTrophy. Young children are introduced to the letters by relating an event of today to one that will happen tomorrow. For example, today's puppy becomes a dog tomorrow.

So, S. (2004). *C is for China.* Illus. F. Lincoln. London: Frances Lincoln Children's Books. This book features an object from China for each letter of the alphabet. The text is very simple and the pictures are like photographs.

Tapahanso, L., & Schick, E. (1999). *Navajo ABC.* New York: Aladdin. English and Navajo words are used to name different aspects of Navajo life.

Thistlethwaite, D. (2001). *My first lift-the-flap ABC board book.* New York: DK Children. There are 45 flaps for children to lift. Every two-page spread features four to seven letters. The pictures are photographs. Some flaps with a picture on them lift to reveal an associated object. For example, under the pizza is a plate.

Williams, G. (2005). *Animal ABC.* New York: Golden Books. Each letter features an animal that begins with that letter.

Wood, A. (2001). *Alphabet adventure.* Illus. B. Wood. New York: Blue Sky Press. This alphabet book is a story about the little "i" who lost his dot. All the other letters help him find it.

Wood, A. (2003). *Alphabet mystery.* Illus. B. Wood. New York: Blue Sky Press. Little X runs away because Charley never uses him. The rest of the letters try to find him. They find him in a castle owned by a monster. The monster permits each letter to choose a gift from his treasure chest. Readers need to match the gift with the corresponding letter.

Zschock, M., & Zschock, H. (2001). *Journey around Boston from A to Z.* Beverly, MA: Commonwealth Editions. This book introduces children to sights in Boston. It is not only interesting for children from Boston but for all children.

Zschock, M., & Zschock, H. (2001). *Journey around Cape Cod and the islands from A to Z.* Beverly, MA: Commonwealth Editions. Each letter features an object, animal, bird, and other things one finds on Cape Cod.

Zschock, M., & Zschock, H. (2002). *Journey around New York from A to Z.* Beverly, MA: Commonwealth Editions. Each letter features sights found in New York. Each letter features an object or scene from New York City.

A.10 Counting Books

Carle, E. (2007). *1, 2, 3 to the zoo.* New York: Putnam. This wordless book encourages discussion about the number of animals going to the zoo on the train.

Carle, E. (2005). *10 little rubber ducks.* New York: HarperCollins. This brightly illustrated book is about counting 10 ducks.

Carter, D. A. (2006). *How many bugs in a box?* New York: Little Simon. Infants and children lift flaps to count the number of bugs in each box. The bugs and boxes are different on each page. The numbers go to 10. This books also encourages discussion about colors, size, and shape.

de Brunhoff, L.(2003). *Babar's counting book*. New York: Harry N. Abrams. Babar's children set off to find and count the objects they see. The numerals are large with the word for the numbers written by them. Some pages have text to tell the story. The illustrations clearly depict the number; for example, there are 9 camels and 10 storks.

dePaola, T. (2003). *Marcos counts: One, two, three*. New York: Putnam. Moffie teaches Marcos to count to 10. Then Marcos repeats the numbers in Spanish.

Falconer, I. (2002). *Olivia counts*. New York: Atheneum. Olivia dons the objects that are being counted. Numerals are in red with the number word and the object in black. For example, "3 three pots of paint." It's a board book and easy for children to follow.

Fleming, D. (1995). *Count!* New York: Henry Holt. This colorful book counts animals up to 10 and then counts by tens to 50. This book also develops vocabulary with words like *bouncing, jumping, wiggling, stretching,* and *snapping.*

Grossman, V. (1995). *Ten little rabbits*. Illus. S. Long. New York: Trumpet Club. This unique counting book features different American Indian blankets for each number. Because each page is sparse in its text, the book encourages discussion between an adult and child. For example, for the number three, the text reads, "Three busy messengers sending out the news." The two-page spread illustration has three rabbit characters giving a smoke signal. The back of the book gives information about the 10 different tribes that were featured.

Haskins, J. (1988). *Count your way through China*. Illus. D. Hockerman. Minneapolis, MN: Carolrhoda Books. This book presents the numbers 1 through 10 written in Chinese characters. Each number introduces an object from Chinese culture.

Hubbard, W. (1991). *C is for curious / 2 is for dancing: A 1, 2, 3 of action*. San Francisco: Chronicle Books. This book contains both the ABCs and the 123s. The book is for toddlers because there are more in the pictures than the object begin counted. For example, "1 IS FOR DREAMING" has a unicorn sleeping across both sides of the page with a cartoon bubble over its head. The bold, bright illustrations depict familiar actions of children.

Inkpen, M. (1995). *Kipper's book of numbers*. San Diego: Red Wagon Books / Harcourt Brace. The text is simple with simple illustrations. For example, "2 Two hedgehogs" is over two playful hedgehogs. Of course, Kipper is on each page.

Katz, K. (2001). *Counting kisses*. New York: Little Simon. This book counts kisses backwards from 10. The numeral and the word spelled out is on the page with a short phrase: for example: "Ten little kisses on teeny tiny toes. 10." This is a board book, but young child would first need to know how to count to 10 the correct way.

Keats, E. J. (1999). *One red sun: A counting book*. New York: Penguin Putnam. There is one number per page. The numeral is in bold black print and the number is spelled below. The number is clearly depicted with the author's illustrations. Four is presented with four colorful birds flying.

Lionni, L. (1995). *Inch by inch*. New York: HarperTrophy. Measurements are introduced to toddlers in this cute story about a little inch worm who proudly measures anything under the sun.

Millard, A. (2001). *My first lift the flap numbers board book*. New York: DK Publishing. Readers lift the number flap to discover the same number of objects under the flap. This book gives the adult and child opportunity to discuss the objects and to count them together.

Priddy, R. (2002). *First concepts: Numbers*. New York: Priddy Books. Readers lift number flaps to discover a picture with the same number of objects as was on the flap. Young children can flip the sturdy flaps on this board book as adults count and name the objects.

Schulman, J. (2002). *Countdown to spring!* Illus. M. So. New York: Random House. This board book counts backwards, beginning with 10. There are more objects on the page than are being counted. There is a phrase, followed by a question, which asks the reader to find the objects. For example, "10 ladybugs crawling all around the crocuses. Can you count them?"

Slaughter, T. (2006). *One, two, three*. Toronto: Tundra Books. On the left-side page is the numeral; on right-side page is an object. For eight, the left-side of the spread has the numeral "8" with eight beach balls on both pages.

Walsh, E. S. (1995). *Mouse count*. San Diego: Harcourt Brace. A simple story about how many mice can get into a small jar. The snake slithering around the jar can prompt a nature discussion about snakes preying on mice.

Wood. A. (2004). *Ten little fish*. Illus. B. Wood. New York: Blue Sky Press. The story is simple. It be-gins, "Ten Little Fish, swimming in a line. One dives down. Now there are . . ." Readers turn the page to see nine fish. At the end of the story, the last fish finds a mate and has babies to make 10 again.

A.11 Color Concept Books

Baker, A. (1999). *White Rabbit's color book*. New York: Scholastic. White Rabbit finds three tubs of paint—red, yellow, and blue. He jumps in and turns his white fur red and then discovers he can mix the colors to get new ones.

Beaton, C. (1997). *Colors/Los colores* (Bilingual first books). Hauppauge, NY: Barron's Educational Series. This book features the basic colors with the words written in English and Spanish.

Carle, E. (2005). *My very first book of colors* (board book). New York: Philomel. The top half of each page features a color, and the bottom half of each page has a picture of an object of that color. The illustrations are brightly colored.

Crew, D. (1993). *Freight train*. New York: Green-willow Books. All the colors are on the cars of a freight train. The text states the color and object. For example, "Red caboose at the back" is illus-trated with a bright red caboose.

dePaola, T. (2003). *Marcos colors: Red, yellow, blue*. New York. Putnam. In this board book, Morgie teaches Marcos colors that end in a rainbow. Then Marcos teaches Morgie the same colors in Spanish.

Ehlert, L. (1990). *Color farm*. New York: Harper Festival. Each right-hand page shows a barnyard animal made of brightly colored geometric shapes. Toddlers can learn color and shapes with this book.

Ehlert, L. (1997). *Color zoo*. New York: Harper Fes-tival. Each right-hand page shows a zoo animal made of brightly colored geometric shapes. Tod-dlers can learn colors and shapes.

Hill, E. (1997). *Spot's big book of colors, shapes, and numbers*. New York: Putnam. Spot instructs readers about colors, shapes, and numbers as they lift flaps.

Holm, S. L. (2009). *Zoe's hats: A book of colors and patterns*. Honesdale, PA: Boyds Mills Press. Illustrations are big with bright colors. A simple phrase names the color: for example, "Red hat" is under a picture of a red Santa Claus hat. "Brown hat" is under a picture of a brown cowboy hat. All hats are worn by a smiling child. At the end of the book the hats reappear and readers are asked to name the colors of the hats.

Hoban, T. (1995). *Colors everywhere*. New York: Greenwillow Books. In this wordless book, there are squares of colors on the side of each page. Readers are asked to say the colors and find them in a photograph. All the photographs are objects children recognize. For example, on one page is a yellow block and a gold block with four baby ducks that have both yellow and gold on them. Readers are asked to say the color and find the two colors on the ducks. This is a great book to help children attend to details.

Mayer, M. (1995). *Little Critter colors*. New York: Random House. Little Critter explores his big, beautiful, colorful world.

Milich, Z. (2006). *City colors*. Toronto: Kids Can Press. The left side of a page has the color printed in large black print with a portion of the object that is on the other side of the page. For example, *purple* has a small section of a purple stool on the left side and purple stools on the right. Parents could cover up the right side and have children look at the left side and guess what the object is.

Pinkney, S. (2002). *A rainbow all around me*. Illus. M. Pinkney. New York: Cartwheel Picture Books. Myles Pinkney's photographs from many cultures accompany the text for each color.

Priddy, R. (2005). *First concepts: Colors*. New York: Priddy Books. One color is featured on each two-page spread. Children lift flaps to discover different objects.

Priddy, R. (2004). *Bright baby colors*. New York: Priddy Books. This board book has one color featured on each spread. One object is large with smaller insets of other objects of that color. For example, on the page featuring *orange,* there is one large orange with smaller pictures of a basketball, tiger, saucepan, orange juice, goldfish, soft orange towel, and a pumpkin.

The book encourages discussion between adult and child as they name the items.

Zemlicka, S. (2001). *Colors of China*. Illus. J. L. Porter. Minneapolis, MN: Carolrhoda Books. This book has the color name written in Chinese characters. The book tells of the significance of various colors in China.

A.12 Concept Books on Shapes and More

Burningham, J. (1996). *First steps: Letters, numbers, colors, opposites*. Cambridge, MA: Candlewick Press. The book is divided into sections: first is the alphabet, second are numbers, third are colors, and fourth are words that are opposites. In each section illustrations make the concepts are easy to understand.

Aigner-Clark, J. (2001). *Baby Einstein: See and spy shapes*. Illus. N. Zaidie. New York: Hyperion Books. There's only a little text in this board book, which puts the emphasis on children finding all the objects on the page of a certain shape. For example, on the *circle* page, the text simply states, "A circle is a crazy thing," leaving readers to find all the objects on that page that are circles. It is a great book for adult to discuss with a child, as the child connects word with picture.

DK Publishing. (2000). *Touch and feel: Shapes*. New York: DK Publishing. The photographs that clearly depict the shapes are on a white background. Many of the photos have parts that are tactile.

Novick, M., & Harlin, S. (2008). *Opposites*. Illus. C. Miesen. Surry Hills, NSW, Australia: Little Hare. In this delightful book children must lift the flap to find the opposite of the word on the flap.

Petty, C. (2006). *Shapes*. New York: Barron's Educational Series. This is an interactive book that teaches young children about rectangles, circles, triangles, squares, ovals, diamonds, crescents, stars, and cones. As readers slide a tab, a word appears that completes a sentence about the shape.

Priddy, R. (2002). *First concepts: Shapes* (board book). New York: Priddy Books. Readers lift flaps to discover what objects are of a certain shape. For example, one page's text reads, "Can you find a little beetle? How many circles can you find?" The reader lifts the flap to find a beetle and then can count the circles on its back. Other objects include a gold coin, a beach ball, a green apple, a globe, a clock, and other familiar objects.

A.13 Series Books for Infants and Toddlers

The Frances Books, by Russell Hoban

Frances is a little badger whose actions and feelings will be familiar to young children. In *Bread and Jam for Frances* (1964, Illus. L. Hoban, HarperCollins), Frances loves bread and jam. Her parents attempt to get her to try different foods, but Frances only likes bread and jam and even sings songs about bread and jam—that is, until her parents only offer her bread and jam because that is all she eats. She finally tries different foods and likes them. In *A Birthday*

for Frances (1968, Illus. L. Hoban, HarperCollins), Frances is jealous because it is her sister's birthday. She sulks all day as everyone else is preparing for the party. She buys a gift for her sister but has a very difficult time actually giving it to her sister. Frances thinks of many reasons why Gloria should not have it. The story is about feelings all children experience: jealousy and selfishness. The characters are animals, and Lillian Hoban's illustrations are in colored pencil, with black and white badgers in colorful settings.

The Max Books, by Rosemary Wells

Max is a toddler bunny who gets into lots of trouble. His sister Ruby is always there to help him out. Toddlers may recognize some of their own adventures in the books. In *Max's Bath* (2004, Viking), Max wears everything he eats because he is very messy. Ruby attempts to clean him up in the bathtub, but Max attempts to eat orange sherbet and grape juice in the tub. It shows the love between a big sister and a little brother. *Max's ABC* (2006, Viking) is an alphabet book. The story begins with ants escaping from the ant farm and crawling up Max to eat his cake. Many letters have a number of different words: *question/quiet, sit/still/smarter.*

When parents want to teach children the importance of keeping a clean room, they can share *Max Cleans Up* (2000, Penguin Young Readers), a comical episode of Ruby trying to help Max clean his room. Ruby tries to clean his room by tossing out old food and other dirty things, but Max stuffs it all in his pockets when Ruby is not looking. The Max books offer creative ways of teaching a lesson about everyday life. In *Max and Ruby's Midas* (2003, Puffin) Ruby attempts to cure Max's sweet tooth by telling him the Greek myth of young Prince Midas. In *Max and Ruby's Busy Week* (2002, Grosset & Dunlap) readers follow the duo from Monday to Sunday, seeing all the activities that Max and Ruby do during the week.

The Manners Books, by Karen Katz

Karen Katz writes books about manners for toddlers. For example in the board book *Excuse Me! A Little Book of Manners* (2002, Grosset & Dunlap), simple text explains the politeness of saying, "Excuse me" that even toddlers can learn. In *I Can Share* (2004, Grosset & Dunlap), toddlers learn the joy of sharing with others. In *No Biting* (2002, Grosset & Dunlap), infants and toddlers learn that biting hurts, and in *No Hitting* (2004, Grosset & Dunlap) infants and toddlers learn that hitting also hurts.

The Rainbow Fish Books, by Marcus Pfister

Marcus Pfister has written a series of delightful stories and concept books about curious Rainbow Fish. In *The Rainbow Fish* (1992), Rainbow Fish, who has beautiful shiny scales like no other fish, learns that when he shares his shining scales with other fish, he gains friends. In other stories, readers discover Rainbow Fish is brave. For example, in *Rainbow Fish and the Sea Monster's Cave* (2001), he enters the scary monster's cave to help a little fish who needs red algae to be cured. And in *Rainbow Fish to the Rescue!* (2001), Rainbow Fish feels bad when the little striped fish is not permitted to play with the other fish because he does not have a shiny scale. When Rainbow Fish realizes that the little striped fish is about to be eaten by a shark, he and his friends swim to confuse the shark and save the life of the striped fish. These stories emphasize learning to help others when they need help and learning to make friends with others even if they are different from you. Rainbow Fish concept books are *Rainbow Fish A, B, C* (2002), in which readers are invited to say the letters of the alphabet as they float by Rainbow Fish; *Rainbow Fish Opposites* (2005), in which children learn about up/down, in/out, and give/take as Rainbow Fish swims through the sea; *Rainbow Fish Counting* (2004), in which children are invited to count the different colored scales on Rainbow Fish; and *Rainbow Fish Color* (2004), in which children learn about the colorful fish of the sea: the blue whale, red starfish, orange seahorse, and of course the most colorful fish—Rainbow Fish. All of these books are board books and unless otherwise noted are published by North–South Books.

The David Books, by David Shannon

These humorous books are about David, who is learning about all different aspects of growing up. The David books (Scholastic) usually feature the main character as a toddler, but *Diaper David* books look at his time as an infant. In *No, David!* (1998), toddler David is learning acceptable social skills. He hears "NO" when he is reaching for cookies from the top shelf, when walking through the house with muddy shoes, when causing water to run over in the bathtub, when running naked outside, when banging on pots and pans, and other antics. In *Oops!* (2005) David spills and makes messes as he learns to feed himself, throw balls, and other activities that toddlers need to learn, while in *David Goes to School* (1999) David shows up late, chews gum, yells out of turn, and misbehaves in other ways.

Infant David learns about the five senses in *David Smells!: A Diaper David Book* (2005).

The Little Bear Books, by Martin Waddell

In the Martin Waddell series about Little Bear (Candlewick Press), each story emphasizes unconditional love. In *Can't You Sleep, Little Bear?* (1998, Illus. B. Firth, Candlewick Press) Little Bear is afraid of the dark, so his mother carries him outside so he can see all the light in the night sky. In *Let's Go Home, Little Bear* (1991, Illus. B. Firth, Scholastic). Mother Bear comforts Little Bear during their walk in the woods. Martin Waddell uses a different, curious, adventuresome bear in *Sailor Bear* (1992, Illus. V. Austin, Candlewick Press), who finds a little boat but gets into big trouble on the rough waters until he is carried safely back to shore.

A.14   A Selection of Rosemary Wells' Books for Infants and Toddlers

Wells, R. (1988). *Shy Charles*. New York: Penguin. Charles is so shy he will not even thank Mrs. Belinski for a treat. His parents try many different things to get Charles not to be so shy, but each one backfires.

Wells, R. (2000). *Noisy Nora*. New York: Puffin. Nora, the middle child of a mouse family, can only be noisy to get her parents to notice her. They give all their attention to the little brother and big sister.

Wells, R. (2004). *Only you*. New York: Viking Children's Books. The story begins with a little bear saying to his mother, "Only you can show me I can do anything I try!" The story is about a mother bear spending quality time with her little bear.

Wells, R. (1997). *McDuff moves in*. New York: Hyperion Books. This delightful book tells of the plight of McDuff until he finds Lucy and Fred. This is another book of Wells that has a rich vocabulary.

Wells, R. (1985). *Hazel's amazing mother*. New York: Dial Books for Young Readers. This book addresses in a humorous way multiple situations that young children experience—wandering off and losing their way back home, being bullied, and feeling the unconditional love of their mother. It also teaches children that if they ruin things of others, they are responsible for fixing them.

Wells, R. (2001). *Yoko's paper cranes*. New York: Hyperion Books for Children. In this story of Yoko's grandparents going back to Japan, children are introduced to the way letters get from one place to the other, some Japanese words, and the art of folding paper into paper cranes and other animals. If children have developed the necessary fine motor skills, parents can help them create paper animals of their own.

A.15   Recommended Story Books for Infants and Toddlers

Asch, F. (2008). *The Earth and I*. New York: Scholastic. A simple story of how the Earth is a friend to a little boy. All the pictures are multicolored. The text is simple: "I help her grow. She helps me grow." The two pictures are of a boy raking and the boy eating. Because the text is simple, the caregiver and child can discuss why the text is true.

Boelts, M. (1999). *Little Bunny's pacifier plan*. Illus. K. Parkinson. Morton Grove, IL: Albert Whitman. Little Bunny received a pacifier from his aunt when he was born. As he becomes a toddler, he has a hard time giving it up. Finally, when his aunt has a baby, Little Bunny knows the perfect gift for the baby—his pacifier.

Bridwell, N. (1987). *Clifford's manners*. New York: Scholastic. Clifford models manners for the reader.

Cannon, J. (1997). *Stellaluna*. San Diego: Harcourt Brace Jovanovich. A little bat falls into a bird's nest and is raised like a bird until her mother finds her.

Carlson, N. (1990). *I like me!* New York: Penguin Putnam Books. A little pig likes herself because she can paint, ride a bike, read, and care for herself.

Freeman, D. (1977). *Dandelion*. New York: Viking Penguin. A lovable lion learns that clothes do not make a man, and you may not really want for what you wished for. He dresses up like a gentleman, but then no one recognizes him.

Freeman, D. (1978). *A pocket for Corduroy*. New York: Puffin. Corduroy goes in search of a pocket after he realizes he does not have one.

Henkes, K. (1989). *Shhhh*. New York: Greenwillow Books. Every person, animal, and toy is sleeping quietly in the house, until the early riser, a little girl, wakes up and blows her toy trumpet. This book has very simple text with few words on a page.

Henkes, K. (2004). *Kitten's first full moon*. New York: Greenwillow Books. When a kitten sees his first full moon, he thinks it is a bowl of milk. He keeps getting into trouble as he tries to paw it and leap for it.

Kirk, D. (1999). *Miss Spider's new car* (board book). New York: Scholastic. The multicolored text uses onomatopoeia to describe the sounds of Miss Spider's car.

Lowrey, J. S. (1942). *The poky little puppy*. Illus. G. Tenggren. New York: Golden Books. A classic story about a curious puppy.

Marzollo, J. (2000). *I love you: A rebus poem*. Illus. S. MacDonald. New York: Scholastic. This poem shows relationships between objects: "Every bird loves a tree, every flower loves a bee, every lock loves a key."

Mayer, M. (1992). *There's a nightmare in my closet*. New York: Puffin. This is a humorous story of how a little boy rids himself of the fear of sleeping alone at night.

McPhail, D. (1988). *Something special*. Boston: Little, Brown. Sam does not think he has any special talents like the rest of the members of his family until he shows his mother how to draw a duck. He realizes that he can draw well.

Miranda, A. (2001). *To market, to market*. Illus. J. Stevens. San Diego: Harcourt Brace. This story begins with the familiar nursery rhyme and then becomes a story of unruly pigs who are running to keep themselves from being captured.

Neitzel, S. (1998). *The bag I'm taking to Grandma's*. Illus. N. W. Parker. New York: Greenwillow Books. This rebus book is about a little boy filling a bag that he is going to take to Grandma's house.

Penn, A. (2006). *A pocket full of kisses*. Washington, D. C.: Child & Family Press Books. Chester is jealous when he sees his mother give his baby brother a kiss in the palm of his hand. Chester thought that the kissing hand was a special gift only for him. His mother assures Chester that she has enough love and kisses for both of them.

Polacco, P. (2004). *Oh, look!* New York: Philomel Books. This humorous story of goats that escape from their pen to have an adventure has repetitive phrases that young children can repeat with parents.

Rohmann, E. (2007). *My friend rabbit*. Brookfield, CT: Roaring Books Press. This almost wordless Caldecott Award book is about a rabbit who tries to help his mouse friend retrieve his toy airplane out of the tree. They solicit the help of many friends in order to reach the airplane. The book encourages discussion because there is no text on many of the pages.

Shaw, N. (1996). *Sheep take a hike*. Illus. M. Apple. Boston: Houghton Mifflin. This is an easy-to-read book with few words on a page. The sheep take a hike and bicker as they go through underbrush and trees, sink in the stream, and get dirty. At the end of the day, they agree it was a great day for the outdoors.

Tafuri, N. (2005). *Goodnight, my duckling*. New York: Scholastic. This board book begins, "Time for bed my duckling." All but one duckling follows its mother. The last duckling gets encouragement from other creatures to follow its mother by wishing the duckling "good-night." However, on one wordless page, readers see a lost duckling in the middle of large lake. Finally, a turtle comes and gives the duckling a ride back to its mother.

Thayer, J. (2005). *The puppy who wanted a boy*. Illus. L. McCue. New York: HarperCollins. Petey, a puppy, wants a boy for Christmas and goes out to find one.

Turkle, B. (1992). *Deep in the forest*. New York: Puffin Unicorn. This wordless book is about a little bear going into a little girl's family's home. He experiences everything that Goldilocks does.

Viorst, J. (1972). *Alexander and the terrible, horrible, no good, very bad day*. Illus. R. Cruz. New York: Aladdin Books. Everything goes wrong for Alexander on this particular day.

Wells, R. (2009). *McDuff and the baby*. Illus. S. Jeffers. New York: Hyperion Books for Children. McDuff is his master's center of attention until a baby comes into the house. When McDuff stops eating, his masters pay more attention to him. The text is simple, and the bright vivid pictures of Susan Jeffers are large and appealing to young children.

West, C. (1997). *I don't care, said the bear*. New York: Candlewick Press. All the animals tell bear that he will meet the moose that is on the loose; however, the bear bravely tells each animal: "I don't care." This defiance gets the bear into big trouble.

Woods, A. (1984). *The napping house*. Illus. D. Wood. San Diego, Harcourt Brace Jovanovich. This humorous, cumulative story is about a sleeping granny who is visited by other inhabitants of the house. Of course, the flea is not sleeping and soon no one else is either.

A.16   Books Representing Common Themes in Children's Literature

Love of Family

Bond, M. (2008). *A bear called Paddington*. New York: HarperCollins. A small bear from Peru sets out on an adventure. He carries a battered suitcase packed with some jars of marmalade. The tag around his neck says, "Please look after this bear." The Brown family finds Paddington Bear at the train station and takes him home to love.

Bunting, E. (1989). *The Wednesday surprise*. Illus. D. Carrick. New York: Clarion Books. A granddaughter teachers her grandmother to read. In turn, the grandmother reads a book to her grandson as a birthday gift.

D'Antonio, N. (1997). *Our baby from China*. New York: Whitman. The author and her husband go to China to adopt their daughter Xiangwei. It is a true story.

dePaola, T. (1981). *Now one foot, now the other*. New York: G. P. Putnam's Sons. Grandfather teaches his grandson to walk. In turn the grandson teaches his grandfather to walk again after he suffers a stroke.

dePaola, T. (1993). *Tom*. New York: G. P. Putnam's Sons. Tom, the grandfather, does many things with his grandson Tom—tells him stories, gives him jobs in the store, and teaches him a trick with chicken feet.

dePaola, T. (1996). *The baby sister*. New York: Scholastic. Tom is delighted to have a baby sister. He helps his mother and even gets to hold his sister.

Dyer, J. (2002). *Little brown bear won't take a nap*. This story is about a little bear that does not want to sleep for the winter, so he goes with geese on a train to warm southern beaches. When he gets down south, he becomes tired and the geese make sure he does not experience any trouble. Later they go back north, and little bear's family welcomes him home with open arms.

Fox, M. (1988). *Koala Lou*. Illus. P. Lofts. New York: Trumpet Club. Everyone loves Koala Lou, but her mother loves her the most: "Koala Lou, I DO love you!"

Fox. M. (1997). *Time for bed*. Illus. J. Dyer. San Diego: Red Wagon. Each page has a different creature telling her baby it is time for bed.

Galdone, P. (1986). *The three little kittens*. Boston: Houghton Mifflin. This is the retelling of the nursery rhyme. The mother kitten loves her three little kittens even though they lost their mittens.

Hill, E. (1999). *Spot's baby sister*. New York: G. P. Putnam's Sons. Spot gets to show his baby sister around his home.

Joosse, B. (1991). *Mama, do you love me?* Illus. B. Lavallee. New York: Scholastic. This story's set in Alaska. A little girl asks her mamma if she loves her. Her mother tells her that she loves her more than various things found in Alaska.

Lewis, R. (2000). *Love you like crazy cakes*. Illus. J. Dyer. New York: Little, Brown. This story is about the author's real experience of adopting a Chinese baby. The loving story is about a mother's incredible love for her daughter. The refrain "Love you like crazy cakes" is repeated throughout the story.

Martin, B., Jr., & Archambault, J. (1966). *Knots on a counting rope*. Illus. T. Rand & B. Martin, Jr. New York: Trumpet Club. This is a dialogue between a blind grandson and his aging grandfather. The grandson asks his grandfather to tell him again about the day he was born.

McBratney, S. (1994). *Guess how much I love you.* Illus. A. Jeram. New York: Scholastic. Mother Hare tells how deep and wide her love is for Little Nutbrown Hare.

McMullan, K. (1996). *If you were my bunny.* Illus. D. McPhail. New York: Scholastic. Verses about the love of a mother for her child are set to different lullabies: "Sleep, Baby, Sleep," "Hush Little Baby," and others.

Munsch, R. (1995). *Love you forever.* Illus. S. McGraw. Willowdale, ON: Firefly Books. A mother sings a love song to her son each night until he grows up and is married. When she grows old, he sings it back to her.

Penn, A. (2006). *The kissing hand.* New York: Scholastic. Mother tells Chester how he can carry her love with him when he is away from her. She kisses his hand; he will have that kiss with him always.

Polacco, P. (1992). *Mrs. Katz and Tush.* New York: Yearling Book. A Jewish grandmother befriends an African American boy. They share and celebrate their differences.

Polacco, P. (2002). *When lightning comes in a jar.* New York: Philomel. An extended family comes to the grandparents' home for a family celebration. The grandmother teaches the children to catch lightning bugs.

Potter, B. (1902). *The tale of Peter Rabbit.* New York: Fredrick Warne. Peter Rabbit runs to Mr. McGregory's garden even though his mother warns him not to. Even after all the trouble he gets into, she still loves him.

Tsubakiyama, M. H. (1999). *Mei-Mei loves the mornings.* Illus. C. Van Wright & Y. H. Hu. New York: Whitman. Set in contemporary China, this book is about the activities Mei-Mei does each morning with her grandpa.

Overcoming Fears

Brown, M. (2004). *Arthur's homework.* Boston: Little, Brown. After helping all his classmates with their homework projects, Arthur is concerned he will be late with his own; however, his friends come to his rescue.

Henkes, K. (1987). *Shelia Rae, the Brave.* New York: Puffin. Even Shelia Rae, who is not afraid of anything, is afraid of wandering too far from her home. She needs her little sister to help her find her way home.

Johnson, T. (1985). *The quilt story.* Illus. T. dePaola. New York: G. P. Putnam's Sons. The story is about all the love wrapped around in a quilt that is passed down from generation to generation.

Magorian, M. (1990). *Who's going to take care of me?* Illus. J. G. Hale. New York: Harper & Row. When Eric's big sister goes to school, he is concerned about who will take care of him. But after school she takes care of him by showing him all the things she learned in class.

MacLachlan, P. (1995). *What you know first.* Illus. B. Moser. New York: Joanna Cotler Books. A little girl is concerned about leaving her prairie home because she is afraid she will forget it. She is assured by her parents that she will never forget what she knew first.

McCully, E. A. (1984). *Picnic.* New York: HarperCollins. In this wordless book, the mouse family is off for a picnic. The pictures show all their adventures. The little mouse becomes fearful when he is lost for a time.

McKissack, P. C. (2001). *Goin' someplace special.* Illus. J. Pinkney. New York: Atheneum/Anne Schwartz Books. Tricia Ann is fearful when she must walk through a segregated town in the 1950s in order to get to the public library, which is free to everyone.

Pérez, L. K. (2002). *First day in grapes.* Illus. R. Casilla. New York: Lee & Low Books. Chico's family moves from farm to farm to pick grapes. Each time, he needs to adjust to making new friends in a new school.

Polacco, P. (1990). *Thunder cake.* New York: Putnam & Grosset Group. Tricia is afraid of thunder storms. Her grandma takes her mind off the storm by baking a thunder cake.

Rey, M., & Rey, H. A. (1966). *Curious George goes to the hospital.* Boston: Houghton Mifflin. Curious George is concerned about going to the hospital but soon learns that doctors are there to help him.

Wells, R. (2001). *Felix feels better.* Cambridge, MA: Candlewick Press. Felix is afraid to go to the doctor but soon learns that the doctor made his tummy feel better.

Overcoming Jealousy

Brown, M. (1999). *D.W., go to your room.* Boston: Little, Brown. D.W. pinches her baby sister and then is sent to her room. She is afraid she will be forgotten and will starve.

Henkes, K. (1989). *Jessica.* New York: Greenwillow. Ruthie creates an imaginary friend Jessica who becomes ill when Ruthie must stay home with a babysitter.

Henkes, K. (1990). *Julius: The baby of the world.* New York: Scholastic. Lily is jealous of her baby brother; she teases him and scares him until her cousin comes and says Julius is disgusting. Lily then makes her cousin kiss Julius and announce that he is the best baby in the world.

Keats, E. J. (1967). *Peter's chair.* New York: Harper-Trophy. Peter is angry when his parents begin to paint his bed pink. He runs away with his chair before they paint it pink. When he sits in his chair, he realizes it is too small, so he suggests that they paint it pink for the baby.

McCully, E. A. (1988). *New baby.* New York: Harper & Row. This is a wordless book. Through pictures alone, readers see the antics of Little Mouse, who is jealous of the newest addition to the family.

Pham, L. (2005). *Big sister, little sister.* New York: Hyperion Books for Children. Little sister is jealous of her big sister because her big sister gets all the perks and new clothes; the big sister is jealous because she thinks her little sister is favored by their parents.

Going to School

Edwards, B. (2002). *My first day at nursery school.* Illus. A. Flintoft. New York: Bloomsbury Children's Books. The narrator tells of his fears of leaving his mother on his first day of nursery school. However, he soon forgets about her when he see all the toys.

Fraser, M. A. (2002). *I.Q. goes to school.* New York: Walker & Co. I.Q. is afraid everyone will make fun of him at school because he is smart; he only wants to be like everyone else.

Henkes, K. (2000). *Wemberly worried.* New York: Greenwillow Books. Wemberly worries about everything, especially going to school for the first time. She quickly finds another shy girl, and they become friends. At the end of the day they tell their teacher not to worry as they will be back in the morning.

Hill, E. (2004). *Spot goes to school.* New York: Puffin. Readers see Spot enjoying his first day of school. Spot paints and does other fun activities.

Building Friendships

Carlstrom, N. W. (1998). *Guess who's coming, Jesse Bear.* Illus. B. Degen. New York: Aladdin Paperbacks. Jesse Bear builds a friendship with a cousin who is older and somewhat bossy.

dePaola, T. (2001). *Hide-and-seek all week.* New York: Grosset & Dunlap. It takes friends an entire week to decide on rules for hide-and-seek.

Henkes, K. (1988). *Chester's way.* New York: Scholastic. Chester and Wilson have their routine broken when Lily moves into the neighborhood. They need to learn how to accept her.

Henkes, K. (1991). *Chrysanthemum.* New York: Trumpet Club. Chrysanthemum's classmates make fun of her name until their favorite music teacher announces that she loves the name and is going to give the name to her baby.

Keats, E. J. (1999). *Apt. 3.* New York: Puffin Books. Two brothers living in an apartment follow the sounds of a harmonica. They find a blind man playing it and befriend him.

Milne, A. A. (2001). *Winnie-the-Pooh and friends.* Illus. E. H. Shepard. New York: Dutton Children's Books. Each story tells of the friendship between Pooh and his many friends.

Rey, M., & Rey, H. A. (1999). *Curious George goes to the beach.* Boston: Houghton Mifflin. Curious George and the man with the yellow hat have fun together at the beach.

Wiles, D. (2001). *Freedom summer.* Illus. J. Lagarrigue. New York: Atheneum/Anne Schwartz Books. A white boy and his African American friend find many public places being boarded up after desegregation. They do not understand why adults would do that just because African Americans are now welcome in all places.

Woodson, J. (2001). *The other side.* Illus. E. B. Lewis. New York: Putnam Juvenile. Clover, an African American girl, and Ann, a white girl, are told by their mothers not to cross over the fence to play with one another; they become friends and sit on the fence.

A.17 Additional Recommended Picture Books

Boelts, M. (1994). *Dry days, wet nights.* Illus. K. Parkinson. Little Bunny wants to be big by not wearing diapers. His parents are understanding when he wets the bed each night. Finally, one night he does not.

Boelts, M. (2007). *Before you were mine.* Illus. D. Walker. New York: G. P. Putnam's Sons. A young boy is talking to his new puppy, imagining where, with whom, and what the puppy did before the little boy rescued the puppy from the shelter.

Brown, M. (1976). *Arthur's nose.* Boston: Little, Brown. Arthur does not like his nose, so he attempts to try on new noses; however, in the end he likes his own nose better than any other.

deRegniers, B. S. (1964). *May I bring a friend?* Illus. B. Montresor. The narrator is invited to meet with the king and queen for tea, breakfast, lunch, dinner, apple pie, and Halloween. The narrator brings friends each day, all of whom the king and queen welcome. Finally, the king and queen go to the zoo for tea on the seventh day.

Gerstein, M. (2003). *The man who walked between the towers.* New Medford, CT: Roaring Book Press. Philippe Petite walked on a wire he strung between the Twin Towers in New York City, dancing and performing other tricks. The police arrested him and sentenced him to perform in the park.

Gliori, D. (1996). *Mr. Bear to the rescue.* New York: Orchard Books. Mr. Bear battles a night storm that has destroyed an owl's nest, a beehive, and a rabbit hole. He saves the creatures, invites them to his home, and helps reconstruct their homes.

Gliori, D. (2001). *Flora's blanket.* New York: Orchard Books. Flora cannot sleep because she lost her blanket. The family searches all over but cannot find it. As her father is finally tucking her into bed, he finds the blanket under her pillow.

Hader, B., & Hader, E. (1993). *The big snow.* All the woodland animals are preparing for winter. Some birds fly south, other animals find warm places to stay for the winter. The couple in the little stone house put out seed, nuts, and bread crumbs for the creatures.

Himmelman, J. (2008). *Katie loves the kittens.* Katie, a dog, loves her master's little kittens, but his barking, leaping, and wagging tail scares them. He learns like many children must that one needs to be patient and let the kittens warm up to him.

Juster, N. (2005). *The hello, goodbye window.* Illus. C. Raschka. New York: Hyperion. The grandchildren see Nanna and Poppy through the kitchen window as they come for a visit, and they later see them wave goodbye through the same window.

Kajikawa, K. (2009). *Tsunami!* Illus. E. Young. New York: Philomel. Ojisan, a wealthy man, does not go down to the village to celebrate the harvest. As he looks down on the celebration on the beach, he sees the beach getting bigger and bigger as the water recedes out to sea. When he sees the big wave approaching, he sets his rice fields on fire so that all the villagers come up the mountain to put out the fire. This act saves them all. The collage illustrations depict the dark chaos the tsunami brings.

Keats, E. J. (1962). *The snowy day.* New York: Viking Press. Young Peter wakes up to a snowy white world. He plays all day in the snow and dreams of drifting snow as he falls asleep that night.

Keats, E. J. (1971). *Apt. 3.* New York: Viking. Sam hears a harmonica coming from another apartment. He and his brother go to the door of different apartments and hear the noises within. Finally, they come to the right apartment and discover the player is a blind man. They become friends. Dark colors of blue, black, gray, and green depict the apartment building and the rainy day.

Kerr, J. (2002). *The other goose.* New York: HarperCollins. Katerina, a beloved goose of the village, longs to have a goose as a friend. She thinks she always sees another goose, but readers know it is really only her reflection in a shiny car. One day Katerina foils a bank robber's attempt to steal the village's money, and Katerina is granted her wish—a boy goose as a friend! The pastel colors convey the villagers' affection for Katerina.

Lamb, A. (2006). *Sam's winter hat.* Illus. D. McPhail. New York: Scholastic. Sam loses his winter coat, mittens, and hat; but with the help of his friend and father, he finds them.

Lee, M. (2001). *Earthquake*. Illus. Y. Choi. New York: Frances Foster Books/Farrar, Straus and Giroux. Set during the 1906 San Francisco earthquake, a Chinese family awakes in the early morning to the rumble of the earthquake. They quickly pack everything they can and walk to a tent city. Dark hues of brown, black, and gray convey the fear and despair of the moment. Even the fire in the background is darkened by the smoke that has filled the city.

McBrier, P. (2004). *Beatrice's goat*. Illus. L. Lohstoeter. New York: Aladdin. Beatrice, an African girl, is given one goat, which gives birth to another goat. The goats provide milk for the family and enough extra to sell for money so that Beatrice can go to school and the family can move into a house.

McCully, E. A. (1991). *Mirette on the high wire*. New York: G. P. Putnam's Sons. Mirette's mother runs a boardinghouse where acrobats, jugglers, actors, and mimes stay. One days a retired master wire-walker comes. Mirette watches him and learns how to walk the tight wire; later she gives the man courage enough that he decides to perform again.

Rubin, A. (2008). *Those darn squirrels*. Illus. D. Salmieri. New York: Clarion Books. Old Man Fookwire, a grumpy man, loves birds. When he attempts to keep them around for the winter, the pesky squirrels meet and devise a way to steal the bird food. Of course, the birds leave. Then the squirrels feel bad and attempt to make it up to Old Fookwire.

Rylant, C. (2002). *Little Whistle's medicine*. Illus. T. Bowers. San Diego: Harcourt. The toys come alive at night in Toytown store. Soldier always reads stories to the toys until one night he is not well. Little Whistle finds a cure for Soldier, using the doctor's and nurse's kits in the store. Happily, all fall asleep to the sound of Soldier's story.

Rylant, C. (2002). *The ticky-tacky doll*. Illus. H. Stevenson. San Diego: Harcourt. A little girl loves her ticky-tacky doll that Grandma made. However, when she starts school, she cannot take the doll with her. In school she does not count or learn numbers because her mind is on her doll. Grandma's solution is to sew a little ticky-tacky doll that can stay in her backpack while she learns her numbers and letters.

Sayre, A. P. (2001). *Crocodile listens*. Illus. J. M. Stammen. New York: Greenwillow. The usually mean Nile crocodile just sits and listens even though his prey is close by because she is protecting her eggs and her young from predators. The books encourages children to learn more about African animals such as warthogs, monitor lizards, and thick-knee birds.

Shannon, D. (2004). *A bad case of stripes*. New York: Blue Sky Press. Although Camilla Cream loves lima beans, she stops eating them to fit in with her friends. But on the first day of school, she develops a bad case of the stripes. When doctors can't find anything wrong with her, she must endure changing colors until lima beans come to the rescue.

Shannon, D. (2000). *The rain came down*. New York: Blue Sky Press. This is a hilarious tale of animals and people who become grumpy and very noisy as the rain comes down: "honking, yelling, bickering, and barking." Suddenly the rain stops; all is quiet and serene, and all creatures get along with one another.

Shannon, D. (2004). *Alice the fairy*. New York: Blue Sky Press. Alice can do all types of useful magical things with her magic wand because she is a temporary fairy. She can turn oatmeal into candy, turn her dad into a horse, and draw pictures on water. Sometimes, however, her magic gets her into trouble.

Shannon, D. (2006). *Good boy, Fergus!* New York: Blue Sky Press. This book prompts participation from readers because so much of the story and humor is conveyed through the illustrations. Any child with a dog will understand the relationship between Fergus and his master.

Shannon, D. (2008). *Too many toys*. New York: Blue Sky Press. Spencer has too many toys; they are piled all over the house. The crowded illustrations show the mess. Finally, Spencer and his mother "haggled and wrestled and argued" over which toys to put into a box to give away. While his mother goes to sit for some tea, Spencer empties the box of toys because he decides the box is "the best toy ever!"

Staake, B. (2008). *The donut chef*. New York: Golden Book. A popular baker encounters competition from other bakers who make donuts a little more outlandish than most. Finally, one day a little girl comes in his shop and asks for a glazed donut.

Steig, W. (1969). *Sylvester and the magic pebble.* New York: Simon & Schuster Books for Young Readers. Sylvester finds a magic pebble that can make his wishes come true. When a lion frightens him, he wishes he were a rock. He becomes one. His parents miss him. One day, as they are picnicking on the rock, the father finds the magic pebble and wishes Sylvester were there because he would love the pebble. As the father says the words, Sylvester becomes himself again.

Stevens, J., & Crummel, S. S. (2008). *Help me, Mr. Mutts! Expert answers for dogs with people problems.* Orlando: Harcourt Brace. Dogs write to Mr. Mutts, who is an expert on dealing with people. Each page is a letter from a dog and a reply from Mr. Mutts with sound advice. At the end of each letter, Mr. Mutts warns the dog about the family cat who thinks she is queen of the house. Of course, the cat posts a response. This humorous book can be used to encourage children to write creative letters.

Taback, S. (1999). *Joseph had a little overcoat.* New York: Viking. When Joseph's little coat becomes old and shabby, he makes it into a jacket and then into smaller items of clothing. The cut-out pages permit children to predict what piece of clothing it will become next.

Waddell, M. (1996). *Small Bear lost.* Illus. V. Austin. Cambridge, MA: Candlewick Press. Small Bear gets left on the train and attempts to find his way home. The pictures help tell the story as day turns to night and he is still not home. Finally at night, a little girl and her mother walk past Small Bear, sleeping near their house.

Waddell, M. (1996). *What use is a moose?* Illus. A. Robins. Cambridge, MA: Candlewick Press. Jack is attempting to find a use for the moose he found in the woods. When Mother sends the moose back to the woods because she has no use for a moose, Jack cries that he really loved the moose. Mother agrees that being loved is a very good use for a moose. So Jack finds the moose, and they build a house for it. The moose's antlers became a ladder for Jack as he builds the house.

Wells, R. (2003). *Felix and the worrier.* Felix tries not to worry, but the worrier also appears! On his birthday, Felix gets a puppy. Since the worrier is worried about dogs, the worries leaves. Felix is rid of the worrier.

Weninger, B. (2005). *Miko wants a dog.* Illus. S. Roehe. New York: Penguin Young Readers. Miko wants a dog, but his mother won't let him have one. One day Miko's neighbor gets a dog. Since Miko is so good with the dog, the neighbor lets Miko play with him anytime he wants to.

Wild, M. (1999). *Rosie and Tortoise.* Illus. R. Brooks. New York: DK Publishing. Rosie, a rabbit, is excited about her new baby brother. But because he is so tiny, Rosie ignores him. She is afraid she will hurt him. Finally Rosie's parents convince her that her brother Tortoise is big enough to hold.

Willems, M. (2004). *The pigeon finds a hot dog!* New York: Hyperion Books. When Duckling asks Pigeon about the taste of a hot dog, Pigeon begins to explain the wonder of a hot dog until he realizes that Duckling is tricking him into sharing it with him.

Willems, M. (2008). *The pigeon wants a puppy.* New York: Hyperion. The pigeon wants a puppy. He sweetly persuades, he sulks, and finally throws a tantrum, demanding a puppy. But when the slobbery pooch comes, the pigeon is not so sure he wants a puppy. Maybe a walrus would be better.

Willems, M. (2009). *Naked mole rat gets dressed.* New York: Hyperion. Wilbur, a naked mole rat, likes to get dressed. All the other mole rats make fun of his clothes. However, when Grandpa mole comes for a visit, he comes all dressed up because he agrees with Wilbur. All the other mole rats start wearing clothes.

Winter, J. (2008). *Wangari's trees of peace: A true story from Africa.* Orlando: Harcourt Brace. The planting of trees in Kenya creates the entire Green Belt of Kenya. This book is great to use when studying environmental issues.

Woodson, J. (1998). *We had a picnic this Sunday past.* Illus. D. Greenseid. New York: Hyperion Books for Children. A family is gathering with their favorite foods for a picnic. Like usual, Cousin Trevor and Moon Pie come empty-handed. Everyone fears that Cousin Martha will again bring a dry pie; however, she arrives with a store-bought cake because she was too busy to bake.

Woodson, J. (2000). *Sweet, sweet memory*. Illus. F. Cooper. New York: Hyperion Books for Children. This is a tender story of a granddaughter remembering her grandfather after his death.

Yolen, J. (1989). *Owl moon*. Illus. J. Schoenherr. New York: Philomel. A father and young child learn patience as they go owling one winter night in the woods. Finally, they spot one, and the little child stands in awe at the great owl until it flies away.

Yolen, J. (2005). *Grandma's hurrying child*. Illus. K. Chorao. San Diego: Gulliver Books. This story is told as a flashback when Maddy asks Grandma to retell the story of how she hurried across three states to greet Maddy when she was born.

Yolen, J. (2006). *Dimity duck*. Illus. S. Braun. New York: Philomel. This story uses onomatopoeia: Dimity Duck waddles, toddles, wiggles, waggles, giggles, gaggles, whooshes, and splashes throughout the day.

Yolen, J. (2007). *Baby Bear's big dreams*. Illus. M. Sweet. Orlando: Harcourt. This is a rhyming story of what a Baby Bear will do in two years when he is all grown up—stay up late and play all day.

Yolen, J. (2007). *Sleep, Black Bear, sleep*. Illus. B. Dyer. New York: HarperCollins. This rhyming story is a lullaby to all hibernating creatures—skunks, badges, snakes, toads, and others. They are reassured that spring will follow the cold winter.

Yorinks, A. (1986). *Hey, Al*. Illus. R. Egielski. New York: Farrar, Straus and Giroux. A janitor and his dog Eddie do everything together. However, they have some problems—their house is too small and cramped, and their life is a struggle. A mysterious bird comes and sets them on an island, where they live a life of ease. However, as they begin to turn into birds, they finally realize that the grass is not always greener on the other side. In the end they make it back home.

Young, E. (2006). *My Mei Mei*. New York: Philomel. The story is based on the author's experience of adopting a Chinese daughter. The oldest daughter is excited about the new sister until she arrives. She cannot play, and the younger daughter gets all the attention. The two sisters become best friends as the younger child grows. The collage illustrations resemble portraits in a family's photo album.

A.18 Orbis Pictus Award for Outstanding Nonfiction For Children

These books are excellent examples of quality nonfiction. Please note that some books on this list may not be appropriate for young children. As when choosing any book to share, consider the age, interests, and reading level of your audience.

2009 *Amelia Earhart: The Legend of the Lost Aviator* by Shelley Tanaka, illus. by David Craig (Abrams Books for Young Readers)

2008 *M. L. K.: Journey of a King* by Tonya Bolden (Abrams Books for Young Readers)

2007 *Quest for the Tree Kangaroo: An Expedition to the Cloud Forest of New Guinea* by Sy Montgomery, photos by Nic Bishop (Houghton Mifflin)

2006 *Children of the Great Depression* by Russell Freedman (Clarion Books)

2005 *York's Adventures with Lewis and Clark: An African-American's Part in the Great Expedition* by Rhoda Blumberg (HarperCollins)

2004 *An American Plague: The True and Terrifying Story of the Yellow Fever Epidemic of 1793* by Jim Murphy (Clarion Books)

2003 *When Marian Sang: The True Recital of Marian Anderson* by Pam Muñoz Ryan, illustrated by Brian Selznick (Scholastic)

2002 *Black Potatoes: The Story of the Great Irish Famine, 1845–1850* by Susan Campbell Bartoletti (Houghton Mifflin)

2001 *Hurry Freedom: African Americans in Gold Rush California* by Jerry Stanley (Crown)

2000 *Through My Eyes* by Ruby Bridges (Scholastic)

1999 *Shipwreck at the Bottom of the World: The Extraordinary True Story of Shackleton and the Endurance* by Jennifer Armstrong (Crown)

1998 *An Extraordinary Life: The Story of a Monarch Butterfly* by Laurence Pringle (Orchard Books)

1997 *Leonardo da Vinci* by Diane Stanley (Morrow Junior Books)

1996 *The Great Fire* by Jim Murphy (Scholastic)

1995 *Safari Beneath the Sea: The Wonder World of the North Pacific Coast* by Diane Swanson (Sierra Club Books)

1994 *Across America on an Emigrant Train* by Jim Murphy (Clarion Books)

1993 *Children in the Dust Bowl: The True Story of the School at Weedpatch Camp* by Jerry Stanley (Crown)

1992 *Flight: The Journey of Charles Lindbergh* by Robert Burleigh, illus. by Mike Wimmer (Philomel)

1991 *Franklin Delano Roosevelt* by Russell Freedman (Clarion Books)

1990 *The Great Little Madison* by Jean Fritz (Putnam)

From www.ncte.org/awards/orbispictus

A.19 Informational Books About Zoo Animals

Arnold, K. (2005). *Elephants can paint too!* Photographer K. Arnold. New York: An Anne Schwartz Book/Atheneum. This unique book tells of an art teacher who teaches children to paint in the city and teaches elephants to paint in the jungle. The photographs depict both children and elephants painting and show their artwork.

Gibbons, G. (1991). *Zoo.* New York: Holiday House. Various animals are described with detailed labels of their physical features and habits.

Gibbons, G. (2008). *Elephants of Africa.* New York: Holiday House. The book has detailed illustrations of the elephant's physical features, its habitat, and its trunks and ears.

Lang, A. (2004). *Baby koala.* Photographer W. Lynch. Markham, ON: Fitzhenry & Whiteside. The book describes the first year of a koala's life as it lives with its mother.

Markle, S. (2007). *Zebras.* The photographs show zebras in their natural surroundings and being hunted by predators. The text also explains how herds stay together and how they help and protect each other. The text is intriguing as it tells about attacks from many different types of predators.

Morecroft, R., & Mackay, A. (2003). *Zoo album.* Illus. K. Lloyd-Diviny. Basic information is given about mammals, birds, reptiles, and amphibians.

Murray, P. (2001). *Rhinos.* Beautiful full-page photographs accompany facts about rhinos' physical features, their food source, their enemies, and their young.

Penny, M. (2001). *Black rhino.* Austin, TX: Raintree Steck-Vaughn Publishers. The habitat, life cycle, and dangers faced by the black rhino are dis-

cussed. The photographs show the rhinos in their natural environment.

Simon, S. (1998). *Wild babies.* Various wild animal babies with their technical terms are described as well as their habitats.

Simon, S. (2002). *Baby animals.* Baby animals often found in zoos are described in their natural habitats.

Smith, R. (1995). *African elephants.* Photographer G. Ellis. Minneapolis: Lerner Publications. The photographs help young readers understand elephants' natural environment in Africa. The text describes the size of the elephant, explains the use of their trunk, gives their eating and drinking habits, and explains their life span.

Staub, F. (1994). *Mountain goats.* Minneapolis: Lerner Publications. The photographs help readers understand mountain goats' natural environment. The text gives details about their environment, their surviving in the cold, their family structure, their manner of communicating, their enemies, and their life span.

Stewart, M. (2002). *Elephants.* New York: Children's Press/Scholastic. The photographs show the elephants in their natural surroundings in Africa. The text explains their size, trunks, life span, and enemies.

Stewart, M. (2002). *Rhinoceroses.* New York: Children's Press/Scholastic. Basic facts of rhinos in African and Asia are given. Discussion includes the danger that rhinos face.

Stewart, M. (2002). *Hippopotamuses.* New York: Children's Press/Scholastic. Content includes information about the physical features of hippos,

their habitat, their life span, their enemies, and
their source of food.

Stewart, M. (2002). *Zebras.* New York: Children's
Press. The photographs show zebras in their natural environment in Africa. The text explains their
food, their family structure, and their enemies.

Squire, A. O. (2005). *Leopards.* Photographer B.
Coleman. New York: Children's Press/Scholastic.
The photographs show the leopards in their

natural environment. The text gives basic
information about the leopard's physical characteristics, their hunting habits, and their enemies.

Squire, A. O. (2005). *Jaguars.* New York: Children's
Press/Scholastic. The photographs of the jaguar
in its natural setting help young readers understand its environment. The text describes how
they hunt, where they live, how they raise their
cubs, and what dangers they encounter.

A.20 Informational Books About Space

Landau, E. (2008). *The moon.* New York: Children's
Press. The text gives basic information about the
moon: its position in space, its phases, the book
also describes the famous lunar landing.

Rey, H. A. (1982). *Find the constellations.* The
illustrations and text help readers locate many
constellations in the night sky.

Simon, S. (1985). *Saturn.* Photographers NASA &
K. Cudworth. New York: Morrow Junior Books.
The focus of the book is on Saturn—its physical
features, its relationship to other planets, and
other facts about the planet.

Simon, S. (1992). *Mercury.* Photographers D. Van-
derhoff & Jet Propulsion Laboratory. New York:
Morrow Junior Books. The focus of the book is
on Mercury—its physical features, its relationship
to other planets, and other facts about the planet.

Simon, S. (1992). *Venus.* Photographer NASA & J.
Lindemann. New York: Morrow Junior Books.
The focus of the book is on Venus—its physical
features, its relationship to other planets, and
other facts about the planet.

Simon, S. (1998). *Destination: Jupiter.* Photographers
NASA & K. Cudworth. New York: Morrow
Junior Books. The focus of the book is on
Jupiter—its physical features, its relationship to
other planets, and other facts about the planet.

Simon, S. (2000). *Destination: Mars.* Photographers
R. Dreiser & NASA. New York: Morrow Junior
Books. The focus of the book is on Mars—its
physical features, its relationship to other planets, and other facts about the planet.

Simon, S. (2002). *Destination: Space.* New York:
HarperCollins. The book describes what has
been seen through the Hubble Space Telescope
as it has orbited Earth since April 1990. The in-
depth information is for children who are really
enthusiastic about space.

Sipiera, P. P. (1997). *Comets and meteor showers.*
New York: Children's Press. This is an introduction to comets, explaining where they come
from, how they travel, why they are important,
and how they relate to meteor showers. Two
sections question whether a comet killed the
dinosaurs and whether they bring bad luck.

Checklists

B.1   Checklist for Poetry Books

○ The poem is appropriate for the age level of the children

○ The use of language sparks the imagination and fits the meaning of the poem

○ The poem's figures of speech are within the conceptual grasp of the children

○ The imagery is fresh and vivid

○ The poet takes into account the knowledge level and experiences of children, using images to which they can connect

○ The poet gets his or her point across in a way that engages young children through sound, rhythm, rhyme, or content

○ The poem invites children to respond in their own way

B.2   Checklist for Books for Infants or Toddlers

○ The book is in an age-appropriate book category, such as concept books or books with repetitive text, rhymes, or humor

○ The book is made of appropriate materials, is sturdily constructed, and does not have any small parts that could potentially cause choking

○ The book provides sensory stimulation

○ The book has a rich vocabulary

○ The book features the characteristics of print

○ If it is a storybook, it has simple, easy-to-follow, sequential plots, and its content reflects the daily experiences of infants or toddlers

○ If the book is a concept book, it introduces the subject matter clearly and consistently

○ The book uses a combination of rhyme, humor, and repetitive text to engage children

○ *Optional:* The book has tabs and flaps for children to manipulate

B.3   Checklist for Fiction Books

Evaluating the text

- ○ Protagonists are round and multidimensional with the personalities and behaviors of real people
- ○ Antagonists, even when flat characters, are believable
- ○ Characters are not stereotypes
- ○ Plots have tension or surprise and suspense, and are believable and logical
- ○ Plots are sequential and do not rely heavily on flashbacks
- ○ Plots and themes promote positive moral development and are relevant to children's experiences
- ○ Settings essential to the plot or theme are accurate and realistic
- ○ Stories told from a first-person point of view reflect children's feelings and experiences
- ○ The tone is appropriate to the plot and theme of the book
- ○ Word choice is vivid and the words effectively create a mood or mental picture in readers' minds
- ○ Sentence length varies, with some simple, compound, complex, and compound–complex sentences
- ○ Literary devices, including similes and metaphors, personification, allusion, puns, hyperbole, assonance, alliteration, onomatopoeia, and rhyme, are used effectively
- ○ If the book is wordless, the illustrations vividly depict action that progresses step by step throughout the book

For fantasy:

- ○ The story has aesthetic or emotional appeal
- ○ The rules of the fantasy world are followed consistently

For realistic fiction:

- ○ The characters are believable and well developed without being stereotypes
- ○ The dialogue is easily understood without relying on slang or extreme dialect

For historical fiction:

- ○ The work is based on research and is historically accurate
- ○ The time period is clearly described
- ○ The illustrations are accurate and do not contain anachronisms

(continued)

Evaluating the illustrations

- ○ Artistic technique is skilled and the medium suits the story
- ○ The mood created by the illustrations is appropriate to the story's theme and enhances the plot
- ○ The illustrations show action or create suspense in a way that moves the plot forward
- ○ Visual information provided in the text matches the illustrations
- ○ The illustrations are appropriate for the age of the children

B.4   Checklist for Informational Texts

Accuracy

- ⟁ Facts are current and complete
- ⟁ Fact and theory are balanced
- ⟁ Varying points of view are included
- ⟁ Stereotypes are avoided and the text is free of biases
- ⟁ The author's qualifications are adequate
- ⟁ Scope and authenticity of detail are appropriate

Organization

- ⟁ The book has a logical development and clear sequence
- ⟁ Interrelationships are indicated
- ⟁ Patterns are provided (such as moving from general to specific or simple to complex, etc.)

Design

- ⟁ The design is attractive and promotes readability
- ⟁ The illustrations complement text
- ⟁ The placement of illustrative material is attractive and aids comprehension
- ⟁ The media, format, and type are appropriate

Style

- ⟁ The writing is interesting, stimulating, and reveals the author's enthusiasm for the subject
- ⟁ Curiosity and wonder is encouraged
- ⟁ Appropriate terminology and a rich language are used

Overall

- ⟁ The readability and scope of details are age-appropriate
- ⟁ The pages have visual appeal, using white space and font size effectively
- ⟁ Definitions of terms are clear and pronunciations for new terms are given
- ⟁ Information is well organized, using an organizational structure such as sequence, explanation/description, compare/contrast, cause/effect, problem/solution

Adapted from NCTE, 2008, pp. 1 and 2 of 2. http://www.ncte.org/elem/awards/orbispictus/106877.htm

Worksheets

C.1   Character Profile of a Round Dynamic Protagonist

Name: _____   Date: _____

Book

Beginning

Traits

Draw a picture of the main character

End

Traits

Evidence

Character Name

Evidence

Changing Event

C.2   Character Profile of a Round Static Protagonist

Name: _____   Date: _____

Book

Character Name

Draw a picture of the main character

Trait #1	Trait #2	Trait #3

Evidence	Evidence	Evidence

C.3 Character Profile of a Flat Antagonist

Name: _____ Date: _____

Book

What antagonist says about protagonist:

Evidence

Character Name

Draw a picture of the main character

What antagonist does to protagonist:

Evidence

What antagonist does with protagonist:

Evidence

Relationship between antagonist and protagonist:

Evidence

Name: _____ Date: _____

Name of the book:

Author:

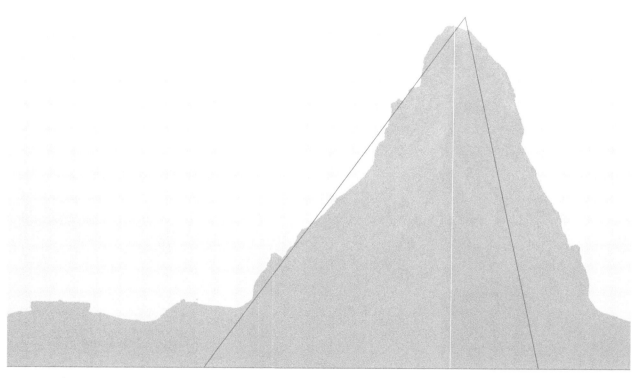

Beginning   Middle   End

C.5 3-2-1 Chart

Name: _____ Date: _____

Name of the book:

Author:

3 Three things I never knew before I read the book:

1.

2.

3.

2 Two things I found interesting:

1.

2.

1 One question I still have:

1.

C.6 K-T-W-L Chart

Name: _____   Date: _____

K (Know)	T (Think I know)	W (Want to learn)	L (What I learned)

Name of the book: _____

Author: _____

C.7   **Fiction Versus Fact Chart**

Name: _____   Date: _____

Subject:

FICTION	FACT
Book(s):	Book(s):

C.8   Detective Worksheet

Name: _____   Date: _____

Subject: _____

What is it?

Where does it
come from?

What is it made of?

What is it for?

References

Adams, M. J. (1990). *Beginning to read: Thinking and learning about print*. Cambridge, MA: MIT Press.

Akerson, V., & Young, T. (2004). Nonfiction know how. *Science and Children, 41*(6), 48–51.

Alexander, L. (1981). The grammar of story. In B. Hearne & M. Kays (Eds.), *Celebrating Children's Books* (pp. 3–13). New York: Lothrop Publishers.

Alexander, L. (1998). Fantasy and the human condition. *New Advocate Magazine, 1*, 70–75.

Allington, R. (2001). *What really matters for struggling readers: Designing research-based programs*. New York: Longman.

Altwerger, A., Diehl-Faxon, J., & Dockstader-Anerson, K. (1985). Read-aloud events as meaning construction. *Language Arts, 62*, 476–484.

American Academy of Pediatrics. (1997). Press statement in Washington, D. C. Chicago: American Academy of Pediatrics.

American Academy of Pediatricians. (2000). www.medem. com.

American Association of Publishers. (2005). Fact sheet on the importance of reading to infants and young children. Retrieved from www.publishers.org/main/Conferences/Conf_Pub/conf_Pub_01_10.htm.

American Library Association. (2005). Terms and criteria: Randolph Caldecott Medal. Retrieved from http://ala.org/ala/mgrps/divs/alsc/awardsgrants/bookmedia/caldecottmedal/caldecottterms/caldecottterms.cfm.

Anders, P., & Lloyd, C. (1996). The significance of prior knowledge in the learning of new content-specific ideas. In D. Lapp, J. Flood, & N Farnan (Eds.), *Content area reading and learning: Instructional strategies* (2nd ed.) (pp. 323–338). Boston: Allyn & Bacon.

Anderson, D., & Pempek, T. (2005). Television and very young children. *American Behavioral Scientist, 48*(5), 505–523.

Anderson, R. C. (1996). Research foundations to support wide reading. In V. Creany (Ed.), *Promoting reading in developing countries* (pp. 55–77). Newark, DE: International Reading Association.

Anderson, R. (2004). Role of the reader's schema in comprehension, learning and memory. In R. Ruddell & N. Unrau (Eds.), *Theoretical models & processes of reading* (5th ed.) (pp. 594–606). Newark, DE: International Reading Association.

Anderson, R. C., Hiebert, E. H., Scott, J. A., & Wilkenson, I. A. G. (1985). *Becoming a nation of readers: The report of the Commission on Reading*. Washington, D. C.: National Institute of Education.

Anderson, R. C., Wilson, P. T., & Fielding, L. G. (1988). Growth in reading and how children spend their time outside of school. *Reading Research Quarterly, 23*, 285–303.

Backes, L. (2006). Straight talk about talking animals. Retrieved from www.fictionfactor.com.

Bates, E., Marchman, V., Thal, D., Fenson, L., Dale, P., Reznick, J. S., Reilly, J., & Hartung, J. (1994). Developmental and stylistic variation in composition of early vocabulary. *Journal of Child Language, 21*, 85–123.

Beck, I. L. (2004, April). *Igniting students' knowledge of and interest in words*. Presentation at the Florida Middle School Reading Leadership Conference, Orlando, FL.

Beck, I. L., McKeown, M. G., & Kucan, L. (2002). *Bringing words to life: Robust vocabulary instruction*. New York: Guilford.

Begley, S. (1996, February 19). Your Child's Brain. *Newsweek*, 55–58.

Bellugi, U. (1971). Simplification in children's language. In R. Huseley & E. Ingram (Eds.), *Language acquisition: Models and methods* (pp. 95–119). New York: Academic Press.

Berk, L. (2006). *Child development* (7th ed.). Boston: Pearson.

Bettelheim, B. (1989). *The uses of enchantment: The meaning and importance of fairy tales*. New York: Random House.

Bloom, K. (1998). The missing link's missing link: Syllabic vocalizations at three months of age. *Behavioral & Brain Sciences, 21*(4), 514–516.

Bradley, B. A., & Jones, J. (2007). Sharing alphabet books in early childhood classroom. *The Reading Teacher, 60*(5), 452–463.

Brassell, D. (2006). Inspiring young scientists with great books. *The Reading Teacher, 60*(4), 336–342.

Brazelton, T. B. (1983). *Infants and mothers: Differences in development* (Rev. ed.). New York: Delta/Seymour Lawrence.

Brown, A. L., Sullivan-Palincsar, A., & Armbruster, B. B. (2004). Instructing comprehension: Fostering activities in interactive learning situations. In R. Ruddell & N. Unrau (Eds.), *Theoretical models & processes of reading* (5th ed.) (pp. 780–809). Newark, DE: International Reading Association.

Brown, R. (1970). The first sentences of child and chimpanzee. In R. Brown (Ed.), *Psycholinguistics: Selected papers* (pp. 208–231). New York: Free Press.

Bruner, J. (1965). *On knowing: Essays for the left hand.* New York: Atheneum.

Bruner, J. (1971). *The relevance of education.* New York: Norton.

Bruner, J. (1983). *Child's talk: Learning to use language.* New York: Norton.

Bruner, J. (1987). *Making sense: The child's construction of the world.* London: Metheun.

Caswell, L. J., & Duke, N. K. (1998). Non-narrative as a catalyst for literacy development. *Language Arts, 75*(1), 108–117.

Cazden, C. (1972). *Child language and education.* New York: Holt, Rinehart and Winston.

Chomsky, N. (1974). *Aspects of the theory of syntax.* Cambridge, MA: Harvard University Press.

Christakis, D., Zimmerman, F., DiGiuseppe, D., & McCarty, C. (2004). Early television exposure and subsequent attentional problems in children. *Pediatrics, 113*(4), 708–713.

Chukovsky, K. (1963). *From two to five.* Berkeley, CA: University of California Press.

Clarke, D. (2002). Making measurement come alive with children's storybooks. *Australian Primary Mathematics Classroom, 7*(3), 9–13.

Clay, M. (1982). *Observing young readers: Selected papers* (Rev. ed.). Exeter, NH: Heinemann.

Clay, M. (1991). *Becoming literate: The construction of inner control.* Portsmouth, NH: Heinemann.

Clay, M. (1991). Introducing a new storybook to young readers. *The Reading Teacher, 45*(4): 264–273.

Clay, M. (1993). *An observation survey of early literacy achievement: Auckland, New Zealand.* Portsmouth, NH: Heinemann.

Clay, M. (2001). *Change over time in children's literacy development.* Portsmouth, NH: Heinemann.

Collier, J. L. (1982). www.answers.com/topicJamesLincoln Collier-historical fiction.

Comer, J. P. (2004). *Leave no child behind: Preparing today's youth for tomorrow's world.* New Haven, CT: Yale University Press.

Comer, J. P. (2005, June). Child and adolescent development: The critical missing focus in school reform. *Phi Delta Kappan, 86*(10), 757–763.

Comstock, G. (1991). *Television and the American child.* Orlando: Academic Press.

Cote, N., & Goldman, S. R. (2004). Building representations of informational text: Evidence form children's think-aloud protocols. In R. B. Ruddell & N. J. Unrau (Eds.), *Theoretical models and processes of reading* (5th ed.) (pp. 660–683). Newark, DE: International Reading Association.

Cowley, G.. (2000, Fall/Winter). For the love of language. *Newsweek, 136* (17A), pp. 12–15.

Cox, B. E., Fang, Z., & Otto, B. W. (2004). Preschoolers' developing ownership of the literate register. In R. B. Ruddell & N. Unrau (Eds.), *Theoretical models and processes of reading* (5th ed.) (pp. 281–312). Newark, DE: International Reading Association.

Crain, W. (2000). *Theories of development: Concepts and applications* (4th ed.). Upper Saddle River, NJ: Prentice Hall.

Curtiss, S. (1977). *Genie: A psycholinguistic study of a modern-day wild child.* New York: Academic Press.

Daniels, H. (2002). *Literature circles* (2nd ed.). Portland, ME: Stenhouse.

Danko-McGhee, K., & Slutsky, R. (2007). *Early art experiences on literacy development.* Reston, VA: National Art Education Association.

Davis, K. (2004). *Letter to parents.* Camp Hill, PA: Children's Book-of-the-Month Club.

DeDroff, L. (1990). Informational books: Topics and structure. *The Reading Teacher, 53*(4), 496–500.

DeTemple, J., & Snow, C. E. (2003). Learning words from books. In A. vanKeeck, S. A. Stahl, & E. B. Bauer (Eds.), *On reading books to children: Parents and teachers* (pp. 16–36). Mahwah, NJ: Erlbaum.

Dickens, C. (1853). *Bleak house.* New York: Bantam.

Doralek, D. (2003). When pictures are worth a thousand words: The nonfiction books of Gail Gibbons. *Young Children, 58*(2), 22–23.

Duke, N. (2003, March). Reading to learn from the very beginning: Information books in early childhood. *Young Children,* 14–20.

Duke, N. K. (1998, February). Empirical confirmation of the scarcity of informational texts in early grades. Paper presented at the Harvard Graduate School of Education Student Research Conference, Cambridge, MA.

Duke, N. K., & Kays, J. (1998). "Can I say 'once upon a time'?": Kindergarten children developing knowledge of information book language. *Early Research Quarterly, 13*(2), 295–318.

Duncan, L. G., & Seymour, P. H. K. (2000). Socio-economic differences in foundation level literacy. *British Journal of Psychology, 91,* 145–166.

Dundee, A. (1985). The psychoanalytic study of folklore. *Annals of Scholarship, 3,* 87–96.

Durkin, D. (1966). *Children who read early.* New York: Teachers College Press.

Duthie, C. (1994). Nonfiction: A genre study for the primary classroom. *Language Arts 71*(8), 588–595.

Eggen, P. D., & Kauchak, D. (1992). *The psychology of the child.* New York: New American Library.

Elias, M. (2004). Short attention span linked to TV. Retrieved from www.usatoday.com/news/nation.

Elkind, D. (2007). *The hurried child: Growing up too fast* (3rd ed.). Cambridge, MA: Da Capo Lifelong Learners.

Enciso, P., & Rogers, T. (1999, Summer). Gender representations: Reaching beyond the limits we make. *New Advocate, 12*(3), 285–297.

Engelmann, S., & Bruner, E. (1995). *Reading mastery 11: Direct instruction—storybook 2.* Columbus, OH: SRA Macmillan/McGraw Hill.

Erikson, E. (1963). *Childhood and society* (2nd ed.). New York: Harper & Row.

Ernst, K. (1998, April). Drawing improves literacy. *Teaching Pre K–8, 27*(7), 28–29.

Ferreiro, E., & Teberosky, A. (1982). *Literacy before schooling.* Exeter, NH: Heinemann.

Feuerstein, R. (1979). *The dynamic assessment of retarded performers: The learning-potential assessment device, theory, instruments and techniques.* Baltimore: University Park Press.

Fisher, C., & Natarella, M. (1979). Of cabbages and kings: Or what kinds of poetry young children like. *Language Arts, 56,* 380–385.

Fisher, C., & Natarella, M. (1982). Young children's preferences in poetry: A national survey of first, second, and third graders. *Research in the Teaching of English, 16,* 339–353.

Fisher, D., Flood, J., Lapp, D., & Frey, N. (2004). Interactive read-alouds: Is there a common set of implementation practices? *The Reading Teacher, 58*(1), 8–17.

Flood, J., & Lapp, D. (1995). Television and reading: Refocusing the debate. *The Reading Teacher, 49*(2), 160–163.

Forman, E. A., & Cazden, C. (2004). Exploring Vygotskian perspectives in education: The cognitive value of peer evaluation. In R. Ruddell & N. J. Unrau (Eds.), *Theoretical models & processes of reading* (5th ed.) (pp. 163–186). Newark, DE: International Reading Association.

Fountas, I., & Pinnell, G. S. (1996). *Guided reading: Good first teaching for all children.* Portsmouth, NH: Heinemann.

Frazier, J. (1915). *The golden bough: A study of magic and religion.* London: Macmillan.

Galda, L., & Beach, R. (2004). Response to literature as a cultural activity. In R. B. Ruddell & N. J. Unrau (Eds.), *Theoretical models & processes of reading* (5th ed.) (pp. 852–869). Newark, DE: International Reading Association.

Gallas, K. (2003). *Imagination and literacy: A teacher's search for the heart of learning.* New York: Teacher's College Press.

Gambrell, L. B., Morrow, L. M., & Pennington, C. (2002). Early childhood and elementary literature-based instruction and current perspectives and special issues. In M. L. Mamil, P. B. Mosenthal, P. D. Pearson, & R. Barr (Eds.), *Handbook of reading research* (Vol. 3). Mahwah, NJ: Lawrence Erlbaum.

Gardner, H. (1980). *Artful scribbles.* New York: Basic Books.

Gardner, H. (1983). *Frames of mind: The theory of multiple intelligences.* New York: Basic Books/HarperCollins, Hancock.

Gardner, H. (1993). *Multiple intelligences: The theory in practice.* New York: Basic Books.

Gee, J. P. (2004). Reading as situated language: A sociocognitive perspective. In R. B. Ruddell & N. J. Unrau (Eds.), *Theoretical models and process of reading* (5th ed.) (pp. 116–132). Newark, DE: International Reading Association.

Giblin, J. C. (1987). *From hand to mouth.* New York: Harper.

Glazer, J. (2000). *Literature for young children* (4th ed.). Upper Saddle River, NJ: Merrill.

Goldhaber, D. (2000). *Theories of human development: Integrative perspectives.* Mountain View, CA: Mayfield.

Goleman, D. (2006). *Emotional intelligence: Why it matters more than IQ.* New York: Bantam Books.

Golinkoff, R., & Hirsh-Patek, K. (1999). *How babies talk: The magic and mystery of language in the first three years of life.* New York: Dutton.

Goodman, E. (2008, January 25). Transcending race and identity. *Boston Globe.*

Goodman, K. (1994). Reading, writing and written texts: A transactional sociopsycholinguistic view. In R. B. Ruddell, M. R. Ruddell, & H. Singer (Eds.), *Theoretical models and processes of reading* (pp. 1093–1130). Newark, DE: International Reading Association.

Goswani, U. (2002). Early phonological development and the acquisition of literacy. In S. Neuman & D. Dickinson (Eds.), *Handbook of early literacy research* (pp. 111–125). New York: The Guildford Press.

Greenberg, M. T., & Kuschle, C. A. (1993). *Promoting social and emotional development in deaf children.* Seattle: University of Washington Press.

Greenberg, M. T., Kuschle, C. A., Cook, E. T., & Quamma, J. P. (1995). Promoting emotional competence in school-age children: The effects of the PATH curriculum. *Development and Psychopathology, 7,* 117–136.

Gullatt, D. (2008, April 1). Enhancing student learning through arts integration: Implications for the profession. *High School Journal, 91*(4), 12–25.

Guthrie, J. T., Van Meter, P., McCann, A. D., Wigfield, A., Bennett, L., & Poundstone, C. C. (1996). Growth in literacy engagement: Changes in motivations and strategies during concept-oriented reading instruction. *Reading Research Quarterly, 31,* 306–332.

Haase, D. (2005). Psychology and fairy tales. In *Fairy tale companion: The Oxford companion to fairy tales* (pp. 404–408). Oxford: Oxford University Press.

Halliday, M. A. K. (1977). *Explorations in the functions of language.* London: Elsevier Science Publishers.

Halliday, M. A. K. (1994). The place of dialogue in children's construction of meaning. In R. B. Ruddell, M. R. Ruddell, & H. Singer (Eds.), *Theoretical models and processes of reading* (4th ed.) (pp. 70–82). Newark, DE: International Reading Association.

Hancock, M. R. (1996, May). State children's choice awards: Instructional insights through children's literary preferences. Paper presented at the 41st Annual Convention of the International Reading Association, New Orleans, LA.

Hancock, M. (2004). *Acceleration of literature and response* (2nd ed.). Upper Saddle River, NJ: Pearson/Merrill/Prentice Hall.

Hannibal, M., Visiliev, R., & Lin, Q. (2002). Teaching young children basic concepts of geography: A literature-based approach. *Early Childhood Journal, 30*(2), 81–86.

Harste, J. C., Burke, C. L., & Woodward, V. A. (1994). Children's language and world: Initial encounters with print. In R. B. Ruddell, M. R. Ruddell, & H. Singer (Eds.), *Theoretical models and processes of reading* (4th ed.) (pp. 48–69). Newark, DE: International Reading Association.

Harste, J. C., Woodward, V., & Burke, C. (1984). *Language stories and literacy lessons.* Portsmouth, NH: Heinemann.

Heath, S. B. (2004). The children of Trackton's children: Spoken and written language in social change. In R. B. Ruddell, M. R. Ruddell, & N. J. Unrau (Eds.), *Theoretical models and processes of reading* (5th ed.) (pp. 187–209). Newark, DE: International Reading Association.

Heller, M. (2006). Telling stories and talking facts: First graders' engagement in nonfiction book clubs. *The Reading Teacher, 60*(4), 358–369.

Huck, C., Hepler, S., Hickman, J., & Kiefer, B. (1997). *Children's literature in the elementary school* (6th ed.). New York: Brown & Benchmark.

Huck, C., Kiefer, B., Hepler, S., & Hickman, J. (2003). *Children's literature in the elementary school.* New York: McGraw Hill.

Huesmann, L. R., & Moise-Titua, J. (2003). Longitudinal relations between children's exposure to TV violence and their aggressive and violent behavior in young adulthood: 1977–1992. *Developmental Psychology, 39*(2), 201–221.

Hughes, F., & Seta, C. (2003). Gender stereotyping: Children's perceptions of future compensating behaviors following violations of gender roles. *Journal of Research, 49,* 27–38.

Hymes, J. (1981). *Teaching the child under six* (3rd ed.). Columbus, OH: Merrill.

IRA/NAEYC (1998). Learning to read and write: Developmentally appropriate practices for young children. A joint position statement of the International Reading Association and the National Association for the Education of Young Children. *Young Children 53*(4), 30-46. Available: http://www.naeyc.org/files/naeyc/file/positions/PSREAD98.PDF.

Jacobs, J. & Tunnell, M. (2004). *Children's literature briefly* (3rd edition). Upper Saddle River, NJ: Pearson.

Jacobson, L. (1998). Reading group, NAEYC issue literacy recommendations. *Education Week, 17*(42), 13. Retrieved from www.edweek.org/ew/articles/1998/07/08/42read.h17.html.

Jennings, C. M. (1992). Increasing interest and achievement in mathematics through children's literature. *Early Childhood Research Quarterly, 7*(2), 263–276.

Jordan, N. (2005). Basal readers and reading as socialization: What are children learning? *Language Arts, 82*(3), 204–213.

Juel, C., & Minden-Cupp, C. (2004). Learning to read words: Linguistic units and instructional strategies. In R. B. Ruddell & N. J. Unrau (Eds.), *Theoretical models and process of reading* (5th ed.) (pp. 313–364). Newark, DE: International Reading Association.

Justice, L. M., & Ezell, H. K. (2004). Print referencing: An emergent literacy enhancement strategy and its clinical applications. *Language, Speech and Hearing Services in Schools, 35,* 185–193.

Kamil, M., & Lane, D. (1997). A classroom study of using information text for first-grade reading instruction. Paper presented at the annual meeting of the American Educational Research Association, San Diego, CA.

Kantrowitz, B. (2000, Fall/Winter). 21st Century Babies. *Newsweek, 136* (17A), pp. 4–7.

Kellogg, R. (1970). *Analyzing children's art.* Palo Alto, CA: Mayfield Publishing Co.

Kiefer, B. (2009). *Charlotte Huck's children's literature in the elementary school.* New York: McGraw Hill.

Kiefer, B., Hepler, S., & Hickman, J. (2007). *Charlotte Huck's children's literature in the elementary school.* New York: McGraw Hill.

Kletzien, S. B., & Szabo, R. J. (1998, December). Information or narrative text? Children's preferences revisited. Paper presented at the National Reading Conference, Austin, TX.

Kohlberg, L. (1984). *Essays on moral development: Vol. 2. The psychology of moral development.* New York: Harper & Row.

Koolstra, C. M., van der Voort, T. H. A., & van der Kamp, L. J. (1997). Television's impact on children's reading comprehension and decoding skills: A 3-year study. *Reading Research Quarterly, 32*(2), 128–152.

Kovanich, K. (2007, September 4). Study shows students' lack of geography knowledge. *Northern Star Internet News.* Retrieved from http://archive.uwire.com/2007/09/04/facebook-app-shows-students-lack-of-geography-knowledge

Krashen, S. D. (1993). *The power of reading: Insights from the Research.* Englewood, CO: Libraries Unlimited.

Kuczaj, S. (1982). *The language development: Syntax and semantics* (Vol. I). Hillsdale, NJ: Lawrence Erlbaum Associates.

Kurkjian, C., & Livingston, N. (2005). The right book for the right child for the right situation. *The Reading Teacher, 58*(8), 786–795.

Labbo, L., Love, M. S., Prior, M. P., Hubbard, B. P., & Ryan, T. (2006). *Literature links: Thematic units linking read-alouds and computer activities.* Newark, DE: International Reading Association.

Lamaze International. (2003). The infant development system. Retrieved from http://lamaze.my-babytoys.com.

Lamb, S. J., & Gregory, A. H. (1993). The relationship between music and reading in beginning readers. *Educational Psychology, 13,* 19–26.

Lane, H. B., & Wright, T. L. (2007). Maximizing the effectiveness of reading aloud. *The Reading Teacher, 60*(7), 668–675.

Lasky, K. (1990). The fiction of history: Or what did Miss Kitty really do? *The New Advocate, 3*(3), 157–166.

Lehr, S. (1995). *Battling dragons: Issues and controversies in children's literature.* Portsmouth, NH: Heinemann.

Leontiev, A. N., & Luria, A. R. (1968). The psychological ideas of L. S. Vygotsky. In B. Wolman (Ed.), *Historical roots of contemporary psychology* (pp. 362–382). New York: HarperCollins.

Lieberman, A. F. (1993). *The emotional life of the toddler.* New York: Maxwell Macmillan International.

Lowenfeld, V. (1963). *Your child and his art.* New York: Macmillan.

Lukens, R. J. (2003). *A critical handbook of children's literature* (7th ed.). Boston: Allyn & Bacon.

Machado, J. (2006). *Early childhood experiences in language arts* (8th ed.). Clifton Park, NY: Thomson Delmar Learning.

Maduram, I. (2000). "Playing possum": A young child's responses to information books. *Language Arts, 77*(3), 391–397.

Mann, L. (2006). Jacqueline Woodson Biography. Retrieved from www.jacquelinewoodson.com/bio.shtml.

Many, J. (2004). The effects of reader stance on students' personal understanding of literature. In R. B. Ruddell & N. J. Unrau (Eds.), *Theoretical models and process of reading* (5th ed.). (pp. 914–928). Newark, DE: International Reading Association.

Mason, J. M. (1984). Early reading from a developmental perspective. In P. D. Pearson, R. Barr, M. L. Kamil, & P. Mosenthal (Eds.), *Handbook of reading research* (pp. 505–543). New York: Longman.

Mason, J. M., Herman, P. A., & Au, K. H. (1991). Children's developing knowledge of words. In J. Flood, J. M. Jensen, D. Lapp, & J. R. Quires (Eds.), *Handbook of research on teaching the English language arts* (pp. 721–731). New York: Macmillan.

McKay, G. (1986). Poetry and the young child. *English in Australia, 75,* 51–58.

McGowan, T., & Guzzetti, B. (1991). Promoting social studies understanding through literature based instruction. *The Social Studies Journal, 82,* 16–21.

McInerney, D., & McInerney, V. (1998). The goals of schooling in culturally diverse classrooms. *The Clearinghouse, 71*(6), 363–366.

McMath, J. S., King, M. A., & Smith, W. E. (1998). Young children's questions: Nonfiction books. *Early Childhood Education Journal, 26*(1), 19–27.

Meyer, B. J. F., & Poon, L. W. (2004). Effects of structure strategy training and signaling on recall of text. In R. B. Ruddell & N. J. Unrau (Eds.), *Theoretical models and processes of reading* (5th ed.) (pp. 810–851). Newark, DE: International Reading Association.

Miller, P. H. (2002). *Theories of developmental psychology* (4th ed.). New York: Worth Publishers.

Monson, D., & Sebesta, S. (1991). Reading preferences. In J. Flood, J. Jensen, D. Lapp, & J. Squire (Eds.), *Handbook of research on teaching the English language arts* (pp. 664–673). New York: Macmillan.

Morrow, L. M., & Gambrell, L. B. (2002). Literature-based instruction in the early years. In S. B. Neuman & D. K. Dickinson (Eds.), *Handbook of early literacy research* (pp. 348–360). New York: Guilford.

Mukai, G. (2000). Teaching about Japanese-American internment. *The Indiana Social Studies Teaching Unit.* Retrieved from www.indiana.edu/-ssdc/interndig.htm.

Murphy, S. J. (1999, March). Learning math through stories. *School Library Journal,* pp. 122–123.

Myers, P. A. (2005). The Princess Storyteller, Clara Clarifier, Quincy Questioner, and the Wizard: Reciprocal teaching adapted for kindergarten students. *The Reading Teacher, 59*(4), 314–324.

Mynard, S. (2005, December). The place of dramatic role playing in the early years. *Early Years Update.* Retrieved from www.teachingexpertise.com/articles/drama-in-the-early-years-1143.

Nagy, W. E., & Scott, J. A. (2004). Vocabulary process. In R. B. Ruddell & N. J. Unrau (Eds.), *Theoretical models and processes of reading* (5th ed.) (pp. 810–852). Newark, DE: International Reading Association.

National Council of Teachers of English (2008). NCTE Orbis Pictus Award for Outstanding Nonfiction for Children. Retrieved from www.ncte.org/elem/awards/orbispictus/106877.htm.

Neugebauer, S. R., & Currier-Rubin, R. (2009). Read-alouds in Calca, Peru: A bilingual indigenous context. *The Reading Teacher, 62*(5), 396–405.

Neuman, S. B. (1988). The displacement effect: Assessing the relationship between television viewing and reading performance. *Reading Research Quarterly, 23,* 414–440.

Neuman, S. B. (1999). Books make a difference: A study of access to literacy. *Reading Research Quarterly, 34*(3), 286–311.

Nodelman, P. (1999, Fall). The boys in children's books. *Riverbank Review,* pp. 5–7.

O'Donnell, M., & Wood, M. (2004). *Becoming a reader: A developmental approach to reading instruction* (3rd ed.). Boston: Pearson.

Ogle, D. (1986). K-W-L: A teaching model that develops active reading in expository text. *The Reading Teacher, 39*(5), 564–570.

Olweus, D. (2002). A profile of bullying at school. *Educational Leadership, 60,* 12–17.

Oyler, C. (1996). Sharing authority: Student initiations during teacher-led read-alouds of information books. *Teaching and Teacher Education, 12*(2), 149–160.

Oyler, C., & Barry, A. (1993, December). Urban first-graders intertextual connections in the collaborative talk around information books during teacher-led read-alouds. Paper presented at the National Reading Conference, Charleston, S.C.

Oyler, C., & Barry, A. (1996). Intertextual connections in read-alouds of information books. *Language Arts, 73*(3), 324–329.

Oyler, C., Barry, A., Moss, B., Leone, W., & Dipillo, M. (1997). Exploring the literature of facts: Linking reading and writing through information trade books. *Language Arts, 74*(4), 418–429.

Palmer, R., & Stewart R. (1997). Nonfiction trade books in content are instruction: Realities and potential. *Journal of Adolescent & Adult Literacy, 40*(8), 630–642.

Palmer, R., & Stewart, R. (2003). Nonfiction trade book use in primary grades. *The Reading Teacher, 57*(1), 38–48.

Pappas, C. (1991). Fostering full access to literacy by including information books. *Language Arts, 68*(3), 449–462.

Pappas, C. (1993). Is narrative "primary"?: Some insights for kindergarteners' pretend readings of stories and information books. *Journal of Reading Behavior, 25*(1), 97–129.

Peterson, R. & Eeds, M. (2007). *Grand conversations: Literature groups in action.* New York: Scholastic.

Piaget, J. (1964). *The psychology of intelligence.* Boston: Routledge and Kegan Paul.

Piaget, J. (1974). *The language and thought of the child.* New York: New American Library.

Piaget, J., & Inhelder, B. (1969). *The psychology of the child.* New York: Basic Books.

Poussaint, A. & Linn, S. (2008). Raising children free from prejudice: setting an example. *Family Education.* Available: http://life.familyeducation.com/slideshow/race/37422.html.

Putnam, L. (1991). Dramatizing nonfiction with emerging readers. *Language Arts, 68*(6), 463–369.

Raymond, A. M. (1995). Engaging young children in mathematical problem solving: Providing a context with children's literature. *Contemporary Education, 66,* 172–174.

Raymond, J. (2000a, Fall/Winter). Kids, start your engines. *Newsweek, 136* (17A), pp. 8–11.

Raymond, J. (2000b, Fall/Winter) . The world of senses. *Newsweek, 136* (17A), pp. 16–18.

Richgels, D. (2002). Informational texts in kindergarten. *The Reading Teacher, 55*(6), 586–595.

Roper Survey (2006, May 2). Young Americans still lack basic global knowledge. *National Geographic Magazine.*

Rosenblatt, L. M. (1994a). The transactional theory of reading and writing. In R. B. Ruddell, M. R. Ruddell,

& H. Singer (Eds.), *Theoretical models and processes of reading* (4th ed.) (pp. 1067–1092). Newark, DE: International Reading Association.

Rosenblatt, L. M. (1994b). *The reader, the text, the poem: The transactional theory of the literary work.* Carbondale, IL: Southern Illinois University Press.

Rosenblatt, L. M. (1995). *Literature as exploration* (5th ed.). New York: Appleton-Century-Crofts.

Rosenblatt, L. M. (1996). *Literature as exploration.* New York: Modern Language Association.

Ruddell, R. B. (2004). Researching the influential literacy teachers: Characteristics, beliefs, strategies, and new research directions. In R. B. Ruddell & N. J. Unrau (Eds.), *Theoretical models and processes of reading* (5th ed.) (pp. 979–997). Newark, DE: International Reading Association.

Ruddell, R. B., & Ruddell, M. R. (1994). Language acquisition and literacy processes. In R. B. Ruddell, M. R. Ruddell, & H. Singer (Eds.), *Theoretical models and processes of reading* (4th ed.) (pp. 83–103). Newark, DE: International Reading Association.

Rymer, R. (1994). *Genie: An abused child's flight from silence.* New York: HarperCollins.

Sadlier, W. (2000). *Nursery rhymes and phonemic awareness.* New York: Sadlier–Oxford.

Saffran, J. R. (2005, March 17). How do infants acquire their native language: What learning processes underlie the acquisition of words? Retrieved from www.waisman.wisc.edu/infantlearning/infantlang.html.

Saffran, J. R., Aslin, R. N., & Newport, E. L. (1996). Statistical learning by 8-month-old infants. *Science, 274,* 1926–1928.

Schnorr, R. F., & Davern, L. (2005, March). Creating exemplary literacy classrooms through the power of teaming. *The Reading Teacher, 58*(6), 494–506.

Shatzer, J. (2008). Picture book power: Connecting children's literature and mathematics. *The Reading Teacher, 61*(8), 649–653.

Shin, F. (2004). Books, not direct instruction, are the key to vocabulary development. *Library Media Connection Journal, 22*(4), 20–21.

Shonkoff, J., & Phillips, D. (Eds.). (2000). *Neurons to Neighborhoods: The science of early child development.* Washington, D. C.: National Academic Press.

Sidelnick, M., & Svoboda, M. (2000, October). The bridge between drawing and writing: Hannah's story. *The Reading Teacher, 54,* 174–184.

Singer, J., Singer, D., Desmond, R., Hirsch, B., & Nicol, A. (1988). Family mediation and children's comprehension of television: A longitudinal study. *Journal of Applied Developmental Psychology, 9,* 119–123.

Skinner, B. F. (1957). *Verbal Behavior.* Englewood Cliffs, NJ: Prentice Hall.

Smith, F. (1988). *Understanding reading: A psycholinguistic analysis of reading and learning to read.* Hillsdale, NJ: Lawrence Erlbaum.

Snow, C. E., Burns, M. S., & Griffin, P. (1998). *Preventing reading difficulties in young children.* Washington, D. C.: National Academy Press.

Solomon, D., Watson, M., Battistich, V., Schaps, E., & Delucchi, K. (1992). Creating a caring community: Educational practices that promote children's preschool development. In F. K. Oser, A. Dick, & J. L. Patry (Eds.), *Effective and responsible teaching: The new synthesis.* San Francisco: Jossey-Bass.

Stanovich, K. E. (2004). Matthew effect in reading: Some consequences of individual differences in the acquisition of literacy. In R. B. Ruddell & N. J. Unrau (Eds.), *Theoretical models and processes of reading* (5th ed.) (pp. 454–516). Newark, DE: International Reading Association.

Strickland, D. S., Ganske, K., & Monroe, J. K. (2002). *Supporting struggling readers and writers.* Portland, ME: Stenhouse.

Striker, S. (2001). *Young at art.* New York: Henry Holt.

Sulzby, E., & Teale, W. H. (1987, November). Young children's storybook reading: Longitudinal study of parent–child interaction and children's independent functioning. Final report to the Spencer Foundation. Ann Arbor, MI: University of Michigan.

Thompson, R., & Aldridge, K. (2001, December 30). Children's attitudes about race form early. *The Cincinnati Inquirer.*

Tiedt, I. (1970). Exploring poetry patterns. *English Education, 47*(8), 1083–1084.

Tobin, A. W. (1981). A multiple discriminant cross-validation for the factors associated with the development of precocious reading achievement. Unpublished doctoral dissertation. Newark: University of Delaware.

Trelease, J. (2001). *The read-aloud handbook* (5th ed.). New York: Penguin Books.

Trelease, J. (2006). *The read-aloud handbook* (6th ed.). New York: Penguin Books.

Trousdale, A. (1989, June). Who's afraid of the big bad wolf? *Children's Literature in Education, 20*(2), 69–79.

Untermeyer, B., & Untermeyer, L. (1962). *Beloved tales.* New York: Golden Press.

Van DeMille, O. (2000). *Teaching a generation of leaders for the twenty-first century: A Thomas Jefferson education.* Cedar City, UT: George Wythe College Press.

Vardell, S. (2006). *Poetry aloud here!* Chicago: American Library Association.

Vukelich, C., Christie, J., & Enz, B. (2002). *Helping young children learn language and literacy.* Boston: Allyn & Bacon.

Vygotsky, L. (1962, 1976). *Thought and language.* E. Haufmann & G. Vaka (Eds. & Trans.). Cambridge, MA: Harvard University Press.

Vygotsky, L. S. (1934, 1978). *Mind in society: The development of higher psychological processes* (M. Cole, B. John-Steiner, S. Scribner, & E. Souberman (Eds. & Trans.). Cambridge, MA: Harvard University Press.

Walker, B. (2004). *Diagnostic teaching of reading* (5th ed.). Columbus, OH: Merrill.

Walton, B. (2007, January 10). More children learn more than one language. *USA Today.*

Weber, B. (2004, July 8). Fewer noses stuck in books in America, survey finds. *New York Times.* Retrieved from www.nytimes.com.

Wells, G. (1985). *The meaning makers.* Portsmouth, NH: Heinemann.

Wells, R. (2004). *Rosemary Wells biography.* Available: http://us.penguingroup.com/nf/Author/AuthorPage/0,,1000033951,00.html.

Welmer, M. (2007). Reading informational texts: Using the 3-2-1 strategy. *Read-Write-Think, IRA/NCTE.* Retrieved from www.readwrtethink.com.

Winn, M. (1985). *The plug-in drug.* New York: Viking Press.

Wright, J., Huston, A., Murphy, K., Peters, M., Pinon, M., Scantlin, R., & Kotler, J. (2001). The relations of early television viewing to school readiness and vocabulary of children from low-income families: The Early Window Project. *Child Development, 72*(5), 1347–1366.

Yaden, D. B., Smolkin, L. B., & MacGillivray, L. (1993). A psychogenetic perspective on children's understanding about letter associations during alphabet book readings. *Journal of Reading Behavior, 25,* 43–68.

Yellin, D., Blake, M., & Devries, B. (2008). *Integrating the language arts* (4th ed.). Scottsdale, AZ: Holcomb Hathaway.

Yopp, R. H., & Yopp, H. K. (2004). Review-predict-confirm: Thinking about the language and content of informational texts. *The Reading Teacher, 58*(1), 79–83.

Young, C., & Maulding, W. (1994, September 1). Mathematics and Mother Goose. *Teaching Children Mathematics,* 36–38.

Zipes, J. (1985). *Fairy tales and the art of subversion: The classical genre for children and the process of civilization.* New York: Routledge.

Zipes, J. (1997). *Happily ever after: Fairy tales, children and the cultural industry.* New York: Routledge.

Author & Title Index

Subject Index